AF352097

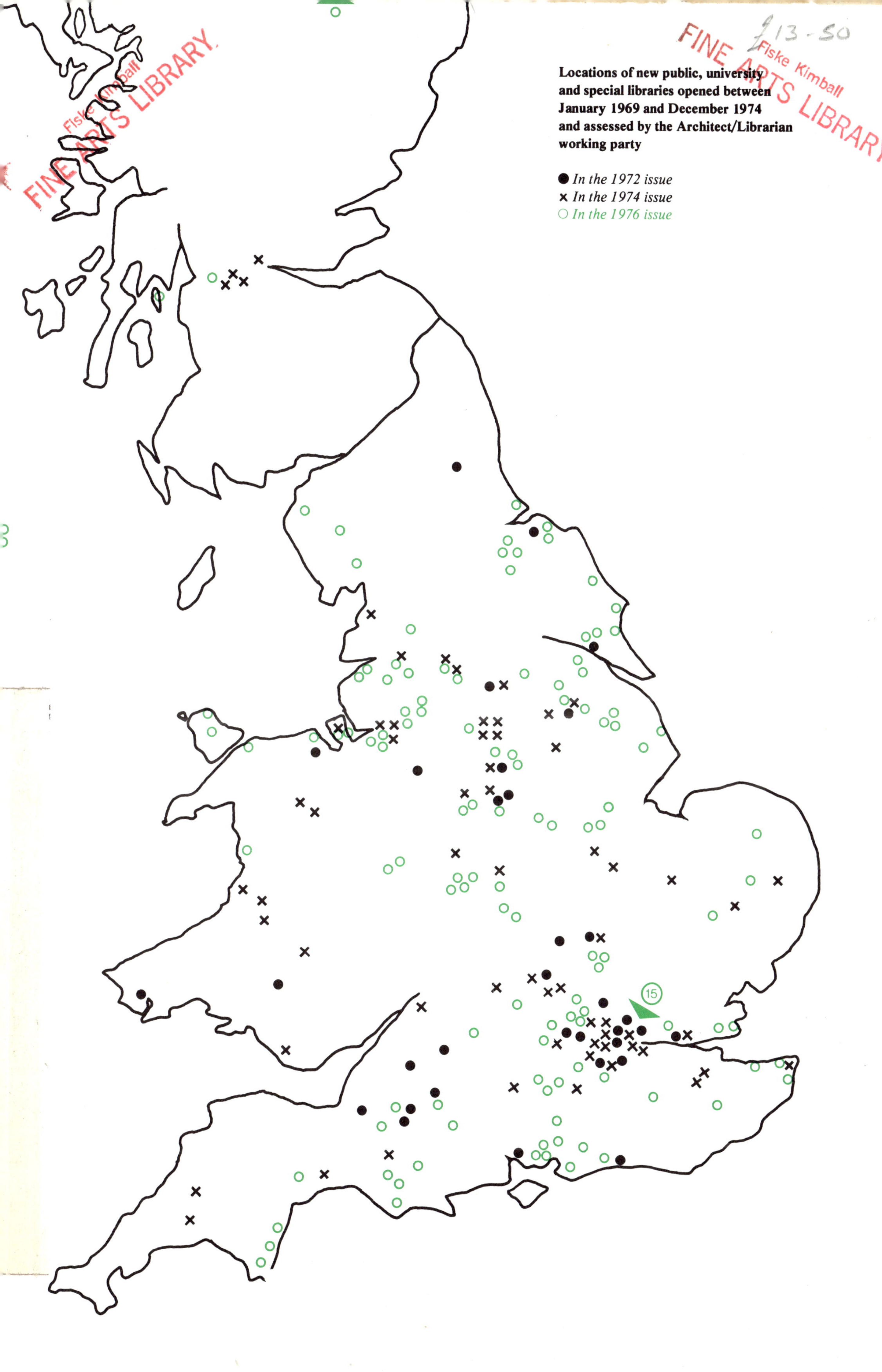

Locations of new public, university
and special libraries opened between
January 1969 and December 1974
and assessed by the Architect/Librarian
working party

● In the 1972 issue
✕ In the 1974 issue
○ In the 1976 issue

New Library Buildings 1976 Issue

New Library Buildings 1976 Issue

Years 1973–1974

Edited by Herbert Ward FLA

Members of the Editorial Board:
E J Carter MA, RIBA, FLA
N T Diamantis B Arch, RIBA
N Reuter RIBA
L H Sidwell ALA
G Thompson FLA
G K V Tomlinson RIBA, AA Dip

Produced with the assistance of the London and Home Counties Branch of The Library Association

The Library Association

First Published by the Library Association
7 Ridgmount Street, London WC 1E 7AE

1976

ISBN 0 85365 089 6

British Library Cataloguing in Publication Data

New library buildings: architect – librarian
    assessments.
    1976 issue; years 1973–1974.
    ISBN 0–85365–089–6
    1. Ward, Herbert, b. 1912.
    2. Library Association – London and Home Counties
    Branch – Architect-Librarian Working Party
    727'.8'0941   Z679
    Library architecture – Great Britain

Architectural plans re-drawn
by Mrs J Diamantis

Lamport Gilbert Printers Ltd., Reading

Contents

		Population Served	Floor Area square metres	Page
Berkshire County Council	Crowthorne	11,000	188	**79**
Buckinghamshire County Council	Burnham	18,000	568	**81**
	Farnham Common	5,000	177	
	Stokenchurch	3,800	90	
	Little Chalfont	6,000	143	
Cheshire County Council	Barnton	4,000	260	**87**
	Winsford	27,500	929	
Cumbria County Council (formerly Westmorland County Council)	Ambleside	6,000	371	**92**
	Keswick	5,000	280	
	Seaton	5,000	165	
Devon County Council	Churston Ferrers	6,000	217	**96**
	Honiton	5,800	374	
	Kingsbridge	3,600	297	
	Teignmouth	11,500	444	
Derbyshire County Council	Blagreaves	10,000	1,263	**104**
	Killamarsh	5,500	136	
Doncaster Metropolitan District Council (formerly West Riding County Council)	Sprotbrough	10,563	535	**107**
	Bawtry	3,500	232	
	Bentley	15,000	250	
	Hatfield	14,000	300	
	Intake	13,725	225	
Dorset County Council	Chickerell	2,300	80	**110**
	Colehill	2,300	100	
	Gillingham	4,000	94	
	Puddletown	1,000	80	
Durham County Council	Chester-le-Street	36,000	450	**116**
	South Moor	10,000	175	
	Annfield Plain	—	—	
	Chilton	10,000	140	
	Spennymoor	30,000	340	
Essex County Council (formerly County Borough of Southend-on-Sea)	Shoeburyness	5,000	569	**121**
(formerly Urban District of Thurrock)	Corringham	15,000	492	
Hampshire County Council	Farnborough	50,000	1,884	**125**
	Fleet	28,000	1,185	
	Yateley	20,000	464	
	Fareham	75,000	2,439	
	Waterlooville	36,000	1,115	
	Stubbington	15,000	490	
Humberside County Council (formerly City and County of Kingston-upon-Hull)	Ings	20,000	395	**136**
(formerly East Riding County Council)	Hornsea	15,000	598	
(formerly Lindsey and Holland County Council)	Crowle	3,100	155	
	Messingham	2,225	130	
Kent County Council	Faversham	15,000	560	**142**
	Sandwich	2,000	140	
	Seal	2,000	140	
Lancashire County Council	Shadsworth	10,000	394	**146**
	Nelson	—	—	
	Leyland	23,690	442	
	Livesey	6,400	261	
	Wheatley Lane	1,000	48	
Leicestershire County Council	Wigston Magna	30,000	1,087	**154**
	Birstall	13,000	447	

Introduction

In our first volume of assessments of new library buildings we reported on more than thirty; in the next issue, twice that number. The Library Association were able to tell us that 72 had been opened during the two-year period up to December 1974. However, to make sure that none had been missed, a notice was inserted in the May 1975 issue of the *Library Association Record* asking Chief Librarians to notify me direct if they had not advised the Library Association. There was little response so a further notice was inserted some months later. We now know that around 150 new library buildings were erected in that period.

The result for us was an unexpectedly overburdened schedule; thus a planned two days leave to visit three new libraries in one area some 200 miles from London would reveal more than twice that number needing to be visited.

It soon became apparent to us that during the run-up to the Local Government reorganisation deadline date of April 1974 officers of the new and larger Authorities, as well as those Authorities due to lose their identity, were either so involved, or so saddened, that the reporting of new libraries became a later-or-never task, to be dealt with 'some time' but certainly not at that moment. In our view the pre-reorganisation Chief Officers were mainly leaving this to the newly appointed top men.

Our aim has always been to make these reviews as complete a record of worthy new British libraries as possible and to include some not-so-good library buildings in order to point out to future planners what we consider to have been unfortunate errors of judgement or missed opportunities. In spite of the difficult circumstances affecting this issue another 138 new library buildings have now been assessed by us. These bring the total for the six-year period that we have covered to 240 new public, university and special libraries recorded, a range scaling down from Birmingham's Central Library of 21,368 m² to small Branch Libraries of 130 m².

My great appreciation, and that of my librarian and architect colleagues, is sincerely expressed to the following distinguished members of the two professions who volunteered the extra help needed for us to reach out to new libraries in Scotland, Wales, Northern Ireland and Dublin: Mr J. Hardie Glover, OBE, ARSA, FRIBA, FRIAS and Mr Andrew Merrylees, DipTP, ARIBA, ARIAS (both of Sir Basil Spence, Glover and Ferguson of Edinburgh); Mr William C. McVeigh, ARIBA, of Belfast; Mr Philip F. Geoghegan, BArch, DipArch, RIBA, of Dublin and Mr Gilbert Turner, FLA, the former Borough Librarian of the London Borough of Richmond-upon-Thames, who now lives in North Wales.

Our thanks are also extended to all the Chief Librarians or their senior representatives as well as, in many cases, the Architects, who made time in their very busy work schedules to receive us so hospitably and to guide us around their libraries, and readily allowed our questions to be fired at them. This to us is a most rewarding factor within our work and underlines the value that these professional colleagues place on our independent assessments of the results of their efforts. We acknowledge too, their kindness in making photographs and plans available to us for reproduction.

Although the time and the energy needed to make so large a number of visits for this volume have been willingly and freely given by the members of the Architect/Librarian Working Party, the costs of travel alone would have rendered the production of this volume financially impossible had it not been for the generosity of the London and Home Counties Branch of the Library Association in making a grant of £1,500 towards those costs. As it was this Branch's Conference, held at Hastings in 1967, which launched the idea of Architect/Librarian co-operation in the design and planning of new Library buildings, it is particularly appropriate that they should want to continue their interest and to help practically in this work, rather than see it founder now under the ever rising burden of increased costs.

As the members of the Architect/Librarian Group have now been visiting and assessing new library buildings for over six years, it may be appropriate to mention some significant, and in our opinion beneficial, trends. Many pre-April 1974 Library Authorities which had been developing individual styles and approaches to library design then found themselves in the shake-up of boundary changes and emerging with a different status. Whilst one hopes that this may benefit the majority and not see too much damage done to others, one fears the possibility of disadvantageous effect on some which had already shown clearly a distinct competency in design.

The linking of libraries with other local buildings (so widely practised in West Germany and Scandinavia) opens up more possibilities for the future. Several examples of the developing practice in England, described in the text of this issue, show close links with other services such as a College of Further Education, Health or Sports Centres, Schools and public halls, and by greater integration of the library into shopping centre facilities. Yet, in many areas, one feels that the siting of a library is more a question of an empty site rather than the result of positive planning to meet the exact needs of a community. Not everyone wishing to use a library has use of a car, so proximity to good public transport becomes vital.

Many architects—and even librarians—seem to find counter design a real problem and some guidance for them is an obvious need. The design of counter areas for efficiency—as well as showing consideration for the staff who man them—is critical. Small failings assume enormous importance to counter staff when these are encountered hundreds of times a day and thus lead to a disproportionately jaundiced view. Some staff were quite outspoken to us about this.

But perhaps the most important impression gained is the evident satisfaction of the public when a new library is built and opened for them. Everywhere these are described as vastly better than the old buildings which have been replaced—and with even more enthusiasm when there was no previous library provision. It is easy in the present economic climate, with capital projects being axed in all directions, to become despondent about the future of

library building. But there are signs, and we all have hope that
this setback will only be a temporary situation, that new libraries
will be built, *must* be built; this need is underlined by the fact
that in spite of cutbacks in hours of opening, new libraries still
tend to show better issue figures than the former buildings. Good
buildings breed a demand for more, and people with a poor
library service can be expected to demand, especially within the
wider Authorities, an equivalent library service to that for a
neighbouring community which has been blessed with a new
building; they have the right to claim similar benefits and the
hope of all of us in the two professions is that they will get them
before the children in those areas lose-out on the opportunities
which we have seen so enthusiastically grasped by the young
people in the vicinity of a newly opened library.

The members of our Working Party receive my very sincere
personal thanks for their tremendous help, given so readily and
cheerfully, in spite of the unexpectedly heavy load and time
factor problems. Without that enthusiastic co-operation, this
particular issue in the series would never have been produced.

August 1976   Herbert Ward

Birmingham District Council

So much has already been written about this building that the present account can only attempt to pick out themes and points related to our general policy in revisiting new library buildings.

The awe-inspiring outside appearance and sheer scale of the project are, at first sight, daunting as are the statistics. With an area of 2 hectares (over 5 acres), this is the largest public library building in Europe. A million books on over 30 miles of shelving (with a capacity for expansion to house half as much again), 1,260 seats for readers, all figures are impossible to imagine in terms of a building which does anything but dominate. The truth, however, is that it is anything but dominating. From first entering, the reader or enquirer, child or adult, visitor or member of staff finds him or herself quietly and efficiently received and guided to the part of the complex to which they are aimed with no fuss. Once there the individual spaces are of comprehensible scale and size and of incomparable quality. The explanation for this apparently effortless success lies in the method by which the impossible has been achieved. In the result we see the exemplification of that co-operation between designer and client which has been the 'raison d'être' and battlecry of this publication for two previous issues and forms a constant theme of the present volume.

One can only be relieved that the City Council's resolution in July 1935 to build a new library was not implemented earlier, for the history of public library building from 1938 until work started on the design of the present building in 1964 can scarcely be regarded as a time of great achievement in this field. Too many monumental white elephants litter our towns and cities for the two professions to look back with much pride on their work in the library field. The stagnation of the war, followed by the battle between modern and academic traditionalist architecture, left little time or opportunity for the kind of meticulous, inventive and fresh design approach which is evident in the Birmingham building. It is interesting that many of the buildings reviewed in this volume are of similar quality and stem from a similar design approach, so that the period from 1964 may well prove to be something of a golden era of library buildings to rival that which led earlier this century to Carnegie libraries, which must at that time have seemed miraculous.

From October 1964 onwards regular meetings were held between the architects and the Librarian and his staff, consultations being constant and detailed. Since the building is planned immediately above the inner ring road tunnel and the bus station above that, and forms part of a larger complex, the design problems may be imagined. When completed the whole building group will include the School of Music, Athletic Institute, Drama Centre, offices, shops, public houses, car park and bus station. Because of its scale the Libraries form the most important feature of the whole scheme which is conceived as a series of low blocks of three to four storeys grouped around open courtyards, connecting above the road system so that pedestrian routes are completely segregated from traffic. The design of the whole centre will follow that of the library with materials and details matching.

The site adjoins an area of fine Victorian civic buildings grouped around Victoria Square. Architectural styles range from the austere classicism of the Roman temple which is the Town Hall to the exhuberant Gothicism of the Museum and Art Gallery to the east, so that a totally modern building, equally monumental in its own terms, was the only possible architectural solution. It says much for the architect's skill that there is no sense of incongruity between the new and the old buildings, all of which face on to the new Chamberlain Place from which the Library is entered. A delightful, high Victorian fountain occupies a place of honour in this open space and is surrounded by a grand sweep of curved stairs leading up to the Libraries.

The fact that the building is referred to as the Central Libraries, in the plural, is reflected clearly in the plan, for there are in effect two buildings touching at a corner. The seven-storey Reference Library in the form of an inverted ziggurat built around a large open courtyard is raised high above the public pedestrian way, with its lowest floor on a level with the top floor of the three-storey Lending Library. It was hoped that the large area beneath the library would form an outdoor exhibition but unfortunately such big buildings generate winds which funnel beneath them so that such spaces become draughty and unpleasant. When the remainder of the development is complete this effect may however be modified, but it is doubtful if the square will ever be a very sympathetic space as the English climate is not conducive to outdoor activities in the same way as, for example, Mediterranean countries where such a solution would undoubtedly be enormously popular. It is to be hoped that one day tree planting and other landscaping will be undertaken, for the hardness of all the finishes needs the contrast of natural growth to show the architecture off to best advantage.

Projecting from a corner of the Reference block the Lending Library follows a gentle curve which is a welcome relief from the rather rigid, rectangular quality of its neighbour. Whilst the Reference block is inward-looking with mainly solid outside walls, the Lending block looks outwards from its long windows with their projecting balconies. Finishes are limited to abrasive blasted concrete for structural beams and colums, and simulated Portland stone concrete for the precast panels, giving a unity to the exterior of the building which is vital because of its large volume and complexity.

Entering the building one is immediately in a pleasant lobby which is used for a succession of changing exhibitions. However, when we visited it there was nothing on display and the area presented a somewhat temporary, untidy appearance, exaggerated by the intrusive desk which had been set up as a security checkpoint—a precaution against possible terrorist attacks on the building by the IRA. We were told that the time-gap between exhibitions was minimal but to us it seemed that provision of some light curtaining to hide the empty area, or whilst setting up or dismantling exhibitions, would be worthwhile. A flight of steps leads down to the Children's Library which faces on to a small landscaped garden and with a separate side entry—again unfortunately closed for security reasons. This area is most imaginatively designed though on the

QUICK R
UP
LENDING
LIBRARY
VISUAL
AIDS
MUSIC
LIBRARY
REFERENCE
DEPTS

small side. The accent is on informality and a fascinating feature is the provision of a room for various activities, screened off from the library, where children may draw, paint and do virtually anything which depends on using books to gather information and ideas. A large pin-board displays the results of such work. Children are encouraged to use this area in any way that they can imagine and the results are exciting. The old idea of dispensing books to children to read at home is therefore only one aspect of this department's service and the busy hustle of the place shows the children's appreciation.

From the entrance hall, steps lead up to the main Reception counter beyond double doors. At this counter a well informed and charming receptionist dispensed information and gives directions to the library services with great efficiency and friendliness, establishing an atmosphere for the whole service. The desk stands at one end of a long hall with escalators at the other, leading up to the Lending Library and flanked by the Quick Reference Department and Commercial Information Desk. This very popular and efficient department is placed at the lowest level, closest to the main entry point because it is intensively used by business people in the city centre. A highly trained staff of very bright young librarians is in constant attendance to deal with queries of a specific nature related to every aspect of commercial life; the switchboard, tucked away behind, enables telephoned enquiries to be answered by the same staff with equal expedition. Entry is through gates controlled by an electrical system to maintain security and to limit pilfering.

The use of escalators for the main circulation of the building was a courageous decision, taken at the outset. Quite apart from its obvious advantages in handling large numbers of people there are other benefits not obvious from the plans. Quietness is all important and ease of vertical movement in this tall building is much better achieved by this means than by lifts which tend to divide the building into layers. But most exciting is the purely aesthetic benefit; the movement of the escalators enables visitors to stand and quietly contemplate their movement through the building, to see the skilful interlocking of spaces and the subtle progression of the volume of the building.

Arriving at first floor level one enters the Lending Library past parallel 'In' and 'Out' counters which can be doubled-up by manning duplicate parallel counters at peak periods. The large lending department is split into three sections with a main open access bookstack area which is balconied to overlook the main entrance hall; a reading lounge and foreign lending areas on mezzanine floors at higher and lower levels are reached by means of short staircases bridging the tall central void above the entrance hall. The lounge is a delightful area in which to relax and gaze out over the centre of the city, relishing a magnificent view. Above the Lending Library is another gallery which gives access to the offices of the Librarian and his chief officers. This overlooks the lending area so that the sense of space and varied views are of great interest and excitement. A lift from the main entrance lobby stopping at all levels enables disabled readers to reach all areas. Readers registration and workrooms for staff are unobtrusively placed in a projecting wing to the north, admirably planned but out of sight.

To reach the Reference Library one must pass along a glazed bridge with views into the Reference Library square, passing a cloakroom where coats and bags must be left. This does help to control pilfering but creates something of a bottleneck at closing time. From this level the escalator journey to the first Reference Library floor is in two stages split by a control where visitors are issued with a date stamped entry card which must be given up on leaving the library as a further security check. At this level there are also generous public lavatories, and access is gained to staff offices, interlibrary loans, processing, and other departments. Some of the workrooms slung beneath the main library floors and heavily glazed to allow the feeling of space to penetrate, are very bleak and cold though well planned and conveniently located.

Arriving at the first of the five Reference floors one is immediately aware of a total change of atmosphere and in the presence of an extraordinary architectural conception of great subtlety. The external walls are solid except for a narrow strip of high-level window, the inner courtyard walls full-glazed but with an external shelf which helps counteract the vertiginous effect of the view into the deep light-well.

As one ascends from floor to floor, always in the same corner of the building, the space increases in size at each floor because the outside walls of the square are stepped out at each level.

Internally the square plan is divided into public open access areas on the two wings radiating from the escalators and closed access stack areas on the other two sides of the square, with staircases, ducts and lifts at each corner. The open access areas are further varied by the use of large voids in the middle—first of one wing then, at the next level, of the other. The structure is supported on an inner ring of 12 huge cruciform columns with an outer ring of large columns like fins. Floors are of *in situ* concrete with an interesting coffered ceiling, into which lighting is fitted. The design of the structure is totally flexible so that any of the library floors may be totally replanned should the need arise, adequate floor loading taking account of even rolling stack requirements.

Enquiry counters are located close to the top of each escalator and on each floor the two public wings are devoted to different subject classification ranging from Music with a splendid listening room equipped with many earphone and record deck pads to Science and Technology, Fine Arts, History and Topography. On the sixth floor the famous Shakespeare Library, with its priceless collection of material, occupies part of one wing elegantly equipped with a special glass-fronted bookcases and glass-topped display cases. Closed stacks are manned by staff and books can be requested from a number of counters related to each subject area.

Behind each of the main enquiry counters a corner workroom occurs, with connections from floor to floor by staff stairs and lift. These rooms are extremely useful and well planned but might perhaps have benefited by the introduction of the occasional window at low level to supplement the ubiquitous high-level strip, and to give staff a view out.

On the top floor the whole aspect of the building changes dramatically, for a sloping roof has been used, consisting of precast concrete units neatly clipping together to cover the building. The underside is visible and creates a magnificent space above the Local Studies Archives area with its long counter and galleried upper floor, reached by a small white, cast iron, antique spiral staircase. The same sloping roof forms the ceiling to the large staff canteen which has access in fine weather to a spacious roof terrace whilst Muniment Rooms and Plant occupy the other two sides of the seventh floor.

Fittings through the library have been elegantly designed and detailed by the Architects using oak with black lino tops and this, together with the universal red carpet, exposed aggregate concrete columns and smooth coffered ceilings produce a consistent interior of immense distinction and sophistication. Detailing throughout and attention requirements, lettering etc is scrupulous and immaculate and has been matched by the quality of execution.

This has produced overall the most distinguished and professional library built in this country and must, in future, form a reference point of excellence to which others responsible for new libraries should turn. It is, of course, impossible for this to be the norm, as few Authorities can afford the resources lavished on this building, but the philosophy and the meticulousness of the preparation of a brief and the solution in architectural terms are always possible. In close co-operation lies the answer. A knowledgeable, analytical client who knows what he wants and an intelligent architect who can subjugate his architecture to the needs of the brief are all that are needed. A tall order, perhaps, but go and see Birmingham Libraries and see what can be done through skill and goodwill.

GKVT   HW

Authority	Birmingham District Council (formerly City)
Designation	Central Library
Date of opening	June 1973
Population served	1,084,000
Name of Architect	John Madin Design Group John H D Madin, DipArch (Birm), J A Maudsley, CBE, RIBA, DipTP, MRTPI, City Architect and subsequently W G Reed, MCD, BArch, RIBA, MRTPI
Name of Librarian	W A Taylor, MC, FLA
Special features:	
a) site	City centre adjacent to city buildings on bridged-over section of inner ring road
b) architecture	Concrete structure cast on site with precast concrete cladding panels
c) function	—
Mechanical Services:	
a) heating	} Air-conditioned
b) ventilation	
c) lighting	Mainly fluorescent with some tungsten and down-lighting spotlights
d) acoustics	Carpeted; coffered ceilings in reference areas. Acoustic tiled ceiling in lending area
e) other	Escalator circulation throughout
Areas: in square metres	
a) lending	1,477
b) reference	10,028
c) reading	in (b)
d) special activities	—
e) children	295
f) control	—
g) library staff admin.	1,128
h) exhibitions	278
i) lecture hall	— (not yet completed)
j) circulation	836
k) services	3,130
l) lavatories	66
m) stack	4,130
Total area:	21,368
Book volumes:	
a) adult lending	115,000
b) adult reference	963,050
c) children	45,000
d) stack	in (a) or (b)
e) other	(15,000 gr: 1,400 cas: 375,000 illus. none included in total)
Total:	1,123,050 (books only)
Costs in £ p:	
a) site	—
b) building	4,091,589
c) furniture & fittings	592,000
Total Cost (ex fees):	£4,683,589
Cost per square metre:	£220

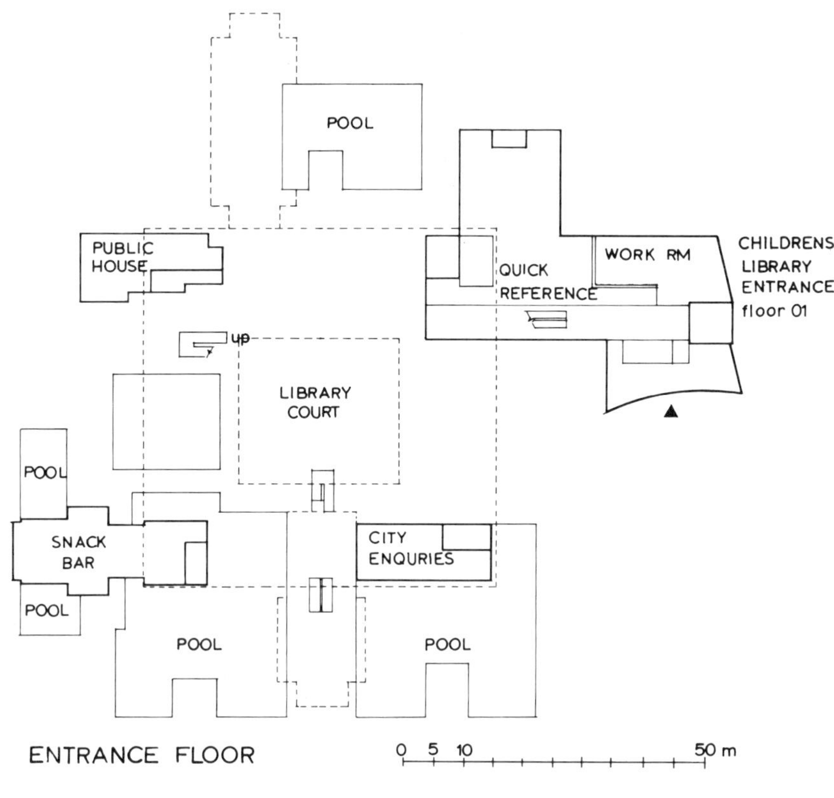

ENTRANCE FLOOR

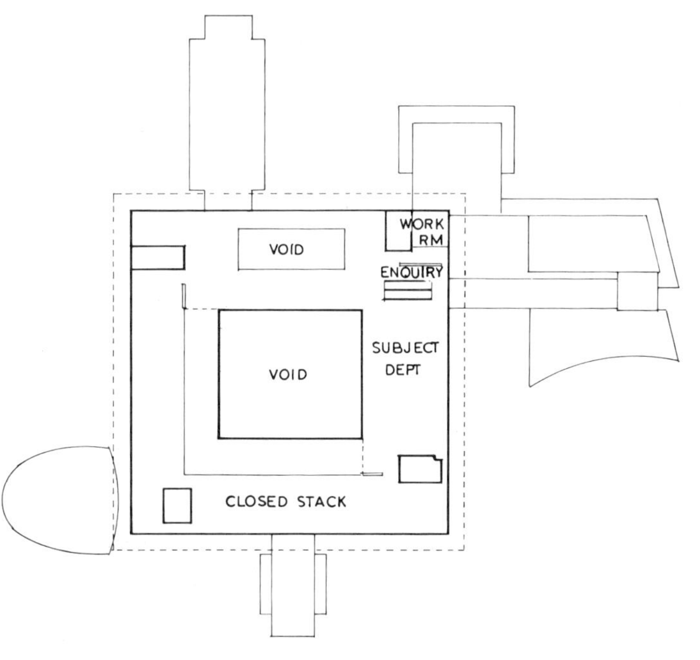

TYPICAL REFERENCE LIBRARY FLOOR

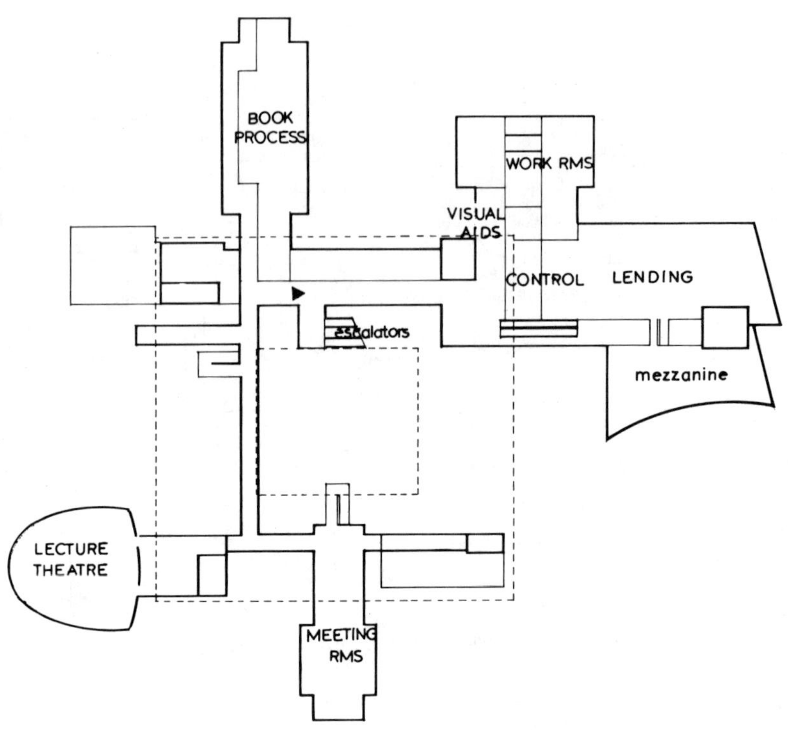

FIRST FLOOR

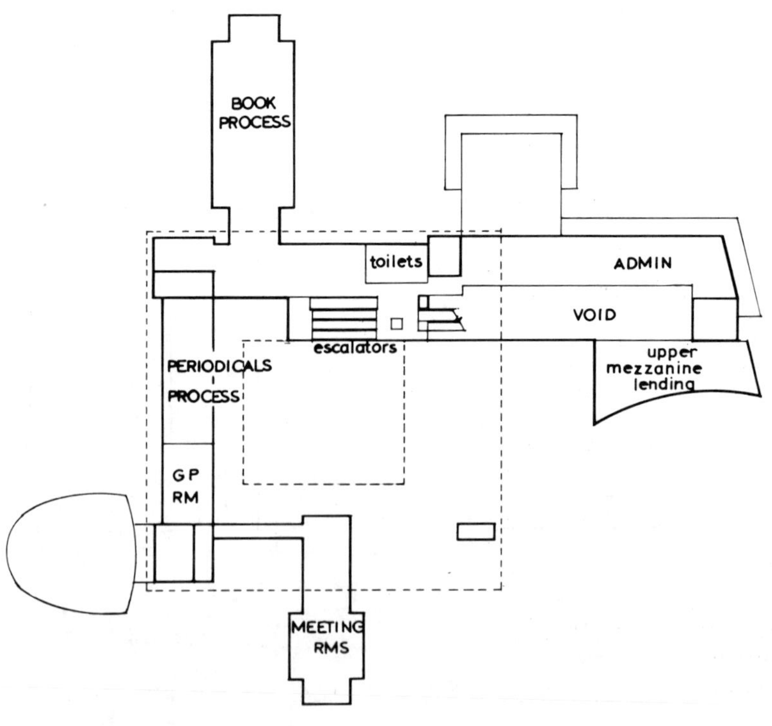

SECOND FLOOR

Birmingham District Council (formerly Borough of Sutton Coldfield)

This library, which was planned when Sutton Coldfield was a Library Authority in its own right, forms part of the system of libraries administered by the City of Birmingham. The population of the town is about 85,000, so that there is a substantial shopping centre here, though Birmingham offers considerably more comprehensive facilities only 20 minutes away by car.

The advantage of having a site at the very centre of the shopping area has been gained by an enterprising deal negotiated between the previous Authority and Sainsburys who, as part of the joint development, built a supermarket and a parade of small shops over service areas linked to a multi-storey car park. For this benefit the library had to make one major sacrifice but one which, in the circumstances, seems reasonable; it had to move up on to the first and second floors. In fact, because the site slopes steeply, the shopping parade with a delightful small courtyard which form the approach to both library and supermarket, are at an upper floor level when approached from the side street where most buses disgorge their passengers, though these are on a level with the main shopping street and another large shopping complex beyond.

The development has many elements each expressed within a limited range of materials, but predominantly in red brick. The library block is of rectangular form with a steady rhythm of pairs of narrow vertical windows alternating with panels of brick to side elevations above a band of travertine, a material which is also used in the undercill panels. More variety occurs on the façade overlooking the main street where two large angled bay windows introduce an element of fun. Unfortunately signposting to the library is hardly adequate but this was due to a financial stringency decision of the Council—not its officers.

Mention has been made of the entrance courtyard which is charming, just right in scale, well sheltered and sunny with low planking and an interesting grit blasted concrete mural incorporating themes of local historical significance. From this space the library is approached through a luxurious lobby with rather grand stairs to the first floor: there is a lift available for readers who are less active. Good notices ensure that there is no doubt as to the direction in which the main facilities lie, although they are out of sight. A feature of the lobby is the indoor planting and attractive display area.

At first floor level there is, on the stair landing, a fine (illuminated) display of the former Authority's mayoral regalia, appealing no doubt to civic pride. A door leads directly into a music and gramophone record library which the librarian admits is much too small for its intensive use. Since it is adjacent to the generous Lending Library, into which it could easily have extended, this was an error which can be remedied, sooner, one hopes, than later. The Lending Library is approached from a corridor which also gives access to the Children's Library and a meeting room seating about 100 people and well equipped with a stage and facilities for exhibitions, and with audio equipment. The library counter is U-shaped with clear 'In' and 'Out' channels. An interesting feature is that at times of peak demand additional staff can be drafted in to additional counters parallel to each channel, thus doubling the normal capacity for issue and return of books.

Layout of the Reska bookshelving is fairly conventional but a pleasant area of seating at the far end where the triangular bays introduce much interest. The windows generally are rather heavily detailed, which is a pity for in such a deep building, which must obviously rely mainly on artificial light, the windows are principally for visual relief. Views to the outside are somewhat limited and it does not help to have even these cut into pieces by the dark anodised aluminium frames. Whilst in no way advocating a return to period design, there are lessons to be gained from the detailing of the Georgian or Victorian windows, painted white and moulded so as to effect a modelling of the light and to give a varied progression from the dark of the room to the light of the sky.

Children's libraries always present to the designer a challenge to produce a particular solution in terms of scale and character whilst recognising the needs of children. In this case there is little to learn from the design which is on the full side. Pleasant views to the old parish church on its hill contribute something but scarcely enough.

The Reference Library is at second floor level, again rather conventionally laid out. However there is a welcome variety of differing types of seating, desks, semi-carrels and rather well detailed enclosed carrels (although the top is open) and with just the right amount of glazing to prevent claustrophobia. The staff area is enclosed in a completely internal room yet having a glazed partition rather than the usual counter. This is perhaps a little inhibiting to members of the public requiring information.

Beyond the carrels there is a pleasant section of the library devoted to local history with a specialist readers' adviser at a desk. Since this is again the area with the triangular window bays the atmosphere here is lively with good views up and down the main road.

A rolling stack with overflow of about 10,000 books is planned on this floor in a rather curious position, opening off a totally internal fire escape stair. A huge office is provided for the Librarian with more modest rooms for the Deputy and secretaries, and an excellent staff room with civilised provision of a well-equipped kitchen which is hidden behind a wall; this enables good furnishing to produce a domestic atmosphere. All too often the design of staff rooms does not appear to recognise sufficiently the professional status of librarians—but here staff are treated as such.

The general form of the library, with its deep plan, is consciously economical and is aimed at energy conservation; but it is a pity that the opportunity for introducing some top lighting on the upper floor was missed. Admittedly there is a caretaker's flat which occupies much of the roof space but with even some perimeter rooflights the building could have been made more lively. On the whole, however, this is a good building excellently sited at the centre of gravity of the town.

GKVT   HW

Authority	District Council of Birmingham (formerly Borough of Sutton Coldfield
Designation	Central Library, Sutton Coldfield
Date of opening	November 1974
Population served	87,000
Name of Architect	Jas A Roberts,
Name of Librarian	B J Cahalin, FLA
Special features:	
a) site	Within main shopping precinct and over shops
b) architecture	Hand-made brick
c) function	—
Mechanical Services:	
a) heating	Air-conditioned
b) ventilation	
c) lighting	Fluorescent strip; some spotlighting
d) acoustics	Double glazing; carpeted; acoustic tiles
e) other	—
Areas: in square metres	
a) lending	604
b) reference	445
c) reading	in (b)
d) special activities	74
e) children	232
f) control	—
g) library staff admin.	278
h) exhibitions	130
i) lecture hall	120
j) circulation	372
k) services	—
l) lavatories	92
m) stack	60
Total area:	2,407
Book volumes:	
a) adult lending	60,000
b) adult reference	10,000
c) children	20,000
d) stack	10,000
e) other	8,500 gr, cas, pictures
Total:	108,500
Costs in £ p:	
a) site	—
b) building	500,000 (approx)
c) furniture & fittings	70,000
Total Cost (ex fees):	£570,000 (approx)
Cost per square metre:	—

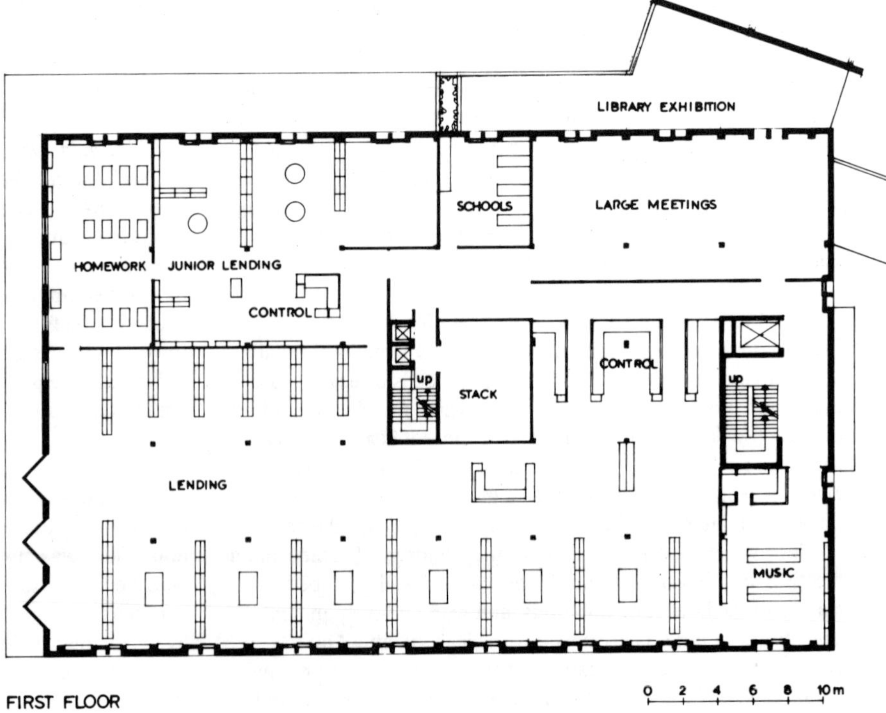

FIRST FLOOR

Berkshire County Council (formerly Borough of Maidenhead): Maidenhead District Library

Not many small towns are the objects of architectural pilgrimages from international travellers–to see the new public library! This is happening constantly at Maidenhead, helped by its proximity to Heathrow Airport, but mainly due to the quality of the architecture by one of this country's most talented architectural partnerships–Ahrends, Burton and Koralek. The new library is stunning, in the sense that it is a building that stops one short, and challenges all one's preconceptions about 'what is a library building'?

In 1966 the architects were commissioned to prepare a feasibility study to consider possible extensions to the old library, to bring it up to the standards laid down in the Public Libraries and Museums Act 1964. It was estimated that additions would cost £160,000, and a new building £180,000. They were commissioned to design a new building, using the feasibility study as the basis for the brief; work started on site in 1970, and the new library was opened early in 1974. The brief provided library facilities for a population of 60,000, in accordance with DES recommendations; with the provision of lending, reference, music and children's library facilities; a divisible meeting room, exhibition space, coffee bar, staff and administration space, book stack, and a mobile library garage. Under boundary reorganisation it is the District Library for Windsor and Maidenhead, population 130,000, and serves nine branch libraries.

The site is ideally placed in the centre of the town, near to the main High Street shopping, and to the nearby bus station, and is backed by the neo-Georgian Council Offices, circa 1962. The site slopes steeply down to the east where there is a belt of fine mature trees, and a stream that has recently been cleared, now the basis of a linear water garden. A new bridge across the stream brings a path from the bus station, past the library, and this will connect with a central area pedestrianisation scheme when it reaches the library. The old library was still in use when the new library was being built, but it has now been removed and the site is laid out as a memorial garden. This leads up to the library entrance and replaces the former war memorial, on which site the new library is built.

The architect Le Corbusier maintained that 'the plan is the generator', and the plan of the Maidenhead Library should be studied for its simplicity, clarity, and logic; but this may be lost at first glance at the apparent complexity of the external form. The cranked sloping path from the memorial garden leads one under a first floor balcony, forming an entrance canopy, through the entrance doors, past the exhibition space to the control counter which is backed by a staircase and lift which form the centrally placed service core, whilst on one side is the readers' adviser. From this central 'core' radiate the Music Library, periodicals area, Lending Library, and the Children's Library, with its own enclosed amphitheatre garden. A second staircase leads up from the entrance to the Reference Library and meeting rooms above, forming a first floor gallery which occupies about half the area of the ground floor, and overlooks the lending library and exhibition space. The Librarian is situated on the ground floor near to the centre, and the lift and service stair lead down to the lower floor, allocated to administration, bookstack, staff rooms, and the mobile garage.

Following another dictum of modern architecture 'form follows function', the square plan is logically covered by a square space frame roof, resting on eight cruciform shaped concrete columns. From this roof, covered with corrugated metal decking, glazed walls appear to be suspended onto a red brick enclosure, which projects outwards all round the building to form hooded enclosures for book shelves and secluded reading areas. Internally there is a very simple vocabulary of finishes. Brick is used extensively for walls and some floor paving; concrete structure is exposed while ceiling soffits are plastered, except for the exposed metal decking of the roof. Carpet is used extensively as a floor finish–although the tiled entrance and exhibition area was noticeably noisy–perhaps due partly to the modern trend in footwear.

Environmentally the building works. Windows are double glazed, and the space frame roof forms a wide overhang to prevent glare from the sun. Heating is from fan-assisted night storage heaters. The main lighting is from industrial type 400-watt mercury vapour lamps suspended within the roof structure, with localised fluorescent tubes, and recessed tungsten downlights. Mention was made in passing of a 'drumming on the tin roof in heavy rain.

Detailing is immaculate throughout and the design of fittings and choice of furniture is excellent, be it the charging counter, the mobile and lockable record browsing trolleys, or the purpose designed library tables, derived from the same architects' Trinity College, Dublin Library. The design and furnishing of the staff restroom would qualify for a colour spread in *House and Garden*, and must be the envy of visiting librarians.

The whole forms an interesting separation, yet integration, of interior building and external enclosure; a dichotomy which has produced sharp divisions between the building's admirers and critics. It is a building with an 'image'; you cannot miss or ignore it; the beautiful cedar tree around which this new building at one corner seems to fit is almost breathtaking by its closeness when viewed from the Reference Library. The librarian reports that however divided people's opinion is about the library's external form, its interior is universally admired and appreciated, borne out by a readership of about 50%. With such a range of colours internally though (chosen by the architects) one could think that some people might not find this entirely pleasing–red brick, brown tiles, russet carpet, orange display boards mainly–but some are magenta–purple for the stair carpet and window-seat cushions, maroon girders and black window frames.

It was in 1967 that Peter Ahrends spoke at the Library Association's London and Home Counties Library Conference, on the subject 'What is a Library Building?'; eventually from that conference developed the working party of librarians and architects that prepares this publication now. It is at Maidenhead that Peter Ahrends' partner, Paul Koralek, has given a startling answer to that question, and at the same time produced one modern British library that deserves the description 'great architecture'.

NR HW

Authority	Berkshire County Council (formerly Maidenhead Borough Council)
Designation	Central Library
Date of opening	February 1973
Population served	47,000
Name of Architect	Ahrends, Burton & Koralek
Name of Librarian	J C Powell, FLA
Special features:	
a) site	Steeply sloping site between bus station and main shopping area
b) architecture	Reinforced concrete frame under space deck roof. Fair-faced concrete with red brick infilling.
c) function	To provide full range of services for town of Maidenhead and act as District Library for much larger area
Mechanical Services:	
a) heating	Fan assisted night storage heaters
b) ventilation	Natural. Extractor fans in meeting rooms
c) lighting	400 w mercury vapour lamps suspended in ceiling with localised fluorescent tubes and recessed tungsten downlights
d) acoustics	Double glazing. Carpeted floors
e) other	—
Areas: in square metres	
a) lending	441
b) reference	274
c) reading	—
d) special activities	69 (Music library)
e) children	155
f) control	—
g) library staff admin.	287
h) exhibitions & circulation	144
i) lecture hall	116
j) circulation	—
k) services	163 (including garage)
l) lavatories	80
m) stack	149
Total area:	1,880
Book volumes:	
a) adult lending	30,000
b) adult reference	10,000
c) children	8,000
d) stack	30,000
e) other	—
Total:	78,000
Costs in £ p:	
a) site	—
b) building	215,000
c) furniture & fittings	16,000
Total Cost (ex fees):	£231,000
Cost per square metre:	£123

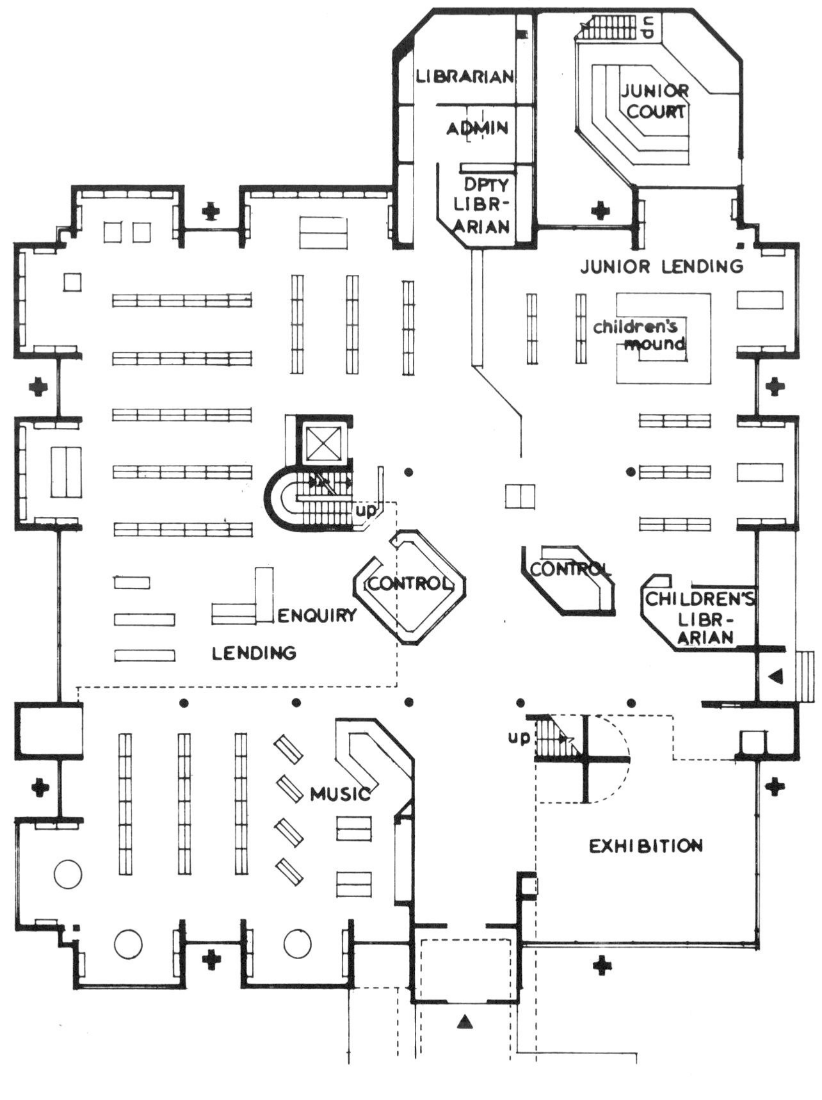

GROUND FLOOR

Berkshire County Council (formerly Buckinghamshire County): Slough Central Library

The new central library at Slough was commissioned by Buckinghamshire County Council from a brief prepared in the 1960's. Work began in 1971, and under boundary reorganisation in 1974 the Berkshire County Council inherited virtually a completed building in the design of which they had no part.

Slough has the inevitable inner ring road system, relieving the old High Street, and the new library occupies an island site at one end of the High Street, facing across a huge traffic roundabout to the Technical College (which, unlike the library, splendidly announces its identity high up on the front elevation, for the guidance of car drivers as well as pedestrians). Also nearby is the bus station, and multi-storey car park (there is no library-users car park). The latter approach is through an extensive system of pedestrian underpasses and sunken walkways, better landscaped and rather less graffitied than most, and from its sunken level provides the most dramatic view of the new library.

The building is basically a three-storey block, with a prominent high ceilinged 'piano nobile' first floor. There is no room for enlargement, but is so generously planned that future lack of accommodation must be the least of its problems. The piano nobile first floor contains only the adult lending library; control, bookstacks, children's library and school library service on the ground floor; reference library, staff administration and rest areas, with public meeting rooms on the top floor.

Simply expressed the disposition of accommodation presents no problems, but in use several weaknesses, but also some opportunities, have arisen. The ground floor has two main entrances, one facing the pedestrian underpass, and the other towards the High Street. Inside, two entrances lead to separated 'In' and 'Out' control counters, with the two public lifts and main staircase beyond. These factors have led to considerable problems of staffing, cross-circulation, and confusion amongst users. This should be resolved when a less space-consuming charging system than Browne is introduced; all charging can then be concentrated in one counter. The children's library is on the ground floor, facing the traffic roundabout, but its story room is situated across the entrance hall; however the staff have created a space in the library itself. An extensive area for the school library service is also on the ground floor, adjacent to the mobile library garage.

The first floor of about 1,100 m² is entirely occupied by the adult lending library, living up to one of the main requirements of the brief, for as much space without internal walls as possible. This floor is a generous open space, made additionally so by a ceiling height of over 5 metres. The space is broken only by the main service core containing the lifts, and the main staircase rising through to the floor above. The readers' adviser is placed near to the lift and stairs, with reasonable surveillance over the space. At present it is not stocked to capacity and shelves are generously spaced around the floor; there is plenty of seating, and space for exhibitions; it has even proved a successful space for concerts. The high ceiling would even permit the introduction of a mezzanine floor in the future, if that much expansion were

envisaged. The staff generally consider it an ideal space to work in.

The reference library on the top floor has 20,000 books, ample seating, and six large study carrels. The ceiling height is relatively low, and windows are deliberately restricted to keep out traffic noise, but with additional daylight from rooflights, fitted with a complicated wood louvre system. The main library administration and staff restrooms are on this floor. Originally the library was envisaged as a virtually independent Central Library, requiring more administrative area than is needed now. The redundant area has been reallocated as a suite of meeting rooms; the largest of these links with the reference library, providing an overflow study area at busy time–an excellent idea. It is questionable whether staff areas should be on the top floor, requiring all staff to go there at the beginning and end of the working day. The meeting rooms present a serious security problem, since they have no separate entrance from the street or lift or stair access; this means that evening users have to walk up through the roped-off lending library.

The internal environment seems entirely satisfactory. The library is quiet, even the open adult lending library, helped by the extensive use of carpet tiles. Heating is provided on the ground floor by fan convectors built into the furniture units, plus radiators on the north side of the building. The first and second floors are heated by underfloor water-filled heating cells. Additional heating can be supplied by a number of small fan convectors housed in the bookcase units on the outer wall. Surprisingly the librarian reports that the first floor underfloor heating is often not needed, as there is sufficient warm air rising up the stairwell from the ground floor.

Appearance-wise the design of the exterior appears too pompous for a humane social and educational activity; an element of gigantism which somehow belies the informal relationship of books, information and people that characterises a modern library service. Large rectangular stone faced panels project around the first floor, giving a somewhat fortress-like appearance, and yet they only provide wall space inside for bookshelves. This rather formal civic type library building can be seen as something of a 'maverick' (even if a distinguished one) in the series of extremely attractive and informal libraries produced by the librarian/architect team of Buckinghamshire Council.

At Slough, Berkshire has acquired an outstandingly fine building, both in appearance and accommodation, redolent of the ambitions of an era before the present economic stress and appropriate to the needs of one of the fastest growing industrial towns in southern England. It is a building which has, at present, certain planning and circulation faults, but it is the open nature of the planning concept which should permit any future changes needed to remedy these faults.

It is interesting to compare this building with the Berkshire County Library at Bracknell, reviewed in the 1974 edition of *New Library Buildings*. Bracknell library was designed for an actual population of 60,000, and an ultimate one of 100,000; the population of Slough is now about 100,000. The total area of Bracknell, also on three floors, is about 1,400 m², that of Slough is about 3,350 m²; Bracknell cost £128,000 in 1971, Slough £412,000.

EJC   NR

Authority	Berkshire County Council (formerly Buckinghamshire)
Designation	Central Library, Slough
Date of opening	November 1974
Population served	100,000
Name of Architect	F B Pooley, CBE, RIBA County Architect of Buckinghamshire succeeded by P R Markcrow. Job Architect D O Till
Name of Librarian	C Rippon, FLA
Special features:	
a) site	Island site near town centre
b) architecture	Free standing; 3 library floors; *in-situ* concrete frame construction; white concrete finishes internally and externally
c) function	—
Mechanical Services:	
a) heating	Fan convectors built into furniture units plus radiators in certain rooms. Also on 1st and 2nd floors underfloor water-filled heating cells.
b) ventilation	Natural
c) lighting	Fluorescent strip
d) acoustics	—
e) other	Carpeted
Areas: in square metres	
a) lending	1,098
b) reference	650
c) reading	in (b)
d) special activities	190
e) children	148
f) control	—
g) library staff admin.	—
h) exhibitions	576
i) lecture hall	—
j) circulation	—
k) services	—
l) lavatories	—
m) stack	678
Total area:	3,340
Book volumes:	
a) adult lending	35,000
b) adult reference	20,000
c) children	6,000
d) stack	—
e) other	15,000 Schools library
Total:	76,000
Costs in £ p:	
a) site	
b) building	412,000
c) furniture & fittings	
Total Cost (ex fees):	£412,000
Cost per square metre:	£123

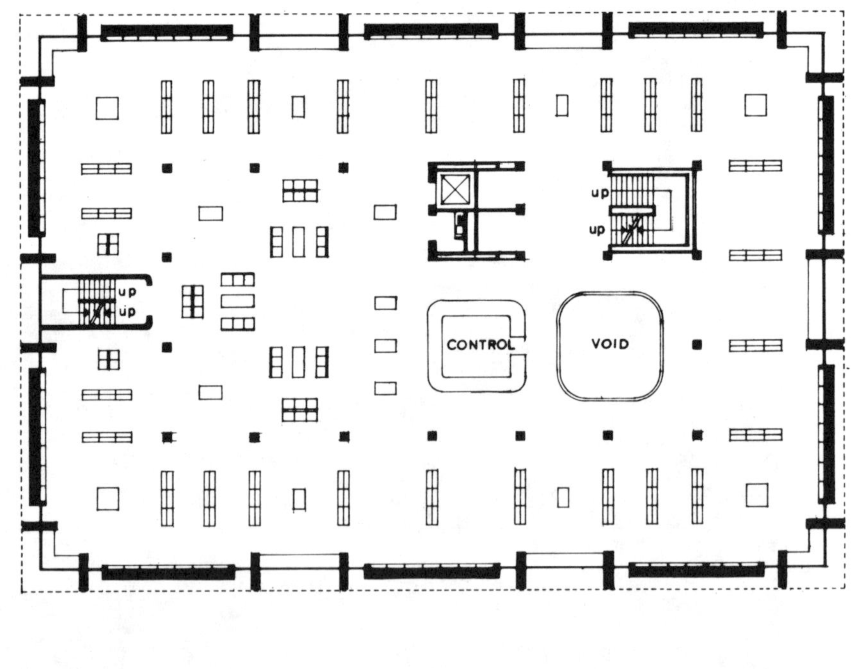

FIRST FLOOR

Bradford District Council (formerly Borough of Bingley)

Bingley has changed a lot since it was an archetypal West Riding manufacturing town. Today, despite some light industry, it serves largely as a dormitory for nearby Bradford. Dark buildings and the general feeling of independence hint at the old tradition. Leading off the High Street is a modern shopping centre which has no particular character about it but ends (temporarily?) with a genuine, huddled open market. Here is the entrance to the new library; an entrance hall containing exhibitions of local interest (in this case steam engines) and the stairs and lift to the library itself. Outside the library is a piece of modern sculpture (illustrated) which provokes by its pointlessness.

The entrance therefore is ideally placed because a comprehensive cluster of small shops, to say nothing of the market and the large parking areas nearby, make it a real focal centre, despite the fact that it is the *back* of the shopping centre: the frontage, on the main road, seems less popular and not so busy.

There are some very odd features indeed about this library. It is approached by an area which is too wide to be a corridor and too narrow to be anything else and ends in a somewhat pointless exhibition space. A pair of stone baffles, now being removed, protected the counter. I call them baffles: nobody seems to know what they were for and their aim certainly baffles me. A collapsible partition nearby hints at flexibility but it is in entirely the wrong position.

The exhibition area ends in a row of steps, which, it is suggested, were to have been used as a podium. At the top of the steps is a kind of emergency exit which the staff insist was decreed by planners as another entrance for readers, even though it leads only on to a partially derelict upper floor of the shopping centre: upper floors of shopping centres normally are derelict.

The building was created by a developer with the Council's architect as consultant. Apart from the crazy planning mentioned above it has some interesting features. There is a very attractive and practical Vilatex synthetic carpet with under-floor heating and some cute segment tables in the children's library. The cases in this area are on castors so that they can be pushed aside to make room for story hours. The plastic laminate sliding fronts to the cupboards over the children's shelves, decorated with transfers, are attractive.

More than any library I have met this one suffers from the change of Authority. Apart from the general planning muddle, the offices and workrooms have been altered from their original purpose and the result is not particularly to be recommended. Nevertheless, and this is the ironical point, the people of Bingley use it and appear to like it. The lift to the main floor appears to be efficient and acceptable and in the busy and cheerful atmosphere in which I saw it working, it is difficult to think of it as the badly planned muddle which I have described.

GT

Authority	Bradford Metropolitan District
Designation	Bingley Public Library
Date of opening	March 1973
Population served	25,475
Name of Architect	Executive Architect Fewster and Partners Consultant Architect Sir John Burnet Tait and Partners
Name of Librarian	Mrs F de Graff, ALA
Special features:	
a) site	First floor level
b) architecture	Papered walls
c) function	—
Mechanical Services:	
a) heating	Electric underfloor
b) ventilation	—
c) lighting	Fluorescent
d) acoustics	Ceiling tiles
e) other	—
Areas: in square metres	
a) lending	500
b) reference	63
c) reading	47
d) special activities	—
e) children	51
f) control	48
g) library staff admin.	95
h) exhibitions	67
i) lecture hall	—
j) circulation	78
k) services	32
l) lavatories	19
m) stack	—
Total area:	1,000
Book volumes:	
a) adult lending	45,752
b) adult reference	2,174
c) children	8,512
d) stack	—
e) other	—
Total:	56,438
Costs in £ p:	
a) site b) building	104,000
c) furniture & fittings	20,000
Total Cost (ex fees):	£124,000
Cost per square metre:	£75

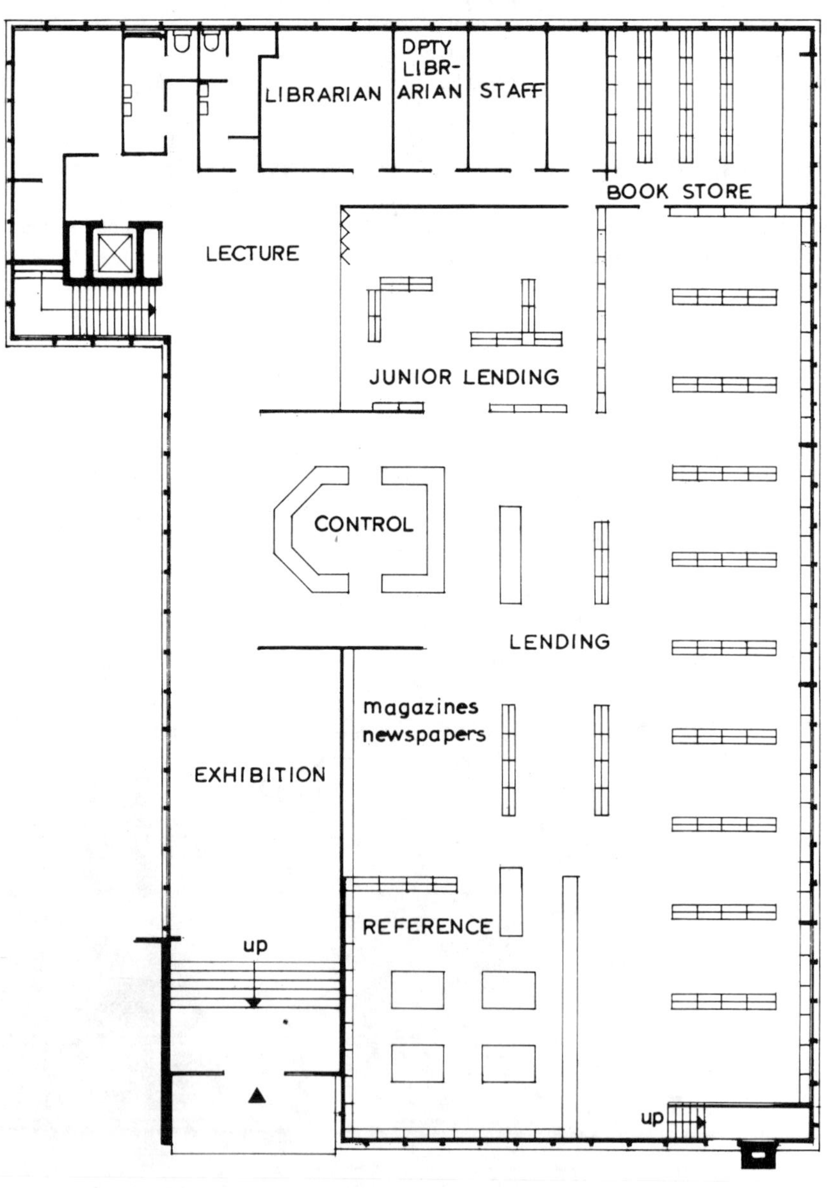

GROUND FLOOR

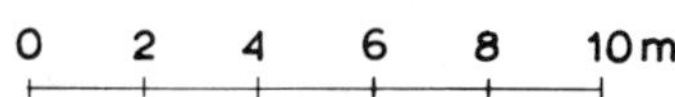

Essex County Council (formerly County Borough of Southend-on-Sea)

Earlier visits to the former Central Library in this Thames Estuary town (170,000 population) had suggested that its prominent corner site, near to the main shopping areas, was a good one, and the use of the building gave proof of this. The decision therefore to erect the new Central Library on a large site immediately to the north of this building (leaving that to be developed as a comprehensive local history museum) seemed sound enough, particularly as the new library was to link into the main Civic Centre complex and the Courthouse. However, visiting the new Central Library twice within three months and discussing this question of siting with the Librarian, it can be seen that the planning of that 'corner' as a huge roundabout, is now so heavily trafficked that pedestrians wanting to move between the shops and the library must go via a 'flyover' footbridge reached by means of escalators. This we were told had produced disadvantages for maximising library use, although a large building at that roundabout, housing the staff for centralised VAT does provide extra library borrowers; undoubtedly no-one, certainly not ourselves, can fail to be impressed by this building which is not only striking in its design, particularly internally, but impresses by its careful planning, quality furnishing and decor and its immaculate attention to detail.

During the five years for the project to be developed the original Borough Architect was succeeded and it was with this architect that we spoke. He was generous in his praise of the librarian client, who he said, had demonstrated such positive views on what he desired and had maintained close collaboration with his team throughout all stages.

A large, if metered, car park is reached from the main road by ramp to an upper deck which leaves the library user but a few yards to walk to reach its impressive entrance. Already noticed had been the inviting appeal of the library, seen through the bronze glass infilled curtain wall which rises between the perimeter columns to a second floor level. This glass not only ensures a mellowing image but fulfils its main purpose of absorbing heat to reduce solar gain. The cream precast concrete for the second floor perimeter wall blends well with this glass, which is held by bronze anodised aluminium mullions and transoms.

Entering through the automatic doors the visitor's immediate impression is one of space, vertically and horizontally, created by the central well of varying dimensions at each of the three public levels. Administration offices occupy a smaller area above that with the plant room one level higher. This two level 'topper', noticed when approaching the building, detracts a little from the overall visual appeal.

Functionally, the plan for a vertical core in the centre of the building to handle reserve stocks (on rolling stacks) which serve the floors that 'float' outwards from it, is highly successful. The walls of this core present a pleasing aspect, being deep bronze in colour and bold in relief. They consist of sculptured ceramic tiles (approximately the shape and size of a large brick) which are bonded on fibre glass, made up into panels which are then bolted to the wall.

Equally noticeable is the 'Flotex' carpet with an attractive black and grey motif which was specially designed in conjunction with the Architect. Mention was made here by the architect of care in choice, as some carpets when edged at balcony level with metal guard rails can give rise to minor electrical shocks for some people.

Descending by staircase from the ground floor lending area into the 'well' of the Junior Library, there is noticeably plenty of area for circulation and for project work, natural lighting coming through a glass wall (facing south into a courtyard area to link with the planned Local History Museum). Artificial lighting is by fluorescents above the wall shelves supplemented by 1000 watt Kolorark lamps in recessed fittings above the well'. A meeting room was in full use by a class of secondary school pupils who were being introduced to the purpose and use of this new library by a senior member of staff. Adjacent to this room is the air-conditioned, 112-seater lecture hall; brightly furnished in yellow, the comfortable seats with note-taking rests are set on a steep rake to give all-over clear view for demonstration lectures, training sessions, films etc, put on by both library and outside organisations. These facilities, available day and evening make the provision of a cafeteria much needed, and indeed, here is one offering good service and pleasant atmosphere. Reached by stairs from the hall foyer, itself a small exhibition area with hessian-lined walls where the full range of municipal entertainment and activities in the town are displayed, this cafeteria is sensibly located so that its kitchen servery runs into the staff room area, which is generous in space, furniture and facilities.

The first floor has, on its north side, Art, Music and Picture Lending, together with exhibition space which leads into Language and Literature on the west. Beyond the well, that is to the south, there is what seems a too-generous area for magazines and newspapers in relation to the very important sections on this floor.

The second floor houses the Reference and Study area with approximately 60 seats, and Local History. Southend being a repository for the Essex County Records requires substantial space for this material and again it is hard to satisfy present requirements (let alone future ones) with Commerce, Technology, History, Travel and Biography as well as the Humanities at this level. A smaller third floor houses the 'top' administration and support staff, while the mechanical services are above that.

This building, in operation, is a tribute to the careful and clear thinking which went into its planning—initially by the Borough Librarian, developed through working parties and by continuing dialogues with Borough Architect colleagues (two during the period) and then senior staff allocated to the scheme. Materials of quality were carefully selected so that each made its contribution to a harmonious blend. Similar care is clearly revealed in the detailing, be it the positioning of power sockets or the handles of doors. All this ensures pleasure for the users as well as satisfaction at the efficiency possible in such a building.

Librarians and architects faced with the planning of a large library should not, even if at long distance from this south-eastern tip of England, fail to make a visit there. Fast trains from London as well as an arterial road make it easily possible to make that part of the journey in an hour. It would be hard to imagine either professional not then thinking the trip to have been well worthwhile.

GKVT HW

Authority	Essex County Council (formerly County Borough of Southend-on-Sea)
Designation	Central Library
Date of opening	March 1974
Population served	164,000
Name of Architect	R Horswell, DipArch, RIBA, DipTP, Borough Architect (in succession to N P Astins, RIBA) A C Membery, DipArch, RIBA, Project Architect
Name of Librarian	L Helliwell, FLA
Special features:	
a) site	Part of Civic Complex; Council Suite Offices; Court House and Library with car park
b) architecture	To complement existing buildings: *in-situ* concrete frame clad at second floor with cream precast concrete panels over anti-sun bronze glass wall
c) function	Central Library and HQ for whole library system
Mechanical Services:	
a) heating	Accelerated hot water feeding underfloor coils and plenum plant served by modular gas-fired boilers
b) ventilation	Four zoned plants supplying warm filtered air through ceiling mounted diffusers. Lecture theatre has own air-conditioning
c) lighting	Fluorescent in library areas plus 1,000 W MBIF 'Kolorark' lamps over well to illuminate Children's Library. Spotlight tracks in exhibition and display areas
d) acoustics	Suspended ceilings; 'Trectex' glacier tiles
e) other	—
Areas: in square metres	
a) lending	1,040
b) reference	635
c) reading	174
d) special activities	116
e) children	272
f) control	95
g) library staff admin.	510
h) exhibitions	140
i) lecture hall	125
j) circulation	895
k) services	450
l) lavatories	102
m) stack	205 58 cafeteria 46 meeting room 72 loading bay
Total area:	4,935
Book volumes:	
a) adult lending	40,000
b) adult reference	10,000
c) children	6,000
d) stack	66,000
e) other	8,000 (inc gr, mf, LH illus)
Total:	130,000
Costs in £ p:	
a) site	in Civic ownership
b) building	687,778
c) furniture & fittings	92,000
Total Cost (ex fees):	£779,778
Cost per square metre:	£159

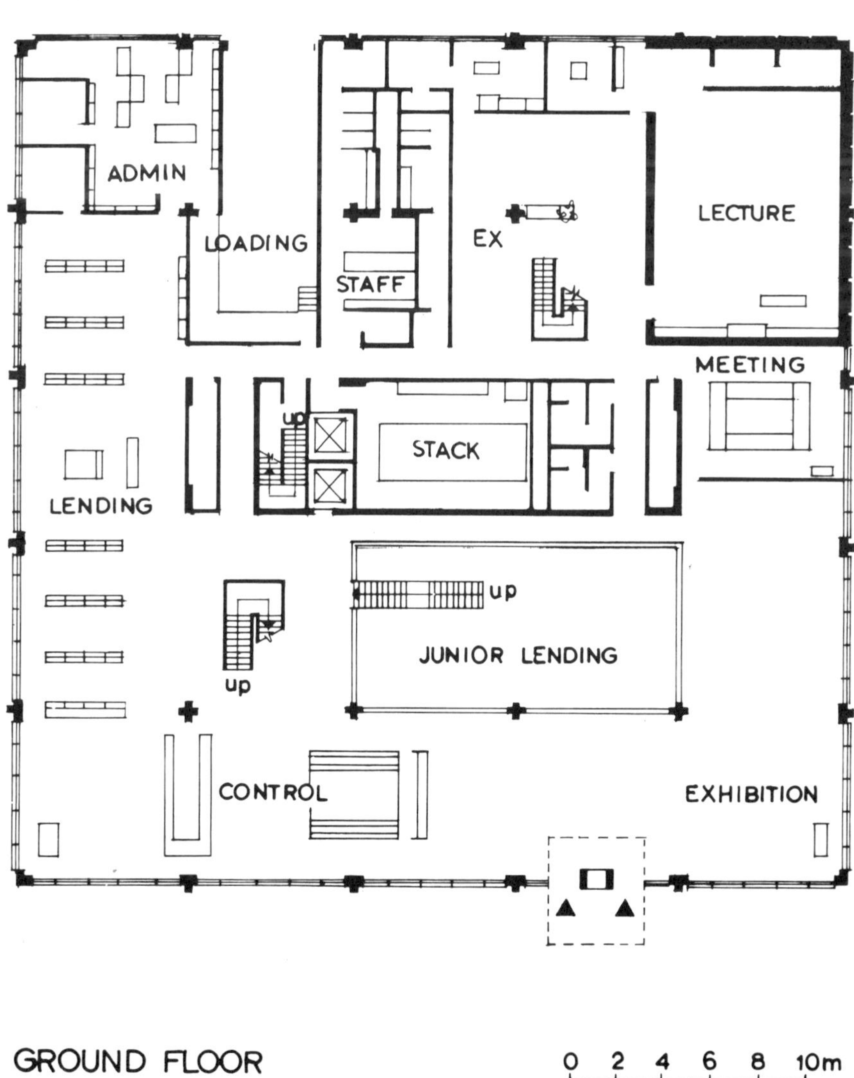

GROUND FLOOR

The library is grouped with the Town Hall and a Department of Employment building, within a pedestrian precinct, and situated just off the main shopping street–and, in addition, near a cinema which is still actively operating. A large, closed-access Town Hall staff car park has been provided at the rear, the public being catered for with car parking next to a recreation ground and boating pool; thus there are plenty of reasons why people will be drawn to this location.

The precinct is attractively laid out with raised plant beds, lit from anodized bronze lighting columns, while the paved area is interspersed with patterns of red brick. Rather than ramps for handicapped persons this paving slopes gently up to the main entrance.

The building is constructed in reinforced concrete with red face brickwork to the panels and plinths. The windows are bronze anodized aluminium with Armorclad glass. The entrance with wide double doors, well capable of allowing wheelchairs, has a glass frontage and sides, with strip metal ceiling well lit by fluorescent and tungsten downlighting, while secondary doors help to exclude winter draughts.

Within, on the left side, is a 'delayed discharge counter' with work area behind and an enquiry desk adjacent, while on the opposite side is a large counter to cater for 'Bookamatic' issuing. Immediately ahead are terrazzo stairs with wooden rails and glass side panels; the stairs seemed too narrow on this busy Saturday morning (an issue of over 4,000 was expected that day). To its side is a large direction panel to the upper floors–two main and each with a mezzanine.

The texture sprayed concrete ceiling has a waffle pattern and within each of the 5×5 groupings is housed a 3×3 grouping of tungsten discharge lamps within acrylic diffusers. These lights take about a minute from switch-on to reach full intensity; emergency lighting has also been installed. At this time however a 50% restriction on artificial lighting was in force.

Peculiarly noticeable was the cloaking to shoulder height of some of the cylindrical support columns by the use of plastic sheeting. This was stated, on enquiry and examination, to be a prevention against personal injury and damage to clothes as the columns have a very coarse abrasive surface which has given rise to quite serious complaints.

The ground floor is allocated to a claimed 'Popular Library' although this contains History and Biography as well as Fiction and not the usually attempted range of subjects. Floor to ceiling height drops from here at about 18 ft to around 8 ft 6 in under the mezzanine floor. Also at ground level is the Children's Library (rather surprisingly, with its high issues, it has no separate entrance–equally surprising, the staff have no separate entrance). An activities room is adjacent, used also for staff training and for weekly lunchtime gramophone recitals, piped from the Music Library on the mezzanine above. There is no basement (the distance to the sea can be measured in yards), and rolling stack storage is at ground level. At the mid-level there are further shelves for non-fiction subjects which are completed on

the next mezzanine. This latter is reached via the main floor level on which is the Reference Library and Study Area. Carrels for use as language laboratories are available. Asked why, when the rest of the library was so busy, the 'Ref' was almost unused (certainly not one of the 80 desk places was occupied at 10 am), the answer was that Portsmouth was so near; even though access is by ferry only, that library is only a mere 15 minutes away.

Up to the second mezzanine where the rest of the shelving is so regimented that in some places these are only 4 ft 6 in apart. With Dewey classes 000–799 to be housed here plus an exhibition area, it really is tight. Administration, with book hoist connection from the delivery area, and the staff accommodation (small with 11 chairs only, but attractive) are on the floor above which also gives access to a roof patio.

Points also noted were (a) the nice choice of colour in the carpeting–but the underfloor heating is far from popular with staff in such a busy library, (b) circulation and browsing (with seating) areas on the ground floor are less than one would have considered desirable (c) the passenger lifts do not go to every floor and, astonishingly, not even to Administration and (d) even with 4,000-a-day users, toilets have to have restricted access due to abuse; this was regretted but 'general public toilets are nearby'.

The publicity about this library indicates that the need for a new Central Library was realised and a plan conceived 25 years earlier, so it has been a long time in coming to fruition. The Gosport Authority are to be congratulated in achieving their goal, at least before the present financial restraints, and the Hampshire County Council should be proud to have inherited such a library building which is so well used.

HW

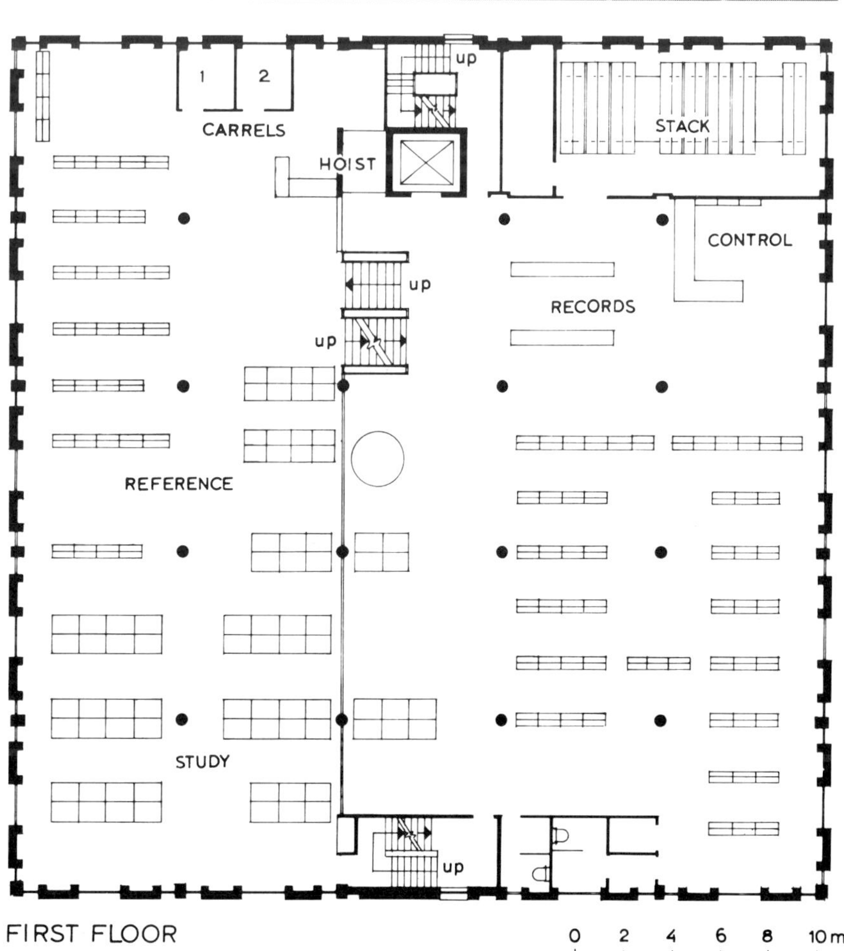

Authority	Hampshire County Council (formerly Borough of Gosport)
Designation	(Gosport) Central Library
Date of opening	July 1973
Population served	83,500
Name of Architect	W H Saunders and Son, Portsmouth (now Southampton)
Name of Librarian	Miss J C Lockhart, AMBIM

Special features:

a) site	Restricted; in civic precinct but adjacent to shopping centre
b) architecture	Reinforced concrete; faced brickwork; armorclad glass
c) function	Formerly Central Library (now District Library) serving large town principally a naval and light industrial area

Mechanical Services:

a) heating	Electric underfloor
b) ventilation	Natural
c) lighting	Tungsten discharge in acrylic diffusers recessed in waffle ceiling
d) acoustics	Texture sprayed ceiling; carpeted
e) other	—

Areas: in square metres

a) lending	
b) reference	1,635
c) reading	
d) special activities	Music
e) children	145
f) control	in (a)
g) library staff admin.	222
h) exhibitions	—
i) lecture hall	—
j) circulation	in (a)
k) services	in (g)
l) lavatories	7
m) stack	75
Total area:	**2,084**

Book volumes:

a) adult lending	70,550
b) adult reference	7,200
c) children	14,200
d) stack	—
e) other	41,000 gr cass
Total:	**132,950**

Costs in £ p:

a) site	12,750
b) building	197,823
c) furniture & fittings	7,000
Total Cost (ex fees):	**£217,573**
Cost per square metre:	**£104**

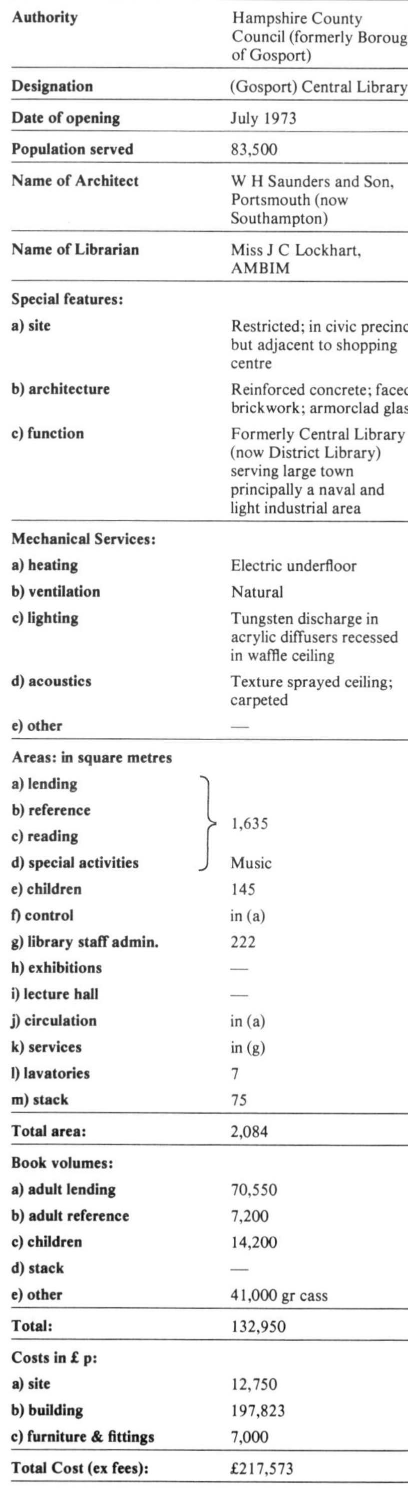

Humberside County Council (formerly Borough of Scunthorpe)

Who's afraid of the big bare wall? Paraphrasing the old nursery rhyme, Scunthorpe's new, almost windowless library, with patterned brick walls, and brick ventilation shafts rising above the roof, challenges one's preconceptions of what a library should look like; but in a different way to the equally unusual Maidenhead Library. The librarian takes as a compliment an early comment, 'It doesn't look like a library; it seems like a warehouse'. The analogy is right, as it is a building devoted to the display and storage of books, with few internal walls, and no windows to interupt this conception.

Scunthorpe is a town of about 70,000, close to the Rivers Humber and Trent, and a town whose importance derives from the extensive ironstone beds nearby, producing about 12% of the country's ingot steel, and 16.5% of its pig iron. A new Central Library has been envisaged since the 1930's, and a succession of premises have been used until the present building was built. The new library is located in the central Market Square, and forms the focal point of the town centre development. It forms one side of a very attractive paved and planted square, with shops and stores on two sides, and a new market building on the fourth side. The entrance to the library is through a large glazed pyramid, leading you into the brick box containing the library.

The main factors considered in planning the new building were:
(a) The need to plan for the expansion of the library service.
(b) The need to cater for possible changes in the type of library service.
(c) The natural development of the library service into other leisure activities.
(d) The desire to provide an informal, relaxed, and welcoming atmosphere.
(e) To provide library services which allow for population growth.

From this statement of aims the idea of a building without windows evolved, and it was not a conscious decision to design a windowless building. Rather, at an early design stage it was seen that the twin concepts of Office Landscaping and Integrated Environmental Design (IED) would achieve these aims, and also give other benefits, including:
(a) Economy in construction and running costs.
(b) Economical use of space.
(c) A controlled air-conditioned environment.
(d) High standards of lighting.
(e) High standards of interior decor and furnishings.
(f) Flexibility in library arrangement, book display, and the development of library services.
(g) An attractive environment for staff and public.

The building is on five floors, with the site sloping away from the front entrance, allowing a separate entrance to the lower ground floor. This gives access to a fully equipped library theatre seating 250 people; there is a meeting room which has its own sound and lighting equipment, so that it can be transformed into a discotheque for young people; and there is a large bar serving refreshments to library, theatre, and discotheque users. The ground floor, approached through the glass pyramid, has a general enquiry area for the library, and for local and tourist information. There is an exhibition space and a control area for all the library's loanable material, including records and paintings. There is also the main administrative area, including the Divisional Bibliographical Department and Schools Library Service. There is a Children's Library, with its own toilet provision.

The first and second floors house the main library areas. On the first floor there is the Popular Library, catering for recreational and light reading, with an emphasis on informality and display, to encourage people to relax and browse. There is also the Arts Library, which includes books, periodicals, paintings, play-sets, gramophone records, music scores etc. The second floor is devoted to the Reference and Research Library, and is designed as the main reference and study department, including books and periodicals on all subjects, except for the arts, and has an integrated reference and lending stock. Both library floors have reserve stacks fitted with manually operated rolling stacks. The top floor houses the plant room, and as an afterthought, the librarian's office accommodation. Access to the upper floors is by lift or stairs. Public toilets are provided on each floor.

Structurally the building has been designed as a brick envelope, and has in-situ reinforced concrete floor slabs and columns internally. The roof is steel framed and clad in slate. The decision to opt for open planning in both library, staff and administrative areas, influenced the basic form of the building, and resulted in an integrated lighting, heating, and ventilation system. The heat from the fluorescent lighting provides the main heat source for the building, and it is recirculated via a full air conditioning plant. In cold weather a district heating system supplements the main heat source.

Internally the floors are carpet tiled, and there is a predominantly green colour scheme, which combined with the lack of windows and fluorescent lighting, gives a bright, yet restful effect. Both library floors have ingenious hinged mobile bookcases, which fold open to form a 'Y' arrangement. These, combined with the fact that the windowless external walls provide much area for bookshelves, reduces the dominating effect of serried rows of bookshelves, and so contributes to the informal effect.

Scunthorpe's new library is completely unique in form and style—Dutch architecture of the 1920's is probably the nearest in feeling, if not form. It is different, yet on its own terms the solution is a perfectly valid one, but it raises some important issues, which only time and experience will provide answers. The building was planned before the tremendous increases in fuel charges, and therefore its cost-in-use should be studied. A well insulated windowless building is going to be economical to heat, and when that heat largely derives from fluorescent lighting, which in itself is economical, then it could still be an economical proposition today. One can question how many windowed buildings suffer from heat gain in the summer, and heat loss in the winter, and even with windows, use artificial lighting indiscriminately and inefficiently.

Another interesting aspect of windowless buildings is the
psychological one, and the reaction of staff and users to the lack
of contact with the outside world. In one sense when the users
go through the glass pyramid entrance of Scunthorpe Library
they are entering a dream world, where modern technology
provides an ideally efficient internal environment. Not only is
there the analogy of the warehouse, but also the department
store, and Scunthorpe definitely has this feeling.

It is to be hoped that one of the library journals will ask the
librarian to monitor these aspects of his library over a year or
two of use, and write about them, as they are interesting, but
controversial, approaches to library building.

NR   HW

Authority	Humberside County Council (formerly Scunthorpe)
Designation	Central Library Complex
Date of opening	July 1974
Population served	70,000
Name of Architect	Brian Brook, Borough Architect, Scunthorpe in succession to Charles J Weekes, F D Parkes, Project Architect
Name of Librarian	R G Roberts, DMS, FLA FIM Ent
Special features:	
a) site	In main shopping precinct; adjacent to car park
b) architecture	Brick clad exterior with no windows; entrance in form of smoked glass pyramid; office landscaping and integrated environmental design
c) function	Central control of library system plus film theatre
Mechanical Services:	
a) heating	Integrated air-conditioning and heating throughout building
b) ventilation	
c) lighting	Tungsten, fluorescent and spot varying 500–2,000 lux
d) acoustics	Heuga carpet tiles; hessian walls; sprayed fibre ceiling
e) other	—
Areas: in square metres	
a) lending	812
b) reference	976
c) reading	in (a) and (b)
d) special activities	204 (meeting room)
e) children	140
f) control	in (a)
g) library staff admin.	464
h) exhibitions	in (a) and (b)
i) lecture hall	248 (film theatre)
j) circulation	in (a) and (b)
k) services	—
l) lavatories	100
m) stack	in (a) and (b)
Total area:	3,714
Book volumes:	
a) adult lending	26,320
b) adult reference	22,530
c) children	3,920
d) stack	36,240
e) other	—
Total:	89,010
Costs in £ p:	
a) site	not known
b) building	656,000
c) furniture & fittings	65,700
Total Cost (ex fees):	£721,700
Cost per square metre	—

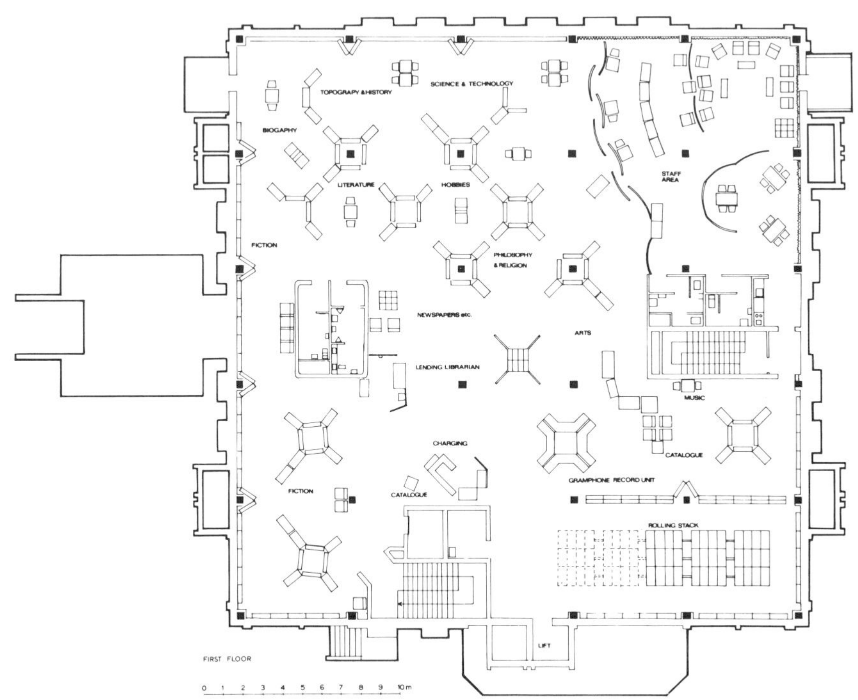

Kent County Council (formerly Borough of Margate)

It would be nice to be able to be as complimentary to this library as one feels the architecture deserves for it is an attractive building in purely aesthetic terms, but there are so many functional shortcomings that it is already somewhat notorious in the county. Forming part of a large complex which also includes a shopping centre, courthouse, offices for the District Council and car parking the library enjoys an ideal position directly on to the main square of the town—a big enclosed breezy seaside town square of considerable character. Here the life of the town eddies round its library in a way that would make most librarians green with envy.

The failure to meet practical requirements may stem, in part, from the change in function resulting from local government reorganisation but this does not explain or excuse the more obvious errors. Designed originally for Margate Council as their Central Library, this building, now within the Kent system, acts as one of 14 Divisional Libraries calling for a large administrative staff; but this does not account for the total lack of thought given to the staff accommodation, the miserly little staff room with sink in the corner, the unpleasant internal office for the Children's Librarian which is an abandoned corridor. Nor does it explain the strangely ambiguous design of the entrance hall after passing through a lobby into which a mysterious stair, apparently from municipal offices somewhere above, discharges—that is when the ugly collapsible iron gate is drawn aside. The entrance hall has no permanent provision for display though Marler Hayley units are employed when any exhibits are available. A large permanent pin-board would have prevented this space becoming cluttered with movable display.

The counter, which has a U-shaped layout, is obviously intended to be for one-way circulation but since no indication of direction is given, readers are confused. When the new librarians from the County Service inherited the building this was spotted and an attempt was made to change the arrangement to allow a long counter backed by the workroom to be substituted. But the architects remained adamant that it was too late. It is surely never too late to correct an obvious mistake. The workroom, which also acts as a closed stack, is fitted with rolling stacks but ideas of how it should be used as a workspace appear to have been hazy. Since no back connection is provided to the staff accommodation or offices, all staff circulation is through the library. The positioning of the main telephone switchboard in the main counter enclosure is almost too obvious a mistake to comment upon, but this is now being removed. The public areas, it must be said, are of delightful quality and finished to a very high standard with yellow carpeted floor, handsome red brick walls with splayed corners enclosing stairs and rooms; fine grit blasted concrete structure and a ceiling of white plastic egg-crating which disguises the light tubes and warm air heating ducting. This is district controlled giving some problems for the library on Saturdays. The lights are behind grilles and maintenance is difficult and costly. Additionally the insertion of these grilles reduces the ceiling height which makes this seem disproportionate to the loftiness of the ground floor department.

At first floor level the Reference Library and overflow of the Lending Library are delightfully lighted around the perimeter by a continuous triangular rooflight but unfortunately at night no one had thought to provide artificial light in this area which is of Stygian darkness and coldness, only partly alleviated by spotlights from the lighting track thoughtfully fitted around the edges of all ceilings. The Children's Library is completely undifferentiated from the Adult areas and consists of a corner of the Lending Library. For story hours it is possible to use the large meetings room at first floor level but this is a long trail away and too big and formal for the purpose. Adults using this room in the evening approach by the stairs previously mentioned in connection with the lobby, but a security risk exists in that the stairs lead up to the municipal offices. Furthermore no lavatories or tea-making room are provided so that the staff room and lavatories have to be used if needed. This is resented by staff, is inconvenient and again breaches security, thus causing problems of supervision.

The triangular rooflight from the library continues over the meetings room but since there is no partition carried up into this space, sound passes readily from the one into the other, seriously limiting its usefulness, eg for recorded music concerts. So much criticism is very sad in such a superficially beautiful and expensively finished building; but, after all, function is all important and basic faults cannot be overcome at a later stage.

GKVT HW

Authority	County of Kent (formerly Borough of Margate)
Designation	Planned as Margate Central Library but opened as Thanet Divisional Library HQ
Date of opening	December 1974
Population served	30,000
Name of Architect	P Taylor, Technical Director, Fewster and Partners. Job Architect
Name of Librarian	G E Clarke, FLA (Margate)
Special features:	
a) site	Corner site of main square on bus and traffic routes
b) architecture	Traditional
c) function	Now Thanet Divisional Library HQ also controlling 7 branches
Mechanical Services:	
a) heating	Gas-fired, warm air via ceiling
b) ventilation	District controlled air conditioning
c) lighting	Mainly fluorescent above plastic egg-crate ceiling; light track and tungsten spotlighting
d) acoustics	Carpeted; acoustic tiled ceiling
e) other	—
Areas: in square metres	
a) lending	414
b) reference	332 (incl music and art)
c) reading	in (b)
d) special activities	—
e) children	in (a)
f) control	in (a)
g) library staff admin.	65
h) exhibitions	133
i) lecture hall	94
j) circulation	120
k) services	—
l) lavatories	18
m) stack	121
Total area:	1,297
Book volumes:	
a) adult lending	20,750
b) adult reference	4,120
c) children	4,760
d) stack	8,000
e) other	2,692
Total:	22,322
Costs in £ p:	
a) site	40,000
b) building	170,000
c) furniture & fittings	20,200
Total Cost (ex fees):	£230,200
Cost per square metre:	£171 ex site

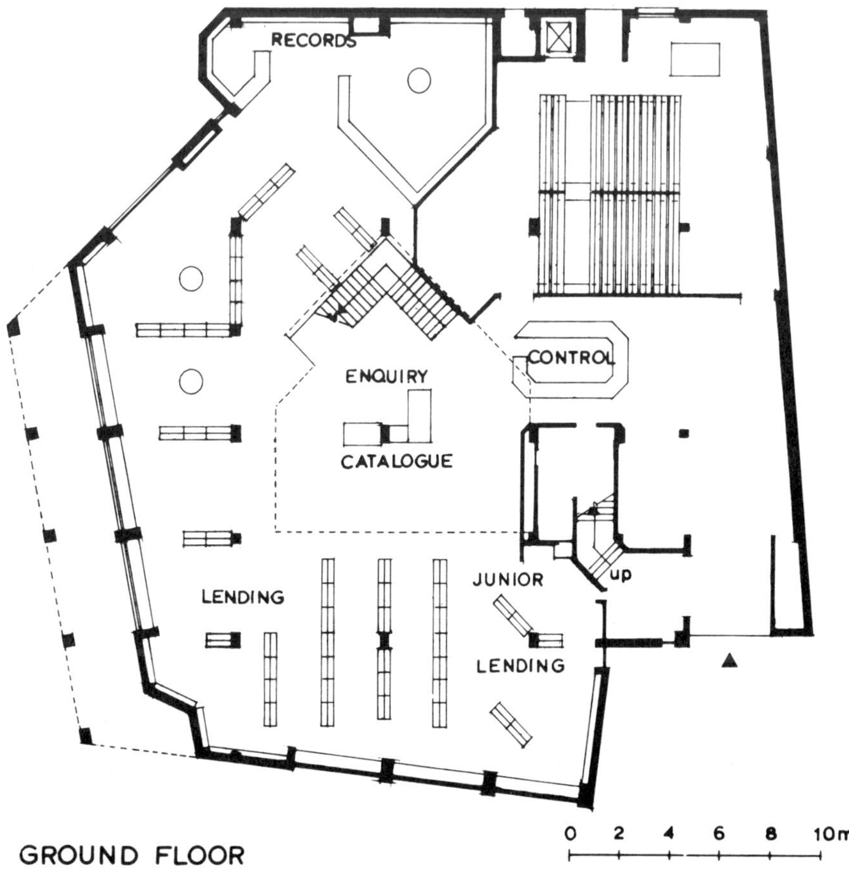

GROUND FLOOR

Northamptonshire County Council (formerly Urban District of Wellingborough)

Wellingborough is one of some 35 'expanding towns', in which the Greater London Council sponsors and designs housing, factories, and sometimes ancillary developments such as shops and community buildings. These expanding towns aim to provide opportunities for London families to move out to better surroundings. Wellingborough was originally planned to expand to a population of 80,000, but it is now felt that 60,000 is a more realistic figure, and the present population is about 40,000.

In 1969 the Wellingborough UDC approved the proposals of Northamptonshire Planning Department and the GLC for the redevelopment of the town centre. As the first stage a group of shops were to be built on a car park facing the market square. At the same time the UDC decided to build a new Central Library, and a central site was considered essential, and it was decided to build the new library above the planned group of shops. It was also decided that as this was to be the first stage of redevelopment, the new building would be seen as 'setting the tone' of the new town centre.

It is at this point that there is some mystery over the role of client, and the author of the Architect's brief. The Greater London Council's Architects' Department designed the library for Wellingborough UDC which, immediately on completion, was transferred to Northamptonshire County Library, under boundary reorganisation. No local librarians seem to have been involved in the compilation of the brief, and the GLC is not a Library Authority—so who is the author, and was any librarian involved?

The brief called for a floor area of about 1120 m², which was to be flexible in arrangement, so that a later extension of 750 m² may be used to amplify existing functions, or to provide for new ones. Within this figure the main library space was to incorporate lending, reference, children's facilities, and a periodicals area; additionally staff accommodation and facilities, bookstack, mobile library garage, and public toilets. It will be seen from the photograph that the new building certainly does 'set the tone' of the central area, and relates well to the adjoining decorated gothic church; but in its obvious handsomeness there are some very real functional and environmental problems.

The entrance hall is three-storeys high, and glazed on the front from top to bottom; seen inside from the top it is a very exciting spatial experience. But this exciting space is the source of several problems. First, the entrance doors face the prevailing winds so that, in cold and windy weather, staff at the control counter can only remain there for short periods. The control counter is an 'L' shape, tucked around the staircase with the short arm facing the entrance resulting in a great deal of cross-circulation by users doubling back on themselves to get to and from the staircase up to the library. The staircase is imposing but appears extremely steep for a heavily used public building, especially when coming down. There is a lift connecting the three floors of the library but it is one of the few lifts in the town, and older people are still reluctant to use it. The openness of the stair well also has a funnel effect, allowing noise from the control counter and wind from the entrance to reach the upper floor. ·

These are all well-founded criticisms, possibly arising from the lack of briefing and oversight by an experienced librarian at the early stages of design. It is not the job of a reviewer to recommend palliatives, but possibly the solution might be to move the control to the first floor library space and use the entrance hall for exhibitions, although realising that 'yobs' and 'vandalism' will be immediately mentioned. All the public areas of the library are on the first floor, and the space has much to commend it. Entering from the top of the stairs there is an advice desk and the lending area directly ahead, with reference area and study carrels beyond and the children's library to one side. Above, on a mezzanine overlooking the main library, and approached by a spiral staircase (the main stairs and lift also go to that level), is the staff work space. The roof steps down away from the mezzanine, and is at its lowest at the furthest end, where the carrels are situated. At each step of the roof are glazed clerestorys, and there are intermediate 'northlights'. The façade facing the market square is largely glazed, although this is only above the height of bookshelves that line the external walls.

Again, the environmental problems negate the positive points about the quality of the space itself. Unfortunately the northlights face north-west, and the market façade faces south-west, with a consequent build-up of heat in sunny weather. Interestingly, the architect's description of the building shows an awareness of this problem; I quote: 'In this case the roof is available to give an evenly distributed natural light. In other buildings where this has been done difficulties have arisen with the heat build-up inside the building whenever the sun shines. In order to overcome this problem here, the rooflights are orientated towards the north and, to accommodate this, the roof structure is angled across the building'. Further investigation showed there was an earlier design which had a spaceframe roof, with rooflights that faced directly north. For some reason, probably economic, the roof and the very interesting design it covered, were shelved; the only remnant of that design being the curiously angled study carrels at the end of the building. The moral is very clear—north is different from north-west, and beware of sun shining down on roof glazing. Incidentally there are problems in cleaning the glazing, resulting in high cleaning charges. There is one other fault, which concerns the lighting system, as only two switches control all the lighting in the main library area, so that it is impossible to localise lighting. As a saving measure, a number of the fluorescent tubes have been removed.

This review has dwelt on the problems in one library of access, circulation, noise, glare, lighting, and the internal environment. In fairness, there is a very positive side to this library. The atmosphere and sense of space within the library are very attractive, and the mezzanine overlooking it (complete with very healthy trailing plants), is an interesting way of providing open-plan staff working areas. The architect's report states 'the placing of this building will consequently have a significant role in determining the personality of the town'. Despite its faults, this new library is a positive addition to Wellingborough, in an excellent location.

NR

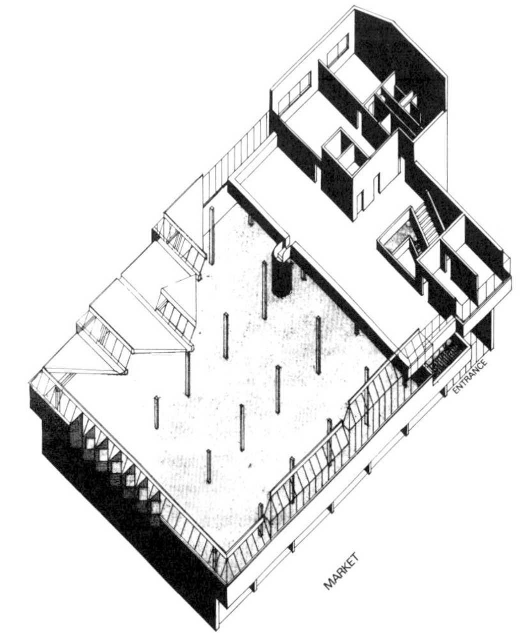

Authority	Northamptonshire County Council
Designation	Wellingborough Library
Date of opening	July 1974
Population served	42,000
Name of Architect	GLC
Name of Librarian	Miss H D Parker (then Chief Librarian now Wellingborough District Librarian)

Special features:

a) site	Overlooking Market Square in centre of Wellingborough
b) architecture	—
c) function	Library service with open areas to accommodate displays and meetings

Mechanical Services:

a) heating	Two gas boilers, thermostatically controlled
b) ventilation	Six extractor fans; windows; louvre windows
c) lighting	Fluorescent and spot
d) acoustics	—
e) other	Lift; book hoist; fire hose reels

Areas: in square metres

a) lending	682 (includes areas of (f), (h) and (j))
b) reference	121
c) reading	30
d) special activities	Not applicable
e) children	129
f) control	included in (a)
g) library staff admin.	175
h) exhibitions	included in (a)
i) lecture hall	Not applicable
j) circulation	included in (a)
k) services	75
l) lavatories	32
m) stack	74
n) garage	74
Total area:	1,396

Book volumes:

a) adult lending	63,683 (not including books on loan)
b) adult reference	5,457
c) children	7,982 (not including books on loan)
d) stack	17,133
e) other	—
Total:	94,255

Costs in £ p:

a) site	
b) building	Separate amounts under these headings are not available
c) furniture & fittings	
Total Cost (ex fees):	£295,855
Cost per square metre:	£142

Viewing this Central Library (which was planned to serve North Shields and Tynemouth and not the whole of the new North Tyneside area) only three days after viewing Scunthorpe's, the contrast in principles of design could have hardly been more noticeable. The populations for which these two libraries were planned to serve are similar at 70,000—although with Local Government reorganisation that figure has tripled in each case. The new library has been included in the first phase of a comprehensive planning development which, when completed, will include a commercial and shopping precinct. The planners had the inspired idea of closing off one corner of Northumberland Square, and pushing the library building forward, beyond the previous building line. This has the double advantage of giving the building additional prominence and producing 'cheap' site land; also allowing the footpaths of the square to provide direct pedestrian access to the main doors of the library.

It is first seen across the lawns and flowerbeds of Northumberland Square (the central bus stop for the town) with the large white letters CENTRAL LIBRARY standing out in relief against the dark brick to herald the library as such—if, indeed, anyone had not by then identified the building from that distance across the square. The floor to ceiling glass for the front and east elevations stand in direct opposition to Scunthorpe's windowless library. A small sloping plinth of brick and the pebble-dashed concrete provide a pleasing variety of surfaces. To the rear of the building there is, at present, ample car parking space on waste ground, although it seems that some of that is planned for shopping development.

The wide entrance to the library is reached by steps or ramp (and concern for the handicapped is evident throughout the building) but before going to the twin-sided control area one may pass to the left into a well-appointed cafeteria (administered by the Area Librarian for purchase of supplies and staffing), while to the right is the large Arts Room planned and fitted for a wide range of facilities from exhibitions to film programmes, stage productions and meetings of societies (180 seats). The somewhat low ceiling however, does not make it ideal for music. Public toilets are adjacent.

The 'In' counter caters for Browne charging (tokens for fiction) and receives all users, adults and children, and there is immediate access to book hoists for return of books to the correct department and sections of a department. A 'popular' library is immediately to the left on this ground floor with 'the more general non-fiction' at this level. Bearing in mind Southend's change of mind on this problem of what is general or popular non-fiction, the question asked here was answered by their decision to use 'dummy' books where readers may need to be directed to the integrated lending and reference departments at first floor level.

The atmosphere in this popular library is welcoming with the readers' adviser well placed; the room is long and wide and with good ceiling height, so this wide expanse of windows gives good views of the lawns and flowerbeds. Although the building is not air conditioned the air is cleaned and recirculated through ceiling and wall ducts. Double glazing with toughened glass (to withstand the very high winds experienced here in winter) excludes traffic noise so that on this very hot day a cool and relaxed feeling was engendered. When necessary, heating is by electric under-floor supplemented by warm air.

Browsing areas, tables, chairs and full carpeting (and acoustic-tiled ceiling for noise reduction) add to one's pleasure. The island shelving, which admittedly has to be plentiful because the windows allow no wall shelving on two of the sides, perhaps seems too strictly regimented. Here is another contrast with Scunthorpe whose 'Y' pattern of low shelving is possible because their lack of windows ensures a high proportion of books on the walls.

Access to the first floor (the only upper floor) is by a wide carpeted staircase, with rubber and steel nosings: generous handrails, at two heights, in West African mahogany combine well visually with the buff walls as well as providing a double safeguard against accidents, particularly to children whose department is at the upper level. Lifts are available, especially for wheelchair cases, as well as separate ones for consignments of new books etc received via the rear delivery bay and destined for the administration department. Similarly books returned by readers go up by the hoist from within the counter area.

The value of the scheme of colour identification for sections becomes more apparent in the integrated lending/reference area (a visual estimate put this floor at 150 ft long), as books received at this level by book hoist have their appropriate colour or colours flashed from the sides of the hoist column so that the appropriate staff allocated to those sections can collect the books and deal speedily with them. Matching colours for spine numbering by Dymotape and for tier guiding are also of assistance in reshelving. Directional signs in these colours lead to General Studies (Green), Commerce and Technology (Red), the Arts including Records, Cassettes and Picture Lending (Yellow), (which, however, are on subscription and a borrowing fee) and then Children's Library and Story Corner (Blue). Each have roughly equal space across the width of the room, and include tables, comfortable browsing chairs and displays of relevant periodicals. The open well, also handrailed, is above the ground floor control counter area which allows maximum natural light to be given there. Eight study carrels are provided, with typewriters being made available for a small charge per hour when required. Lack of space on the ground floor has meant that the Arts and Children's Libraries have had to be sited on the first floor, and that the Children's Library is reached by going through the Arts Library. Surprisingly, this has worked well.

The reorganisation situation which made this the centralised administration and book reserve for the new North Tyneside library system was emphasised by the librarian in terms of lack of space for this new requirement. A major complication was the discovery after, rather than before, that railway tunnelling ran directly under the building which not only created structural problems needing urgent solution but also the unexpected provision of rubber and steel cushion pads to offset vibration.

But the major disappointment of this was the need to abandon the plan for substantial use of the basement for reserve book storage. Thus a large quantity of books had to be crammed, at two levels, into the rear of the building so that administration and bibliographical services space (including service to schools), is crowded. Again, these needs have been made much greater with local government reorganisation.

The refreshment area had been planned primarily to encourage students to use the library for long periods. It has however proved very popular with everyone, and it has become one of the town's meeting places, and there are queues at most times of the day. It has helped the library's figures, and has had an excellent public relations impact, many people now know of the library because of it.

Although there are only two floors, and a lift and prominent staircase, there seems some difficulty in acquainting some people with the upper floor facilities. Some old people are naturally reluctant to use the lifts. There is an open well over the ground floor entrance, but its relatively small size seems to 'funnel' noise from below of machinery at the control counter and of people talking.

This is a building which is impressive not only in design and use of materials but in concept. Its impact on the community is undoubtedly great and this library is their pride–reflected in high use with 4,000+ issues per day. The statue in the gardens of an elderly fish wife with the 'wooden dolly' on her back, is a stark reminder of the conditions of former years when such folk had to make their way up from the fish quays with a heavy load of fish on their backs which they needed to sell in the market on the higher levels of the town. She, with a drawn countenance that cries fatigue, faces this library with all its benefits, being open and free to everyone, whatever, to resurrect a phrase of the past, their 'station in life'.

NR   HW

Authority	Metropolitan Borough of North Tyneside (formerly Tynemouth)
Designation	Central Library
Date of opening	November 1974
Population served	206,700
Name of Architect	Booth, Hancock and Jackson and Partners (Harrogate)
Name of Librarian	Richard Blundell, FLA
Special features:	
a) site	Corner of existing Northumberland Square; built over railway tunnel still in use
b) architecture	Piled foundation carrying reinforced concrete frame with brick infilling
c) function	Headquarters for service to North Tyneside; Area Library for North Shields
Mechanical Services:	
a) heating	Gas fired, low pressure hot water in offices; ducted warm air elsewhere
b) ventilation	Mechanical extract
c) lighting	Modular fluorescent to 300 lux in offices and stack; 600 lux for public areas
d) acoustics	Ceiling tiles; carpet tiles; double glazing
e) other	Special lighting for stage presentations; listening rooms
Areas: in square metres	
a) lending	
b) reference	1436 (and includes e)
c) reading	
d) special activities	49
e) children	See (a)
f) control	45
g) library staff admin.	112
h) exhibitions	240
i) lecture hall	—
j) circulation	263
k) services	124
l) lavatories	66
m) stack	128
Total area:	2,463
Book volumes:	
a) adult lending	
b) adult reference	120,000
c) children	
d) stack	
e) other	8,650 gr; cass; pic
Total:	128,650
Costs in £ p:	
a) site	not available
b) building	424,981
c) furniture & fittings	46,310
Total Cost (ex fees):	£471,291
Cost per square metre:	£171 ex site

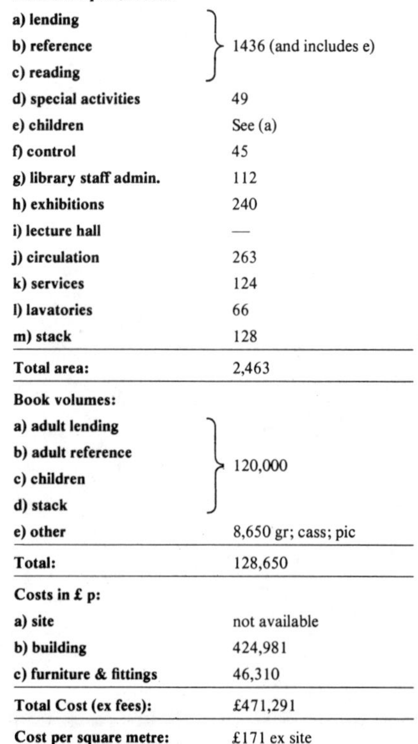

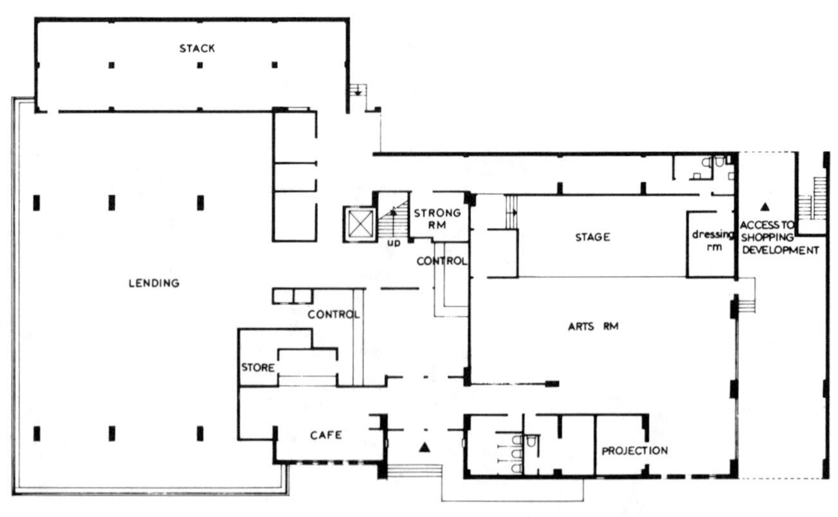

GROUND FLOOR

Oxfordshire County Council:
Oxford Central Library

Oxford may be the city where 'there are more books and librarians per square yard than anywhere else', but it has taken 70 years to move from the Town Hall to a new building 300 yards away, part of the new Westgate Shopping Centre.

In 1966 the City of Oxford presented a Redevelopment Plan, which included the controversial Christ Church Meadow relief road; based upon extensive commercial development from the city centre southwards towards the run-down residential area of St. Ebbs. The city council decided to finance and operate the development, and work on site began in January 1970. The site itself slopes away from the city centre, facilitating the separation of shop and pedestrian levels from the basement delivery and service areas. Multi-storey and extensive ground car parks are on the southern periphery, access into the centre is by travelators, lift, staircases, and ramps for the disabled.

The original road from the city centre at Carfax has been pedestrianised (except for bus access), and leads into the main shopping mall, a distance of about 200 yards. The shopping mall is about 11 yards wide and leads through the centre to the car parking area beyond, with several large stores, and many individual shops opening off it, and at the end of the entrance arcade there is an internal 'square', covered with a glazed pyramid. Approaching the Westgate Centre from Carfax the first feature to be seen is the entrance to the new Central Library, situated intentionally just outside the shopping mall. The estates manager had wanted the library entrance in the middle of the mall, so that library users would be forced to pass the shops, but the Librarian resisted this. Inside the mall there is a row of shops on the right, above which extends the library, with some of the library staff offices looking down into the enclosed 'square'; on the left of the mall is Selfridges store.

The library inevitably has had to be something of a compromise, being above ground floor level, and with a long and narrow plan form dictated by the dimensions of the shopping units beneath. Additionally, the entrance is at the corner of one end of the long building. However, approaching from Carfax, you cannot miss the building, and its site is certainly prestigious in commercial and convenience terms. One of the prices to be paid for being part of a commercial development has proved to be the prevalence of theft and vandalism. The centre has attracted 'yobs' and 'layabouts', and these have drifted into the library, destroying fittings in the building, and using the toilets to strip stolen goods and change into stolen clothes.

Inside the ground floor entrance there is a pram-park, and from the entrance a lift and a well detailed staircase take users to the main first floor library area. Once on the first floor there is still a considerable penetration of the building needed to reach the main library area, so wasting space. In pure planning terms an entrance in the centre of the building would probably have produced a more efficient use of space, but the client's insistence on an entrance outside the shopping mall is quite justified. In the intermediate area between staircase and library, users pass through an enclosed reception area, designed to isolate noisy clerical procedures, and which also forms a display space.

The main library area—a general collections room of about 1,200 square metres, is on two levels, with the centre of the room open to the floor above, and lit from above by a series of roof skylights. The room is divided into subject areas, with integrated bookstock for lending and reference, and with each subject area having seats for browsing, and study tables. There are also nine lockable study carrels available for hiring, equipped with benches and electric socket outlets for audio-visual aids and typewriters. The main space has very few windows, and these are basically vertical slits, their size dictated by fire regulations within the shopping mall. The main daylighting comes from the skylights, which admit a great deal of sunlight, and with it the problems of glare and heat gain. The lighting is assisted by the placing of lighting built into the bookshelves, so that it shines down onto the books. The room is carpeted throughout. Precast beams and columns are used inside the building, twinned, so that air-conditioning ducts and wiring are fitted in the space between. At the far end of the general collections room there are the staff, service, and storage areas, with lift and staircase access to the service entry dock at the basement level. In the general collections room a staircase links the two floors, but it only links the staff areas.

The Children's Library overlooks the front area, the centre of the room occupied by browser boxes for small children, and bench seats for mothers. There is provision for local history collections, the city archives, and special collections, appropriately including one on the motor car. There is a special study room for 120 students at separate tables. A lecture theatre had been envisaged, but the budget would not allow for it, so that the exhibition space can be transformed into a lecture room for 150 people. The periodical room has display racks which incorporate lockable storage for back numbers. There is a dark room which is available for staff and library users. There is a coffee area off the first floor foyer, but this has produced problems of noise and loitering, the noise certainly increased by the hard finishes in that area, and it is a space which is not easily controlled.

Other interesting facets of the library should be briefly mentioned. The library is one of the first integrated computerised libraries in the country. Attention to small details, so important in the overall effect is demonstrated by two interesting designs: drop boxes for books in the lobby have been fitted with catch traps for cigarettes; the Librarian and architect devised with Watkins and Watson a battery operated book trolley, that made library staff's work easier in moving books along the 40 metres length of the library.

The nature of the commerical development at Westgate has meant that the 5,100 square metres library has little scope for expansion, either upwards or outwards. Generally this would be seen as a disadvantage, but the librarian rationalises the situation quite simply. The larger the library the more remote the relationship between staff and users. With an eventual stock of 400,000 books, and access to the many university collections, together with interlibrary loans and subject specialisation schemes, the users of Oxford's Central Library will be able to get good service for many years to come from the building as built.

One point that was very evident was the close relationship between the project architect and the library staff. For three years the architect was almost a member of the library staff, collaborating with them on every aspect of the planning and equipment of the new building. This collaboration has been commemorated by the architect being created 'Honorary Librarian of the City of Oxford'!

NR

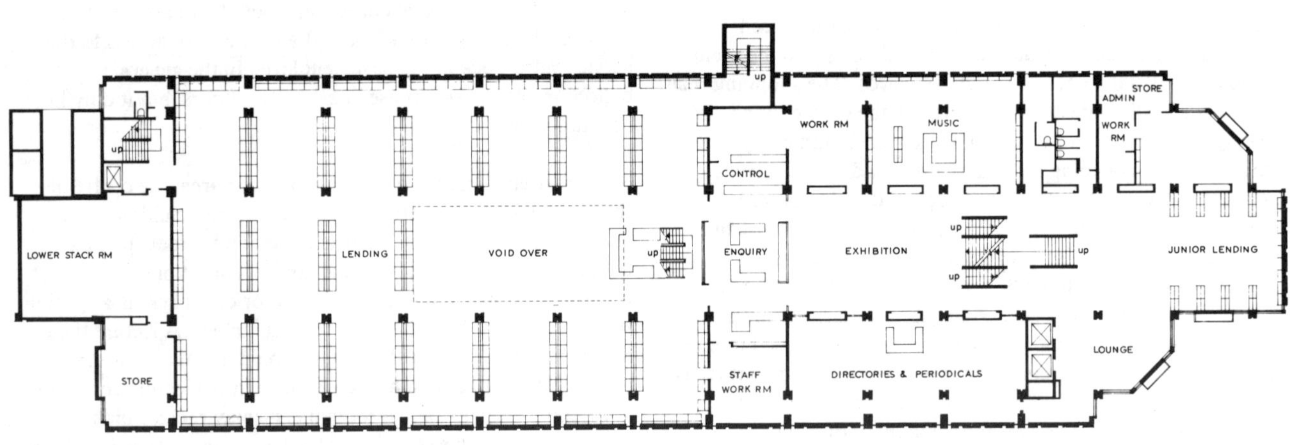

GROUND FLOOR

0 2 4 6 8 10m

Authority	Oxford County Borough Council
Designation	Central Library
Date of opening	21st May 1973 (Official opening: 31st October 1973)
Population served	114,220
Name of Architect	D Murray, DipTP, ARIBA, MRTPI, FRSA, City Architect and Planning Officer
Name of Librarian	J P Wells, MA, FLA, City Librarian and Information Officer
Special features:	
a) site	On first and second floors above ground floor shops, within a Central Shopping Precinct.
b) architecture	Precast concrete framed structure with cladding of facing brick panels separated by floor to floor double-glazed slit windows
c) function	Central Library
Mechanical Services:	Comprehensive air-conditioning equipment, together with tungsten and fluorescent lighting effects supplemented by natural light from large double-glazed roof lights; wall to wall carpeting, acoustic ceilings maintain a pleasant environment. Comprehensive smoke-heat detector system. Burglar alarm protection
a) heating	
b) ventilation	
c) lighting	
d) acoustics	
e) other	

Areas: in square metres	
a) lending	
b) reference	2,140
c) reading	150
d) special activities	100
e) children	210
f) control	50
g) library staff admin.	565
h) exhibitions	
i) lecture hall	185
j) circulation	1,600
k) services	160
l) lavatories	60
m) stack	280
Total area:	5,500
Book volumes:	
a) adult lending	
b) adult reference	98,000
c) children	14,000
d) stack	10,500
e) other	29,000
Total:	151,500
Costs in £ p:	
a) site	8,000 per annum ground rent
b) building	528,000
c) furniture & fittings	45,000
Total Cost (ex fees):	£573,500
Cost per square metre:	£104.27

Staffordshire County Council (formerly Borough of Tamworth)

An ideal situation, a beautiful library, well thought out and doing a good job, plus optimism. When this building was planned the population of Tamworth was around 40,000. It is now over 50,000 and there is talk of 80,000 or even 100,000 in the near future. Perhaps optimistic planning of this kind is a cause of growth and progress.

The library was built as the Central Library of the Borough of Tamworth and is now the Area Headquarters for South Staffordshire, an area which exactly coincides with the Tamworth Borough boundary, so the library is doing the job it was planned to do, despite reorganisation. It stands right in the heart of this busy market town in the churchyard of the beautiful parish church. It has been designed with two fronts and no back so that approach from the main shopping street and from the bus depot, both across grass and between mature trees, leads to a main and attractive entrance.

A long low building which, when lit up at night, looks rather like a ship, is faced by vertical concrete slats which blend with the surroundings, the contrasting fins reducing the penetration of direct sunlight. The slight oddness of shape at the north end is explained by the fact that this is only Phase 1 and that a second phase can join it at right angles. Phase 2 may only be needed for other cultural activities but it is a sign of the forward-looking ideas that such plans have been prepared.

In the entrance hall is a striking and beautifully sculptured mural created to celebrate the existence of the alphabet. At the other end of the entrance hall is an exhibition area and the second entrance, whose windows are a good advertisement for the library. Inside is an open room with bookcases at right angles to the walls and with a 'popular' periodical reading area in the centre. Because of the sloping site the room is rather below ground level on one side and the narrow windows there provide very little light on the bookcases. The strip lighting above the windows and that high up in the ceiling, and even the taller windows in the higher part of the wall, do not seem to provide as much lighting as the figure of 300 lux stipulated seems to suggest. Incidentally the vertical venetian blinds to these windows are power-controlled to change on lighting conditions.

At each end of the room is a balcony, one for the Music and Discs Library and the other for the Children's Library but they are entirely unconnected. The usual expedient of a complete mezzanine or even a linking cat-walk was rejected by the architect on aesthetic grounds but this does mean a considerable waste of staff time. In fact the open stairs to the Children's Library are not used, access being only from the main closed stairs leading up from the entrance hall.

In the entrance hall is the small control counter which is much too small, as it was designed for a mechanised charging system which has not been provided and the Browne system is too bulky for the space; an 'Out' counter is needed in addition, within the Lending Library itself. Immediately behind the control counter is a workroom to which direct delivery access is available and from which there is a generously large book hoist to the administrative departments above. The general

impression inside the Lending Library is of concrete, but it is most attractively used. Hessian is used extensively to bring up the colour. A thoughtful feature is the use of smoothed concrete edging on to the concrete columns for protection and quick maintenance. My only aesthetic objection to the concrete is that the two large wedge-shaped supports to the open staircases intrude both on the eye and on to the normal walkway.

The second floor, approached by a staircase and passenger lift, leads to an open reference library, a small local history and map room as well as the administrative offices and toilets. The Reference Library gives an impression of too much space and too few books, although there is a collection of newspapers and semi-popular journals in the centre. There are two private study rooms and four double open carrels, but one has the uneasy feeling that it is neither a room for intensive study nor for popular reading: perhaps the mixture is right for such a self-contained town. The Lending and Reference Libraries have different types of furniture, Spur metal in the Lending Library and LDS maple in the Reference. Apparently this was chosen deliberately because of the differing character of the rooms.

The staff room and kitchens are generous and well equipped and there are public toilets (including a special toilet for the disabled) on this floor.

Jutting out from the main building is a first floor homework annexe above the entrance lobby. Leading off the Children's Library it forms a useful films, talks and story hours area and will ultimately link up with Phase 2. Also on this floor is a general meeting room and a bookstack/workroom area which is serving too as an overflow for the very busy programme of children's activities. It also contains a small and utterly silly photographic room which has no possible purpose but which was apparently added at the request of the Ministry. Not only is the whole building attractive and apparently successful but the number of thoughful touches is large: water and cleaners' rooms on every floor; light switches controllable only by keys; push trolleys for parents with children and flower displays on every level. Space precludes any further eulogies but this is a library to be visited and enjoyed.

GT

Authority	County of Staffordshire (formerly Borough of Tamworth)
Designation	Tamworth Central Library
Date of opening	June 1973
Population served	46,960 in 1973: now 52,000
Name of Architect	John Tetlow and Partners
Name of Librarian	V Tyrrell, ALA (now Principal Area Librarian, Stoke on Trent)
Special features:	
a) site	Town centre with established public gardens to front and rear
b) architecture	*In situ* reinforced concrete column and beam structure
c) function	—
Mechanical Services:	
a) heating	Pumped low pressure hot water system serving forced air heaters which supply 10% heated fresh air
b) ventilation	
c) lighting	Diffused fluorescent 300 lux
d) acoustics	Acoustic tiled ceilings; carpeted
e) other	Smoke detection alarm system
Areas: in square metres	
a) lending	410
b) reference	303 + 24 local history
c) reading	45.50 music
d) special activities	26
e) children	177
f) control	—
g) library staff admin.	145
h) exhibitions	35
i) lecture hall	40
j) circulation	—
k) services	—
l) lavatories	43
m) stack	77.50
Total area	1,668
Book volumes:	
a) adult lending	27,000
b) adult reference	8,000
c) children	8,500
d) stack	20,000
e) other	1,600 records
Total:	65,100
Costs in £ p:	
a) site	—
b) building	178,630
c) furniture & fittings	16,621
Total Cost (ex fees):	£195,251
Cost per square metre:	£117

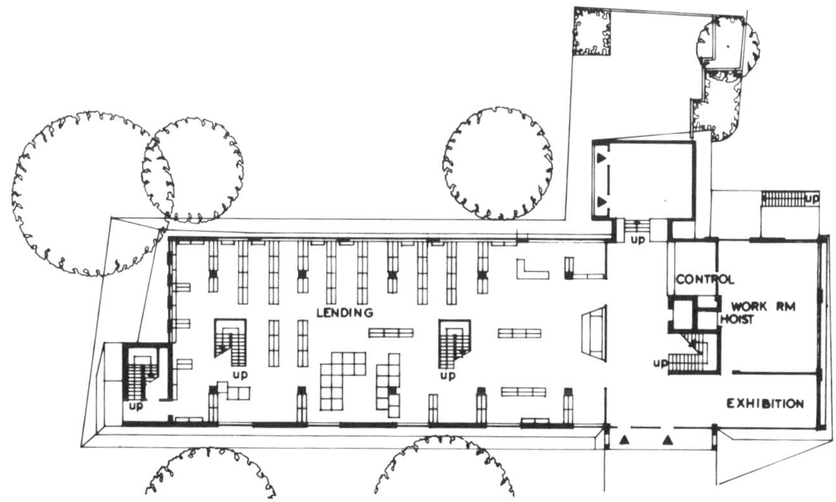

GROUND FLOOR

Stockport Metropolitan District (formerly Cheshire County Council): Marple Library

Marple is a town of some 10,000 population to the south-east of Manchester on a hill looking eastwards toward the Peak District of Derbyshire. Formerly in the county of Cheshire, Marple has now become part of Stockport under local government reorganisation.

The library is on a site some 250 metres off the main shopping street and is approached by a road at the side of the Memorial Park. A car park, serving the library and the adjacent Council offices, clinic and police station provides ample space.

The town is a convenient distance for commuting into Stockport and Manchester and people with cars can reach the library without difficulty. But it is worrying to hear that owing to its siting the library is noticeably less used by those without their own transport who live in remoter council estates. This imbalance would have been less apparent had a more central position been available near to the shops. This said, the present site is a delightful one with sweeping views over the park to the distant hills.

The crisply detailed two-storey building stands in well-landscaped surroundings with trees and shrubs nearby. Brick and concrete paving surrounds the ground floor which is recessed beneath the projecting first floor with black columns standing proud of the white walls and windows. The upper floor is mainly solid with narrow slit windows. The entrance porch with a large Nuway mat is fully glazed with a good external canopy. A large sign identifies the building clearly.

Once inside, virtually the whole of the public accommodation can be seen at a glance, for a large well rises through the first floor to the roof with the Reference Library as a gallery overlooking the ground floor Lending and Children's Libraries. The counter is free standing in the well and is of 'U'-shaped plan. It is efficiently designed with a long book-return counter which needs to accommodate 60 trays. Both fiction and non-fiction issue is by standard Browne method so that a large number of cards have to be on view. There are normally two counter staff with a readers' adviser at a desk slightly apart from the counter. This was originally placed as part of the counter enclosure but had to be moved to make it obvious that the adviser should not be called in for counter duties. The design of counter of hardwood with plastic laminate tops and black steel framing sets the tone for the furnishing of the library which is of a consistently high quality. Luxurious leather and chrome easy chairs and fine tables with chrome framing give an air of sophisticated comfort.

Finishes throughout the building are of a very limited range; white concrete block walls of fine texture, acoustic tile ceilings in aluminium tee framing with neatly integrated fluorescent lighting diffusers and light-brown carpet tiled floors.

Windows are at high level over perimeter bookcases protected from glare by the overhang of the first floor. Bookshelving is by Reska with six shelves on perimeter walls with low free standing centre bookcases. Pin-up boarding covered with hessian is used above the bookshelves in the Children's Library on which lively displays are arranged. In the entrance area Marler Hayley display screens can be used to form changing shapes for exhibitions.

The workroom is in the form of a single-storey block projecting from the side of the building beneath the first floor and is windowless, though with large rooflights. Owing to a late change of heating chamber layout the nearby goods entrance originally planned has been lost and book deliveries have now to be brought in by a fire exit door and through the library. This library acts as one of Stockport's three district libraries with several satellites of its own and therefore serves as a link between the smaller libraries and Headquarters.

The enclosed staircase leading to the first floor is expressed as a strong design element both internally and externally. The half landing is just too low for people to walk beneath so not only is this dangerous but useful space is lost. No heating has been provided in the stairwell which can make for a bitterly cold transition from ground to first floor. Detailing is again very good with terrazzo treads and risers, chunky hardwood handrails and glazed screens which allow constantly changing views into the library from the stairs. The Reference Library suffers greatly because of the open well, with constant disturbance from the public at the counter and plans have been mooted for enclosing the well with glazed screens. This would be a shame aesthetically but the lack of peace and quiet for study is a distinct disadvantage. A large meetings room and exhibition gallery opens off the staircase, at the foot of which is an entrance door enabling the room to be used when the library is closed. This is a handsome room capable of sub-division but appears bigger than necessary. The normal run of small exhibitions tends to get rather lost.

Corridor connection to the staff room with lavatories leading off enables this accommodation to be used in conjunction with meetings though the incorporation of the kitchenette for staff into the staff room necessitates a member of the library staff being on duty during meetings to make tea! Refreshment facilities for evening meetings are not essential but a separate kitchen is. The staff room is delightful, very restful, beautifully furnished with elegantly detailed lockers and kitchen fittings, and with a fine outlook. Intriguing views into the public areas are obtained through narrow borrowed lights in the staff corridor.

The first floor is finished to a similar standard to that of the ground floor and the floor-to-ceiling strips of window with narrow top hung windows for ventilation allow fine views. The ceiling height throughout is rather higher than strictly necessary. Heating is by low pressure hot water distributed by means of unobtrusive skirting heaters painted black. Oil fuel boilers are accommodated in a chamber alongside the workroom.

This is a fine building in which practical problems have been elegantly solved and must be a pleasure for both readers and staff.

GKVT

Authority	Metropolitan Borough of Stockport
Designation	Marple Library
Date of opening	December 1973
Population served	27,000
Name of Architect	Jack Whittle, FRIBA, SP Dip, FRTPI, Philip R Wrightson, Job Architect, FSIA
Name of Librarian	Mrs Barbara Kay, ALA
Special features:	
a) site	Situated in Memorial Park on crest of hill, large car park
b) architecture	White Forticrete concrete blockwork; steel windows in timber frames
c) function	Community library
Mechanical Services:	
a) heating	Oil-fired with skirting heaters
b) ventilation	Natural
c) lighting	Double skin acrylic roof-lights. Fluorescent
d) acoustics	—
e) other	—
Areas: in square metres	
a) lending	186
b) reference	98
c) reading	—
d) special activities	130
e) children	71
f) control	20
g) library staff admin.	87
h) exhibitions	25
i) lecture hall	—
j) circulation	37
k) services	20
l) lavatories	23
m) stack	—
Total area:	697
Book volumes:	
a) adult lending	30,582
b) adult reference	580
c) children	8,584
d) stack	—
e) other	—
Total:	39,746
Costs in £ p:	
a) site	—
b) building	£80,000
c) furniture & fittings	included in above
Total Cost (ex fees):	£80,000
Cost per square metre:	£115

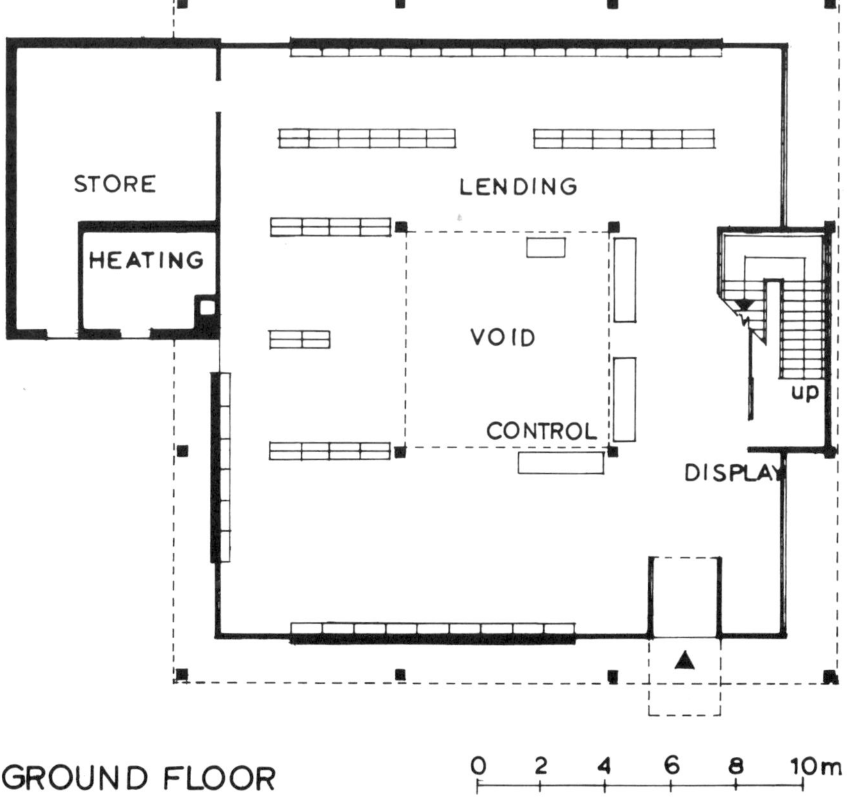

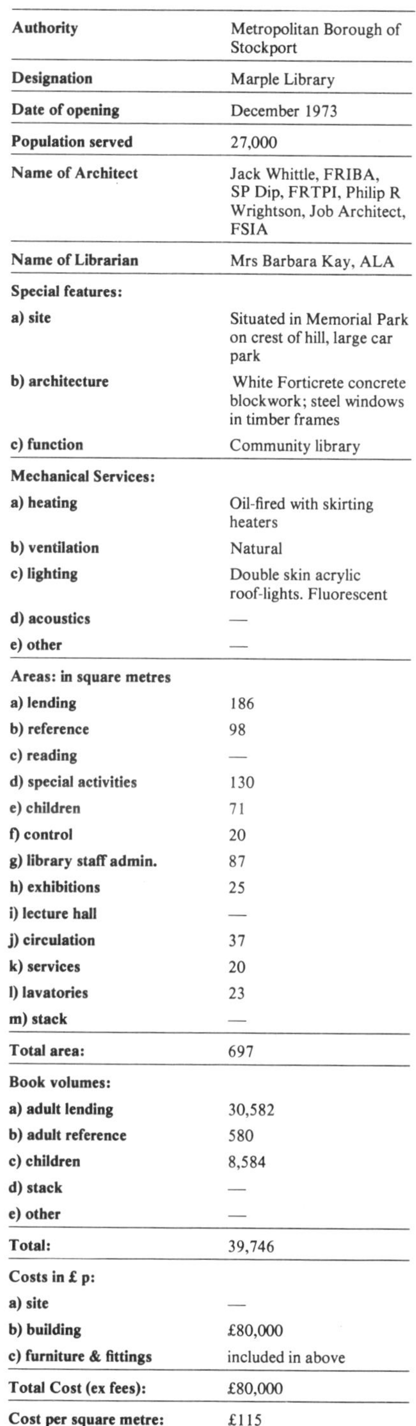

City of London: Guildhall Library

The Guildhall Library forms part of the 'Guildhall Precincts Redevelopment' Phase II and is part of the complex of old and new buildings which house the wide range of activities related to the Guildhall which it incorporates. Essentially a specialist library, it provides reading, reference storage and display facilities for its unique collection of books, maps, prints, manuscripts, newspapers and detailed reference material relevant to London and in particular to the City and its operations.

Though the library is a specially designed unit tailor-made to accommodate the services provided it nevertheless has to fit in with the overall structure; this to a certain extent determines both the character and the arrangement of the spaces. Part of the library, for instance, is directly over the underground car park which serves the overall complex: this resolves itself in a number of levels within what is loosely described as the ground floor. The advantages and disadvantages of this may be a matter of debate but the origin of the configuration is traceable to the character and organisation of the overall complex. The entrance to the library is at ground floor level from Aldermanbury on the west of the building complex, with an exhibition gallery on either side of the entrance hall. The Whittington Room on the right houses in good display cases historic London material and old books; on the other side there is a permanent exhibition of clocks and other timepieces and related literatures, the property of the Clockmakers Company. Both these galleries act as a suitable introduction to the mature and historic background of the library and form a buffer between the outside world and the main reading areas.

Access to the Main Reading Room is through an intermediate space which contains the public side of the counter, stairs to other levels and a quick-reference area.

The Main Reading Room itself is square in shape with its centre portion double in height and lit from the top by a 40-foot square skylight divided egg-crate fashion by deep concrete beams. Perimeter galleries at first floor level accommodate stacks for books of more immediate use; at ground level, below the stacks, two sides are arranged into alcoves using shelving to house specialist reference sections. The northern side below the gallery is occupied by the cataloguing room this is formed by separating an area from the Reading Room by use of a long specially made catalogue card holder fitment, made as all the furniture in selected elm. Books are brought directly to the readers at lavishly proportioned comfortable reading tables, modern but maintaining the tone of the old building. The attendant desk area is screened by the counter and is connected to the main stacks in the basement by a Lamson tube vacuum system and a book hoist.

At what is described as the ground floor but at a level some two metres higher, the Print and Manuscript Rooms form distinct sections, each with its own independent catalogue inquiry desk and staff; these sections share a long row of windows to the north. Because of the functional levels of the underground car park below, variations in the floor levels have helped break up the areas and create useful separation of some functions. The

variation in levels in the reader floor has drawbacks to the extent that certain parts are not immediately accessible to handicapped readers; this in practice is overcome by an arrangement whereby any material is brought to the main reading area for the use of handicapped people on request.

The administration of the library is conducted from the Mezzanine floor and the accommodation consists of well appointed Librarian and Deputy Librarian's offices, room for secretaries, a general office with sales facilities for reproductions and, on the same level but on a gallery overlooking the Manuscript and Print Rooms a Conference Room is formed by screening with double sided bookcases which accommodate larger books. This arrangement is successful and the screening provides adequate noise insulation. The lower ground floor which is reached both by lift and stairs from the Entrance Hall houses the Newspaper Room, cloakrooms and a small theatre for the public and the full range of staff facilities for the library staff. The Newspaper Room provides storage in specially designed cases for its unique collection of uninterrupted runs of the more serious newspapers. There is a small number of reading tables and provision for photocopying and an insulated typewriter booth for use by readers. The theatre has seating for 56 is well equipped for lectures and projection of films and can draw upon additional equipment available in the Guildhall complex. Staff canteens, restrooms, kitchens, cloakrooms and lockers are very well appointed and lavishly furnished.

The Main Book Stack is in the basement and contains the balance of the collection of books in metal rolling stacks and is connected with the reading rooms by a Lamson tube vacuum system and book hoists. At the same level are the well equipped facilities for repair and restoration of manuscripts. The library is air-conditioned throughout. A high illumination level is maintained overall with fluorescent lights. Noise interference is reduced with absorbant surfaces and luxurious carpeting over all public areas. Fire detection is by smoke detectors and for fighting by means of water hose reels on all floors in strategic positions. The general level of furniture and fittings is very high and in keeping with the Guildhall traditions and finance. Elm with vinyl leather coverings and thick piled carpet squares dominate and set the tone of the public areas. The furniture is all specially designed and very well made. There is an overwhelming feeling of luxury and lavish good taste.

Generally a successful and carefully thought out building it nevertheless is part of a larger complex from which it has to take its flavour and some of its shape and certainly the lavishness of its appointments; this does not materially undermine its functions as a library or its success as a building but it sets it apart as a one-off example of a very special library.

ND

Authority	Corporation of City of London
Designation	Guildhall Library
Date of opening	October 1974
Population served	Night 5,200, Day 350,000
Name of Architect	Sir Giles Scott, Son and Partners
Name of Librarian	Godfrey Thompson, FLA
Special features:	
a) site	Rebuilding on bombed site
b) architecture	To integrate with 15th century Guildhall
c) function	Library of historical research
Mechanical Services:	
a) heating	Full air-conditioning
b) ventilation	
c) lighting	Fluorescent 500 lux
d) acoustics	Carpet and acoustic tiles in all public areas
e) other	Lamson pneumatic tube system; 3 book hoists; 1 passenger lift
Areas: in square metres	
a) lending	—
b) reference	1,480
c) reading	
d) special activities	—
e) children	—
f) control	—
g) library staff admin.	285
h) exhibitions	128
i) lecture hall	77
j) circulation	247
k) services	414
l) lavatories	84
m) stack	1,827
Total area:	4,542
Book volumes:	
a) adult lending	—
b) adult reference	42,000
c) children	—
d) stack	147,000 printed books 70,000 mss units
e) other	23,000 maps 17,000 photos 1,500 trade cards 30,000 prints 42,000 other items
Total:	372,500
Costs in £ p:	
a) site	Not available: integral part of administrative complex
b) building	
c) furniture & fittings	
Total Cost (ex fees):	—
Cost per square metre:	—

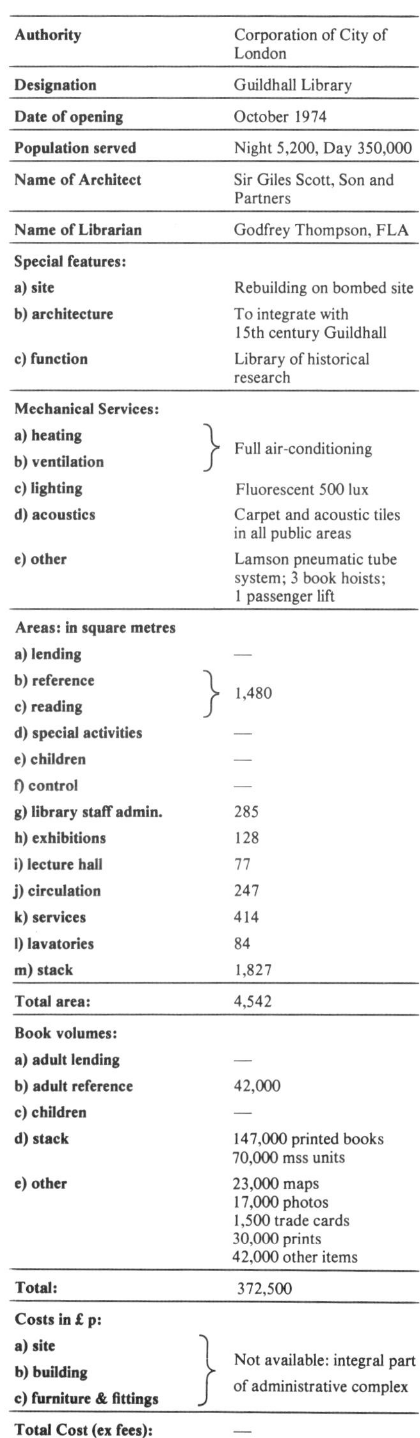

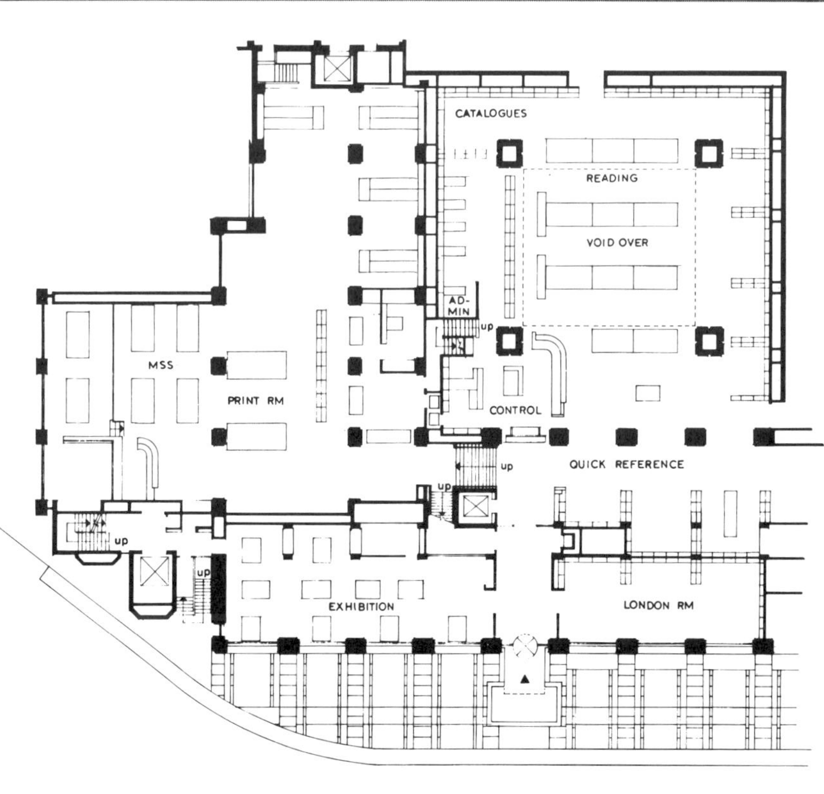

GROUND FLOOR

London Borough of Barking

The siting of the new Central Library (which replaces one destroyed by fire) is in some respects near to the ideal for a municipal library, as it lies on the route between one of the major car parks for the town centre, within a one-way traffic circulation system, and the larger shops. However the detailed placing of the building in relationship to the Town Hall and to the large town square between the two buildings is curiously ambiguous and seems to miss opportunities that could have been grasped. This criticism, however, may be mitigated when the future planning intentions within this central area become clearer.

At present the main entrance to the library is off an alleyway near one corner of the square so that this focal point faces the back of several very unattractive old buildings which have been painted in a sombre dark red colour, serving to make them even more obtrusive.

The façades of the library building in brown brick at first floor, with strips of vertical timber windows, glazed with anti-sun glass, over a podium of a different colour brick with a horizontal strip of windows between, is blandly modern yet rather lacking in any positive qualities. Whilst this positioning may be acceptable and is one way of fitting a large building into a jumbled architectural context it lacks much immediate appeal and presents an unduly municipal image.

It has always been part of our belief that libraries should, by their design, positively attract and entice their users and in this respect there is little to indicate, particularly when approaching from the car park, that this building is in fact a library and not just another commercial building. Inside, however, very definite attempts have been made to make the building attractive but, in our view, the results are somewhat heavy-handed and over elaborate.

After passing through the thoughtfully-provided electrically operated doors into a draught lobby, from which access is gained to the Children's Library, the visitor enters the main Lending Library. Here he is presented, immediately opposite, with a view into a small but attractive landscaped court (which, perhaps sensibly in our climate, is not provided with any means of access for the public) presenting a lively prospect of planting, sculpture, moving water and a variety of paved surfaces and natural features set against a heavily textured wall. This is a welcome prospect for casual readers who are offered a number of comfortable chairs near to this area for relaxation.

The main counter is sensibly placed beneath a well in the building which runs up through both floors to provide excellent natural light from a large rooflight immediately overhead. On the day that we visited the library there was some glare from this source but this probably only occurs in high summer and is not too serious. The open well serves to draw attention to the upper floor which houses the reference and music collection and to give a generally spacious atmosphere. However the very fussy and overwrought detail of the gallery handrails is out of all proportion to its importance and is evidence of a general tendency to over-design relatively unimportant features at the expense of more vital elements.

This tendency is again apparent in the reception desks on both floors which have been taken to unnecessary lengths to achieve an architectural effect quite unrelated to functional considerations; their inflexibility suggests that any future adoption of new methods of charging would almost certainly involve costly alterations and even wasteful scrapping of much of the fittings.

At the far end of the library is a three-storey book store, well equipped with electrically operated moving stacks. A reservation must, however, be made about the position of this room which is totally unconnected with, and remote from, the book-entry and workrooms. Since the store is also some distance from the counter and there is limited shelf capacity in the lending library, this siting is likely to lead to additional staff movement with delay in obtaining books from the store for the public as well as complicating purely routine administrative procedures.

A feature of the Children's Library is a carpeted pit designed for younger children together with a raised platform used for story hours. This absorbs rather a large proportion of the total space with the result that too little is left for book display and stock which thus tend to be crowded.

The relationship of the Children's Library to the main entrance is sensible and convenient for parents visiting the Library with their children, but some visual connection with the Lending Library would have improved the functional and aesthetic relationships.

Useful Library Activities and Community Activities Rooms are situated beyond the Lending Library, and these spaces can be shut off from the library for use by the public out of opening hours. The latter also doubles as additional sitting space during times when this area is not used separately. The Library Activities Room is well equipped with visual aids and projection facilities, and thought has been given to accommodating the wheelchairs of handicapped people. This follows the recent tendency in new libraries, but it is unfortunate that no provision has been included for any catering facilities which would have made the public rooms much more flexible and useful. Lack of any refreshment here is a considerable loss to the library during normal opening hours. Although the problems associated with catering in libraries are well known we cannot believe that these are so incompatible that they should lead to the exclusion of what must today be considered a vital provision in new libraries. Visiting Barking immediately after seeing Southend Central Library's catering provision for the public and how it was being used, emphasised this. We were told that in Barking there are alternative commercial sources available locally, but this does not meet the point.

It was gratifying to note that in contrast with some recent buildings, provision had been made for toilet accommodation to be available to the public and in particular to wheelchair users.

Here again some problems are to be expected but this is a provision which can surely never again be ignored.

At first floor level the Reference and Music libraries are adjoining and visually undivided though here another worrying detail of planning is apparent. In several places in the library low mobile screens have recently been introduced to segregate areas within the open plan in order to direct the public towards counters or to restrict access to other parts. This infers insufficient consideration having been given initially to the way in which the building would be used by the public or of changes in the way in which free circulation can be permitted as a result of experience. We were told that preparations were being made for the introduction in reference areas of an electronic system for combating that and that this would necessitate stricter channelling of readers past service points. In either case the screens intrude seriously on the apparent openness of the plan giving us the impression of a temporary street barrier.

Staff accommodation seems adequate and reasonably well arranged within itself, but too remote from the main reception desk and lacking in any flexibility for future expansion or change, although demountable partitioning has been used.

Furniture is well considered functionally but lacks any great design consistency and is in places unduly sparse. Direction

signs and guiding are generally not very good; in particular the use of very small lettering on tier guiding makes life difficult for the casual visitor looking for any individual subject. Whilst it is recognised that professional staff are always available to direct an enquirer to any specific subject or even book, it must be recognised that the vast majority of readers will prefer browsing; thus all guiding should be clearly visible and helpfully readable from a distance.

It is no pleasure that we have felt it necessary once more to make criticisms similar to those that we have levelled at libraries which were featured in earlier issues, for Barking offers outstanding features in its service; in particular that all services are given without charge (including reservations and picture lending) and that no fines or recovery fees are levied for overdue material.

Some of the faults undoubtedly arose out of the distressing circumstances of building of the library to replace the former building which was destroyed by arson. This must have resulted in pressure so as to minimise the time in replacing the service as well probably as from needs of economy. Nevertheless some seem unfortunately to have arisen, as so often, from a lack of clarity in the brief.

GKVT   HW

Authority	London Borough of Barking
Designation	Central Library
Date of opening	June 1974
Population served	157,600
Name of Architect	S J Harris, RIBA, Borough Architect, A B Ablitt, RIBA, Principal Assistant
Name of Librarian	E W McManus, FLA
Special features:	
a) site	Independent site within existing central area of municipal and shopping environment
b) architecture	Modular frame using traditional construction with modern technology, especially use of materials
c) function	Centralised service, including picture, lending and service to schools
Mechanical Services:	
a) heating	Comprehensive plenum system working on heat recovery basis; double glazing
b) ventilation	Fresh air supply automatically controlled; air-conditioning in Lecture Hall
c) lighting	Air handling luminars of B21–2 to IES code standards
d) acoustics	Carpet tiles and hessian walls; impact and airborne treatment
e) other	—
Areas: in square metres	
a) lending	676
b) reference	542
c) reading	in (a)
d) special activities	80
e) children	168
f) control	66
g) library staff admin.	134
h) exhibitions	—
i) lecture hall	120
j) circulation	148
k) services	174
l) lavatories	84
m) stack	1,418
Total area:	3,610
Book volumes:	
a) adult lending	58,110
b) adult reference	10,478
c) children	12,338
d) stack	38,349
e) other	5,275 gr, cass, (pic 210)
Total:	124,550
Costs in £ p:	
a) site	Council owned
b) building	414,344
c) furniture & fittings	45,000
Total Cost (ex fees):	£459,344
Cost per square metre:	£114

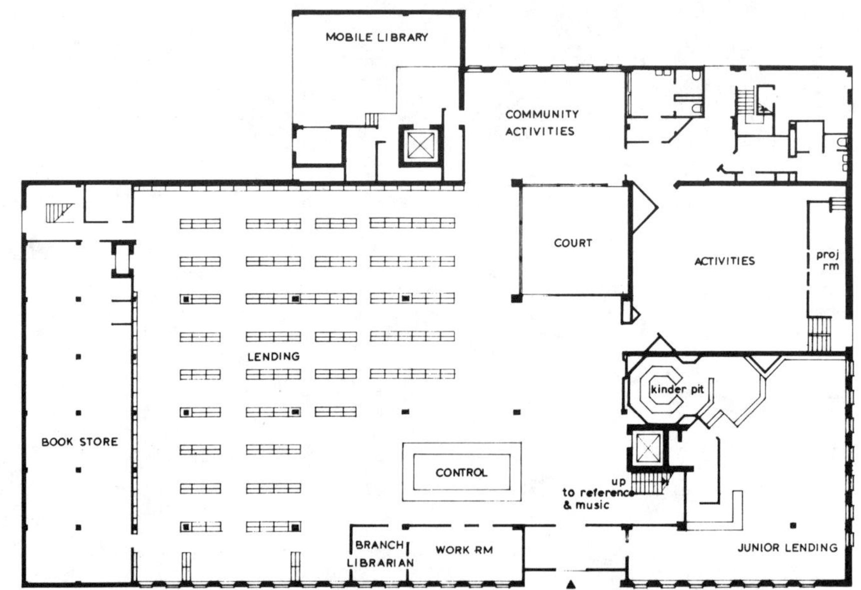

GROUND FLOOR

Argyll and Bute District of Strathclyde Regional Council (formerly Bute County): Rothesay

Rothesay is the main town on the Island of Bute in the Firth of Clyde and has a definite air of relaxed self-sufficiency about it. It is a traditional holiday spot for Glaswegians, many of whom eventually retire there. The use of the library is fairly constant over the seasons, the visitors filling in the local fall-off during the summer.

The library is in a new leisure centre which forms part of one side of a quiet square in the middle of which stands the ruin of Rothesay Castle surrounded by a moat. The area is just off the main shopping street on the opposite side from the busy steamer terminal. The new building, a two-storey, white rough-cast structure sits comfortably in the square and quietly makes its own contribution to the immediate environment. The building generally is solid, with pierced openings, but the public part of the library on the ground floor has been expressed differently with floor-to-ceiling glazing broken up with a quick vertical rhythm of mullions. These superimpose a domestic scale on the large glass areas and give a degree of privacy while still maintaining views out from inside.

The entrance hall is shared with the other leisure centre facilities and a public staircase links the library on the ground floor with the staff offices, etc, on the first floor. The general atmosphere of the library comes as no surprise due to the glimpses into it on approaching the building, but the immediate impression is one of lack of space in spite of, or maybe because of, the high ceiling and glazed walls. The circulation space seems just a little bit too tight, the book stacks seem a fraction too high and the tables with four chairs would have difficulty in accommodating four adults. The fully glazed walls do, of course, mean that all stacks are free standing in the centre of the floor and circulation is around them. The library is quite obviously a social meeting place and a lot of talking takes place but it does not seem to disturb the users.

The Children's Library is at the rear of the main library, separated from it by a timber glazed screen and has its own ramped entrance to allow easy access by prams; wheelchair users also use this entrance. The ceiling in the Children's Library is lowered and timber-lined as are the walls. The furniture, in matching timber, is of a small scale and there is more floor space—altogether a much more successful space than the main library.

The building was planned as a County Library with relatively large administrative facilities but is now being operated only as a branch library. The staff areas on the first floor are therefore mostly unused; a very depressing sight and one would imagine some better use could be made of the space. At this upper level the only criticism of layout is the positioning of the staff common room in a windowless area in the centre of the building, while the water storage tanks occupy an adjoining space with an outside wall.

Heating is by means of low pressure hot water underfloor heating around the perimeter which eliminates cold radiation and condensation. There are also a number of electric storage heaters in the lending library. High-level clerestory windows open for natural ventilation but are insufficient to cope with the solar gain experienced at certain times. The windows are not remote controlled and are difficult to reach. There are no facilities for shading of the large windows and this leads to some slight book damage as well as occasional excessive heat gain. Both artificial and natural lighting are excellent. Noise attenuation between the library and the other parts of the leisure centre is not unreasonable.

This is a library which could have been so much more successful with very few alterations.

AM

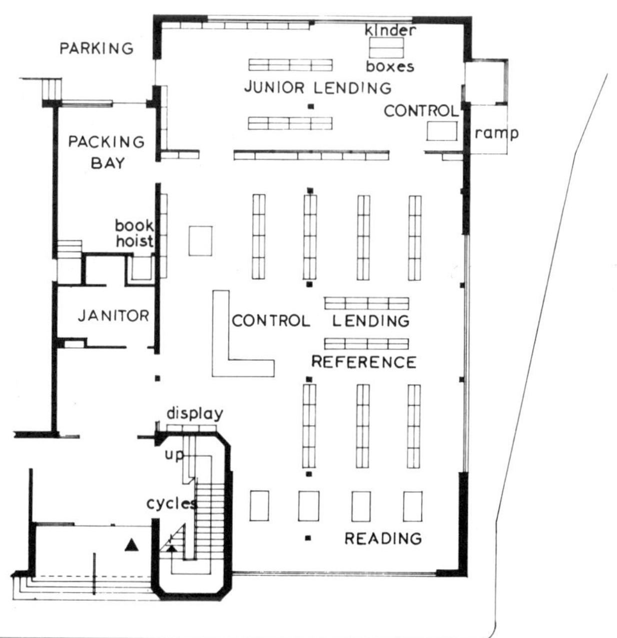

GROUND FLOOR

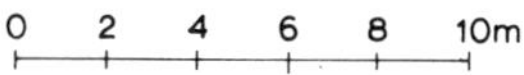

Authority	Argyll and Bute District of Strathclyde Regional Council (formerly County of Bute)
Designation	The Moat Library and Leisure Centre, Bute
Date of opening	November 1974
Population served	8,500
Name of Architect	Robert B Rankin and Associates (Glasgow and Ayr)
Name of Librarian	Martin O'Dowd, MA, ALA, DipLib
Special features:	
a) site	Restricted but corner site facing rear of Rothesay Castle overlooking moat
b) architecture	Traditional roughcast brick with steel frame
c) function	Serving islanders and holiday makers
Mechanical Services:	
a) heating	Oil-fired underfloor heating
b) ventilation	Natural
c) lighting	Fluorescent strip diffused
d) acoustics	Carpeted in main area: acoustic tiled ceiling
e) other	—
Areas: in square metres	
a) lending	168
b) reference	} in (a)
c) reading	
d) special activities	—
e) children	74
f) control	in (a)
g) library staff admin.	106
h) exhibitions	6
i) lecture hall	in Leisure Centre
j) circulation	—
k) services	28
l) lavatories	33
m) stack	100
Total area:	564
Book volumes:	
a) adult lending	9,600
b) adult reference	750
c) children	2,500
d) stack	17,000
e) other	50 gr: language
Total:	29,900
Costs in £ p:	
a) site	7,804 } includes Leisure Centre
b) building	138,253
c) furniture & fittings	2,750
Total Cost (ex fees):	£148,807 (Library only: estimated £65,850
Cost per square metre	£117

London Borough of Brent: Tokyngton

Tokyngton Library is pleasantly situated in Monks Park, next to Tokyngton Recreation Ground on the banks of the small River Brent south of Wembley, just 200 yards from the shopping parade in Harrow Road. Although there is parking space for about 10 cars one suspects that most readers approach on foot, for the library serves mainly the area of housing enclosed by the river, Harrow Road and the railway by Wembley Stadium.

The main library is on the ground floor, with staff accommodation upstairs approached by a spiral staircase. These rooms are within the pitched, mansarded black asbestos cement slate roof, with double glazed timber roof windows. The remainder of the library is flat roofed and of complex shape. The large black bulk of the mansard roof dominates the building. The purply-red brickwork contrasts well with the black slates which are also used for the roof fascias. The walls of the low block are divided into panels by vertical slit windows and each panel has in addition a high-level horizontal slit window. An entrance canopy of V shaped plan, supported on stout brick boxes projects strongly from the front of the building and this, together with the all glass screen and front doors, provides a welcoming approach. This impression is reinforced upon entering by the very well detailed canopy, with diagonal red stained boarding and concealed fluorescent lights. The counter faces the entrance and follows the V shape of the canopy to cleave the readers to the right for the 'In' counter and left for the 'Out' counter; low screens on either side allow views into the Children's Library on one side and Reference on the other. Ample provision for pinning up notices makes this a lively space and the intriguing view of the whole library beyond, is attractive and satisfying.

The Adult Library lies behind the counter and is a striking space with quite excellent natural lighting. The horizontal and vertical slit windows mentioned above, are now seen to be part of a total concept of lighting of considerable originality and subtlety. The vertical slits on both sides of the library are linked by rooflights running right across the building. These are formed by parallel laminated timber beams supporting flat glass rooflights. The beams rest on piers at the ends of each section of wall which form neat recesses for the bookshelving. Further rooflighting slits occur on either side of the first floor block so that even here there is good natural daylight. The materials of the interior are nearly all natural and maintenance-free, brick walls, timber beams and aluminium windows in timber frames. The ceiling between the beams is finished with grooved fibreboard acoustic absorbent material and this, together with the green nylon carpet tiles on the floor, ensures a good, quiet environment.

Bookshelving is mainly six shelves high and a row of free standing shelves ranges down the middle of the room. In the Children's Area five shelves are used on walls and three in free standing bookcases. Shelves are in metal and the ends of bookcases in timber. Ample and varied comfortable seating is provided. The counter works well, although a number of minor adjustments had to be made after opening. A happy feature is that the returned book trolley fits snugly against the end of the 'In' counter and looks as if it is part of the desk. There is ample space for storage and well thought out accommodation for cards.

The staff room with built in kitchen, lavatories, workroom and book storage are at first floor in a series of rooms approached by the spiral staircase which has an original turret-like window with a broad view over the playing fields to the south. The roof windows are set in sloping walls which are painted white, giving a pleasantly domestic feeling to the rooms in contrast with the openness of the public spaces. An electric book hoist from the children's library near to the counter delivers to the workroom. This is a most useful feature but its placing is unfortunate for it largely blocks the view of the children's library from the desk.

The artificial lighting is well thought out, as is the daylighting. Rows of fluorescent lights, on either side of each downstanding rooflight slit, are supplemented by clusters of shiny, brushed aluminium tungsten downlighters which add a warm quality to the fluorescent light. Heating is by underfloor off-peak electric coils with hot air blowers in the porch to overcome draughts. A second set of doors might have provided a more economical answer to reduce draughts and heat loss. When the cost of off-peak electricity eventually increases to the normal price of daytime electricity the effect on running costs is likely to be serious. The meters, waste bins, letter box and hot air blower are all very sensibly and unobtrusively arranged in concealed cupboards to either side of the porch.

Landscaping is simple with a number of mature trees in front of the library and a tarmac car parking area at one side. The library is almost completely blocked off from the adjacent recreation ground by a sports pavilion which is attached to the south end of the library, but this helps with the enclosure of the courtyard off the children's library which is used for story hours on warm days. The courtyard, whilst it has some shrubs and trees, is tarmac paved with some concrete pavings set in strips opposite the library windows. This could have been a major asset but instead is rather a bleak area which, at a casual glance, might be taken for a vehicle entry or service yard—such are the associations of tarmac. Signposting is by means of a rather ugly triangular notice on a central stalk looking like an afterthought, when it was discovered that the original sign, which is uncomfortably placed on the building, is almost invisible from the road.

It is evident that this library is reasonably popular, issuing about 2,600 books per week. It is a very pleasant building with particularly imaginative lighting and it deserves to be better known and more heavily used.

GKVT

Authority	London Borough of Brent
Designation	Tokyngton Library
Date of opening	September 1973
Population served	10,000
Name of Architect	A Beckett, RIBA, DipTP, MRTPI (former Borough Architect) R Box, DipArch (North Poly) RIBA, Job Architect
Name of Librarian	Mrs L Pennells, ALA
Special features:	
a) site	Adjoining recreation ground, quiet suburban road
b) architecture	Brick
c) function	Branch public library
Mechanical Services:	
a) heating	Underfloor electric
b) ventilation	Natural
c) lighting	Fluorescent; good daylighting
d) acoustics	Acoustic tile ceiling; carpet
e) other	—
Areas: in square metres	
a) lending	272
b) reference	
c) reading	
d) special activities	in (a)
e) children	
f) control	
g) library staff admin.	81
h) exhibitions	—
i) lecture hall	—
j) circulation	—
k) services	—
l) lavatories	—
m) stack	—
Total area:	353
Book volumes:	
a) adult lending	18,056
b) adult reference	329
c) children	11,058
d) stack	—
e) other	—
Total:	29,443
Costs in £ p:	
a) site	—
b) building	44,770
c) furniture & fittings	4,000
Total Cost (ex fees):	£48,770
Cost per square metre	£138

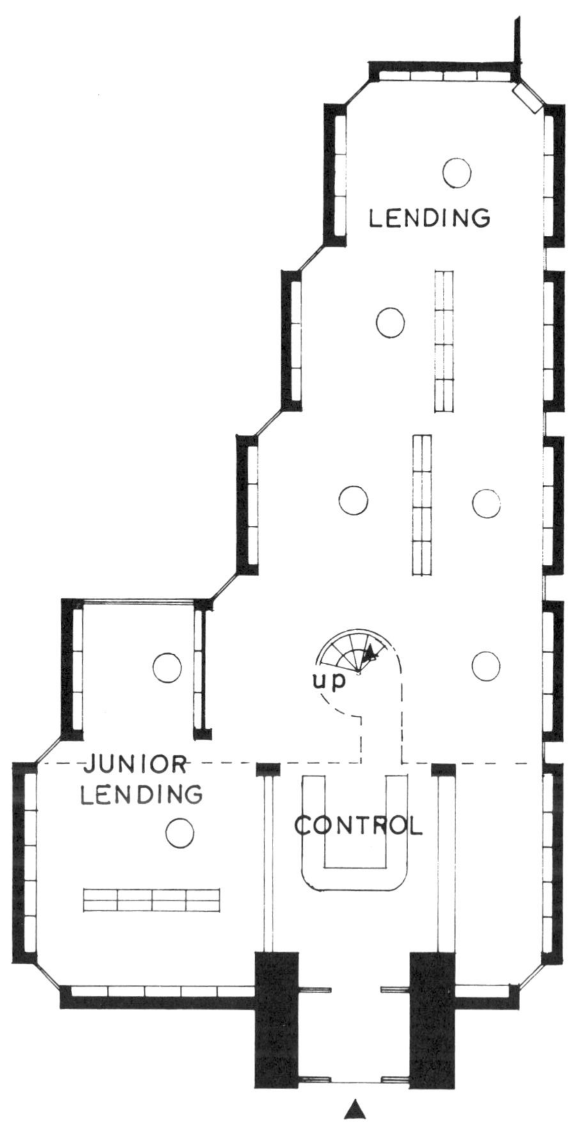

GROUND FLOOR

London Borough of Hackney: Homerton

This Homerton branch stands at the corner of two busy roads and almost opposite the large Hackney Hospital (at which, incidentally, Hackney run the medical library). The population served by this new library is reckoned to be about 20,000 and the building is large enough to do this. It is built in a reinforced concrete frame, clad with London stock yellow bricks while the large windows have precast concrete aprons; there is a small front lawn within a low brick wall, recessed for bench seats—and a reasonable car park at the rear.

The brick-tiled floor entrance hall has spotlighted wall panels, facing the entering public and these take the eye away from the starkness of the walls of concrete blocks, with no skirtings. To the right are public toilets clearly indicated as usable by wheelchair persons; staff toilets and rest room are adjacent. Vigorous direction signs leave you in no doubt as to the route for adult lending, reference and reading room on the ground floor, or to the Children's Library and lecture hall above; the former, perhaps unexpectedly, is upstairs, although this location allows the young people plenty of space for activities and Hackney prefer this arrangement (see Stamford Hill Library in our 1972 Issue).

Adult Lending is on three sides around a central rectangular counter (for Browne issue), itself built around substantial rectangular supporting pillars. The third side leads into a Reading and Reference Library which thus lies to the rear of the entrance hall and corridor. Of reasonable size, and hung with items from the picture lending service, the number of reference works and periodicals seemed low. The Lending Library, carpeted in brown, the warm hardwood counter, with black top surfaces and insets, and similar toned chairs and tables has good natural light from all sides (venetian blinds for use in sunshine); the fluorescent lighting is recessed within a suspended ceiling. The impression is pleasing but for the lack of browsing chairs and the visually obtrusive convector heater wall panels, each nearly two metres high and painted mid-green.

Access to the first floor is by an effective open staircase with inset carpeting on the treads, with metal edging and with toughened glass side panels; attention to detailing here is good. A planted area, well maintained, fits into the floor space. A lift to first floor is provided particularly for persons in wheelchairs visiting the lecture hall and for handicapped children to their library. This Children's Library, large, light, airy and carpeted showed itself near ideal for the heavy use including substantial class visiting.

A substantial fixed counter with wood strip canopy and recessed fluorescents seemed to conflict with the dwarf book cases for the younger children, so low that only a few centimetres separated books from the floor; happy for the under-fives perhaps but forcing the staff to kneel for book tidying. A wall-to-wall display panel with spotlighting if required was eye-catching—but so were those wretchedly large convector heating panels.

The lecture hall was part (approximately two-thirds) flat wood strip floor while the remainder was stepped wall-to-wall and carpeted; seating can be arranged for 130. Equipment includes cine projector and for highlighting any activities there are two buttons each with three floods and four spots. Air flow input and extraction grilles are provided, the former in the step risers, the latter in the ceiling. Use of the hall is by film and other societies.

Adjacent on this upper floor is a Special Collection Room fitted with rolling stacks, which at this level necessitates care in calculating maximum floor loading; otherwise, if the floor sagged the cases would not roll easily.

For an East London Authority with typically high calls on its purse for the priorities of housing and social services, Hackney has shown remarkable good sense in paying careful attention to the development of its library services, ensuring that new buildings are well sited and generous in space to allow a good range of activities. Thus this is another library able to play an effective role in the wider realms of social services, almost certainly preventing dissatisfaction and even delinquency which is so often caused by the absence of good amenities in an area.

ND   HW

Authority	London Borough of Hackney
Designation	Homerton Branch Library
Date of opening	June 1974
Population served	20,000
Name of Architect	Harry Moncrieff, RIBA, FRTPI, Cooperative Planning Ltd. T R W Roberts, RIBA, DipTP, MRTPI, Borough Architect
Name of Librarian	C J Long, FLA
Special features:	
a) site	Corner on main road frontage
b) architecture	Reinforced concrete frame: External yellow brick cladding
c) function	Branch serving south-east of Borough
Mechanical Services:	
a) heating	Gas-fired: fan assisted convectors
b) ventilation	Natural, but system in Lecture Hall
c) lighting	Recessed fluorescent within suspended ceiling
d) acoustics	Carpeted floors
e) other	—
Areas: in square metres	
a) lending	196
b) reference c) reading	93
d) special activities	in (i)
e) children	182
f) control	in (a)
g) library staff admin.	12
h) exhibitions	93
i) lecture hall	115
j) circulation	in (h)
k) services	23
l) lavatories	21
m) stack	355
Total area:	1,090
Book volumes:	
a) adult lending b) adult reference	13,500
c) children	12,000
d) stack	23,000
e) other	—
Total:	48,500
Costs in £ p:	
a) site	58,050
b) building c) furniture & fittings	263,700
Total Cost (ex fees):	£321,750
Cost per square metre:	£290

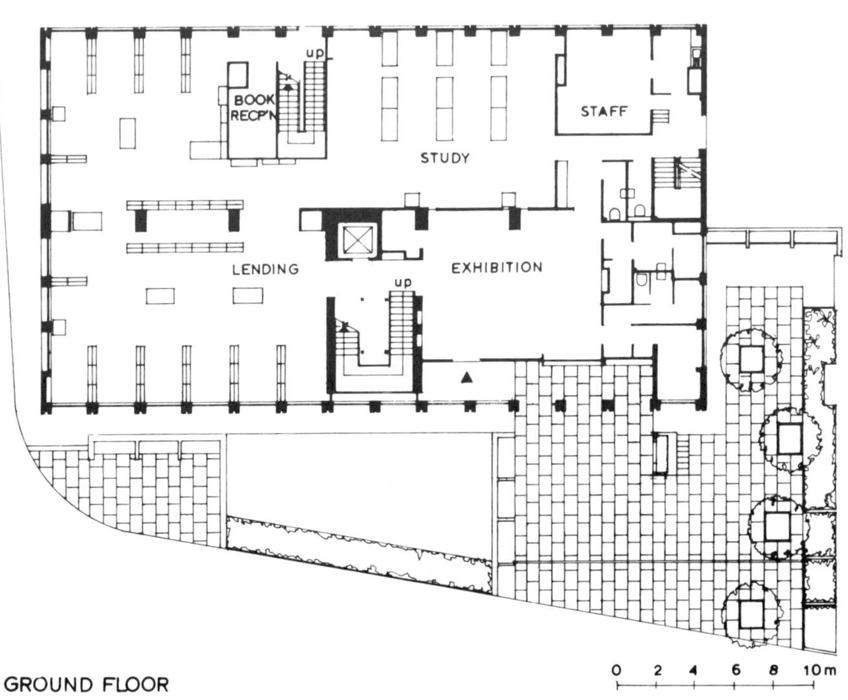

GROUND FLOOR

London Borough of Hillingdon: Yiewsley

Yiewsley lies to the north of the M4 on the road from London Airport to Uxbridge at the very edge of London, near to the Colne Brook which marks the beginning of the Green Belt. Originally the Library was housed in an old Chapel, only a few yards from its present position, which is on a traffic roundabout 400–500 yards from the shopping area of the High Street. The roundabout is a busy one with another main road meeting the High Street and has on the other corners a petrol filling station, a motor showroom and a builder's merchants, which seem scarcely compatible neighbours.

In 1970 the Council bought the site, selecting their own developer and carefully laying down the conditions under which the library was to be built in return for the developers obtaining offices for letting. This has resulted in an attractive financial proposition. Not only has the library been obtained free of cost to the ratepayers but even the original land cost has been recovered and part of the rent for the offices is received by the Council which helps to pay running costs. The only capital cost to fall on the ratepayers has been for furniture and fittings.

However, a high price has been paid in terms of amenities enjoyed by the library. The siting of the building takes no account whatsoever of the traffic noise, being set directly on the edge of a narrow pavement, exactly on the corner where heavy traffic is gathering momentum in low gear after the roundabout. The offices are at first floor but the library at the lower level takes the full brunt of the noise. This has been exacerbated by the design, which consists of a single long room parallel to the road with windows full-height and length. A car park is situated at the back of the building and here high-level windows admit additional noise.

The entrance to the library, which is poorly indicated with only a single sign facing the road, is at the recessed corner of the building at the roundabout end, with doors to the offices at right angles in the same corner. It is very easy to drive straight past the building without recognising its function. An entrance porch is provided with space for prams, a large mat, umbrella rack and pin-up boards for notices. The counter, which is straight and facing down the library, has good visibility for supervision, but in spite of this there have been cases of vandalism. A small workroom and store space opens out behind the counter which has been sensibly and generously planned. The rather bleak staff room has only high-level windows and a single fluorescent tube, a sink, cooker, cupboards and metal lockers, all cheerless and unwelcoming.

An attempt to mitigate the traffic noise in the library by fitting internal windows independent of the outside ones, with curtains between the two for appearance only, does not achieve the desired effect. There are no ceiling tiles to deaden the room acoustically, though the carpeted floor helps somewhat. The large windows which face west admit much evening sun creating glare and the building tends to be hot in the warmer months. No air-conditioning is employed and the only means of ventilation, when the windows are kept shut, is by two very inadequate extractor fans at one end of the room. It is possible to open windows on both sides–if the resultant smell and noise can be ignored. Lighting is a mixture of fluorescent and tungsten; the heating by underfloor electric coils will prove increasingly expensive to run as cheap off-peak electricity is phased out, though it is cheap to instal.

The layout of furniture and fittings is sensible but rather dull, as might be expected in such a restricted shape, but there is ample space for readers, with tables and 15 chairs. Browser boxes and six tiny chairs are provided for children whose department is near to the counter, whilst at the far end of the room an area can be curtained off for small meetings. Four semi-carrel desks and a photocopier are placed near to the counter and the catalogue, immediately inside the doors. Shelving is of standard metal pattern supplied by Reska with four shelves generally in centre stacks and five on the east wall beneath the windows. Shelf capacity is almost 9,000 and issues run at about 124,000 issues per annum.

An unusual feature of the library service is the provision of an up-to-date facility for members of the community to learn foreign languages by way of tape cassettes. Initially, courses in French, German, Spanish, Italian and Russian are available and this may later be extended. Arrangements can be made with the Librarian but the cassettes are handled only by staff, with the student listening through earphones at one of the desks. Language records for loan are also available. There is a free telephone by the counter for use by the public who may wish to contact the Council's advisory and information services and departments. Leaflets on council services and a job vacancies board are placed prominently in this area. The civic information and language learning facilities, if popular, are ideas which may be used in other libraries in this borough.

This library, although architecturally not very interesting, is significant for the means of financing used by the Council. Authorities who follow their example should take heart and, while driving a hard bargain, make sure that it is not at the expense of the quality of design and finish, for this is something which can never be remedied, nor can basic siting which is the most important single factor in the design.

GKVT

Authority	London Borough of Hillingdon
Designation	Yiewsley Branch Library
Date of opening	May 1973
Population served	17,500
Name of Architect	Shangler Risdon Associates
Name of Librarian	Philip Coleham, FLA
Special features:	
a) site	Main road
b) architecture	Conventional RC frame brick clad
c) function	Branch public library
Mechanical Services:	
a) heating	Electric off peak underfloor
b) ventilation	Natural plus 2 fans
c) lighting	Fluorescent
d) acoustics	—
e) other	—
Areas: in square metres	
a) lending	
b) reference	
c) reading	223
d) special activities	
e) children	
f) control	10
g) library staff admin.	20
h) exhibitions	—
i) lecture hall	—
j) circulation	in (a)
k) services	1
l) lavatories	2
m) stack	—
Total area:	274
Book volumes:	
a) adult lending	11,916
b) adult reference	227
c) children	2,945
d) stack	—
e) other	—
Total:	15,109
Costs in £ p:	
a) site	—
b) building	— Nil to council (see text)
c) furniture & fittings	5,500
Total Cost (ex fees):	£5,500
Cost per square metre:	£20

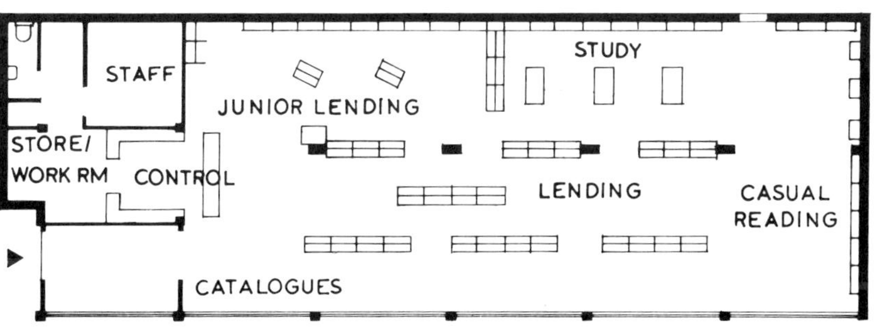

GROUND FLOOR

London Borough of Islington: John Barnes Library

This is a most interesting branch, for its siting must have presented considerable planning problems. It is set back from the quite steeply inclined Camden Road and the even steeper rise of Dalmeny Avenue. This has necessitated the facilities being at two levels with direct footpaths to each—adult activities at the upper and, at the lower, children's together with an assembly room for joint use by the library and by the public for meetings and social functions; this latter area is capable of isolation from the library as required.

Approaching up the footpath slope to the main entrance, one is struck by the bold design of the main building, principally of solid brickwork (to meet, it was said, the requirements of the librarian for maximum wallshelving) but with two oriel windows, rectangular in shape, which are opposite to what proves to be the reception area. There are also corner floor-to-ceiling windows and these give views out on to the lawn which fronts on to Camden Road. These windows link with an angled roof glazing to provide generous natural lighting overhead. Heating is by gas fired boiler supplying hot water to fin convectors below the wall skirtings and in the ceilings. Fluorescents are continuous and are concealed in those parts of the ceiling which are boarded. Adequate display panels in the entrance and reception area give immediate information to the potential user as to the facilities offered; the walls here are of exposed facing brick. A continuous control counter of angled design, with a central wicket gate for staff use, is shaped to route the public into the adult library. This control counter is in two sections for service, the one for audio materials and the other for books; backing this is the workroom and book store and adjacent staff rest areas.

No separate study area had been included but public suggestions soon made it desirable to provide these; in fact, only a few small tables could be included near the browsing area by the oriel windows and between the ten island bookcases which, arranged in two ranks give a somewhat crowded feeling. The plastic tiled floor is very well maintained but there is a noticeable noise factor.

The Children's Library and Assembly Room having their separate entrance, there is no public internal connection between the upper and lower floors, although there is a narrow staff staircase. This young person's library is on two slightly different levels with a separated study and homework area at the higher and with workroom to the rear of that. This study area has a good view of the garden courtyard which incidentally can also be viewed by adult users by access from their Lending Library on to a flat roof where seating is provided. Small alcoves in the Children's Library give an added attractiveness to this pleasant room.

The assembly accommodation can seat about 100 for social functions and there are good kitchen and public toilet facilities.

It is reckoned that the population in the vicinity is about 15,000 (that is excluding those in Holloway Prison, which is close by, and which has special provision for library service given by Islington Council). On the other side of the library is a vast council housing development while in Camden Road some of the private property is commercially used by professional persons for office purposes.

There is much to congratulate this Council's Architect and Librarian upon in the difficulties which they have overcome, yet having made this visit directly after one to Hackney's Homerton branch there were interesting comparisons which gave rise to contrasting feelings of crowdedness in the one and spaciousness in the other. Islington certainly can claim a limited site area for erecting the building but whereas they provide over 30,000 volumes for a 15,000 population, with the consequential need for greater footage of shelving, Hackney differs with 25,000 books for a 30% higher population area. It is an interesting debating point: the ratio of book stock to space for circulating and browsing—which is likely to offer the greater appeal to the users?

ND   HW

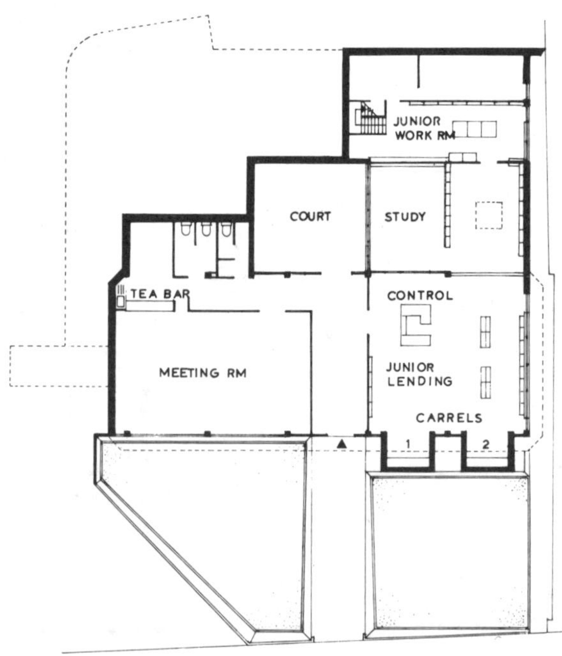

LOWER FLOOR

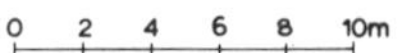

Authority	London Borough of Islington
Designation	John Barnes Branch
Date of opening	December 1974
Population served	15,000
Name of Architect	A E Head, RIBA, DipTP, MRTPI, Borough Architect in association with Andrew Sherlock and Partners
Name of Librarian	C A Elliott, FLA

Special features:

a) site	Limited on steeply sloping corner site necessitating two levels
b) architecture	Reinforced concrete frame with aluminium glazed screens: brickwork to upper floor
c) function	Serving mainly residential area

Mechanical Services:

a) heating	Gas-fired low pressure hot water; fan assisted convectors
b) ventilation	Artificial ventilation through ceiling grilles and outlets
c) lighting	Fluorescent within boarded ceiling
d) acoustics	Acoustic ceiling tiles
e) other	—

Areas: in square metres

a) lending	
b) reference	} 233
c) reading	
d) special activities	—
e) children	148
f) control	68
g) library staff admin.	190
h) exhibition	in (f)
i) lecture hall	77
j) circulation	—
k) services	in (g)
l) lavatories	23
m) stack	—
Total area:	**906**

Book volumes:

a) adult lending	20,000
b) adult reference	100
c) children	10,000
d) stack	—
e) other	2,000 gr
Total:	**32,100**

Costs in £ p:

a) site	15,600
b) building	183,860
c) furniture & fittings	5,000
Total Cost (ex fees):	**£204,460**
Cost per square metre:	**£225**

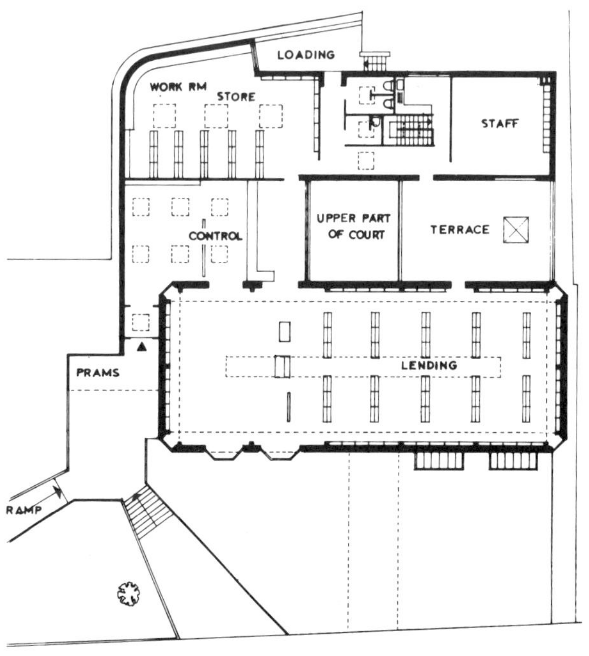

UPPER FLOOR

Royal Borough of Kensington and Chelsea: Brompton

The site on the north side of Old Brompton Road on the borders of Kensington and Chelsea was acquired by the Council during the war after the bombing of the two houses which stood there. Hidden behind advertisement hoardings for many years and with the cost of a new library rising constantly, the Council put off the decision to build it until it was resolved to try to finance the venture by letting out, under competitive conditions, the development rights of the site for flats over a new library. By this means a substantial part of the cost of the building was met without falling on the rates whilst the valuable new block of flats produced a substantial contribution in rateable value whilst benefiting from the undoubted prestige of the library. The Council retains the freehold of the site. This is a useful formula for achieving mixed developments on valuable city centre or town centre sites at little cost to ratepayers and it is hoped that this will become more popular as a method of financing the building of new libraries.

Despite numerous problems typical of congested urban sites, including restrictions of Ancient Lights, library vehicle parking and fire-escape (all greatly complicated by the presence of the block of flats), the library has been fitted into a remarkably tight and difficult site with great ingenuity. It has, predictably, proved very popular with the local residents in this strangely mixed area. Old Brompton Road passes through one of the most sought after and expensive areas of London but the library also draws a substantial part of its readership from the less desirable areas off Earls Court Road which are traditionally the habitat of a shifting population of far-from-affluent students. The very sophisticated finishes, whilst appealing to the very respectable residents of the neighbourhood have been very well-treated and there is remarkably little of the vandalism so often found in city centre libraries.

The exterior view of the library, nestling unobtrusively at the foot of the large block of flats (with its rather gaping loading and parking bay), gives no idea of the comparatively large library space included. The handsome white mosaic clad canopy with its stylish blue and silver lettering does however give a clue to the excellent quality of its internal finishes.

A main entrance porch, with its whole floor a matwell, leads into an equally narrow hallway which opens out quickly into a generous foyer with plenty of pin-up-panels and a long glass-fronted showcase, well stocked with the latest books and other material. Here the floor was in sparkling black terrazzo tiles which the public found slippery and the staff wearisome to the feet. Now it has been carpeted—but in mauve which 'clashes'. Several easy chairs give an immediate sense of welcome. A very well designed 'In' and 'Out' counter, with space for trolleys to stand inside without any interruption of working space, and with built-in desks for readers enrolment and a desk between for a librarian within the counter, show clear evidence of the thought that has been given to the solution of the counter problem. Issue is by the Browne method and about 176,000 adult and 23,000 junior issues per annum are for the most part handled by one assistant with a second at peak times only. This high figure, relative to staff handling it, testifies to the efficiency of the counter design, particularly when bearing in mind that the assistant also handles telephone calls.

Black terrazzo stairs with smoked glass balustrade and hardwood handrails lead at right angles from the entrance hall to a first floor landing giving access to a Meetings Room (with roof balcony and adjacent lavatories) and to the Reference Library. Unfortunately owing to financial restrictions and staffiing problems the Reference Library was delayed in opening to the public. The Meetings Room is hardly used despite the excellent provisions and the proximity of a small room from which refreshments can be dispensed, albeit hazardously, for it is up a short narrow flight of steps quite unsuited to carrying trays of cups or glasses.

The Reference Library promises to be a pleasant, very quiet, well-lighted room lying as it does on the north side of the block, away from the road, with large windows overlooking the roofs of the projecting ground floor lending and children's libraries. This view is not particularly attractive as the roofs of the lower block are somewhat clumsily handled, but the quietness of the position is a great advantage. The choice of enclosed desks, with high divisions between, and with no informal tables, or easy chairs for browsing, seems to make the room sterner than it needs to be.

Returning to the ground floor, the Children's Library lies immediately behind the counter with a rather unnecessary glazed screen partly enclosing it, but since there are no doors, the reason for this is obscure.

The Lending Library is to the right of the Children's and much larger. Both rooms are lighted from large clerestorey windows in a raised centre section, again of rather clumsy design, which arises from a structural solution in the form of bent, reinforced concrete beams which have the great advantage of leaving the floor unobstructed by columns. This rather ungainly structure is a price well worth paying for the uncluttered space that results.

It was noticeable that on the hottest day for many years (about 86°F), the library was comparatively, pleasantly cool, partly no doubt because of the overshadowed situation of the ground floor building between parallel rows of tall terraced houses. In the evening the high-level windows admit late sunshine which is always welcome. As many of the windows can be opened by unsightly remote control gear, ventilation is quite good.

The Children's Library has a raised fibreglass fish and plant pool with fountain, a nice idea if slightly costly in loss of space and somehow a little formal, a tendency too in the rigidly symmetrical furniture layout which somewhat obscures the view into parts of the library. The brown carpet is complemented by deep tier guide panels, of temporary appearance, in orange with rather unsympathetic black hand lettering.

In the Lending Library the brown carpet and acoustic tiled ceiling combine to provide a quiet and dignified atmosphere enhanced by solid mahogany shelf units by Serota with gold-lettered, black tier guiding of smallish not very clear lettering. Lighting is recessed into the tiled ceiling with plastic diffusers used. In the Children's Library this is supplemented by tungsten lights with orange shades which give a rather more pleasant light. Heating is by means of low pressure hot water from a boiler in the basement distributed generally by Hudevad radiators but with fan assisted convectors in the Children's and Lending Libraries. Parallel with the counter and opening off the Lending Department is the Librarian's office and next to the part apparently intended as the Gramophone Record Library when economic circumstances allow this service to be initiated.

Adjacent to the above, off the Lending Library, there is a large but completely internal workroom with a short corridor to the loading bay. This room, whilst adequate for the purpose, with metal shelving, is rather a claustrophobic place in which to work, the inevitable result of having to pack so much accommodation into such a dense building form.

In direct contrast, the Children's Library service for the whole Borough is run from an office on the first floor next to the Reference Library. This is a very pleasant room with big north-facing windows overlooking the same view as the Reference Library; but since the floor of this room is some four steps higher than that in the Reference the asbestos cement clad rooflights of the lower floor do not appear nearly so obtrusive.

The staff do not come off too well for their room (access to which is gained from the entrance hall) is directly facing Brompton Road and the South. It is therefore very hot, noisy and, if the window is open, full of traffic fumes; but there is a cooker, refrigerator and sink for preparing snacks, and adjacent lavatories.

The emergency escape requirements, together with problems of security, are the cause of some concern to the staff, for the library plan is very complex with many possibilities for trouble. It has already been burgled three times and this before the Reference Department was even open. In particular the position of the lavatories will be a constant worry. This is a universal library problem and is seldom solved successfully.

The librarians complain that the artificial lighting is too bright generally. The tendency in recent years to design for high lighting intensities in new libraries has led to some reaction by the users and staff, as noted in our review of St Pancras Library in the 1974 issue of the publication. It is perhaps time for a reappraisal on rather more scientific than emotional or prestige-making lines, of just what constitutes a sensible level and quality of illumination for libraries.

All-in-all this is an excellent library where the best has been made of a very difficult restricted site and is significant particularly for the method by which it was financed and built.

GKVT

Authority	Royal Borough of Kensington and Chelsea
Designation	Brompton Branch Library
Date of opening	May 1974
Population served	30,000
Name of Architect	John MacAlpine, MC AA, Dipl RIBA
Name of Librarian	S C Holliday, FLA succeeded by W S Hudson FLA
Special features:	
a) site	On main road: bombed terraced housing
b) architecture	Brick and concrete construction, ground and first floor of block of flats
c) function	—
Mechanical Services:	
a) heating	Gas-fired central heating
b) ventilation	Natural plus fans to pump in cold air
c) lighting	Fluorescent strip in ceiling panels. Some tungsten in Children's Library
d) acoustics	Ceiling treatment in Reference Library
e) other	—
Areas: in square metres	
a) lending	223
b) reference	112
c) reading	—
d) special activities	—
e) children	84
f) control	56
g) library staff admin.	158
h) exhibitions	46
i) lecture hall	58
j) circulation	56
k) services	63
l) lavatories	28
m) stack	232
Total area:	1,116
Book volumes:	
a) adult lending	13,000
b) adult reference	1,720
c) children	3,000
d) stack	17,380
e) other	—
Total:	35,100
Costs in £ p:	
a) site	12,000
b) building	112,000* (cost to Authority £30,000)
c) furniture & fittings	15,000
Total Cost (ex fees):	£139,000
Cost per square metre:	£124

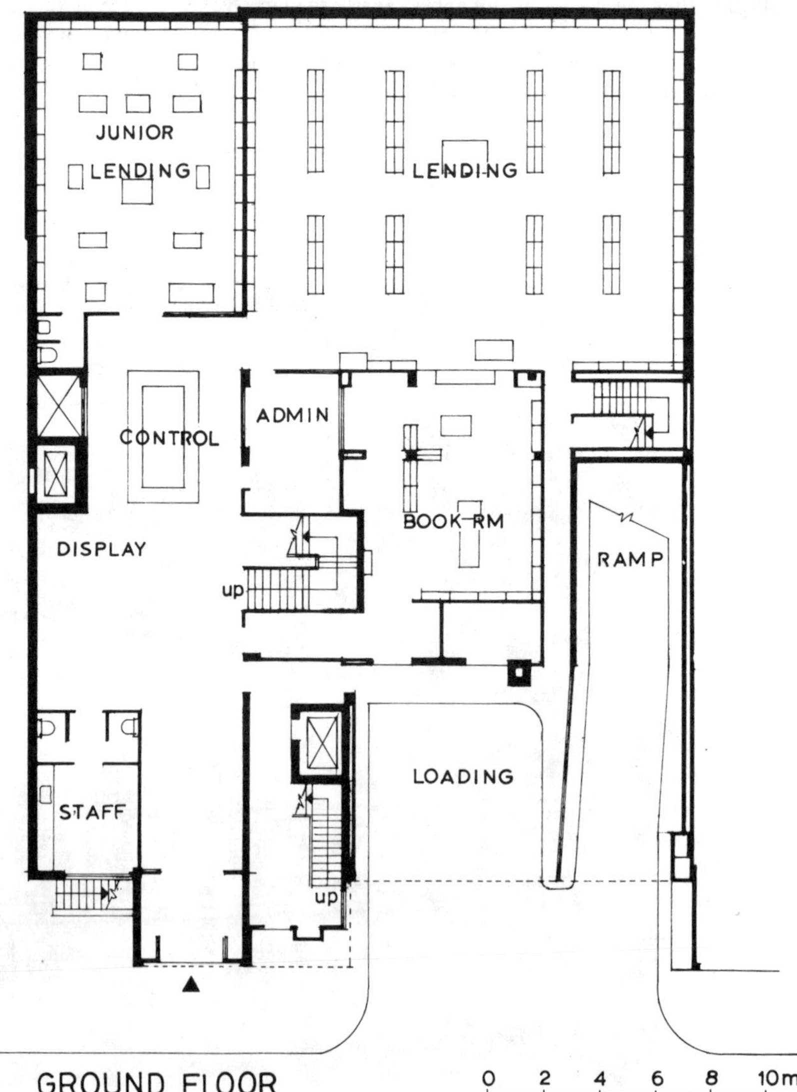

London Borough of Redbridge: South Woodford

Although this library was not opened to the public until January 1975, the work was virtually completed within this review period and therefore justifies inclusion. Driving towards it, there was the thought that Redbridge has two other libraries opened within recent years, the earlier one being nearly a disaster while the later one ranked an architectural award. It was hoped, therefore, that this visit to South Woodford Library would reveal another library of merit.

Set on a generous main road site, opposite a parade of shops and itself alongside a Health Centre, a Careers Advice Bureau and accommodation for a Registrar of Births, Deaths and Marriages, and with a large school at its back, it is thus ideally placed for 'drawing' power. Wide grass lawns and trees separate it from the busy road while very generous underground car parking is provided–surely a comfort for users of all the services provided. Access from this car park to the front entrance of the library is by wide steps which link with the pedestrian path from the main road to the library and then by steps, or ramp for handicapped persons. This strange combination creates a situation where handicapped persons arriving by invalid cars have to park in the main road as they are unable to negotiate the stairs.

The visual impact of the building may, to some, be impressive but the curious insistence on windows framed in bright blue and with heavy black cills and surrounds, creates a clash with the bright red brickwork of the whole building which also includes two floors of Council flats above.

Entry into the building reveals a wide and deep entrance hall with quarry tiled floor which just a year's wear has already made rather dull and nondescript. Wide poster boards range on each side but it was stated that this area is not used for display or small exhibitions as there is an area for this purpose at lower ground floor level. To the left is the entrance to the Hollis Room (named after a former lady Alderman) which is available for meetings only, and then for not more than 75 people. With excellent kitchen facilities it is surprising that this facility is not widened for other library and social purposes. Public toilets are provided off the entrance. The room is rather cold and austere with only high-level windows behind the speaker's platform, producing considerable glare.

Through the inner entrance doors and one is impressed by height and space, helped by split levels up and down. A large counter (Browne charging system) allows passage to the main lending area (Libraco furniture in beech is pleasing) and to an enquiry desk and gramophone record issue counter. Strangely the records are stored in a tall shelf unit running in front of a low handrail with the record sleeves, for selection, on the lower floor some distance away–this appears to have been an afterthought. Behind this counter is a large south-facing window with venetian blinds. Now one may go up eight stairs to a reading (newspaper and periodicals) and study area, or down to the Music Library, or to an exhibition area and then through to the Children's Library.

All flooring is in grey carpeting, while the balustrades are concrete with metal handrails and railings painted black. From floor-to-ceiling on one side of the counter is a flanking window (approximately 18 ft high) while on each side is a sloping roof-light which stretches across the whole width of the department, giving both a glare and a cleaning problem. Remembering the former disaster of Fulwell Cross Library a question was asked of the effect of these on internal temperatures. 'Last summer it was 110°F by 11 am' came the reply, 'and the counter staff had to learn to endure this'!

The reading and study area, stretching the width of the building, is furnished sparsely with hardwood bench seats and plain topped desks with grey-black polypropylene chairs. A few black vinyl, but armless, chairs are around to give some semblance of relaxation: but there is a chill about this area, with its unpainted block walls and with no curtains to hide those obtrusive heavy blue and black framed windows. Here there is not a warm colour to be seen and had it not been for the bright sunshine outside it might have caused a shiver!

Returning to the main floor level and then down to the small exhibition area disappointingly occupied by a small collection of photographs, pinned to boards, but, it seemed, with no planned arrangement; nor was there a prominent lead-in board. A step or two further to the Children's Library (posts and rope are used to segregate one area from another as needed for the children have their own entrance from the main road). This was said to be a busy section although there were few children in at that time; but the room seemed crowded with so much in it. A 'West Norwood' touch had been attempted but this sunken, carpeted 'pit' was much smaller and was not helped by 'Kinderboxes' occupying much of the surround while even the pit floor was encumbered with more furniture. Although the view from here out to the front lawns is attractive, a long low black radiator, with slatted bench top, stretches across the width of the windows, which have opening catches and so could, if needed, said the Branch Librarian, serve as emergency exits. In the non-public areas there is generous space in a staff room, equipped with kitchen fittings, which is comfortably furnished and has a good view. Offices and toilets, a store and a large workroom complete the accommodation.

On asking about access for delivery of books, furniture etc, as the workroom is at least four or five metres from ground level (because of the underground car park), a curious situation was revealed. There is a small exterior concrete landing outside the workroom with steps to ground level. At the extremity of this landing is a small, electrically driven hoist which is, however, not used–and vandalism was mentioned. The drivers thus 'hump' books and other manageable goods up the stairs and into the workroom but large furniture and equipment have either to be taken through the main entrance doors or somehow through the largest of the windows.

This library serves a catchment area of approximately 20,000 population, mostly in good residential areas and so book issues average 1,000 per day. Considerable road work was in progress for the new motorway less than 100 metres from the library and this may be restricting library use at the moment.

The concept of multiple use of the site is good, and the gas-fired central heating serves the whole complex. The space is generous and the position of the library is a dominant one. Yet this potential seems, in some measure, not to have been used to the maximum, for the building's exterior lacks attractiveness, and could possibly be, to some people, even repellent—and this a great pity indeed.

GKVT   HW

Authority	London Borough of Redbridge
Designation	South Woodford Branch Library
Date of opening	January 1976
Population served	20,000
Name of Architect	D J W Restick, DipArch, RIBA, Borough Architect C J Hockley, Job Architect
Name of Librarian	F C Kennerley, FLA
Special features:	
a) site	Within complex of Health Centre, Careers Advice Bureau and Registrar of births and deaths offices: all to 'sit' between existing trees near new motorway
b) architecture	Reinforced concrete frame; brick faced externally; fair faced concrete block walls internally; split levels for underground car park
c) function	Serving large residential area
Mechanical Services:	
a) heating	Gas-fired central heating for whole complex: Fan heaters
b) ventilation	Natural
c) lighting	Fluorescent strip plus tungsten down lights and spots
d) acoustics	Carpeted
e) other	—
Areas: in square metres	
a) lending	239
b) reference	109
c) reading	in (h)
d) special activities	45
e) children	95
f) control	—
g) library staff admin.	34
h) exhibitions	42
i) lecture hall	58
j) circulation	—
k) services	—
l) lavatories	9
m) stack	250
Total area:	881
Book volumes:	
a) adult lending	18,000
b) adult reference	1,100
c) children	5,000
d) stack	3,000
e) other	1,600 gr
Total:	28,700
Costs in £ p:	
a) site	Not known: part of complex
b) building	106,617
c) furniture & fittings	5,800
Total Cost (ex fees):	£125,760 (ex site)
Cost per square metre:	£142

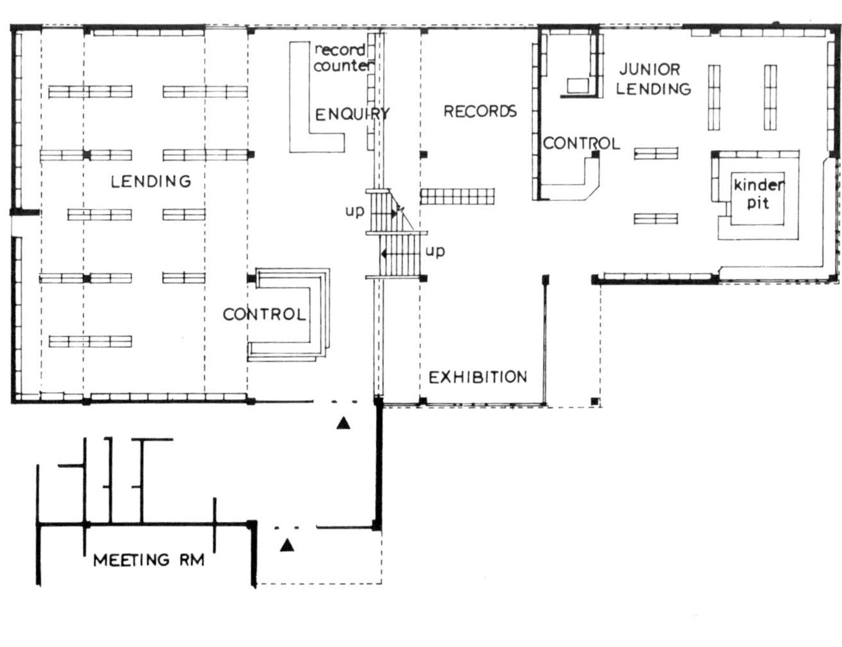

GROUND FLOOR

London Borough of Richmond-upon-Thames: Whitton

Whitton lies between Twickenham and Hounslow and the site of the new library is in Nelson Road. After a long and chequered history of temporary library buildings housed in shops the present site was acquired in 1971. It is long and thin on the approach road to a car park behind the main shopping parade in Whitton–an unpreposessing 1930's development. If obviously convenient for car users it is slightly less so for other members of the public who have to traverse the car park to approach the library from the shops. The site is a very unattractive one and noisy because of its relationship to the road. With this factor its linking to an Old People's Day Rest Centre is a little surprising. The design adopted has been largely dominated by the need to screen off the very unattractive surroundings and to keep out the noise, and this has been achieved reasonably successfully.

The entrance has been placed almost as far from the car park and shops as the site would permit and at the point where the building is at its narrowest so that some planting is possible at the front. The rear wall is on the boundary and is without openings. The small draft lobby leads to an L-shaped counter which wraps round a small office–with the circular Children's Library to right and the Adult Library to the left. Staff rooms are at the far end of the Adult Library off a corridor which leads to a rear entrance.

The counter arrangement is interesting in that it combines a children's issue desk with the adult issue and return areas. Unfortunately not quite enough space is left behind the counter for easy circulation so that the advantage of one member of staff being able to supervise the whole counter when the library is lightly-used is outweighed when the busy times occur. Had the corner of the office been splayed off, sufficient extra space would have been obtained to ease movement.

Whilst the counter incorporates plenty of storage space of diverse sizes it is very uncomfortable in some respects. For example, no knee space is provided beneath the workship in one of the positions where staff are supposed to sit. All returned books are placed in shelves under or behind the counter so that they have later to be loaded on to trolleys which stand some way from the desk instead of being loaded direct. The designer's task has not been easy, however, for record storage shelves have had to be fitted in even though there are, at present, no definite plans for starting a record lending service.

The Children's Library is a circular brick drum with windows placed where they can look out onto Nelson Road, which though not a particularly inspiring view is at least reasonably open. In the middle of the circle the floor drops by a single step to provide a pit where small children can sprawl to read their large picture books. This area however would have been better if it had not been cluttered with kinderboxes for browsing which make the pit very difficult to use. Comparison with a similar feature in the West Norwood Library illustrated in the 1971/72 Volume shows a much more flexible arrangement.

The circular shape adopted has not proved very successful for it is difficult to fit shelving to a circular wall; in consequence the bookshelving takes the form of free standing three-shelf units radiating from the centre which clutter the otherwise attractive shape and conceal some areas from view at the desk. Pin-up panels have been fixed around the perimeter but these are in the form of a strip of the boarding which leaves cold blank areas of wall above and below. Perimeter bookshelving would have provided a much more spacious arrangement and more shelving.

A rather curious rooflight (taking the form of sloping patent glazing on either side of a brick wall built on a concrete beam across an opening in the ceiling) gives good natural daylighting in the Children's Library.

In the Adult Library some views out are are obtained through narrow slit windows between stepped panels of wall which are arranged so that the library gradually opens out from the desk. The atmosphere in this room is very pleasant and not as claustrophobic as the plan might suggest, since the views down the length of the room into the Children's Department are long and varied. White painted fair-faced brick walls reflect much of the light from the large square rooflights and the large square fluorescent light diffusers between and alongside the rooflights. The yellow carpet and white pinhole acoustic tile ceiling together with fixed double-glazed windows make for quiet, but not completely dead, acoustic conditions. The many plants which are carefully looked after by the staff add a further interest.

The bookshelving, which is arranged on the outside walls with five shelves and two free standing bookcases of only two shelves maintains an openness which is missing in the Children's Library. Several chairs upholstered in khaki coloured fabric and hardwood tables arranged informally give opportunities for quiet reading and browsing. Shelving by Library Design and Engineering is in metal but the effect is softened by the beech fascias and ends to the shelving.

Lighting is varied by a number of adjustable ceiling spots in lighting track directed on to perimeter shelving. The warmth of the tungsten lights is very welcome as a contrast to the cold efficiency of the fluorescent.

The Reference Department is beyond the Adult Lending area and up two steps or a narrow ramp with some very obtrusive and ugly handrails. Unfortunately this area is oppressively low, about 2.3 m, though the lighting from the large rooflights and diffusers is as efficient as in the Lending area. The lack of any outside windows does matter here and the rather long thin plan of the room prevents its enjoying the feeling of a balcony that it might have had if it had been planned as a wide, shallow roof at the end of the library rather than as a long tunnel. The furnishing with six tables each having two chairs is rather formal. Very pleasant perspex periodicals display shelving against a natural hessian background helps to brighten a not very successful room.

Why the staff should have been allocated such an unpleasant room is a mystery, for in many libraries attention has been paid to making the staff comfortable in their rare moments off duty. Librarians work long hours, often at times when most people are at home, and it is fitting that they should be treated to civilised surroundings. But in this room, a sink at one side and a tiny cooker on the other, cut up the room; ugly hat and coat hooks and a refrigerator are all placed with little thought. The outlook could hardly be worse, for the window which occurs beneath the back door canopy looks over the dustbins, past the plant room door to the road and car park and the rear of the shops and maisonettes over.

Nearly all the faults of this building stem from the very poor site; not even the considerable ingenuity of the architect could quite mitigate the result which falls way short of the ideal.

GKVT

Authority	London Borough of Richmond-upon-Thames
Designation	Whitton Branch Library
Date of opening	December 1973
Population served	15,000
Name of Architect	M J C Edwards, DipTP (Lond) FRIBA, FRTPI, Borough Architect and Planning Officer
Name of Librarian	Gilbert Turner, FLA
Special features:	
a) site	Adjacent car park
b) architecture	Traditional brick
c) function	Branch public library
Mechanical Services:	
a) heating	Gas-fired boiler; radiators
b) ventilation	Natural plus extract. fans
c) lighting	Mixed
d) acoustics	Acoustic tiles, carpet
e) other	—
Areas: in square metres	
a) lending	
b) reference	
c) reading	268
d) special activities	
e) children	82
f) control	in (a)
g) library staff admin.	42
h) exhibitions	—
i) lecture hall	—
j) circulation	—
k) services	—
l) lavatories	2
m) stack	6
Total area:	400
Book volumes:	
a) adult lending	12,626
b) adult reference	658
c) children	5,945
d) stack	—
e) other	—
Total:	19,229
Costs in £ p:	
a) site	—
b) building	55,300
c) furniture & fittings	5,300
Total Cost (ex fees):	60,600
Cost per square metre:	£151

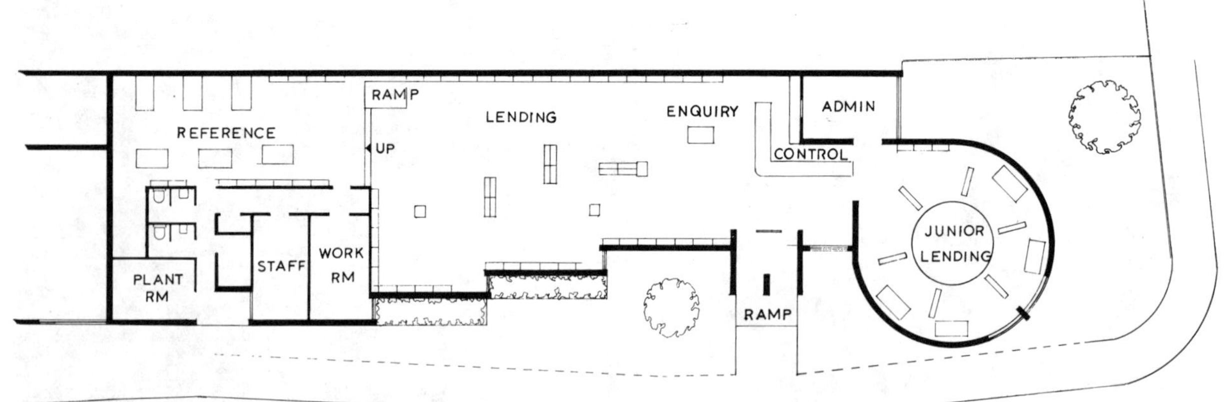

GROUND FLOOR

◁ TO CARPARK

0 2 4 6 8 10m

London Borough of Wandsworth:
York Library

One of the most remarkable features of this library is its neglect by the public. That the staff of seven issue only 1,500 books per week is surprising, until one learns that this building was intended to replace the old Southlands Library, only 500 yards away, which has remained open by popular demand. This is partly because it has a thriving children's library, for which no provision is made in the new building.

Perhaps another explanation lies in the design of the huge new housing estate within which the new library is sited. Unfortunately one of the least attractive developments, it replaces the small scale rows of terrace housing, which typified much of this part of London. Long tall slabs of flats, sometimes raised on columns, allow cold draughts to funnel through to windy piazzas—eminently suited to a southern climate but a nightmare in England. As time goes by it is becoming more generally recognised that such planning, whilst solving many problems of safety, daylighting and economics, poses new and more intractable social problems. People tend to cling to any vestiges of the past, which may explain the attachment to the old library whilst the new building, regardless of its merits, is shunned as belonging to the new order.

The red brick library with timber fascias looks on to the pedestrian shopping precinct and a large paved square which is planted with rather pathetic saplings, too young to contribute much in the way of shelter or decoration. The entrance to the building is rather obscure, being not very well signposted. The main library consists of a single large rectangular room which has windows facing west, with low cills and venetian blinds, on one side, and on the opposite side clerestorey windows above perimeter bookshelving. The west windows look across the bleak square to a wall of nine-storey flats. Within this large room, four long rows of tall Reska metal bookcases march down one side whilst the other half of the room remains empty except for 20 easy chairs ranged, for casual reading, around low tables. This somehow leaves it devoid of any character, despite the warm timber ceiling, the timber ends to the bookcases and the yellow carpet. Too much space is almost more daunting than too little.

The counter by the entrance doors has rather small 'In' and 'Out' signs in awkward positions, so that the public need constant reminding of the correct direction of circulation. The actual arrangement of the photocharging equipment is ill-considered for dealing with any large flow of issues—not significant perhaps at present but later when issues grow it would be a potential cause of much annoyance, particularly since the lighting at the counter is far from good. Counter design is a highly specialised matter and needs to be given more detailed consideration than any other part of the library. The assistant's job here is tedious and repetitive so that any minor faults are quickly magnified.

Plenty of pin-up boarding is provided, most of it in the form of screens, which unfortunately block the view from the counter into the library. Supervision is only partly possible from the desk of the Readers' Adviser. Near the counter a section of the library is screened off to form a corridor and display space with elegantly detailed showcases for books and other material. Behind this screen lies a study area with a row of nine desk places and chairs, again completely hidden from the counter. Also in the corridor is a public telephone with acoustic hood which appears to be very popular in this neighbourhood where not everyone has their own telephone, although this does cause disturbance. Close to this are doors to the Librarian's small, high ceilinged office, with clerestory windows, and to the very claustrophobic internal workroom without any natural lighting, view or even heating; a cheerless place for staff to be expected to work.

The staff room, although it faces south, is an unattractive room lacking privacy, since it becomes something of a passageway being situated between the workroom and the staff corridor. It has cooker, refrigerator and sink in one corner, high ceiling and plastic tile floor. Good lavatories are provided for men, women and oddly a separate one for porters, but five lockers only for the ten staff.

Some time after the completion of the library it was decided to add a public hall with connecting doors to the library so that the two spaces could, if needed, be used together, though a separate entrance is also provided. The hall (110 m^2) has high-level windows, fitted with blackout blinds on all four sides, and a dais. The roof is of similar design and height to that of the library but the supporting columns are placed just inside the internal walls sterilising a 500 mm wide strip around the room. Men's, women's and wheelchair lavatories and a superbly equipped kitchen with long rows of white melamine finished cupboards and a hatch to the hall will prove a useful adjunct when a decision is eventually made as to the actual purpose of the hall which has only once been used (for an inaugural party) since it was finished.

The heating is generally underfloor and is run off the estate district heating mains. One suspects that the high ceilings, so universally used, may lead to high running costs.

It is sad not to be able to be more enthusiastic over such a well-finished building but the ultimate test of success must be whether the public like it and use it.

GKVT

Authority	London Borough of Wandsworth
Designation	York Branch Library
Date of opening	December 1973
Population served	15,000
Name of Architect	Howes Jackman and Partners
Name of Librarian	E V Corbett, MA, FLA, FRSA
Special features:	
a) site	Single storey, free standing in small shopping precinct
b) architecture	Timber framed structure; wide span laminated timber frames; brick externally matching other buildings facing amenity area
c) function	Branch library
Mechanical Services:	
a) heating	District heating: built in convectors; fan circulators and radiators
b) ventilation	Opening windows and mechanical system
c) lighting	Fluorescent overall: tungsten spots for highlighting in public areas; also in offices etc
d) acoustics	Double glazing and carpeting
e) other	—
Areas: in square metres	
a) lending	143
b) reference	51
c) reading	81
d) special activities	—
e) children	—
f) control	—
g) library staff admin.	109 (inc toilets)
h) exhibitions	115
i) lecture hall	—
j) circulation	153
k) services	—
l) lavatories	23 (public)
m) stack	46
Total area:	721
Book volumes:	
a) adult lending	11,559
b) adult reference	878
c) children	—
d) stack	—
e) other	—
Total:	12,437
Costs in £ p:	
a) site	11,000
b) building	132,000
c) furniture & fittings	5,000
Total Cost (ex fees):	£148,000
Cost per square metre:	£205

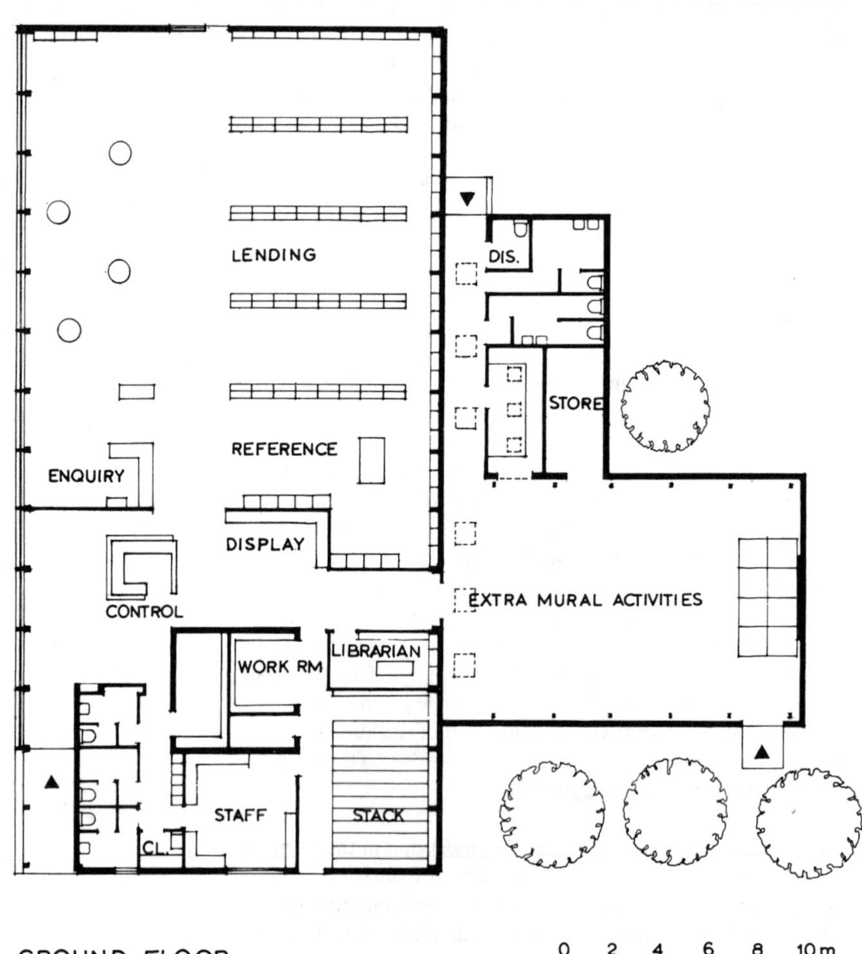

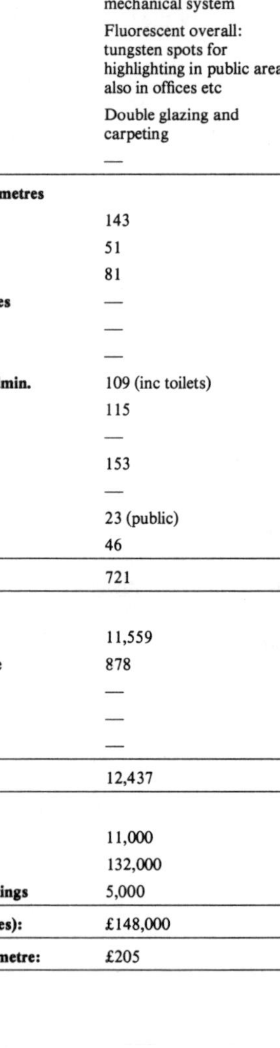

GROUND FLOOR

City of Westminster:
Pimlico

This Library is situated at the south end of one of the most distinguished and interesting new housing developments in London, at Lillington Street in Pimlico opposite the entrance to Pimlico Underground Station.

The housing scheme, which has attracted widespread interest was the result of an architectural competition. It represents a strong reaction against the institutional and regimented type of large scale housing so often seen in the post-war period. The reaction is in the direction of complexity, apparent randomness and an intensely human, almost quirky vernacular design. The library is a late afterthought, somehow shoehorned into a corner of a large block which also contains flats and a clinic.

Facing south on to a noisy road junction, the library occupies a semi-basement position with mezzanine floors and some accommodation at full basement level. When approached from the south, there is a large clear sign but from other directions it is not nearly as apparent that this is a library. Since it serves a wider area than the housing estate itself this is a disadvantage, for the building is hardly recognisable as a library; the large windows are carefully screened with vertical venetian blinds so that it is difficult to make out what goes on inside.

The entrance is down several steps or by a curving ramp for wheelchairs or prams, beneath the corner of the projecting mezzanine floor. There is some space to leave prams outside, while wheelchairs can pass through to the main floor of the library although no arrangements were possible to enable access for wheelchairs to the upper levels.

A clearly lettered signboard by the entrance states opening hours whilst large pin-up boards in the draught lobby allow space for information on local and London activities to be displayed. This pin boarding, finished with red baize set in dark hardwood panelling, runs through into the library up to the control counter.

The main library room at this level contains lending stock, 25 seats and the catalogue which takes the form of an illuminated screen for viewing the filmstrip index. Though it is not a large space, it is so arranged that many areas are not visible from the desk which makes supervision difficult.

On the mezzanine where the remainder of the lending sequence is found, with more seating, supervision is virtually impossible and problems do arise. It was originally the intention that a member of the staff would sit upstairs to keep an eye on the mezzanine but although a desk has been provided, it is seldom practicable to spare anyone for this boring and unproductive task. In any event even from the desk much of the mezzanine is out of sight, so that the risks of vandalism, pilfering and misbehaviour have to be accepted.

Behind the counter is a small workroom with some rolling stacks for reserve stock, an office for the Librarian, luxuriously panelled in blackened hardwood and a staff entrance which widens to become a porters room with store off. The staff complain that it is impossible to keep the workroom tidy but the view into it is very restricted so that this scarcely matters to the public.

As a place in which to work, the workroom is very pleasant, the narrow slit windows allowing views out whilst not revealing too much from outside. Storage, as always in workrooms, is not as generous as staff would wish but the variety of shelving and cupboards seems to satisfy most needs. The installation of rolling stacks is useful but unfortunately, owing to the late appearance of a small duct which restricts the movement of the stacks, totally inadequate space has been allowed for access between the stacks. This is so inconvenient that there are suggestions that one of the stacks may have to be removed to make the arrangement workable. A small book hoist provides a connection to the mezzanine floor for return of books from the counter.

Functionally the counter is reasonably good and well placed in a position for controlling the entrance, the foot of the staircase, catalogue and the approach to the Children's Library which is on a further mezzanine level behind the counter. In one respect however, that of lighting, it is badly served. Where there is so much detailed and finicky work with tokens and cards, the librarians need perfect lighting, without shadows and of high intensity. Instead the designers have provided very dazzling spotlights which cast strong shadows, are far too directional and introduce, at low level over the librarians' heads, a great deal of radiant heat. The effect is very dramatic but extremely uncomfortable for the long periods of rather repetitive work involved at the counter.

Elsewhere in the library the mixture of fluorescent lighting (which are behind diffusers built onto and out from the bookcases) and tungsten lights (either as swivel spots or glass spheres) gives interesting and original illumination, but sometimes inadequate because of the lack of reflective surfaces available. Over the readers' adviser's desk the single dazzling bulb which pops down from the ceiling is ridiculous.

The use of so much tungsten lighting does have another undesirable effect in that it exacerbates the serious problem of overheating from which this library suffers. As originally designed, the library was to have been air-conditioned, a natural decision in view of the orientation and the noise from surrounding flats. The attempt to provide some natural lighting in a building of such a deep plan led to the provision of large windows all of which face south or south-west and though some attempt has been made to mitigate solar heat gain, this is not really effective.

At a late stage in the design, the air-conditioning was omitted as an economy measure and no compensation was made to deal with the potential problems which now plague the building. Even when this library was reviewed in the *Architects Journal* of 23rd April 1975, following a visit by their critic in February, it was noted that conditions were uncomfortable on warm days. The experience of the summer of the same year when temperatures were frequently above 90°F must have convinced the authorities that some measure will have to be taken to make the library

more comfortable. A pathetic attempt to extract some of the
heat by means of two small fans at high-level in the mezzanine is
doomed to failure. Despite this the Adult Library is obviously
popular with some 3,000 books issued per week.

Children have a very small room capable of holding only
a few books. This room which is at a higher level than
the main floor has been enclosed behind glazed screens which
have not been adequately considered since, when furniture is
placed near the screens, the view from the main library reveals
the undersides of tables, the backs of display screens and a
clutter of waste bins and other paraphernalia. Because of the
limited room available for children's books, these have tended to
overflow out on to shelves and to seats obviously not intended
for the purpose, thus giving an untidy impression. Some
difficulties have been experienced with windows which open out
directly into pedestrian alleys at the back of the library to the
danger of the public. The Children's Library has been more
popular than anticipated and issues run at 500–600 per week
despite the fact that there is another and much larger Children's
Library in Lupus Street, which is only half a mile away and has
been open for many years. Any new library will attract a large
number of readers and it may be that the demand will fall back.
If it does not, then it is hard to imagine how the limited
accommodation available will be able to cope with the constant
demand.

The Adult Lending Library has an intriguing atmosphere totally
different from that of most new libraries. No expense seems to
have been spared in the pursuit of this effect. The bookcases are
elaborately and floridly designed in black stained hardwood
matched by the staircase handrail, wall panelling and furniture
in the same material. This, together with the beige carpet which
is turned up as a skirting in places, produces a calm though
rather sedate interior of great quality, interest and is highly
sophisticated. Ceilings are generally finished in a rough
rendering which though painted white, together with the dark
timber, absorb too much of the available light and produce a
rather sombre interior. On the mezzanine level the high-level
windows with adjacent sloping ceiling might have produced a
great flood of lighting but for the fact that the ceiling is in black
timber, again soaking up the light.

The elaborate detailing, whilst providing an interior of much
interest, must have been very costly. One wonders whether the
priorities have not become confused. Functionally there are so
many shortcomings, such as the extreme difficulty of cleaning
windows, overheating, lighting that could relatively easily have
been solved if more money had been available by using simpler
details and cheaper materials.

The staff accommodation is well detailed, a large staff room with
kitchen section being screened off behind an overdetailed wall,
and men's and women's lavatories of sober design. The position
of the staff room at basement level does result in its being a little
bleak.

Interesting aspects of the service offered are the issue of
music cassettes which are attractively displayed and a large

display of paperback books for lending. The latter are
recognised as having a very limited life and are regularly
replenished.

Illustrations of the exterior are misleading as they are seen in
isolation. The Library is so closely integrated into the complex
fabric of the building, of which it forms a part, and the vast
warren of an estate that it has to be seen to be fully appreciated.
Despite all the criticisms of functional shortcomings and
discomforts this is a distinguished library which has turned its
back firmly on the institutional image so often encountered in
public libraries. Its reward seems to be an enthusiastic clientèle.

GKVT

Authority	Westminster City Council
Designation	Pimlico Library
Date of opening	July 1974
Population served	12,000 approx
Name of Architect	Darbourne & Dark
Name of Librarian	K C Harrison, MBE, FLA
Special features:	
a) site	Corner site facing Pimlico tube station
b) architecture	Integral part of Lillington Gardens Estate
c) function	To serve as General District Library for surrounding area, primarily for adult lending
Mechanical Services:	
a) heating	District heating scheme
b) ventilation	Filtered and heated fresh air
c) lighting	Mixed fluorescent and tungsten
d) acoustics	Ceilings and wall areas sprayed with sound absorbent material
e) other	—
Areas: in square metres	
a) lending	
b) reference	230
c) reading	
d) special activities	—
e) children	25
f) control	10
g) library staff admin. incl. stack	49
h) exhibitions	—
i) lecture hall	—
j) circulation	10
k) services	—
l) lavatories	10
m) stack, see (g)	10
Total area:	344
Book volumes:	
a) adult lending	20,500
b) adult reference	250
c) children	7,800
d) stack	—
e) other audio-cassettes	1,300
Total:	29,850
Costs in £ p:	
a) site	18,000
b) building	
c) furniture & fittings	104,000
Total Cost (ex fees):	£122,000
Cost per square metre:	£355

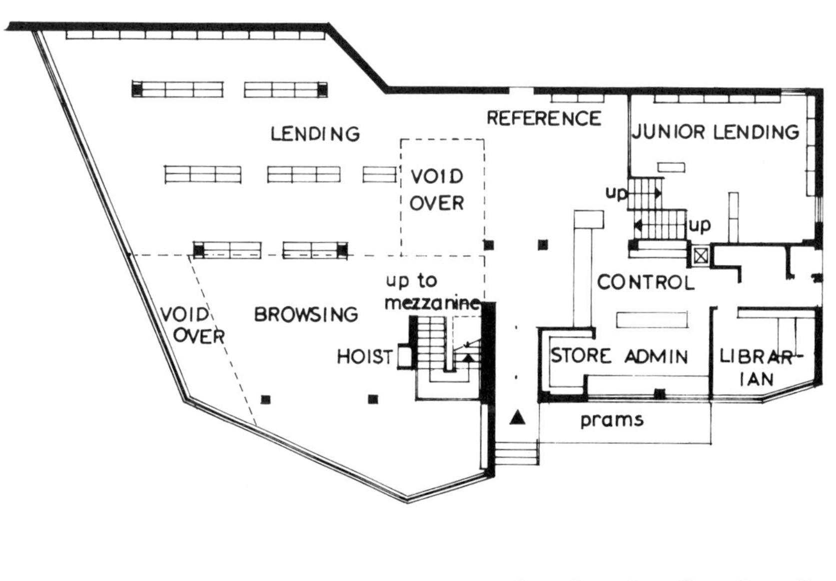

GROUND FLOOR

Bedfordshire County Council:
Toddington, Leagrave (formerly County Borough of Luton) and Barton

Toddington After a heavy week's work in the East End of London it was a delight, on a sunny if frosty morning, to drive out to this delightful village and to stand looking towards the library across the village green. A fine Norman church, some thatched roofs, a pub (next to the library in fact) all fit into a picture book scene.

The library, at that distance, does not reveal itself as such, for there is no 'Library' sign to do this job either on the building itself or as a direction from any point. Later in discussion with the Deputy County Librarian it was learned that the County Librarian and his local staff, as well as the Parish Council, had striven for this but that the County Architect had resisted as it would be out of keeping with the character of the building–and until now his view has carried more weight. Even the hours of opening have to be displayed unobtrusively and therefore are hardly noticeable as a narrow banner at the foot of the window (about eighteen inches above the pavement) which is troubled by condensation.

The site was a narrow one which had previously (but not for many years) been occupied by a dilapidated and structurally unsound house in the centre of an existing terrace and it needed consultations between the County Planners, the Preservation Societies, the Parish Council, County Council Committees and, of course, the Libraries to bring the project to a conclusion–even if it were not one to please everybody.

The illustration does far more than any written description: the decision was not only to retain the principle of two levels and a slated roof, but to introduce the fine dormer windows to replace the former chimney skyline–but these have been described by some as 'brutal and too heavy'. This virtually forced certain aspects of design, eg a mezzanine floor across the front of the building which was, by experience, to be used for reference and local history provision with certain fields of non-fiction on a rotating basis.

The small entrance hall surprises, for instead of the more usual floor covering, illuminated display cases and notice boards, here is a stone floor (ramped for wheelchairs) which is used for cycles, prams, etc. But through a second pair of swing doors there is then a warmer pleasing, welcoming atmosphere–an open-plan library with good natural lighting through the dormers and numerous daylights as well as through full windows at ground level and a glass door at the rear which leads out on to a small seated courtyard. The fair-faced brick of the interior is painted white which adds to this lightness, although the prime reason for this was to keep within tight cost limits. The artificial lighting is by strip fluorescent, behind fascias, for wall cases in the public area and by ring fluorescents within diffusers in the ceilings (acoustic tiled). 'Nylfloor' carpet, copper bronze in colour harmonises with the Afromosia of the counter; this is 'L'-shaped, in sections to provide a work area and privacy for the door to the staff accommodation. Shelving is Terrapin Reska whilst chairs are mainly polypropylene although there is more comfort in the browsing area.

This library (one of five in the South Bedfordshire District) is undoubtedly popular as was readily seen this early Saturday morning; being open only 23 hours per week 80 issues per hour are usual and are quite enough for the one staff member. It is reckoned that this service caters for a population of 4,000, many of whom work in Luton (12 miles) Dunstable (5) or commute to London. But Toddington itself is in the midst of agricultural land which makes it more than just a dormitory village. One peculiar feature of this project is that it was planned for 'a library and the Parish Clerk's Office' so the latter space is located to the rear of the building.

Leagrave, next to be seen, was a sharp contrast, having been planned and built by the County Borough of Luton to serve a population of 16,000 many of whom work at Vauxhalls or Electrolux, but whilst it is considered a working class population the housing is mainly private. Luton is now a District Library Area in Bedfordshire but has agency powers for budget control, purchase of books and related materials, furniture, equipment etc and controls the mobile service.

The planning was initiated by Frank Gardner as Borough Librarian of Luton until 1972, was then succeeded by his Deputy, Mr Howe, until he moved to Scotland. Mr Gardner returned for six months until amalgamation of Authorities in April 1974, after which Mr Hawkes took up duties as the Librarian for the Luton District; this library, at that time, had been open just one week. The original project was for linking buildings for the British Legion and for a Library with a common entrance–but the architect had already been selected by the former. A collaborating Local Authority architect was appointed and then, at a very late stage, the Legion withdrew. This has been a very well used library, having its own car park (reached by a side driveway) at the rear and bounded at the south side by a raised grassed bank abutting a large car park and a Legion club house beyond.

Approaching from Toddington it was pleasing to see this dominating building advertising itself as a Library on both the side and front elevations and with a sign to the driver that there was a car park to the rear. The design might be felt by some to be too solid and heavy, particularly with the dark coloured brick and the first floor overhang. The two tall saplings at the front looked rather sparse at the end of November and their height so close to the building could, when foliage is full, be a disadvantage to the three upper windows which they would obscure; were this space for other than offices one might feel even more strongly about it. Consideration for the handicapped is demonstrated by a ramp at the side and a no-step front entrance–but it was surprising later to learn that there was no toilet facility for these people.

The impression on entering is one of care and quality, with an illuminated display case and publicity space catching the eye, with down lights giving the additional illumination so necessary when moving in and out of a building on a winter's night. Powerful lights from the underside of the exterior overhang also help and, by leaving these on after closing time, these help to minimise hooliganism. Turning left into the circulation and

central area there is a three-seater settee and coffee table flanked
by a trough of chrysanthemums, and plants. This is set against a
brick wall (of the same dark colour) about head high, and this is
just long enough to guide people to the control counter and the
children into their department, the carpeting changing from
green to brown to define their particular area. Bold floor-to-
ceiling patterned curtains throughout, happily complement the
two different colours of carpeting–good points for detail here.
Hessian wall panels allow for the display of children's art in their
area but use of this feature is restrained elsewhere. Furniture is
mainly LDE with some Remploy.

Moving into the adult area the feeling is of too little circulation
area. The long counter (Plessey light pen charging) needs only a
step or two to the Readers' Adviser's desk–good–but tends to be
lost within a group of six other desks for reference use. Leather
arm chairs for the consulting of periodicals (slotted into a black
and white plastic display stand which is quite out of keeping
with the tone of the room) are close by too. To some extent the
cramped feeling is lessened by the use of low bookcases
throughout; even those at the walls are five shelves only. This
permits a view right across the room to a huge window dressed
at the sides by the patterned curtains but with white nets side to
side: it is a pity one only sees through to the car park. A further
bank of chairs for browsing are provided here too while close by
is a Visual Display Unit for those happy with this form of
catalogue.

Two study/listening booths, glass-fronted, are set back to the
side of the counter with the playing decks situated in a small
space adjacent. Here too is the staff entrance to the Children's
Activities Room, the main door being to the right of the inner
entrance door. Curtained at one end (behind which staff gain
access to the front display case) shelving is included along one
wall; it was admitted that experience had made this necessary
for use as a workroom too.

Only the ground floor is for public service, giving rise to a feeling
for a first-time visitor of congestion and lack of good circulation
area. The upper floor is completely set aside for a schools'
library centre (not staffed by library staff), the housebound
readers library service and mobile stacks accommodating
reserve stock, for all of which, a lift (but goods only) has been
provided. No doubt these centralised services have to be
adequately housed but one must ask why, in a newly planned
library for 16,000 persons, priority on space was not given (in
accordance with the spirit of Public Libraries Act's requirements
for a comprehensive service) to provision for exhibitions, films,
lectures etc as well as hirable accommodation for local
organisations, etc. Thus there was a feeling of incompleteness on
leaving this attractive library. The facilities envisaged for the
British Legion land were a multi-purpose hall, club and bar,
large enough for dinner dances and film shows with considerable
car parking. The joint use by the library for its activities would
have been ideal and evidence of the physical link is the size of
the toilets on the first floor of the library (the non-public area
now) which are obviously too lavish just for the few staff. But in
spite of that disappointment this is a library which impresses.

Barton part-time branch is a long narrow brick building set on
part of the site of an existing school, the buildings of which
range from small aged buildings to prefabs. That part of the site
on which the library now sits was the former 'Old School House'
the demolition of which, to make way for this library, caused
some consternation to members of the Parish Council and local
inhabitants. To mark remembrance of it, twelve bricks in pairs
of six are framed and displayed within the entrance to the
library–one brick carries the date of 1791.

The village is 7 miles from Luton, 9 from Dunstable and 15
from Bedford and the surrounding area is rural. With only a
4,000 population there is a claimed 2,700 membership. Being
actually on the main A6 road and with a car park it is feasible
that people do come from a distance. There is a cement works in
the area but the Deputy District Librarian stated that this now
seemed less operational–certainly the clouds of cement dust
which used to be experienced are no longer noticeable. An
attempt to give some aesthetic quality to this plain building
shows in the raised brick-sided beds with mature and elegant
trees, but the small grassed areas looked neglected.

The four wide and deep windows assure good natural lighting
but the entrance is disappointing–small quarry tiles and a 'tatty'
coconut mat. The distance from the entrance to the long, facing
counter is short but even this leaves too narrow a space behind
the counter for staff, with the wall to the so-called staff
accommodation (in which is a large heating unit). It was stated
that the plan indicated that the electric warm-air unit would be
located on the wall at high-level but in fact it is floor-based 6 ft
high, 4 ft wide and 3 ft deep, leaving only room to stand at a
sink! And this heating was not working on the day of my visit so
that the counter staff, facing an ever-opening door, were
remarkable to look so cheerful on this chilly November
morning.

The library is, of course, open-plan with a small children's
section to the right of the entrance. The remainder, if small, also
offers secondary use for small meetings, councillors' surgeries
etc. Seating abounds–orange armchairs, window benches, with
study chairs and tables in the 700 volume reference alcove. The
unusual lovat shade carpeting is pleasing. Lighting is strip
fluorescent and the shelving is Terrapin Reska.

HW

Toddington

Authority	County of Bedfordshire
Designation	Toddington Branch Library
Date of opening	April 1973
Population served	4,000
Name of Architect	J C Barker, DipArch, RIBA, MRTPI, County Architect
Name of Librarian	Colin Muris, MA, FLA
Special features:	
a) site	Narrow site; previously terraced house overlooking green. Developed in conjunction with preservation societies and planners
b) architecture	Loadbearing brickwork to match existing; also roof tiles; dormer windows introduced
c) function	Serving village and some surrounding
Mechanical Services:	
a) heating	Gas-fired, fan assisted convectors
b) ventilation	Natural
c) lighting	Fluorescent strip and ring
d) acoustics	Carpeted throughout
e) other	—
Areas: in square metres	
a) lending	100
b) reference	31
c) reading	in (a)
d) special activities	16
e) children	42
f) control	18
g) library staff admin.	in (f)
h) exhibitions	—
i) lecture hall	—
j) circulation	21
k) services	9
l) lavatories	8
m) stack	10
Total area:	255
Book volumes:	
a) adult lending	5,000
b) adult reference	500
c) children	2,000
d) stack	—
e) other	—
Total:	7,500
Costs in £ p:	
a) site	2,342
b) building	23,612
c) furniture & fittings	500
Total Cost (ex fees):	£25,954
Cost per square metre:	£102

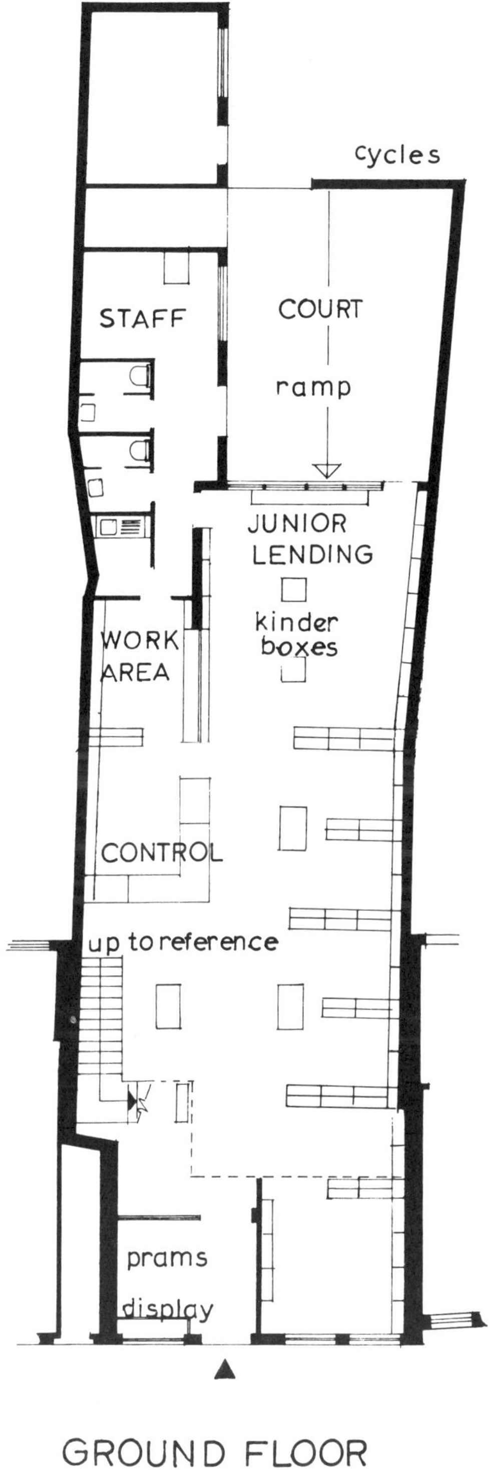

GROUND FLOOR

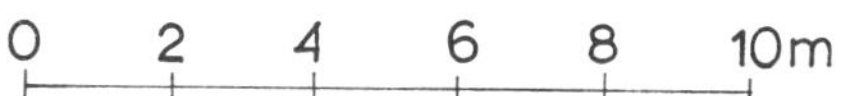

Leagrave

Authority	County of Bedfordshire (formerly Borough of Luton)
Designation	Leagrave Library
Date of opening	March 1974
Population served	16,000
Name of Architect	James L Caldwell & Associates, V Caldwell, BA, BArch, RIBA, Project Architect, J P Colclough, RIBA, collaborating Local Authority Architect
Name of Librarian	Frank Gardner, FLA (succeeded by J A Howe, FLA)
Special features:	
a) site	Main road adjacent to shopping area
b) architecture	Reinforced concrete frame; load bearing brickwork
c) function	District Library with agency powers, also schools library centre
Mechanical Services:	
a) heating	Ducted warm air
b) ventilation	Mechanical
c) lighting	Fluorescent
d) acoustics	Double glazing; carpet tiles; ceiling tiles; hessian clad walls
e) other	—
Areas: in square metres	
a) lending	94
b) reference	43
c) reading	in (a)
d) special activities	30
e) children	48
f) control	12
g) library staff admin.	299
h) exhibitions	—
i) lecture hall	—
j) circulation	—
k) services	—
l) lavatories	17
m) stack	16
Total area:	559
Book volumes:	
a) adult lending	11,685
b) adult reference	341
c) children	6,795
d) stack	—
e) other	604 gr
Total:	19,425
Costs in £ p:	
a) site	—
b) building	91,860
c) furniture & fittings	15,500
Total Cost (ex fees):	£107,360
Cost per square metre:	£192

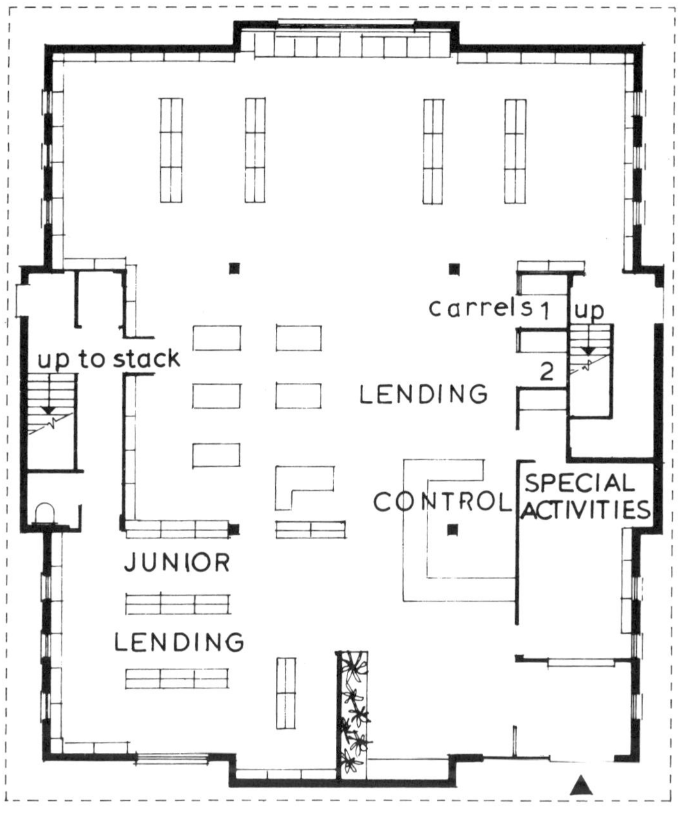

GROUND FLOOR

Authority	County of Bedfordshire
Designation	Barton Branch Library
Date of opening	February 1973
Population served	4,000
Name of Architect	J C Barker, DipArch, RIBA, MRTPI, County Architect, K Travis, RIBA, Project Architect
Name of Librarian	Colin Muris, MA, FLA
Special features:	
a) site	Part of school site with shared car parking
b) architecture	External brickwork; timber roof with pantiles
c) function	Serving village and surrounding area
Mechanical Services:	
a) heating	Electric warm air
b) ventilation	Natural
c) lighting	Fluorescent diffused
d) acoustics	Carpeted
e) other	—
Areas: in square metres	
a) lending	68
b) reference	19
c) reading	18
d) special activities	—
e) children	34
f) control	12
g) library staff admin.	in (f)
h) exhibitions	—
i) lecture hall	—
j) circulation	13
k) services	—
l) lavatories	8
m) stack	4
Total area:	176
Book volumes:	
a) adult lending	6,000
b) adult reference	700
c) children	2,000
d) stack	—
e) other	—
Total:	8,700
Costs in £ p:	
a) site	5,581
b) building	18,246
c) furniture & fittings	1,000
Total Cost (ex fees):	£24,827
Cost per square metre:	£141

Berkshire County Council: Crowthorne

This small branch library was opened on 1st January 1973. Previously, Crowthorne had used for library purposes a room in the old parish hall. An attractive new library was certainly well received; in its first full year of use the book issues were 122,231. Crowthorne has a present population of about 11,000. It has within its boundaries the Transport and Road Research Laboratory, Wellington College and Broadmoor Hospital; increasing numbers of London commuters travel to Waterloo via Bracknell.

The building is sited about fifty metres off the main road, in the corner of a public recreation ground and at the end of an entrance drive to Broadmoor, which makes regular use of the library services, as do the other two large establishments mentioned which, between the three of them, employ over 2,000 of the working population of Crowthorne. It is of simple, square plan with a central area covered by a raised, pitched roof over clerestory windows running round each of the four sides and about a metre in height. The floor of the library then extends on three sides under low flat roof sections with a series of square roof lights set about a half metre forward of the wall shelving. From this perimeter run four island stacks. One corner of the square is taken up by a children's section with low browser box for young children; another by the staff counter beside the entrance door. Behind the counter is the very small staff room/workroom and other staff accommodation. The floor is carpeted within an outer ring of tiles which extend over the counter area. There must have been a lapse in planning co-ordination which led to a heater being sited in front of bookshelves and less than a foot away.

The entrance door opens off a quite small lobby, but one provided with good wall space for notices. Outside, the entrance face of the building has a good covered area, the whole well landscaped. Cars can be parked close to the library entrance. Guiding to the library, especially from the High Street, could surely be improved?

LHS

Authority	Berkshire County Council
Designation	Crowthorne Branch Library
Date of opening	January 1973
Population served	11,000
Name of Architect	R C N Paul, FRIBA, AADipl, County Architect, Royal County of Berkshire
Name of Librarian	Vernon Jennings, FLA, County Librarian, Berkshire
Special features:	
a) site	The site is in the corner of a recreation ground adjacent to the neighbouring housing
b) architecture	Buff brick building with a blue-grey asbestos slated pitched roof over central area surrounded on four sides with flat asphalt roofs. Traditional construction
c) function	Full-time branch library operating as part of a district library organisation based in Bracknell
Mechanical Services:	
a) heating	Off-peak electric storage heaters, fan-assisted and thermostatically controlled
b) ventilation	Natural by means of opening windows; gear operated to clerestory
c) lighting	Electrical tungsten fittings
d) acoustics	Nylon carpeted flooring
e) other	—
Areas: in square metres	
a) lending	
b) reference	
c) reading	
d) special activities	139
e) children	
f) control	
g) library staff admin.	17
h) exhibitions	—
i) lecture hall	—
j) circulation	6
k) services	—
l) lavatories	—
m) stack	—
Total area:	162
Book volumes:	
a) adult lending	
b) adult reference	6,000
c) children	2,500
d) stack	—
e) other	—
Total:	8,500
Costs in £ p:	
a) site	1,300
b) building	19,440
c) furniture & fittings	1,700
Total Cost (ex fees):	£22,440
Cost per square metre:	£138

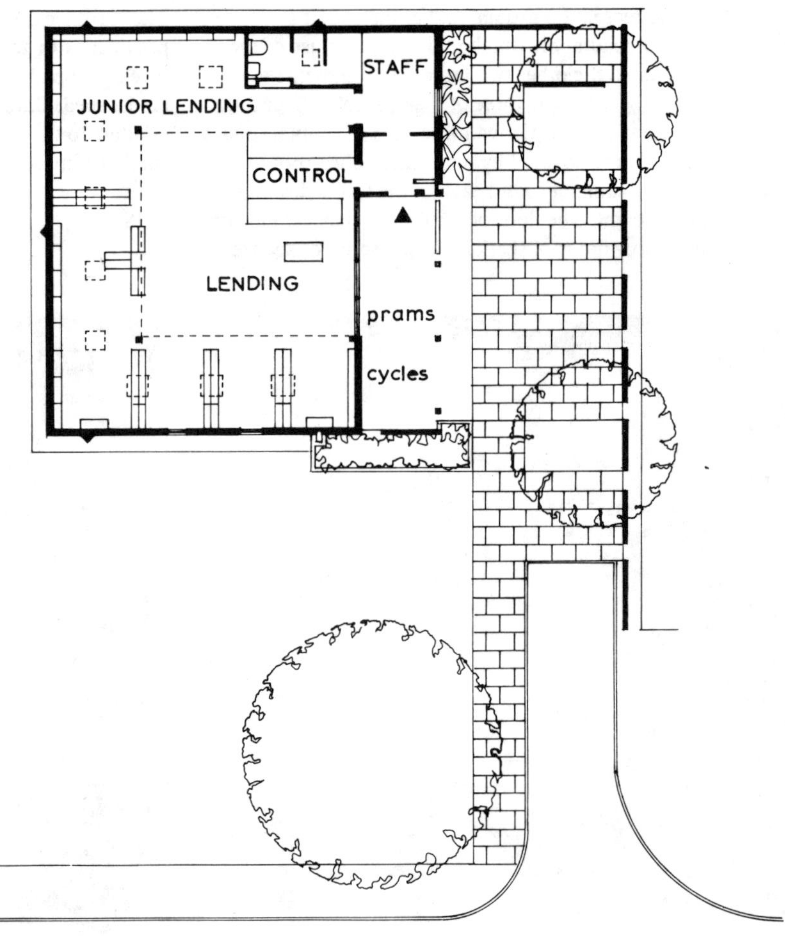

GROUND FLOOR

0 2 4 6 8 10m

Buckinghamshire County Council:
Burnham, Farnham Common, Stokenchurch and Little Chalfont

This county has produced a series of consistently distinguished small libraries, six of which we discussed in the 1972 and 1974 volumes. In the two years now surveyed, four new buildings have been completed, ranging from a large branch at Burnham to a minute one at Stokenchurch, though in the same period and reviewed separately by other contributors is the new Slough library planned and built as a Buckinghamshire project but absorbed, in the recent local government reorganisation, by Berkshire. (See page 14).

Burnham The brochure for the official opening—on 1st October, 1973—of this new branch library begins with a Domesday Book reference. The 'village' now has a population of some 18,000 but its centre is still a very typical English village centre, with a small, narrow main street, pubs and tiny shops, spilling out to a green which in turn opens on to Burnham Park. On the borders of this, in a very attractive position just south of the High Street the new library is placed. It is beside a community hall and the Parish Council offices, well served by a good public car park. Burnham village still has a secluded air. London commuters are inevitably numerous, served by a short rail journey of only 21 miles.

Burnham has quite a library history, from the Workman's Reading Room of 1876 and the first public library service (500 books in two bookcases) established in 1935 at the instigation of the Townswomen's Guild. Two years later there were 488 readers borrowing 10,000 books a year, bookcases and bookstock doubled. By 1955, Burnham was the busiest centre in the county with over 25,000 issues and plans for a new library were mooted in 1957. Since January, 1965, the village has been served by a mobile library only. Now has come yet another of this first-class series of Buckinghamshire libraries, a building quietly distinguished in its impact, even unobtrusive, yet strong enough in line, proportions, textures, to give very real visual satisfactions and draw sufficient attention to itself to attract readers; almost 200,000 books were issued in the first year. It is not surprising that it has received a commendation from the RIBA.

Pitched roofs sweep down to a very low eaves line with purple-brown hand-made clay tiles contrasting crisply with the white textured, rendered walls. The windows are large, rectangular, white painted, set in massive timber frames with dormer windows of similar width above.

The large library block is linked by means of the staff workroom, opening immediately off the counter in typical Bucks style, to a smaller block parallel with it. This has staff rooms, meetings room, kitchen and lavatories. A covered porch links the opposing entrances to the library and to the meetings room area.

The main library gives the immediate impression of wide space, owing its inspiration obviously to traditional timbered country barns. Structurally the roof is supported on two lines of steel columns with trussed rafters above substantial tie-beams which bridge the columns themselves and extend further to the outer walls of loadbearing brickwork. The structural elements are completely clad in oak whilst the ceiling is lined throughout with narrow strips of Parana pine. Together with the Heugafelt carpet tiles on the floor and felt covered pin-up board on wall spaces above bookshelves, this all produces a very warm and comfortable environment.

Some sacrifices are made to achieve this very individual room character. Perhaps the most questionable one is that of limitation of natural lighting, for the windows cannot possibly produce more than a fraction of the light required for this large area, particularly at the point where the central link structure meets the main block. True, in a building as wide as this it would always be difficult to achieve natural lighting evenly, but in a single-storey building possibilities do exist and it may seem wilful to have ignored them and to depend on artificial light to supplement that from the windows.

The fluorescent lights have been integrated with the beam casings and produce a well concealed source of light which is varied by the use of great clusters of sparkling bubbly glass globes with tungsten bulbs hanging in the centre bay and by some downlighters on the columns incorporated into the ends of the beams. For all the subtlety of this arrangement architecturally, the level of illumination on the face of the bookshelves is uneven. Placing the principal lights at right angles to the shelving is not an efficient method of lighting and is not altogether successful.

Acoustics present another slight irritation. The roof form and its hard lining unfortunately result in producing a rather marked aural resonance and a good deal of conversation can be clearly heard at the other end of the library. In consequence, the placing of the Telex machine which provides a frequently audible link with headquarters and between all the county's libraries becomes an assertive factor. It should have been kept away in the depths of the workroom rather than put on the protruding counter. This, serving both adults and children, is placed to the side of the entrance doors. One end of the library is given up to children's use and no attempt is made to provide any separation. However, because the centre of the library is kept largely clear of high furniture, supervision is excellent. The end of the room opposite to the Children's Library is used for reference stock and study purposes.

Total shelf capacity is a little upwards of 10,000 volumes. Future expansion of the book stock can very easily be absorbed, for at present most of the fitted bookcase units are placed around the perimeter with only easy chairs and low tables in the centre, leaving it free for display purposes. It is much used for exhibitions.

The position of the workroom in the link structure is excellent though it is not clear why a separate passage to the staff rooms from the library was considered necessary. There are occasionally problems caused by members of the public penetrating into the staff quarters and there has been theft following entry at this point. Had the workroom been made wider to incorporate this present corridor, the extra space would have been useful to increase storage facilties. There also appears

Authority	County of Buckinghamshire
Designation	Burnham Branch Library
Date of opening	October 1973
Population served	18,000
Name of Architect	F Pooley, RIBA, County Architect, D Turner, RIBA, Project Architect
Name of Librarian	C Rippon, FLA
Special features:	
a) site	Level parkland close to High Street and village centre
b) architecture	Traditional; load bearing brickwork with light steel frame
c) function	Branch library
Mechanical Services:	
a) heating	Electric underfloor off peak with fan heaters
b) ventilation	Natural
c) lighting	Fluorescent with tungsten features
d) acoustics	Heugafelt tiles; panels of felt-faced pin-up areas to walls
e) other	—
Areas: in square metres	
a) lending	300
b) reference	in (a)
c) reading	in (a)
d) special activities	—
e) children	152
f) control	29
g) library staff admin.	36
h) exhibitions	in (i)
i) lecture hall	27
j) circulation	—
k) services	12
l) lavatories	12
m) stack	—
Total area:	568
Book volumes:	
a) adult lending	5,460
b) adult reference	600
c) children	2,880
d) stack	1,410
e) other	—
Total:	10,350
Costs in £ p:	
a) site	2,200
b) building	72,610
c) furniture & fittings	in (b)
Total Cost (ex fees):	£74,810
Cost per square metre:	£121

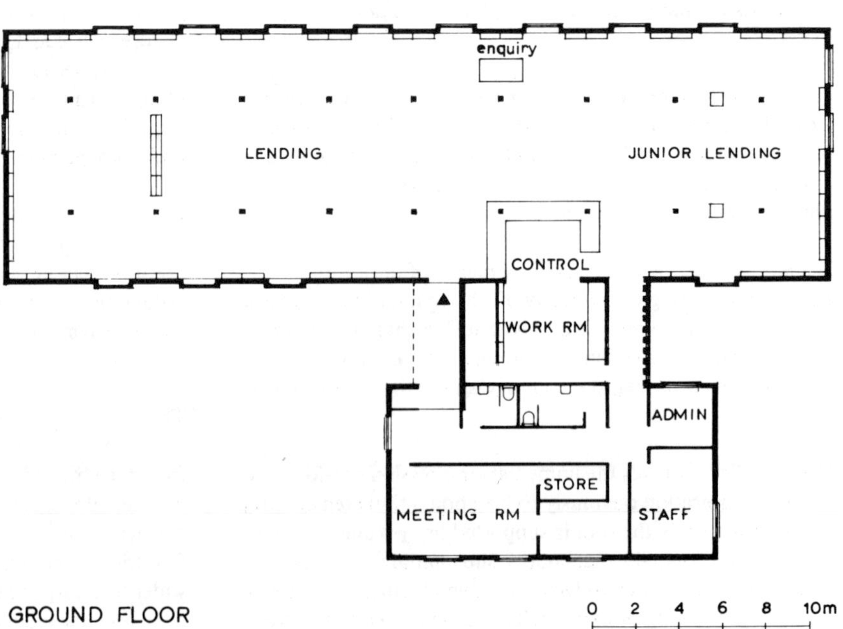

GROUND FLOOR

to be, as it is, rather limited provision of pin-up boarding, so necessary in any workroom.

The staff quarters are good. The staff room itself is possibly as attractive as any that we have come across, though the staff might have preferred to have some part of the room better lit for writing. The staff kitchen can double as a kitchen for the meetings room and the staff lavatories are also available to users of that room. It is therefore a little disappointing to find that the room is small, for no more than 25 people can be comfortably accommodated. Whether this is the reason or that charges are somewhat high, it seems that the room stands empty for much of the time except when it is hired for an occasional small conference or for use at times by the library itself, such as for a children's story hour.

Concrete paving slabs, divided by brick paviors in the forecourt, are flanked by fine planting with berberis, pampas grass and other shrubs. Large slabs of granite from old London Bridge provide seats. Bicycle holders are well used. Decorative lamp standards, with the same handsome glass globes as have been used inside the library, have obviously become targets for local hooligans. Understandably they are not being replaced.

GKVT LHS

Farnham Common This branch serves the villages of Farnham Common and Farnham Royal with their scattered population of about 5,000. Situated in a quiet side road, but only just off the main shopping area, the building is from the outside very simple; again a distinctly vernacular design with two blocks, both with pitched roofs, set at right angles one with the other, making a T-shape; the larger block has hipped ends. The roofs are finished in heather brown machine-made clay tiles and square brown box section gutters with matching downpipes form an unobtrusive edge to the roof above the yellow and grey Sevenoaks stock brick walls. Subtle details such as the brick-on-end sills with splayed tops, and brick-on-end recessed band course just below the projecting roof eaves provide interest whilst maintaining the overall simplicity of approach. Behind the building, spaces for five cars are defined by lines of paving bricks set in the tarmac, clearly but quietly outlining the limits.

Nothing seen outside prepares one for the surprise of the interior. For the architect has with great subtlety produced an interior of considerable distinction. A flat ceiling follows the perimeter of the main block which houses the Lending and Children's Libraries, but in the centre the ceiling rises with sloping chamfered edges to a higher flat section whilst beams supporting the whole roof sail gracefully across the void in the centre. These beams are in hardwood as are the narrow strips, around the top of the walls, which separate wall and ceiling. This strip in turn becomes the fascia of the low canopy over the counter. These and the hardwood skirting impart a unity to the room which is enhanced by the white textured Artex ceiling.

The floor is finished in grey Nairnflex carpet tiles with a large serviceable coir doormat at the entrance and the walls above

and between the bookshelf units are faced entirely with felt-covered pin-boarding so that notices can be placed almost anywhere. This finish is also used above and below the regularly spaced grey-painted softwood windows which are in hardwood frames. The covering fabric is near to yellow in the children's section of the room and brown in the adult's, a rewarding use of colour variation. Fitted bookshelf units round the walls are made with teak veneered and lipped shelves. Brown plastic laminate faced fascias carry hook-on black plastic laminate tier-guides with incised white letterings; very clear and easy to read. Shelves are on Tonk's strip to enable them to be adjusted and the bottom shelf is very slightly tilted. Beneath the bottom shelf, which is not too low, is a hardwood ply-faced panel with a brown plastic skirting matching the fascia. A line of fluorescent light fittings on the ceiling over and slightly in front of the shelves gives excellent lighting.

The workroom opens out behind the counter, following this County's usual policy, and so enables a single member of staff to run the library at slack periods, attending the Telex and doing such work as there is time for away from the counter face. The design of the counter is simple and solid with a generous handbag shelf and plenty of storage space, carefully divided into small pigeonholes and varying sized drawers on the staff side. Large pin-up boards flank the counter and are well used for posters and information of all sorts.

One curious feature is a readers' enquiry desk opposite the counter, which seems to show either a change of mind about the possible level of staffing or a hopeful glance to the future when demand might justify a full-time readers' adviser. At present this looks a little unlikely and the desk is used more for display purposes. Issues are running at about 6,000 a month.

The staff quarters more than live up to the quality of finish of the public areas, with a pleasant carpeted staff room, well furnished, with kitchen corner, two lavatories, meter and bin cupboards and ample store. The staff entrance opens off the car parking area. For the present level of staffing this accommodation is generous.

GKVT LHS

Stokenchurch This library is very small. Of the Buckinghamshire library buildings we have seen, it compares most nearly with that of Stoke Poges, built in 1969. (*Library Buildings* 1972 Issue, p. 33). There, use limitations were not only immediate, related to the small local population to be served, but it was anticipated that the completion of the then planned new County Central Library in nearby Slough would further limit its use. (Now Slough is a branch in Berkshire: such has been the impact of local government reorganisation). Stokenchurch is a different matter, however. It is much more an isolated village, though on the main London-Oxford road. Its population is only in the region of 2,000 (Stoke Poges–5,000) though likely to increase to about double the present figure.

There is little usefully to say by way of comment on design. By comparison with even Stoke Poges it is undeniably an economy

Authority	County of Buckinghamshire
Designation	Farnham Common Branch Library
Date of opening	April 1974
Population served	5,000
Name of Architect	F B Pooley, RIBA, County Architect, D Maxwell, RIBA, Project Architect
Name of Librarian	C Rippon, FLA
Special features:	
a) site	Corner site near High Street and shopping area
b) architecture	Traditional load bearing brickwork; clay plain tiles to pitched roof
c) function	Branch library
Mechanical Services:	
a) heating	Underfloor off peak electricity; controlled fan convectors
b) ventilation	Natural
c) lighting	Fluorescent with tungsten features
d) acoustics	Carpet tiles; felt faced pin-up wall areas; Artex finish ceilings
e) other	—
Areas: in square metres	
a) lending	89
b) reference	in (a)
c) reading	in (a)
d) special activities	—
e) children	42
f) control	13
g) library staff admin.	22
h) exhibitions	—
i) lecture hall	—
j) circulation	—
k) services	5
l) lavatories	6
m) stack	—
Total area:	177
Book volumes:	
a) adult lending	2,800
b) adult reference	150
c) children	1,570
d) stack	550
e) other	—
Total:	5,070
Costs in £ p:	
a) site	7,000
b) building	38,671
c) furniture & fittings	in (b)
Total Cost (ex fees):	£45,671
Cost per square metre:	£258

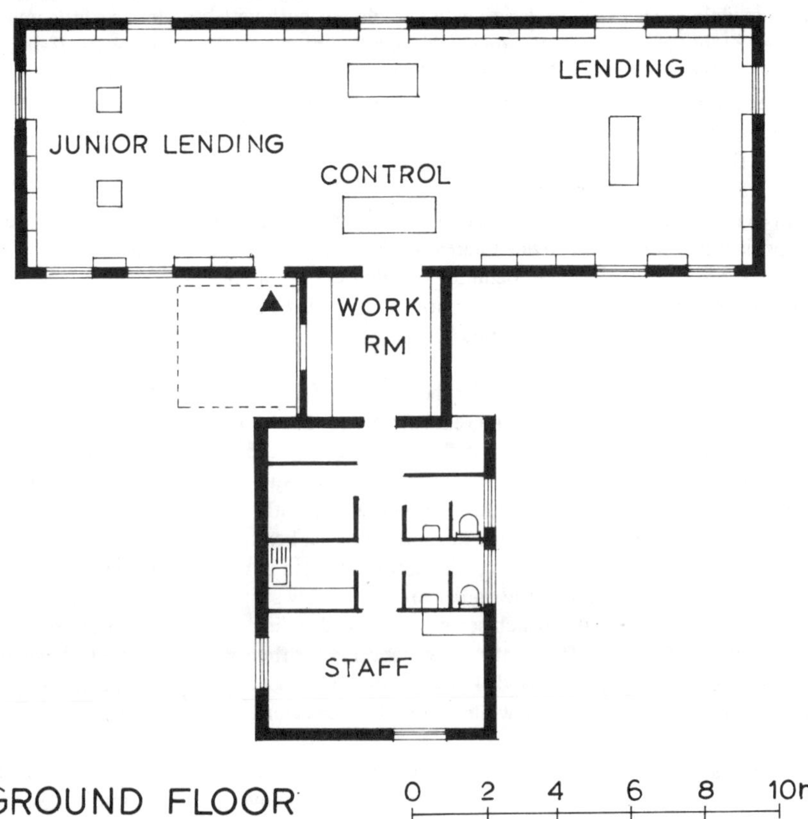

GROUND FLOOR

model, with shallow shelving, for example, on which far too
many books have to be up-ended for good appearance; or
worse, for good selection from the bookstock. It is only open on
four part-days a week, though it manages to issue some 56,000
books a year from its stock of between five and six thousand
which the shelves hold.

GKVT   LHS

Little Chalfont is unlike the other Chalfonts–St Peter and St
Giles which have their village roots in the past, in that it has
developed more recently. Principally it is a dormitory town of
6,000 for commuters to London and to workers in Amersham
some three miles to the north. Set in beautiful country, the town
has developed with restraint and its new library nestles within a
setting of trees, even though it is only a few yards back from the
main road and the start of a line of shops. A village hall and
large car park are adjacent.

Approaching the library between grassed areas, with trees either
side and shrubs flanking the building, the contours of the
building are very similar to those of Lincolnshire's Sutton-on-
Sea (reviewed in this issue; compare photographs of each). The
use of the separate monopitch roofs rather than the low
rectangular box gives the inside a feeling of greater space,
airiness and light. Here too, there is in addition a warmth; wood
strip ceiling of light gold colour to complement the buff multi-
facing brickwork and a Marleytex carpet to blend in.

The counter, which faces you as you enter, is straight and abuts
the returning wall which helps to form the Children's area on the
right and also permits workroom space to the rear (but no
separate restroom, presumably because of the limited hours–23
normally). Heating is by electric underfloor, the lighting is
diffused fluorescent strip set in the pitched roofs with,
additionally, a rectangular set of such lights over the counter
area.

The closeness of two schools and the station bring additional use
by class visits from the former and returning commuters during
the early evening. This is another library in the Bucks style and
to their high standard of quality and originality.

HW

Authority	County of Buckinghamshire
Designation	Little Chalfont Branch
Date of opening	April 1974
Population served	6,000
Name of Architect	F B Pooley, RIBA, County Architect, A Parkes, Job Architect,
Name of Librarian	C Rippon, FLA
Special features:	
a) site	Opposite shops, next to Village Hall and car park
b) architecture	Traditional load bearing brickwork
c) function	Branch library service
Mechanical Services:	
a) heating	Electric underfloor; controlled convectors
b) ventilation	Natural
c) lighting	Fluorescent strip
c) acoustics	—
d) other	—
Areas: in square metres	
a) lending	67
b) reference	—
c) reading	—
d) special activities	—
e) children	23
f) control	23
g) library staff admin.	in (f)
h) exhibitions	—
i) lecture hall	—
j) circulation	23
k) services	3
l) lavatories	4
m) stack	—
Total area:	143
Book volumes:	
a) adult lending	3,390
b) adult reference	125
c) children	1,385
d) stack	540
e) other	—
Total:	5,440
Costs in £ p:	
a) site	225 p.a. (lease)
b) building	16,838
c) furniture & fittings	in (b)
Total Cost (ex fees):	£16,838
Cost per square metre:	£117

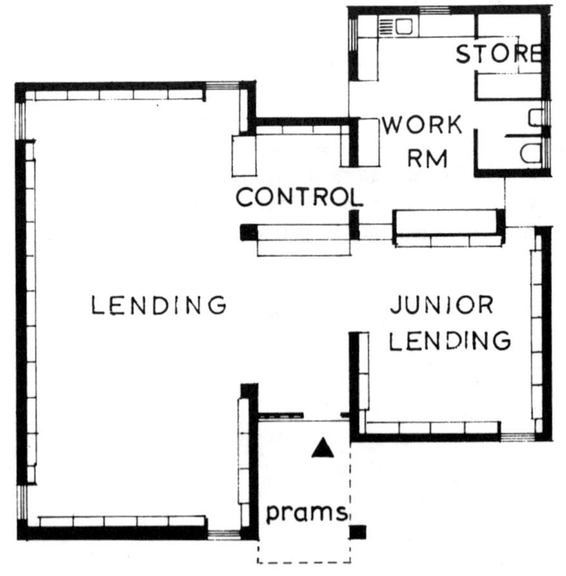

GROUND FLOOR

Cheshire County Council:
Barnton and Winsford

Barnton is a large village just to the north of the Cheshire salt mining town of Northwich, on a ridge overlooking the valley of the river Weaver. There has been much sprawling development over recent years in consequence of which the village has lost all coherence with new estates some way from the original centre and shops.

In the circumstances the choice of library site was obviously a difficult one for it could be sited either in the geographical centre or the historical centre with other public buildings, shops and hall. The site selected is geographically central and adjacent to the primary school though visually there is no apparent reason for its actual siting apart from the availability of the land. There is space for 10 cars and plenty of room for the library to stand in isolation so that it can be seen clearly.

Much of Cheshire is very rural and the design of the library at Barnton is one that has been evolved by the County Architect for use in small rural or suburban communities. Since this library was opened another of identical design has been built at Sandiway to the west of Northwich and others in Chester.

Whilst one may have reservations about the principle of the use of standard solutions, when they are as good as this one any such worries are quickly dispersed. This is an excellent and well-considered design of great simplicity, fine salce and proportions wedded to functional efficiency. The brick walls with narrow window slits and wide corner windows, with dark stained timber fascia to the flat roof above clerestory windows, is of such restrained design that it readily fits into the rather varied and not very distinguished background. In this case there is little landscaping and a few trees and shrubs would be a great help in mitigating the bleakness of the surroundings in this ugly village.

A very low canopy brightly lit at night is of generous size for mothers to leave prams on the warm brown brindled brick paving whilst concrete cycle slabs recognise the popularity of the 'bike' in rural areas. A tiny low draught lobby with coir matted floor leads into the library, with a bin store opening off.

The square plan of the building is open except for staffroom, book store and lavatories along one side, with heating chamber accessible only from outside. A small square display area next to the lobby allows small exhibitions or arrangements of library material to be on show without in any way intruding on the main space. The counter is of a standard design in use throughout the County, composed of well considered units which can be arranged as required in 1250 mm units. In this library the desk is of 'L' shape backed by the bookstore. The structure which is of steel with rectangular columns and brick external walls is conventional but contrived with great finesse of detailing. Despite the large number of columns in the room these are so carefully arranged that they are nowhere intrusive, a point that might well be noted by designers striving needlessly for large columnless open spaces at high cost to the client. In fact the columns make a virtue out of necessity with large roof lights providing first class natural light above and directly over the column echoing the cruxiform arrangement of bookcases forming attractive clusters around centre columns.

Internally the walls are of white painted concrete blocks with full height black door frames with borrowed lights over the hardwood doors. Supervision from the desk is good with the junior section of the room unencumbered with furniture and with a view of the staff. In a small building of this kind it is almost impossible to be out of sight of the counter but some screening is provided by the centre bookcases.

The floor is fitted with beige Heugaflor's carpet tiles and the ceiling finished with large acoustic tiles in aluminium framing with recessed tungsten lights and surface mounted multiple fluorescent lights with plastic diffusers. Ceiling light tracks with adjustable spotlights permit wide variation in lighting arrangements.

Heating from the gas-fired boiler by continuous skirting heaters around perimeter walls is effective and unobtrusive though its position under bookshelving causes some concern on account of possible damage to the books. In addition a fan convector is placed on the inside wall of the lavatories. Natural ventilation is provided by the opening hopper windows all around the room, at high-level operated by long arm poles.

Metal bookshelving is by Reska and arranged in perimeter recesses between windows and in lower freestanding tiers in addition to the cruciform layout round two columns. Plenty of yellow hessian-covered pin-up boards are provided and well used. Sensible furniture has been selected to enhance the intimate bright feeling that has been created. Large corner windows are fitted with venetian blinds which can be used at night to shut out the darkness of the windows, creating a welcoming glow from outside.

On the cold wet January night that this building was visited the exceptionally warm and friendly atmosphere of the library made this a very pleasant place in which to be. The 3000 village readers obviously find it equally sympathetic as the demand for 1900 volumes a week emphasises. The staff of one full-time, two part-time, assisting the librarian, who is responsible for this and Sandiway Library, are well pleased with their lot, which includes a delightful staff room. The Library is open for a $4\frac{1}{2}$-day $33\frac{1}{2}$-hour week.

Winsford: Situated about 13 miles south of the Mersey this small country town has been designated as an overspill area for Liverpool. This will lead to the eventual expansion of this town which had a population of 11,000, to about 40,000. This figure is unlikely to be reached for some time but all the necessary town centre facilities, shopping centre, car parks, civic hall and library have been built some way from the old centre, on a hillside with fine easterly views to the far away hills of the Peak District.

The library is ideally sited at the end of the shopping precinct close to substantial car parks. Though the entrance approach is welcoming, with large west facing windows running the full two-storey height of the building, the side elevation to the adjacent road with few windows is somewhat daunting and fortress-like. This has been done quite deliberately since the road is to be widened and will eventually run close to the wall of the building,

Authority	Cheshire County Council
Designation	Barnton Library
Date of opening	September 1974
Population served	4,000
Name of Architect	G Hamlyn, DipArch, RIBA, County Architect
Name of Librarian	A Wilson, FLA
Special features:	
a) site	Between old village and new estates
b) architecture	Steel framed; glass and brick walls
c) function	Neighbourhood library
Mechanical Services:	
a) heating	Gas-fired convectors and low pressure hot water skirting radiators
b) ventilation	Natural
c) lighting	Fluorescent recessed diffusers (400 lux)
d) acoustics	Carpet; acoustic tiled ceiling
e) other	—
Areas: in square metres	
a) lending	—
b) reference	—
c) reading	—
d) special activities	—
e) children	—
f) control	—
g) library staff admin.	—
h) exhibitions	—
i) lecture hall	—
j) circulation	—
k) services	—
l) lavatories	—
m) stack	—
Total area:	260
Book volumes:	
a) adult lending	8,490
b) adult reference	135
c) children	1,696
d) stack	294
e) other	—
Total:	10,615
Costs in £ p:	
a) site	3,000
b) building	39,982
c) furniture & fittings	3,500
Total Cost (ex fees):	£44,482
Cost per square metre:	£170

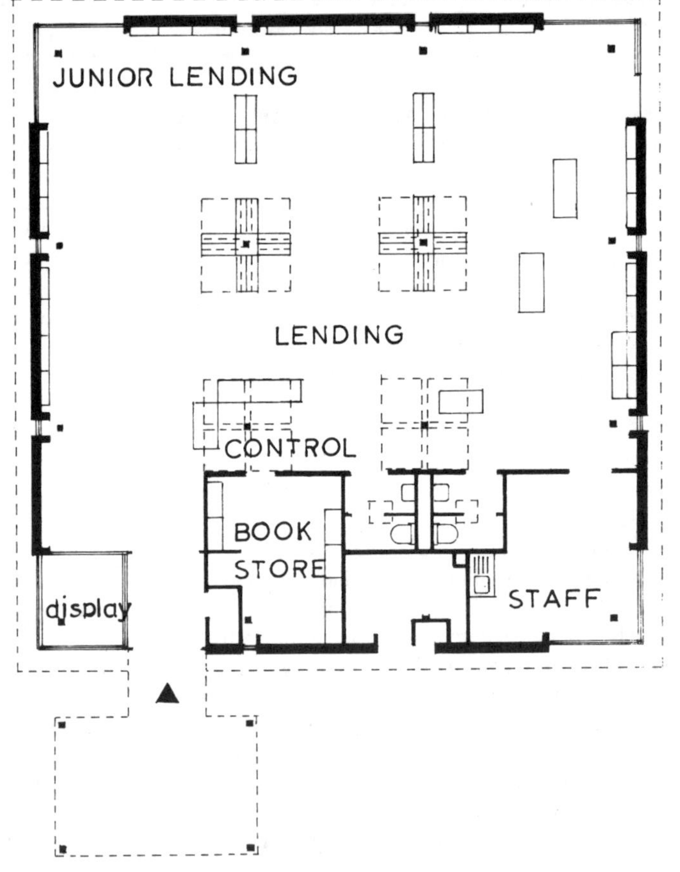

GROUND FLOOR

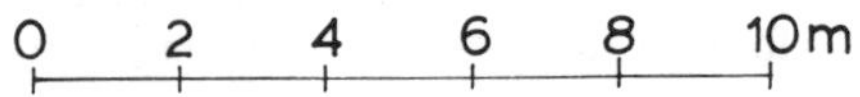

so that windows have wisely been kept to a minimum of narrow vertical slits in the dark grey-brown facing brick. The aluminium windows are glazed with tinted solar glass. Unfortunately the choice of brick and detailing at the top of the walls leads to very unsightly staining in wet weather.

The large entrance canopy with its prominent 'Library' sign provides space for parking prams, clearly visible from within the building. A wide porch with large mats leads into the spacious and intriguing interior with the counter rather far from the doors, beyond the wide flight of steps to the open Children's Library.

The architecture is strong but dominant with groups of four columns taking up an undue amount of space for their function and, in places, sterilising further space around them because of their position. However, because the library is at this stage bigger than required, being related to the eventual population, there is no shortage of space.

Planning leaves something to be desired particularly in the functional arrangement of staff accommodation which is remote from the desk and at first floor level, leading to slow response to changing counter needs. At present this is less of a drawback than it may be when the library becomes busier with steady increase in population. The long thin store at ground floor, which is totally unsuited as a workroom, tends to be used as such since it is the only staff area on this floor and is close to the outside door from the service parking area into the staff stair doubling as a fire-escape from first floor. A small lift is provided.

Book stock is divided between adult lending fiction and popular non-fiction at ground floor and the remainder of non-fiction at first floor with a very limited quick reference stock. There is apparently little local call for a large reference stock which is only available at Chester, some 15 miles away.

An attractive and informal arrangement of freestanding shelf units combined with desk plates, seats and sloping display shelves with display screens and showcases makes the end of the ground floor Lending Library an attractive and lively area with two large windows facing east, one with distant views, the other looking into the quiet landscaped garden shared with the neighbouring clinic.

The Children's Library, close to the desk for good supervision, is attractive. The ceiling runs through but the four steps up reduce the height of this area to an appropriate scale for children. A fine octagonal room opens off the children's area; this, lightly curtained off, serves as a story hour area. This is partly out of sight of the counter, which might lead to trouble with high spirited youngsters indulging in high jinks. Opposite the counter a rather dark, narrow corridor gives access to staff lavatories, which are remote from the staff accommodation at first floor, whilst public lavatories, kept locked, are at first floor level remote from the counter and necessary supervision, a curious reversal of what, from experience, might have been expected.

The first floor library is more conventional and formal in arrangement, than the ground floor; a pleasant space with its large windows at either end. The rooflights do not contribute much to the natural lighting being obscured by a very small plastic eggcrate which cuts down the daylighting to the point of insignificance.

The fine Meeting Hall and Study Room which can, if required be thrown into one large space opens off the upper library. The Hall has a platform with a window behind so that curtains have to be drawn when the platform is in use to avoid speakers being silhouetted. When the rooms are used as one, the shape apparently leads to inaudibility of speakers from the rear Study Room unless speech reinforcement equipment is used. A very curious and poorly detailed tea bar with almost chin high counter and very low sink is situated in the library with ample space for use in the Hall. The placing of the tea bar necessitated that when the library is closed during meetings a caretaker must be present to ensure security of the library which cannot be shut off.

The staff room, which has a fine outlook, is somewhat bleak. It is a pity that lockers and kitchen corner could not have been screened in some way to make the room more civilised.

The Librarian's office is large, but gloomy, with good top light but only a minute narrow vertical strip window for view. This results in a claustrophobic feeling which it shares with the workroom, which has no window at all, though it is on a south-facing wall. The architect's insistence on the slit window aesthetic unfortunately deprives the staff of a cheerful, sunny outlook although it is admitted that the view would have been on to a squalid unloading yard at the rear of shops, unless a high cill line were adopted.

There is no provision for wheelchair users to whom the first floor and Children's Library are inaccessible.

GKVT

Authority	Cheshire County Council
Designation	Winsford Library
Date of opening	August 1974
Population served	27,500
Name of Architect	Tweddell Park and Partners in collaboration with G Hamlyn, County Architect
Name of Librarian	A Wilson, FLA

Special features:	
a) site	New town estate centre adjacent shopping precinct
b) architecture	Reinforced concrete frame; brick walls
c) function	Public library

Mechanical Services:	
a) heating	Gas-fired space heating
b) ventilation	Natural
c) lighting	Fluorescent (400 lux)
d) acoustics	Acoustic panels; carpet
e) other	Electric book hoist

Areas: in square metres	
a) lending	431
b) reference	in (a)
c) reading	in (a)
d) special activities	160
e) children	160
f) control	in (a)
g) library staff admin.	66
h) exhibitions	in (a)
i) lecture hall	in (d)
j) circulation	in (a)
k) services	—
l) lavatories	80
m) stack	—
Total area:	929

Book volumes:	
a) adult lending	18,463
b) adult reference	1,635
c) children	4,140
d) stack	2,777
e) other	400 discs and cassettes
Total:	27,015

Costs in £ p:	
a) site	14,530
b) building	138,850
c) furniture & fittings	8,000
Total Cost (ex fees):	£161,380
Cost per square metre:	£158

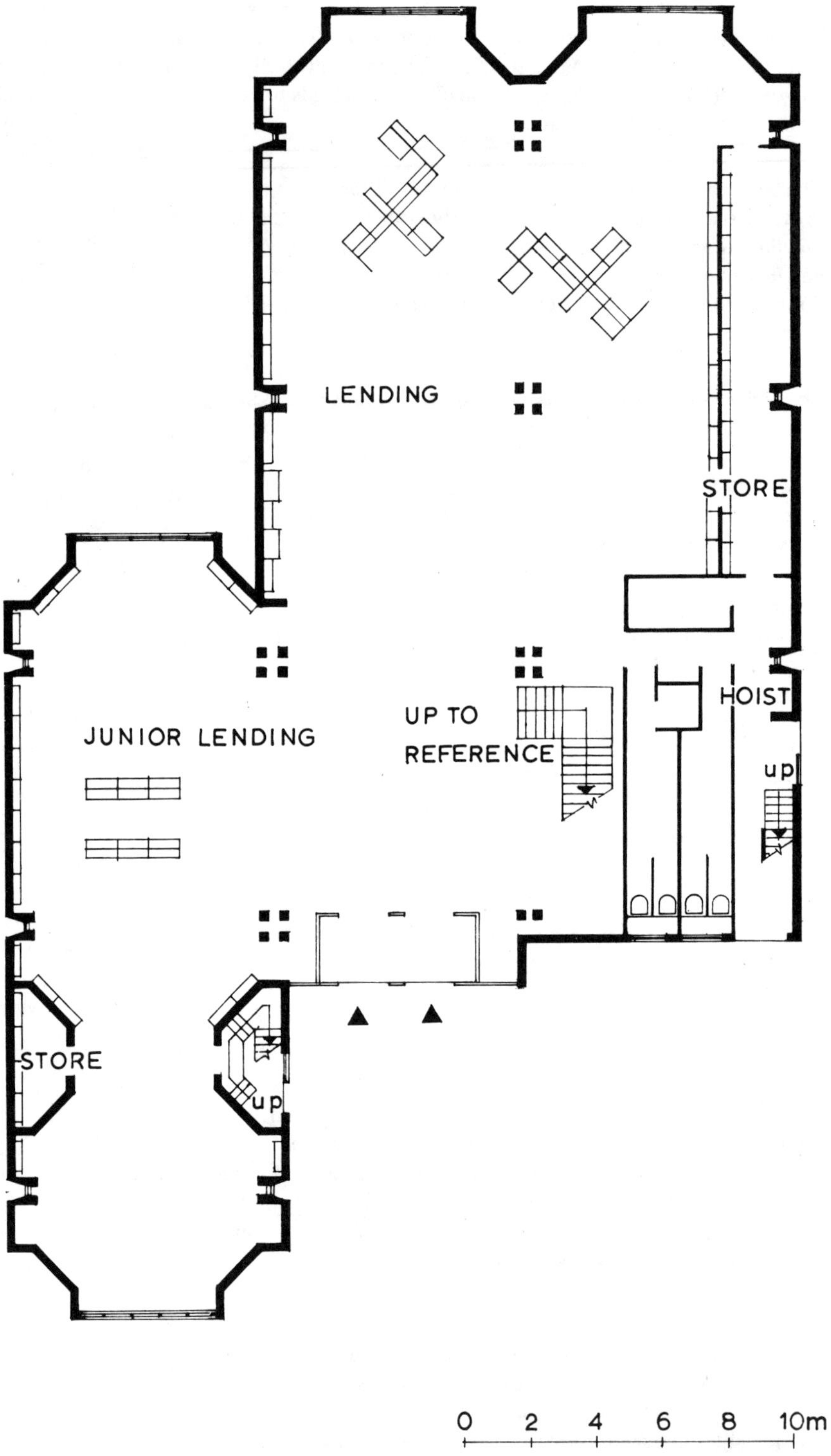

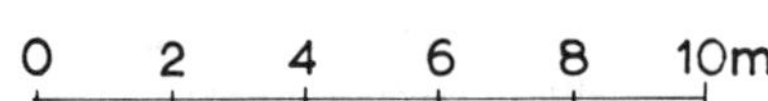

GROUND FLOOR

Winsford

Cumbria County Council (formerly Westmorland County Council): Ambleside, Keswick and Seaton

Ambleside At right angles from the main street of this pleasant lakeland touring centre, heavy with the clump of climbing boots, is a street of houses in the local stone. Some of them have been converted to, or replaced by, shops but all are entirely congruous. The latest is the new small branch library which has been most carefully designed to fit in a cramped site with the terraced houses on either side, not only the local blue slate but the roof line, sizes of windows and all proportions being beautifully maintained. The ground floor has a shop front but it does not look in any way odd in its domestic surroundings. Almost all surfaces on show have used materials to fit in with the blue-grey colour scheme. Both in front of the library and behind it are extensive car parks; this is entirely accidental of course and they are very heavily used in the tourist season but they nevertheless help residents from outlying districts who call for their books.

The entrance through glass doors is to an extensive lobby, the floor covered with dirt-absorbent link matting and the walls with hessian display material. The result is an exercise, some might say an excessive one, in community involvement. The display areas are covered, inch by inch, with notices of all kinds and there is a community events booking diary which residents are encouraged to complete.

The library itself consists only of a single room with access to a brick and flag patio with flowering trees; again everything shows the same excellent choice of materials. The library room is carpeted with Giltex carpet tiles of mixed wool and gives a very attractive appearance indeed. Although the shelving in the library is nothing unusual there are some thoughtful touches such as the covering of all pillars with hessian, thus avoiding the usual finger-marked effect.

The workroom and staff room open off the library, the work-room shelved to the ceiling a touch often neglected in small libraries with a storage problem.

Heating is by hot-air blown from an oil-fired boiler served from a tank in an enclosed yard at the rear. Lighting is recessed fluorescent.

Leading from the library (and also from the lobby so that meetings can be held when the library is closed) is a staircase (with a charming handrail in aluminium) leading to the Armitt Library. This is a special collection presented by a local lady which also incorporates books and funds from other local societies. This library is rich in local history and topography and includes two study carrels and a microfilm reader so that it will be used by serious students of the area. The windows in this pleasant upper room are domestic in scale and curtained to complete the effect.

It is a long time since I have seen a small library which attracted me so much. It is difficult to account for this except by saying that good taste has been used everywhere by Westmorland County Council's architects, for whom it was completed before the new Cumbria County took over.

Keswick The problem of a town like Keswick in the summer is that it is overwhelmed by tourists and it is difficult to consider in a vacuum the needs of the residents. Just behind the old-fashioned centre of the town is a completely modern shopping centre and on a street leading from this is the new library. It has a shop front and some modern stone, but one is conscious immediately of an intense sense of disappointment because the major walls have been covered in pebble-dash, surely a pointless economy when the local grey-blue slate is so tremendously attractive. Outside is a clear and concise notice but no details of the services.

The ground floor is an oblong with a picture-window frontage; the General Lending Library with a counter at the far end of the main room; behind it, with a folding wall, is the Children's Library. The shelving heating, lighting and so on are absolutely functional and adequate enough but one looks in vain for some spark of originality. Upstairs is a half floor which contains a reference and reading area, two large glass partitioned carrels and the Librarian's office. One wonders whether, in such a small library, it is really necessary for the Librarian to have such an isolated office; would he not be better involved directly in service to readers?

From the workroom on the right hand side of the ground floor is organised a highly important mobile library which is garaged alongside. This serves many small outlying areas and its issues are astonishingly high. The library too is well-used. In all, the overwhelming impression is that it is perhaps a little too small for its job and needed that touch of the local slate to bring it to life.

Seaton The main road of Seaton trails rather drearily from Workington, of which it is now little more than a suburb, although there are indications that it was originally an independent village. It has no real centre and an undeveloped piece of road leading off into open country seems an unpromising place for a new branch library. The library itself however is attractive, constructed in a pleasant concrete brick with a sandstone appearance, with an imaginatively curved wall in front (unfortunately damaged by a backing lorry). Once inside, one is struck by the enthusiasm of the users: rarely have I met a library in which the local readers were so much at home. On plan it has little to distinguish itself: an oblong room with a Children's Library leading off, separated if necessary by a folding wall. There is little to catch the eye except perhaps a line of natural light and spotlights over the counter and a charming curtain behind it. The inside walls are of grey brick largely covered with hessian. The flooring has industrial carpet stuck to the screed and is satisfactory enough; the Reska shelving is adequate as is the lighting, fluorescent in diffusers. There are a few low padded chairs and round tables. What could have been a very ordinary little building was redeemed entirely by the cheerful, outgoing personality of the librarian on duty and the reaction it produced on the 'locals' who were obviously happy to use it.

GT

Authority	Cumbria County (formerly County of Westmorland)
Designation	Ambleside Library and Armitt Library
Date of opening	August 1973
Population served	6,000
Name of Architect	D M Butler, ARIBA, for County Architect.
Name of Librarian	—
Special features:	
a) site	—
b) architecture	Local slate walling on front elevation above picture window
c) function	—
Mechanical Services:	
a) heating	Oil-fired warm air by convectors
b) ventilation	—
c) lighting	Fluorescent recessed with diffusers
d) acoustics	Ceiling finishes
e) other	—
Areas: in square metres	
a) lending	65
b) reference	13
c) reading	13
d) special activities	—
e) children	42
f) control	18
g) library staff admin.	37
h) exhibitions	19
i) lecture hall	Armitt Library 79 Lecture Hall 33
j) circulation	37
k) services	10
l) lavatories	5
m) stack	—
Total area:	371
Book volumes:	
a) adult lending	6,700
b) adult reference	300
c) children	1,000
d) stack	1,500
e) other	Armitt Library 8,000
Total:	17,500
Costs in £ p:	
a) site	5,000
b) building	45,000
c) furniture & fittings	1,600
Total Cost (ex fees):	£51,600
Cost per square metre:	£138

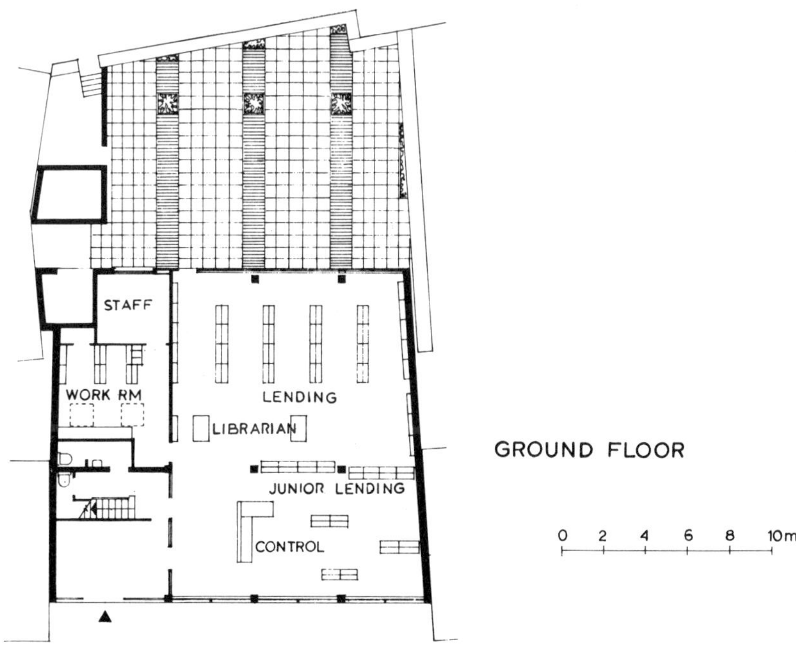

Authority	Cumbria County (formerly County of Westmorland)
Designation	Keswick District Library
Date of opening	March 1973
Population served	5,000 (+ 20,000 in surrounding area)
Name of Architect	J Mellor, for County Architect
Name of Librarian	—
Special features:	
a) site	Shopping area off town centre
b) architecture	Stone; pebble dash; picture window
c) function	Branch library for town plus mobile library for rural area
Mechanical Services:	
a) heating	Gas-fired hot water; blown air
b) ventilation	—
c) lighting	Fluorescent and incadescent mixed
d) acoustics	—
e) other	—
Areas: in square metres	
a) lending	140
b) reference	35
c) reading	—
d) special activities	—
e) children	75
f) control	—
g) library staff admin.	30
h) exhibitions	—
i) lecture hall	—
j) circulation	—
k) services	—
l) lavatories	—
m) stack	—
Total area:	280
Book volumes:	
a) adult lending	7,000
b) adult reference	1,400
c) children	Included in adult
d) stack	2,000
e) other	3,000 mobile stack
Total:	13,400
Costs in £ p:	
a) site	
b) building	£47,000
c) furniture & fittings	
Total Cost (ex fees):	£47,000
Cost per square metre:	£147

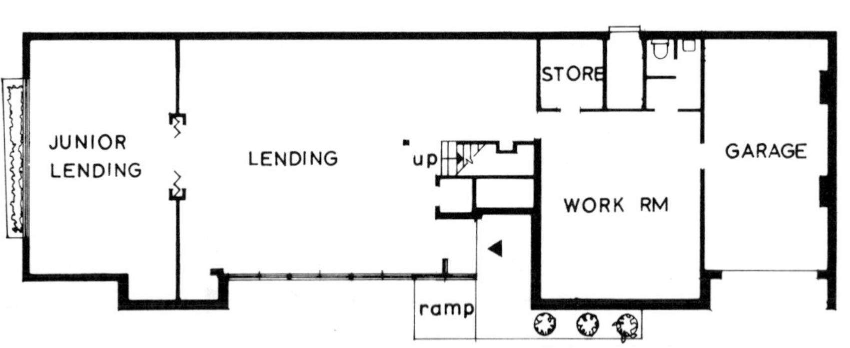

GROUND FLOOR

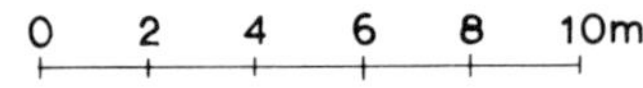

Authority	Cumbria County (formerly County of Westmorland)
Designation	Seaton Branch Library
Date of opening	February 1973
Population served	5,000
Name of Architect	J Mellor, for County Architect
Name of Librarian	—
Special features:	
a) site	—
b) architecture	Concrete brick
c) function	—
Mechanical Services:	
a) heating	Gas-fired underfloor
b) ventilation	—
c) lighting	Natural; fluorescent in diffusers, hanging incadescent and a row of spotlights over counter
d) acoustics	—
e) other	—
Areas: in square metres	
a) lending	—
b) reference	—
c) reading	—
d) special activities	—
e) children	—
f) control	—
g) library staff admin.	—
h) exhibitions	—
i) lecture hall	—
j) circulation	—
k) services	—
l) lavatories	—
m) stack	—
Total area:	165
Book volumes:	
a) adult lending	—
b) adult reference	—
c) children	—
d) stack	—
e) other	—
Total:	7,000
Costs in £ p:	
a) site	—
b) building	—
c) furniture & fittings	1,100
Total Cost (ex fees):	Not given
Cost per square metre:	—

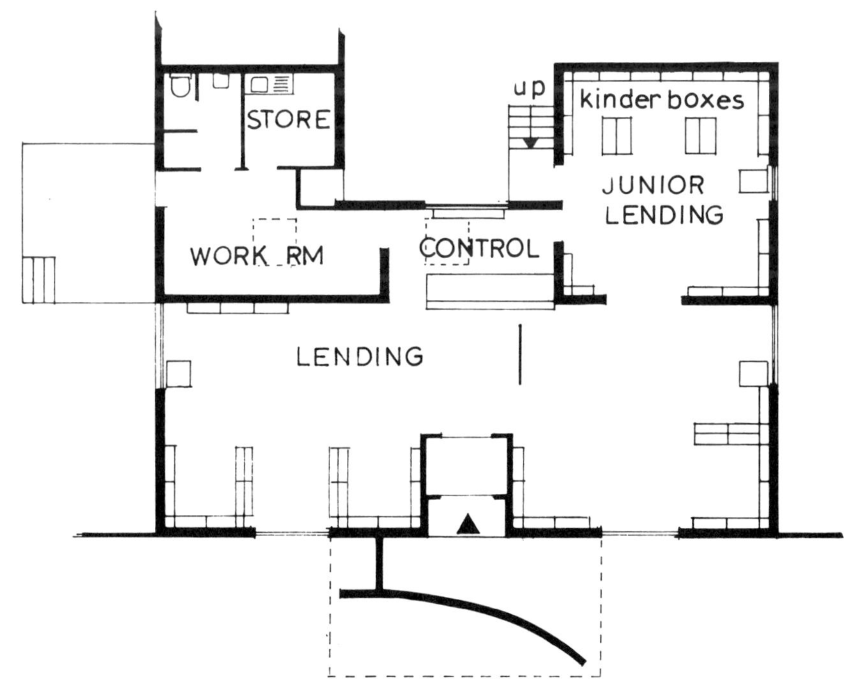

GROUND FLOOR

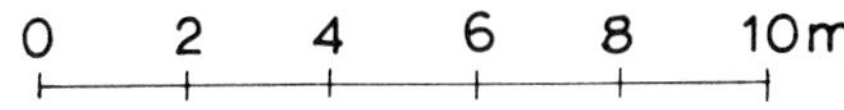

Devon County Council:
Churston Ferrers, Honiton, Kingsbridge and Teignmouth

Churston Ferrers (pop. 8,000), lies between Paignton and Brixham, overlooking Tor Bay. The small, modern parade of shops, restaurant, etc, opposite the library, is now the focal centre of the area and the library is very prominently sited against its background of sea and cliffs. There is ample car parking available immediately outside the library which has a generously-sized and attractive canopy over the front entrance. The building, only a small branch, consists principally of a single rectangular room with northlight clerestory windows running across it. However, to add interest and relate the building to the site, the staff and workrooms take the form of a triangular extension of this rectangle.

The good entrance porch has room for prams and dogs. The crisp appearance of the library is most attractive with its white fair-faced concrete blocks contrasting well with strip windows of dark brickwork up to sill level, black fascia and green plastic coated aluminium roofing. Warm natural coloured boarding on the underside of the canopy makes for a very welcoming introduction to the building. The large clear sign leaves no doubts as to the building's identity. No confusion should arise over the direction of flow round the counter since the 'In' door directly faces the entrance doors whilst the 'Out' door comes into the entrance lobby at right angles. However, the librarian has unfortunately had to place small tables inside the large plate-glass screen to the library as people tend to try to walk through the glass. The atmosphere is exactly right for a small library, bright and cheerful but at the same time restful–undoubtedly attractive. Perhaps a little more might have been made of the exceptional view available from the site by slightly adjusting the positions of windows to take the fullest advantage of it. Supervision of the library from the desk is excellent; the furniture has been intelligently placed to assist in this.

The library was originally planned to be longer by one bay and deliberately provides the possibility that it can later be extended as the population may increase. Staff have been catered for excellently with a most attractive restroom facing the best view and equipped with nicely designed sink, cooker and cupboards. All the services have been tucked away unobtrusively: meters in a cupboard, a tiny yet adequate cleaner's store, space for maintenance equipment, small boiler cupboard, and immaculate lavatories. The entrance to the workroom is close to the counter and to facilitate the occasional use of this room as an election polling station, an external door has been provided which is also used for deliveries.

Throughout the library, clearly apparent close attention to detail, of function as well as of design, must stem from continued co-operation between the architect and his librarian client, who has evidently thought out his attitude to the library and the functional requirements withcare. An exemplary building is the happy result. It is a pity that some faults in building slightly mar the result in places, but these are capable of remedy and in no way diminish the professionals' achievement. Finishes are intelligently chosen, with acoustic tiled ceiling, plastered and painted walls and carpet with antistatic treatment to all floors: a small library building, but one of quality and some distinction.

Honiton Pevsner says of Honiton: 'The town is all one long High Street, quite exceptionally unspoilt.' Though New Street, at right angles to it, lacks the distinction of the High Street, it has a number of fine buildings.

The new library clearly aims at some form of vernacular identity to relate it to existing buildings in Honiton. Such an attempt is desirable in a town of this distinction, but much skill is needed to produce a truly modern building which will fit happily in such context. To be fair, this is rarely achieved and it is all to easy to miss that inherent sense of balanced rightness which characterises a surprising range of our traditional buildings. This new one has been set well back from its older neighbours but the necessity to provide access for a mobile library van, as well as to a private car park along one side of the library (there is a large free public car park directly opposite the building) and for disabled readers' cars which can be parked in front, has resulted in tarmac dominating the foreground. At night, large steel gates are used to shut off the car park whilst opposite are steel folding doors to the mobile library van garage. The approach to the front door is by a wheelchair and pram ramp with handrail, with a pair of double doors at the back of what was intended to be a pram lobby. Because the public naturally tend to want to use these doors, which directly face the entrance, an exhibition screen is now kept permanently placed across the doors to discourage their general use.

The library is planned mainly on the ground floor but with a galleried first floor Reference Library overlooking the main area of the Lending Library below. The rear section is single storey with flat roof; an interesting treatment has been adopted for the front part of the building with a sloping roof revealed on the inside, rising over the well and the first floor, whilst a row of clerestory windows at the bottom of the slope lights the centre section in front of the low rear section.

This Lending Library, directly behind the counter, is a single large space at floor level and the natural lighting effect in the centre produces a pleasant, spacious atmosphere. Natural lighting by means of rooflights could, perhaps, have been introduced at the rear, particularly as the use of a flat roof would suggest such a solution. Instead of this, artificial lighting is needed on all but the brightest days. Windows at the side overlook the car park and a large window at the back gives on to more parking. A slight shift of this window together with some measure of landscaping of the earth bank which rises behind the building, would, surely, have been rewarding. Such a treatment would also have benefited the Children's Library, which is tucked away at the side of the adult Lending Library, right at the back of the building and out of sight of the counter. This relative isolation makes supervision difficult and limits the amount of help and attention that the staff can offer the children.

The workroom, among other things housing a regional bookstock of 3,000 to 4,000 books, lies between the Children's Library and the mobile library vehicle bay to which it gives direct access for loading. It has a door leading from the adult library. This room is well lighted from high-level windows beneath a sloping ceiling, matching that of the adjacent library well. The van bay has a raised side platform for convenient trolley access, whilst stores for maintenance staff and cleaners' use, together with meter cupboard and heating equipment very sensibly open off this platform.

The stairs up to the Reference Library start very close to the counter which allows staff to keep track of readers going up, though, of course, once there they are out of sight. This is a very pleasant space with small windows giving a good view out. Even better, though, if the gallery, on the side overlooking the well, had not such a high parapet wall against which bookcases are placed.

Staff are well provided for with a delightfully informal staff room placed over the van garage. This room, having a dormer window, also serves as office. A well arranged recess, equipped with cooker, sink and a refrigerator, opens off one side and cupboards and shelving are ample. A small lavatory is set between this staff room and the stair landing.

The counter is of the usual 'In' and 'Out' pattern but a space of only just over 1 metre (3 ft 3 in) has been left between the counter faces, hardly sufficient if two assistants are working back-to-back and the counter surfaces are not quite wide enough for trays of issue tickets. No litter bin appears to have been provided for the waste paper that collects at the counter, nor is there properly designed space for storing the various-sized cards and items of stationery. Careful library counter design is surely fundamental and the study of working methods is critically important, since the majority of staff working hours are spent here. What may in itself be a minor fault quickly assumes major importance if encountered hundreds of times in a day, and annoyance out of all proportion to the problem is caused.

Difficulties seem to have arisen over heating, for the form of the building ensures that heat from the ground floor will end up in the somewhat funnelled area of roof space, making the Reference Library too hot whilst leaving the ground floor cold.

No difficulties however have deterred readers, who express themselves well pleased, as is testified by the more than doubling of book issues since the move from the old building.

Kingsbridge Library shares with the Health Centre a most charming and centrally situated site in this small Devon estuary town. Kingsbridge has a resident population of 3,000 but a large summer influx of visitors. Set beyond a well-landscaped garden, the building is close to the town's main car park, the central bus and coach station and only 150 yards from its main shopping street. Its link with the Health Centre brings people right to its door where the warm and friendly character of the interior must surely gain many new readers. Provision is made for a large, covered porch/pram park shared with the Health Centre, and the large glazed screen of the library entrance enables mothers using it to see their prams.

The library, which occupies the ground floor of the two-storey building, is faced with random rubble local stone and has on the approach side mainly clerestory windows, since this long wall is used internally to accommodate the main run of bookshelves. On the first floor, the Health Centre has windows set into a stone wall which, in some places, projects out over the lower floor, providing a slight arcading effect. Within the main entrance of the library a well-designed counter in hardwood faces the doors directly: well-designed, but not, it would seem, anticipating the success of this building, which has been such that the counter is now being lengthened by another bay to accommodate the additional trays of cards necessitated by the increased numbers of readers and book issues.

The library takes the form of a single large, long room for the Lending Department with staff workroom/office, Children's and Reference Libraries along the west side, though the two latter areas are only divided from the main library by movable book stacks. Both Reference and Children's Departments have large windows which face south and west and suffer a little in summer from overheating which it is difficult to alleviate as the windows open insufficiently to allow a good current of air to pass through. Curtains are however provided and these can be used to cut down the glare, whilst being useful in winter by making the library warmly attractive. Some glare is evident from the windows above the bookshelves on the long east wall, which makes the top shelf titles a little difficult to read. Generally, however, because of the depth of the room and the impossibility of rooflights, artificial lighting is necessary throughout the day.

The fire escape door at the extreme end of the library must have been a cause of slight concern to the Librarian from the point of view of security, though it is clearly visible from the counter.

Staff have a small restroom, again facing south and west, equipped with cooker, sink and cupboards, off a lobby which gives access also to the staff lavatories. The building, on this side, faces a steep bank covered with weeds which is eventually to be grassed and planted with shrubs.

Stacks for 3,000 books in the Regional Room supplement the 12,000 volumes on open shelves and provide stock from which the mobile library is supplied. Access to this room is through the staff workroom/office. The mobile library service is run from this building to the various villages of the South Hams district and a fully enclosed bay is provided for the van, with a raised entrance platform off which are located meter cupboard, cleaners' room and maintenance store. The volume of issues from the mobile is considerable, so that the amount of loading and unloading of books makes this provision essential.

Heating is by hot water floor coils from an oil-fired boiler which also supplies heat to the Health Centre. The library obviously benefits from the Centre being above it and is apparently very warm and comfortable in winter. Both warmth and quietness are also improved by the use throughout of carpeting. Bookshelving is by Reska with excellent hook-on and clearly lettered, interchangeable tier guides designed by the architects.

The popularity of the library is testified by the increase in issues from the 85,000 per annum of the old library, which it replaces, to 180,000 in the first full year of the new building's life.

Authority	County of Devon formerly County Borough of Torbay
Designation	Churston Branch
Date of opening	January 1973
Population served	8,000
Name of Architect	M R Hawkins, CEng, MICE, Director of Technical Services; R V Banks, RIBA, Chief Architect; M A Perry, RIBA, Job Architect
Name of Librarian	John R Pike, FLA
Special features:	
a) site	Adjacent main traffic route; area for extension on north side
b) architecture	External walls white fair faced concrete with dark grey textured brick plinth
c) function	Service to locality
Mechanical Services:	
a) heating	Gas-fired; fan assisted convector heaters
b) ventilation	Natural
c) lighting	Fluorescent strip
d) acoustics	Acoustic tiled ceiling
e) other	—
Areas: in square metres	
a) lending	178
b) reference	in (a)
c) reading	—
d) special activities	—
e) children	in (a)
f) control	in (a)
g) library staff admin.	24
h) exhibitions	—
i) lecture hall	—
j) circulation	—
k) services	15
l) lavatories	15
m) stack	15
Total area:	217
Book volumes:	
a) adult lending	6,000
b) adult reference	300
c) children	2,000
d) stack	—
e) other	—
Total:	8,300 (rising to 11,000)
Costs in £ p:	
a) site	13,800
b) building	24,000
c) furniture & fittings	3,000
Total Cost (ex fees):	£40,800
Cost per square metre:	£188

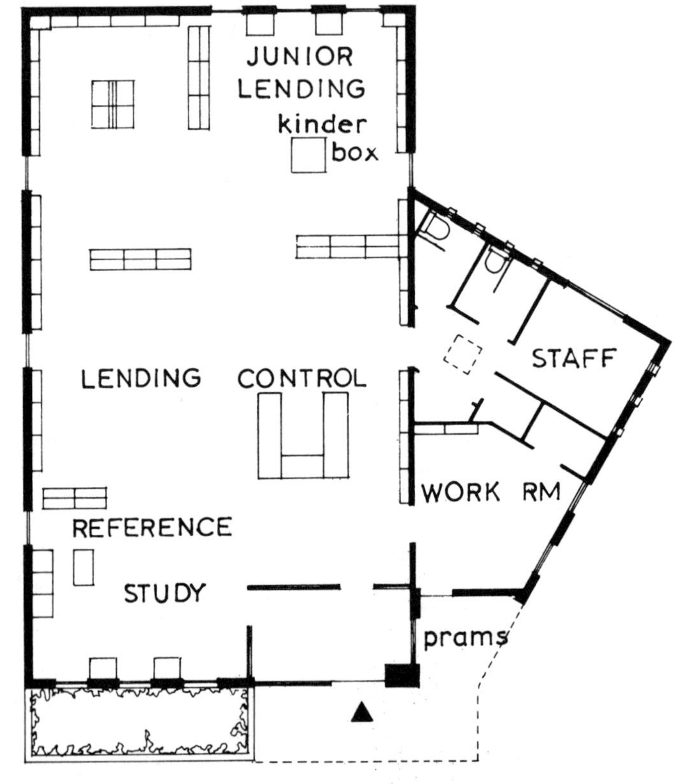

GROUND FLOOR

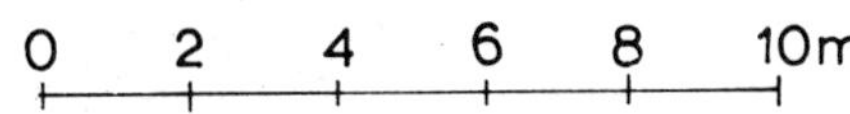

Authority	County of Devon
Designation	Honiton Branch
Date of opening	September 1974
Population served	5,800
Name of Architect	C J Weeks, RIBA, County Architect; B C Hook, Project Architect
Name of Librarian	R G Charlesworth, ALA
Special features:	
a) site	Sloping site; retaining walls needed
b) architecture	Traditional
c) function	Serving locality
Mechanical Services:	
a) heating	Gas-fired; warm air
b) ventilation	Natural
c) lighting	Fluorescent and tungsten
d) acoustics	—
e) other	—
Areas: in square metres	
a) lending	149
b) reference	38
c) reading	—
d) special activities	47 (Regional room)
e) children	27
f) control	—
g) library staff admin.	27
h) exhibitions	—
i) lecture hall	—
j) circulation	43
k) services	40 (inc. garage)
l) lavatories	3
m) stack	—
Total area:	374
Book volumes:	
a) adult lending	12,500
b) adult reference	1,500
c) children	3,500
d) stack	3,500
e) other	—
Total:	21,000
Costs in £ p:	
a) site	4,665
b) building	57,534
c) furniture & fittings	5,278
Total Cost (ex fees):	£67,477
Cost per square metre:	£180

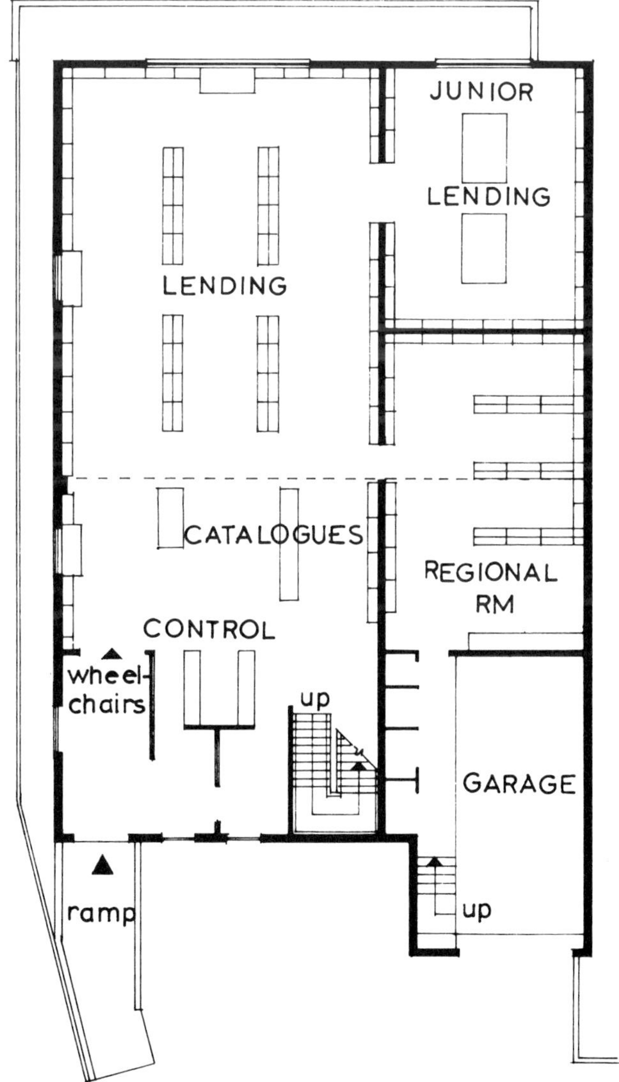

GROUND FLOOR

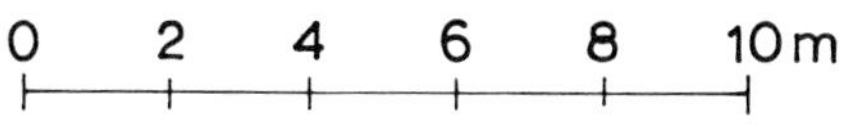

Authority	County of Devon
Designation	Kingsbridge Library
Date of opening	October 1974
Population served	3,600
Name of Architect	B H Thompson, RIBA, succeeded by C J Weeks, RIBA, County Architect; O S Lawes, RIBA, Project Architect
Name of Librarian	R G Charlesworth, ALA
Special features:	
a) site	Restricted and steeply sloping; with health centre
b) architecture	Traditional; concrete frame with brick
c) function	Serving locality
Mechanical Services:	
a) heating	Underfloor; low temperature hot water
b) ventilation	Natural
c) lighting	Fluorescent strip
d) acoustics	Acoustic suspended ceiling; felt floor covering
e) other	—
Areas: in square metres	
a) lending	111
b) reference	25
c) reading	—
d) special activities	13
e) children	32
f) control	in (a)
g) library staff admin.	12
h) exhibitions	—
i) lecture hall	—
j) circulation	3
k) services	60 (inc garage)
l) lavatories	5
m) stack	—
Total area:	297
Book volumes:	
a) adult lending	13,000
b) adult reference	1,200
c) children	2,250
d) stack	4,750
e) other	—
Total:	21,200
Costs in £ p:	
a) site	5,000
b) building	40,633
c) furniture & fittings	1,200
Total Cost (ex fees):	£46,833
Cost per square metre:	£158

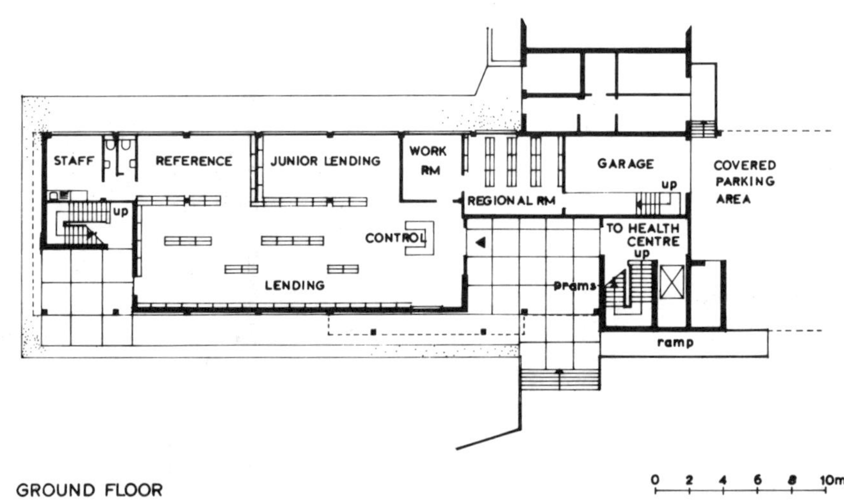

GROUND FLOOR

0 2 4 6 8 10m

PUBLIC·LIBRARY·HEALTH CENTRE

Teignmouth This is a new library building of particular interest for the exceptional nature of the site chosen. It can properly be described as occupying a very central position, just off the main shopping streets. It is also uniquely isolated in what is almost a totally enclosed triangle of land bounded by a high-level motor link road on one side and a deep railway cutting on the other, being finally wedged in on the short, third side by a tall council housing block. Access to it is entirely by pedestrian footpaths and subways, apart from a vehicle approach, shared with the housing estate, which leads to the staff and deliveries door. The new elevated roadway may work wonders for Teignmouth's central traffic flow but is hardly a satisfactory neighbour at such very close quarters for a library; perhaps even less so the railway, which runs right beside and below the longest of the perimeter walls of the adult Lending and Reference Libraries and which is, unfortunately, very noisy.

The choice of site is a factor of fundamental importance in the planning of every new library building. This building should be seen by anyone assessing the peculiar problems created by exceptional characteristics in site location such as these. The pedestrian paths twist their way around the library from the bridge over the cutting to the subways under the road, with the left-over spaces attractively planted with shrubs. It really is a problem site. Isolated, undoubtedly in its own peculiar circumstances, but central too. One access path leads from a point where four roads converge beside the parish church—approximately 100 yards from the library, across the footbridge. Another is again only 100 yards, chiefly by underpass, from a new shopping precinct and Teign Street and the main shopping centre. A site which might well have been given up as presenting too many difficulties should certainly be visited by anyone considering a 'problem' site. What has resulted from the local planners' obviously carefully considered series of solutions is a building which is likely to provoke very varied but probably positive reactions.

Its exterior is far from unattractive despite all the discordances created by such close and unpleasant companions, though signs indicating that it is a library are hardly adequate and though it is evident externally that this is an important public building there are few windows through which the activities of the library can be seen or its actual function guessed. Neither are the approaches as well guided as they should be, especially with so 'hidden' a site.

The long ramp up to the main entrance has a canopy where prams could be parked outside, but since this cannot be kept under any sort of observation from inside the library, this facility is of limited use. Wheelchairs can enter the library, though the ramp is rather steep.

Accommodation principally consists of a large main Lending Library with a high ceiling and clerestory windows and a lower-ceilinged Reference Department at one end and Children's Library at the other. This latter has its own immediate access directly from the entrance hall which also gives access to a separate exhibition gallery. This was originally planned as a reading room but the function was changed almost immediately after the opening. The exhibition space might, perhaps, better be a part of the hall itself, but the Librarian has plans for using the exhibition room for other extension activity purposes so the limitation may become an advantage. On the lower floor a public meetings room with entrance quite separate from that to the main library departments, has been provided. This connects with a lobby to the staff room and its services.

The Lending Library is pleasantly lighted from the high-level windows which are supplemented by narrow slit windows at low level. Not for the first time, we found the design of the counter really inadequate. Insufficient space has been allowed for staff to move about. This is quite unnecessary, for the size of this library is sufficiently generous for more room to have been allowed. No part of any library is more intensively used, so that it is essential that work shall be facilitated by good functional layout of the counter.

A second doubt relates to supervision, which is always a necessary consideration in a library, especially where the staff is small in number. Here the layout of bookshelving adopted is generally across and blocking the lines of vision. It also has fixed shelving. Its design, with hardwood ends and shelves on steel frames concreted into the floor, precludes any easy alterations later. The spacing of bookcases is such that another stack cannot be introduced without major alteration. Since the purpose-designed five-shelf bookcases are tall and have solid backs, the major part of the library is out of view of the staff. In particular the reference section is almost invisible from the desk. Similarly, and more seriously, the view of the Children's Library is blocked from the main counter by a wall and though there is a glazed screen between the rooms this is so placed that it does not assist supervision. It is true that the Children's Library has its own counter provided, but this is not often separately manned.

The cork flooring showed signs of scuffing in front of shelves. In the most heavily used areas, as around the counter, carpet has been used and, in the entrance hall, PVC was not looking very good in wet weather. Double glazing has been used for the windows but ventilation has to be provided in summer by remote controlled opening gear to the high-level windows. Noise is a real enemy.

Despite these criticisms, this is a handsome library and well built. Whether the choice of site was a right one is the interesting speculation here.

LHS   GKVT

Authority	Devon County Council
Designation	Teignmouth Branch Library
Date of opening	February 1973
Population served	11,500
Name of Architect	Edward Narracott and Partners, Torquay in collaboration with Devon County Architect
Name of Librarian	E J Coombe, FLA
Special features:	
a) site	Sloping site
b) architecture	'One-off'; character and materials echo central area development
c) function	Service to town and adjacent
Mechanical Services:	
a) heating	Gas-fired
b) ventilation	Natural
c) lighting	Fluorescent
d) acoustics	Acoustic tiled ceiling; cork flooring
e) other	—
Areas: in square metres	
a) lending	165
b) reference	63
c) reading	43
d) special activities	35
e) children	56
f) control	—
g) library staff admin.	40
h) exhibitions	—
i) lecture hall	—
j) circulation	30
k) services	12
l) lavatories	4
m) stack	—
Total area:	448
Book volumes:	
a) adult lending	15,500
b) adult reference	2,500
c) children	3,000
d) stack	—
e) other	—
Total:	21,000
Costs in £ p:	
a) site	—
b) building	39,518
c) furniture & fittings	5,098
Total Cost (ex fees):	£44,616
Cost per square metre:	£99

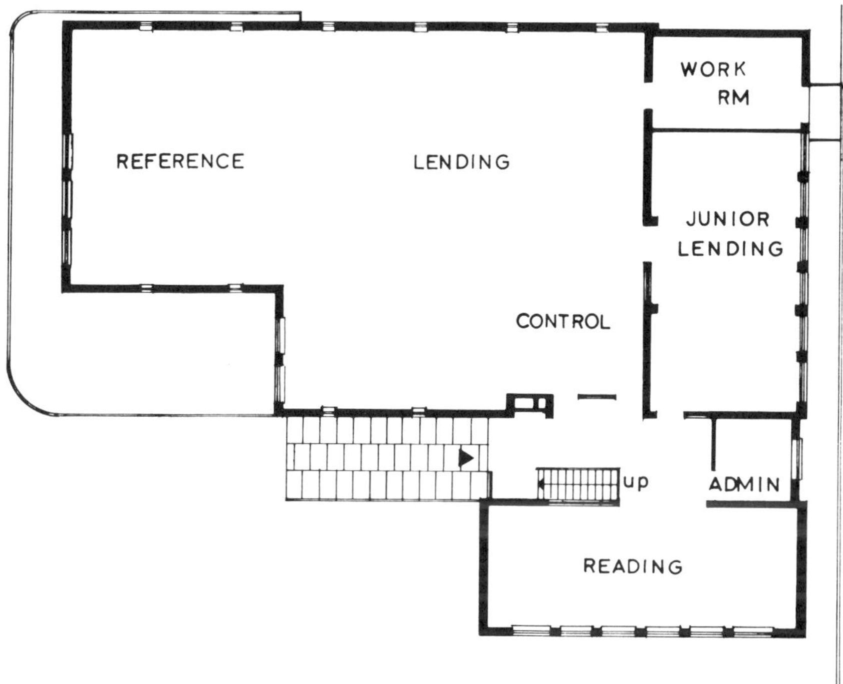

GROUND FLOOR

Derbyshire County Council:
Blagreaves Lane (formerly Derby County Borough Council) and Killamarsh

Blagreaves Lane area has had a chequered library history in recent years. A branch was planned on the site by Derbyshire County but before they could proceed the area was taken over in an extension of Derby Borough boundaries. On reorganisation the whole area has come again under the County.

The complex is most unusual in its function, combining a normal branch library with what is described as a bibliographical unit–which others might call an accessions and book distribution department for the Derby area. In some ways the two functions, public branch library and bibliographical unit, are separate under one roof.

The building is quite intriguing from the outside with its blue-brown brick, patches of white wooden slatting and its irregular but pleasing shape. It stands in a busy surburban shopping centre, $3\frac{1}{2}$ miles from the town centre with a convenient car park in front. A normal lobby leads through a porch on to the control counter, the library leading off to the left of it. To the right of the lobby is a connecting link to the bibliographical unit.

The L-shaped counter serves both the entrance area and the inside of the Lending Library, being located under spotlights and with an intriguing scarlet laminate counter top with scooped out areas for the various sectors of public service–books in, books out, registration, etc. The carpeted Lending Library room is not unusual except that the lattice beams have been left open as a feature in both halves, with an open stairway to the Children's Library which is above the centre of the room. The scarlet motif has been repeated in places throughout the room but otherwise the decoration is white plaster. The Children's Library overlooks the main library room from both sides with balconies which serve also to carry book shelves. The Children's Library is normally unstaffed (although the entrance to the staff room lies through it) and one feels that the temptation to the unsupervised child to throw books on to the heads of adults below must be very strong.

The administrative part of the building, very much the larger, consists mainly of open rooms, which are reasonably efficient but unremarkable. They are shelved with odds and ends of bookcases from old libraries but there can be little objection to this as the public do not have access to it. On the ground floor of the administrative part of the building is a very large bookstack area with rolling compact storage cases, but on the frontage are a series of generously-sized carrels and a seminar room. These have individual windows looking out on to the road and are the only part of this section of the building which are used by readers. The Lending Library staff, heavily outnumbered by the bibliographical unit staff, share common staff and toilet facilities in the office part of the building.

This is a very difficult complex to describe and must sound a weird mixture. In practice it seems perfectly acceptable: the public area attractive, the private area efficient.

Killamarsh is a small village on the very northern edge of Derbyshire and the new library, attached by a covered way to the community centre, has to serve a population of little more than 5000. Moreover there is a very steep hill between two sections of the village, which cannot help.

There is not much to say about the oblong building of traditional construction, carpeted throughout, with gas-fired low pressure accelerated hot water heating using fan convectors. It is in fact a single room with four full-length door-size windows at the sides, a central entrance lobby and open-plan layout. The small rebate areas level with the entrance lobby are used as browsing, periodical areas and closed storage respectively. A space saving feature is that staff toilet facilities are provided in the community centre building adjoining. The counter is a straight desk in the centre of the room and, in the space allocation, children seem to have a good share. A number of tuffets add interest to the low bookcases here.

The library is open only part-time and seems adequate for the purpose, if not particularly exciting.

GT

Authority	County of Derbyshire formerly Borough of Derby
Designation	Blagreaves Lane Library and Bibliographical Unit
Date of opening	October 1973
Population served	10,000
Name of Architect	N I N G Doig, DFC, DipArch, ARIBA, Borough Architect
Name of Librarian	R E Marston, FLA, former Borough Librarian
Special features:	
a) site	Triangular, between garage and shopping parade
b) architecture	System built brick-tile construction
c) function	Branch Library; Bibliographical Unit; Regional Library HQ; Schools Service; Stack, etc.
Mechanical Services:	
a) heating	Gas-fired hot water radiators and fan radiators
b) ventilation	Natural
c) lighting	Fluorescent (diffused); tungsten spots; 300 lux
d) acoustics	—
e) other	Passenger/goods lift; book hoist; emergency lighting system
Areas: in square metres	
a) lending	
b) reference	} 218
c) reading	
d) special activities	20
e) children	58
f) control	25
g) library staff admin.	—
h) exhibitions	—
i) lecture hall	—
j) circulation	—
k) services	—
l) lavatories	30
m) stack	912 (Bibliographical Unit)
Total area:	1,263
Book volumes:	
a) adult lending	15,000
b) adult reference	69
c) children	6,300
d) stack	52,000
e) other	—
Total:	107,000 (includes Bibliographical Unit)
Costs in £ p:	
a) site	Already owned
b) building	107,000
c) furniture & fittings	6,360
Total Cost (ex fees):	£113,360
Cost per square metre:	£84

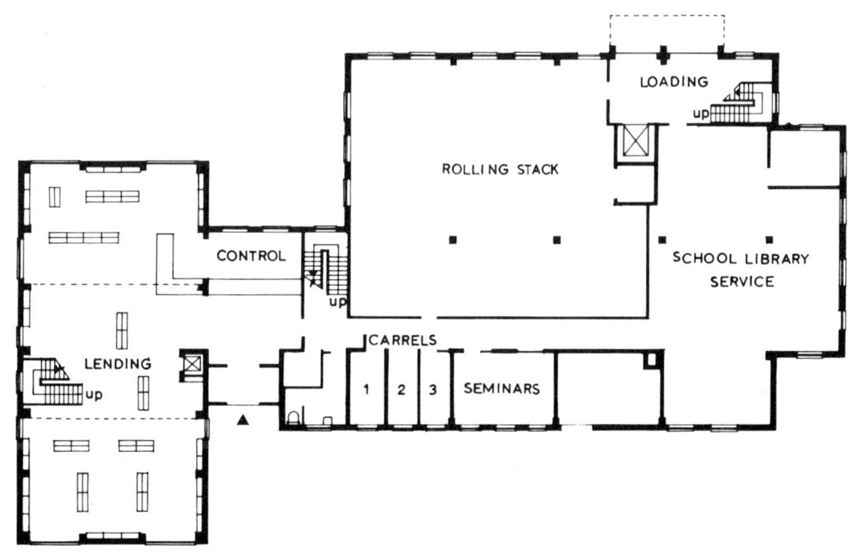

GROUND FLOOR

Authority	County of Derbyshire formerly Borough of Derby
Designation	Killamarsh Library
Date of opening	1974
Population served	5,500
Name of Architect	Consultant R F Ward, DipArch; Chief Officer R W Kerning, DipArch, ARIBA, AMTPI
Name of Librarian	D A South, BA, FLA (now retired)
Special features:	
a) site	—
b) architecture	—
c) function	—
Mechanical Services:	
a) heating	Gas-fired hot water; fan convectors
b) ventilation	Natural
c) lighting	Fluorescent; 350 lux
d) acoustics	Suspended ceiling of acoustic tiles
e) other	Self-contained fire alarm
Areas: in square metres	
a) lending	
b) reference	85
c) reading	
d) special activities	—
e) children	33
f) control	—
g) library staff admin.	11
h) exhibitions	—
i) lecture hall	—
j) circulation	—
k) services	7
l) lavatories	—
m) stack	—
Total area:	136
Book volumes:	
a) adult lending	7,037
b) adult reference	93
c) children	3,390
d) stack	—
e) other	—
Total:	10,520
Costs in £ p:	
a) site	3,921
b) building	13,824
c) furniture & fittings	2,005
Total Cost (ex fees):	£19,696
Cost per square metre:	£144

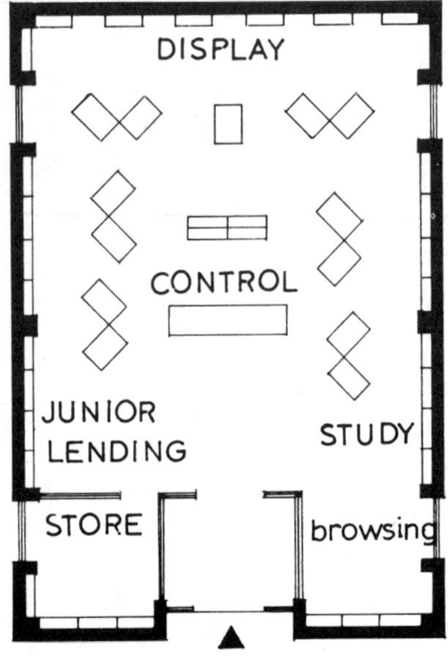

GROUND FLOOR

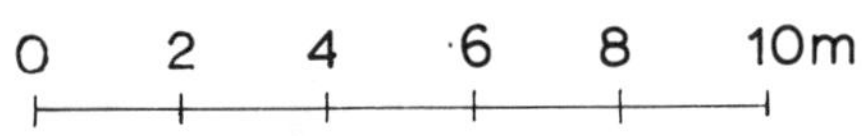

Doncaster Metropolitan District (formerly West Riding County): Sprotbrough, Bawtry, Bentley, Hatfield and (formerly Doncaster Borough) Intake

Sprotbrough Library is quite a striking building set back from a busy main road which runs east/west between the old A1 and over the new A1(M). It has a simple drive-in to car parking space, with then only a step or two before entering the library.

The frontage of the building has a design which succeeds in announcing its specific identity in large light-grey letters with white rims and, as important, arousing such interest as will draw the public towards it to see just what lies beyond. This reveals a large open-plan area with shelving for book stock arranged in alcove fashion; it is all neat, bright and colourful with plenty of space for movement. A centrally placed control desk with adjacent readers' advisory point is well positioned for those who appreciate an immediate opportunity to make an enquiry. This control, which caters for the children as well, is set between supporting pillars and is as spacious as that particular area encourages. The distance which this is set back from the entrance allows for an area for display.

The wide window alcoves each have a bench seat, with comfortable chairs nearby; other cushion-backed seats (with coffee table and periodicals) are for resting at convenient points. These match well with the mottled fawn and brown carpeting. Lighting is mostly fluorescent strip but with some tungsten.

Stairs to the right of the entrance lead to the mezzanine where the siting of study desks and chairs seems appropriate for reasonable private study. The left side has been devoted to a hall for meetings and exhibitions and has direct access from a separate entrance at the far left of the frontage. A recessed, illuminated display case is able to announce the subject if required or can be used for general publicity of the library service. An exterior emergency stairs exit from the hall is provided at the rear.

It was noticed that the exterior window panels on the west (non-public) side of the building which are thus, to some extent at least, protected from mischevious attention, but no doubt receive much sun, have peeled quite badly during the not-so-long period that the library has been open. This and the damage to the front step were the only scars on an otherwise well-cared-for building.

Just prior to going to press we learned of four other libraries in this area opened during the review period but for which no notification had been received. It was impossible for any visits to be made at that late date but a few facts about each are given here.

Bawtry, opened in February 1974, to serve a population of about 3,500, is situated at the north end of the village, bounded by the Great North Road. It is linked to a Further Education Centre and is adjacent to a row of cottages, protected as historic buildings. It is a single storey brick building with a floor area of 232 sq metres and a book stock of 15,000. Cost per square metre was £146. The area serviced by the library includes part of Nottinghamshire as well as West Riding County.

Bentley is a mining town a few miles to the north of Sprotbrough whose library is similar in size and design to that library building.

Hatfield (pop 14,317) lies about 10 miles to the north-west of Doncaster and its library fronts on to the A18. It is a flat-roofed single storey brick structure on a site of 17 m × 58 m. The floor area is 300 m², the book stock 20,000 and the cost per square metre £135. It was opened in May 1974.

Intake (pop 13,725) was planned by the former Doncaster Borough Council as a Branch Library within that system to serve a large suburban estate. The building itself is set in landscaped parkland and is flat-roofed, single storey constructed of industrial timber frame with external brick cladding. A book stock of 18,665 volumes is housed within its 225 m² of floor area; cost per square metre being £156.

HW

Intake

Authority	Metropolitan Borough Council of Doncaster formerly County Council of West Riding
Designation	Sprotbrough Branch Library
Date of opening	May 1973
Population served	10,563
Name of Architect	West Riding County Council; Architects' Department
Name of Librarian	W J Murison, FLA, FLAI
Special features:	
a) site	Main road site in residential area
b) architecture	Two-storey brick; flat timber roof
c) function	Serving locality
Mechanical Services:	
a) heating	Underfloor electric cable
b) ventilation	Natural
c) lighting	Fluorescent strip
d) acoustics	Carpeted
e) other	—
Areas: in square metres	
a) lending	145
b) reference	85
c) reading	27
d) special activities	—
e) children	50
f) control	—
g) library staff admin.	26
h) exhibitions	} 100
i) lecture hall	
j) circulation	—
k) services	—
l) lavatories	12
m) stack	—
Total area:	535
Book volumes:	
a) adult lending	14,395
b) adult reference	885
c) children	5,187
d) stack	—
e) other	—
Total:	20,467
Costs in £ p:	
a) site	2,250
b) building	41,199
c) furniture & fittings	4,900
Total Cost (ex fees):	£48,349
Cost per square metre:	£90

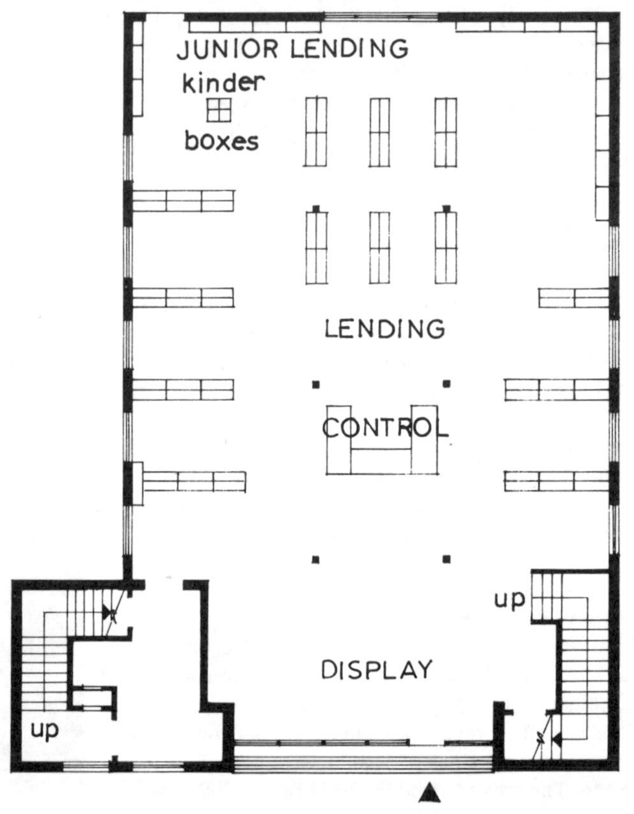

GROUND FLOOR

Bawtry

Hatfield

Dorset County Council:
Colehill, Chickerell, Gillingham and Puddletown

It was interesting, having just visited new libraries in other county services, to come across a markedly different approach to the provision of library services for the rural and village communities as provided by Dorset County Council.

Starting in 1954 many of the villages, including Chickerell and Puddletown, were served by a mobile library visiting them at fortnightly intervals. More recently it has become the accepted policy of the Library and General Purposes Committee 'to provide small libraries in rapidly developing villages in the County, a suitable site or building for conversion being sought in the area'. The Council is now steadily and systematically providing small permanent libraries in such villages of over 1,000 inhabitants; in many cases this is by the conversion of suitable, otherwise redundant buildings as at Chickerell and Gillingham, by additions to existing buildings as at Puddletown or, in the case of larger communities by new architect-designed libraries as at Colehill. The mobile library service is maintained for visiting the smaller and more isolated communities. As the policy has developed, so it seems has local conviction that readers prefer the permanent buildings, however small, because they are more convenient to visit, having longer opening hours, being mainly manned by staff, if often non-professional, recruited locally on a part-time basis. Much emphasis is placed on a personal service to readers, who all become well known to the staff. Book stocks are inevitably very small, the open shelf capacity at Chickerell and Puddletown, for example, being about 3,000 volumes each. Gillingham, also a converted building, has a stock twice this size.

Colehill This is a purpose designed building. Colehill is virtually a suburb of Wimborne pleasantly situated on a wooded hill and very open in layout. The library, is set between two roads, close to their junction and at the edge of a pinewood. There are no other public buildings or shops in the immediate vicinity and the reason for the choice of site, which is scenically quite delightful, is not very apparent. It is not easy to find and there is little signposting to help. Across one of the roads, however, there is a sizeable residential area and certainly for all local readers, once located it cannot be forgotten, for this is a most attractive, almost a notably romantic little building.

The site calls for a structure which must be in sympathy with the wooded landscape and the architects chose to use a prefabricated timber structure of great charm, made by a local firm, J E Lesser and Company. The use of horizontal timber cladding, stained black on the low end-blocks, contrasts well with large areas of glass to ground level on four sides of the central and higher library room. This square, tall, main library is set at 45° to the low blocks and this produces very exciting and dramatic effects, and a great feeling of openness so that the library announces its function very clearly.

A simple entrance lobby, large enough to accommodate prams, leads to the single room library, whilst the staff workroom is placed at the opposite end, off a lobby which gives access to a lavatory and a store.

The counter is under the lower roof of the porch section with an excellent view into all corners of the library and beyond into the surrounding woods. On a warm summer afternoon this is quite idyllic, though on some dark winter days it might well become rather an isolated and eerie experience to be alone in the building. On balance, we believe that the architectural approach is justified on this site and library users do, we were told, appreciate it. The library is open for nineteen hours a week and accommodates some 5,000 volumes on its centred 'island' Terrapin Reska shelving, including selections for children and 'young adults'. Book issues were 66,000 in the first year. Reference provision is limited in view of the proximity of the larger Wimborne library. There was a small display of paintings by local artists and good notice board provision. At £13,420 for the building with a further £1,325 for furniture, this library is certainly economical as well as being most attractive.

Chickerell. It is a small village close to the Chesil Beach coast near Weymouth, roughly a mile inland on the south slope of the hills. The County Architect is a strong believer in conservation, we were told, and was lucky to be able to save the derelict Peto Memorial Room, which has become the new library.

Set in a pleasantly grassed plot of ground this is a brick-faced and rendered building with one end Dutch-gabled and a canopied door, originally the entrance, now attractively replaced by a full-length window. Sir Henry Peto was founder, in 1907, of the Dorset Schools and Villages Booklending Association, forerunner of the present county library services.

The situation of the building, next to the post office and opposite the main row of shops, is right at the centre of the village. It consists of two rooms to which a new porch provides entrance: the first, with control counter by the door, being the Lending Library, includes a children's section. The rear room contains a reference section. A small staff cloakroom with lobby has been built on to the back of the building whilst a minute tea bar and washing-up recess (which doubles as cleaner's room and is screened by a curtain) opens off the back room which is often used by local societies for meetings. This is a most useful facility and could be said to put to shame many a much larger library where such provision has not, but could have been, made. This encouragement and practical help to community life in the village must greatly assist in recommending and familiarising the library to local people. Bookshelves are purpose designed in softwood and together with the warm coloured, carpeted floor, curtains and simple beech furniture are good looking and comfortable.

This small library is open for ten hours each week, these being agreed between the Branch Librarian and the readers in the village. Book issues from the stock of 3,000 volumes run at about 700 per week.

Gillingham In the northern part of Dorset which juts out between Somerset and Wiltshire, the small town of Gillingham has a considerable variety of industry and a thriving market. It is the centre of an exceptionally large parish and has a growing population of some 4,000 to 5,000. Its library until July 1974, functioned from a highly inadequate room in the Methodist church. A long search for alternative accommodation to meet the urgent needs of this expanding community ended that month with the opening of new premises, a converted former National Provincial Bank building at the corner of the High Street and Station Road, almost opposite the main post office and among shops: a very good and prominent central position.

The library consists of one large room accommodating adult lending and reference facilities and a smaller room, on the Station Road frontage, which leads out of the main library and provides a recessed area for children. To the rear are a book store, office and staff accommodation. There is open shelf capacity for almost 6,000 volumes in all.

The building is reported to have been most effectively replanned and furnished internally and very successful in its first year of use. One of us, only, managed to visit this library, owing to the large number of buildings to be fitted into sometimes complex journeys and this visit was also at a time, unfortunately, when the library was closed (it is open for twenty hours a week). Externally one does wish that it could have been made a little more attractive. Almost no view is obtainable through the windows, which have cills high above the pavement level and there is no useful provision for external display to tempt potential users. It is unmistakeably a bank building and rather grim-faced at that.

Few alterations had to be made to adapt the building for library purposes and the cost of converting it was only £1,538 plus £2,100 for shelving and furniture. The site cost was £9,000.

Puddletown Unfortunately the site of this library, which is an addition to the old village hall, is very unattractive, lying as it does directly on the main A31 Wimborne to Dorchester road which carries heavy traffic through the village, particularly at holiday times. The usefulness of the connection with the village hall is, however, the prime consideration. Since it also lies virtually at the centre of the village and as, perhaps one day, there is to be a by-pass, there was nothing else to be done. It does, however, cause the librarian anxiety when the Infants and Primary School children have to cross the road from their building opposite running the gauntlet of cars and lorries; this imposes a duty, which is fortunately rare for librarians, of shepherding them back when they leave.

A new porch with doormats and notice board has been built and double doors lead into the library, with a single door giving access to the village hall's cloakrooms.

The control desk, which is well designed, with plenty of room for reserved books behind it, faces the entrance door with a good view of most of the library. This single room, tucked into a tight site between the hall with its kitchen and the boundary hedge, is pleasantly lighted from above with four large rooflights as well as a large window at the rear. The direct connection with the hall kitchen enables the library to be used in the evenings for local meetings at which, naturally in a country area, refreshments are generally expected.

A warm and friendly atmosphere is created by simple furnishings, carpet and good book display. The bookcases are by Terrapin Reska and accommodate about 3,000 volumes.

As at Chickerell, the library is open for ten hours a week; times have been carefully arranged to suit its readers. The cost of the building, completed in March 1974, was £6,471; shelving and furniture £900.

GKVT   LHS

Colehill

(Statistics not available)

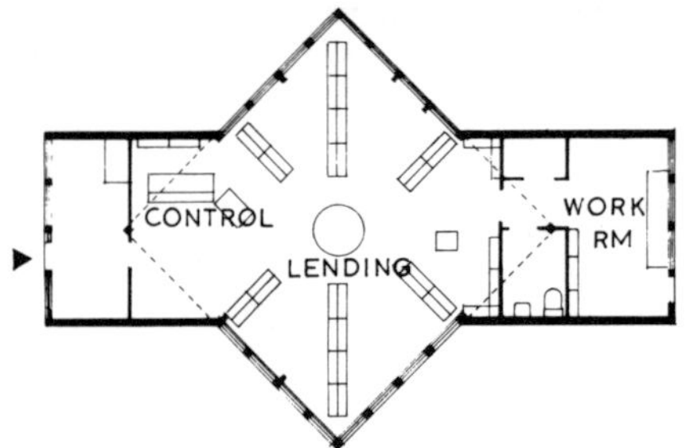

GROUND FLOOR

Chickerell

(Statistics not available)

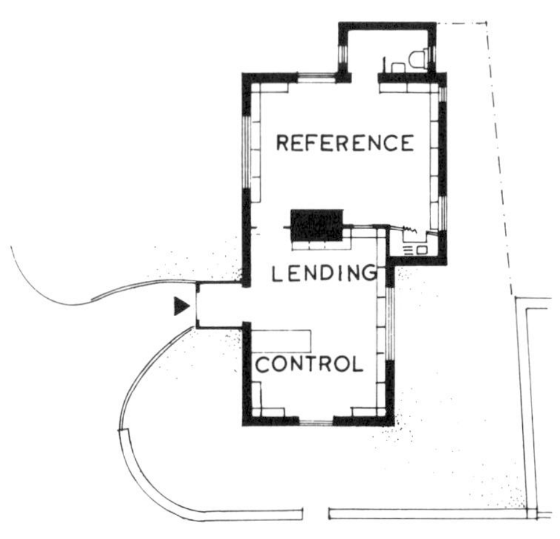

GROUND FLOOR

Authority	Dorset County Council
Designation	Gillingham Branch Library
Date of opening	July 1974
Population served	4,000
Name of Architect	R J Patterson, DipArch (Birm), RIBA, County Architect; K Hughes, Job Architect
Name of Librarian	H E Radford, FLA
Special features:	
a) site	Former bank building; corner site in shopping centre
b) architecture	Conversion of bank premises
c) function	Serving locality
Mechanical Services:	
a) heating	Gas-fired
b) ventilation	Windows do *not* open; fan ventilation
c) lighting	Fluorescent strip
d) acoustics	—
e) other	—
Areas: in square metres	
a) lending	
b) reference	80
c) reading	
d) special activities	—
e) children	10
f) control	in (a)
g) library staff admin.	4
h) exhibitions	—
i) lecture hall	—
j) circulation	—
k) services	—
l) lavatories	in (g)
m) stack	—
Total area:	94
Book volumes:	
a) adult lending	4,750
b) adult reference	150
c) children	1,500
d) stack	—
e) other	—
Total:	6,400
Costs in £ p:	
a) site	9,000
b) building	1,538 conversion
c) furniture & fittings	2,100
Total Cost (ex fees):	£12,638
Cost per square metre:	£135

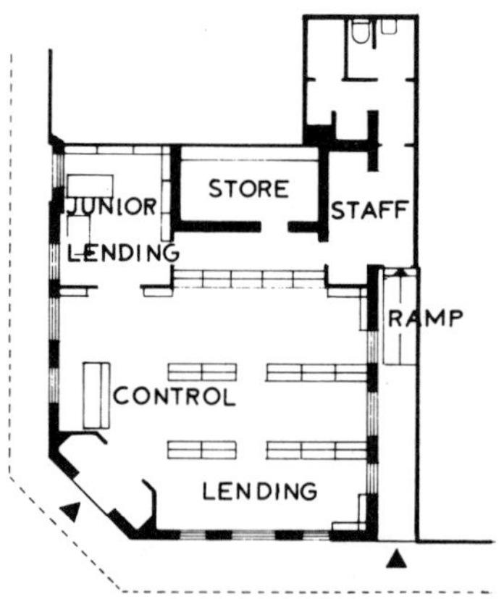

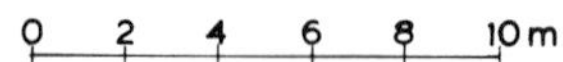

GROUND FLOOR

Puddletown

(Statistics not available)

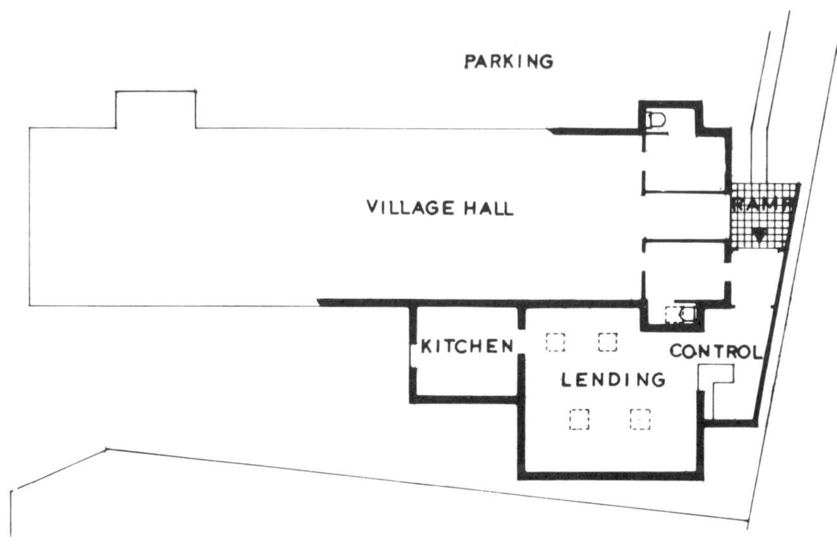

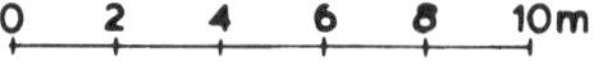

Durham County Council:
Chester-le-Street, South Moor, Annfield Plain, Chilton and Spennymoor

Driving up the A1 to Durham at a time when locally in London plans were being finalised for a 50th anniversary exhibition of the General Strike of 1926, memory recalled the Jarrow hunger marchers from Durham pits. Now the area being visited has been virtually devoid of pits for some years with resettlement of industry up to the north-east taking their place. Answers to questions about the work force in these five communities revealed that unemployment was in some measure being relieved by the needs of the newly located Courtauld, Ever Ready and Black and Decker factories within County Durham. Each of these new libraries has similar types of readership areas and each, to a larger or smaller degree, provided a bright centre against a rather drab background. All were designed by the County Architect's department, yet pleasingly there was something different about each. In the order visited assessments are:

Chester-le-Street, serving a population of 36,000, is fortunate in having a corner site on the main road, among the shops and near a market. With the entrance just off the main street and with a brick side elevation to the traffic it was helpful to be driven by the Deputy County Librarian, as non-local car drivers would pass by as there are no direction signs from the main road to the Library. Another lack is a car park, but this is due to limited site area.

For Library Authority purposes Durham is divided into eight districts but this library, even though it serves 36,000 people, and produces over 1,000 issues a day, ranks only as a branch. It occupies over 7,000 ft^2 (650 m^2) and was a former police station and court before demolition. A wide entrance leads into a display hall with spot illuminated cases; to the left there is a 'General Purposes' room equipped with wall display panelling, screen and chairs for some 50 people. This can be segregated for activities after library hours, but has no kitchen facilities. From the entrance hall to the right is the open-plan library. The large counter, purpose designed for Browne issue, stands on a lino-tiled area while the carpeting does not commence until entering the adult and children's areas. This was common to the other libraries visited, though the colours of the flooring and the facings on the counters varied with each. The beige carpet here was an unfortunate choice showing very many dirt marks–the darker but bolder colours in other buildings were much more effective. Large 6 × 5 ft convectors are in all, panelled with Sundela for display or poster purposes.

Orange coloured, wide easy chairs are there for browsing, while occasional vinyl bench seats in window spaces were a bonus; but strange it was to see these same large chairs in the children's section wasting space when, with quite heavy issues, smaller stools or coloured 'tubs' would have seemed better for the purpose. An attractive feature is the bold wooden frame screen separating the children's section from the counter area. The first floor, which stretches back only as far as the entrance but not over the public departments, is reached by a quality wooden open stairway. Here is the workroom, serviced by an electric book hoist and also the staff restroom–reasonable in size and facilities for the ten staff there.

South Moor, smaller at 2,000 ft^2 (186 m^2) is planned to serve a population of about 10,000, some being drawn from South Stanley, nearby. It stands next to a Boys' Club and Play Group Centre and has four schools in the vicinity.

The exterior shape is unusual, sloping from a lower level, which is over the Children's Library to a greater height over counter and adult section. The supporting cross beams are faced with varnished plywood, while the ceiling itself is wood strip running at right angles to these beams. The walls are in cream emulsion with a contrasting end wall covered by a dignified patterned wallpaper. The green carpet and red lino-tiled counter surround are striking. The counter itself, well designed, is in white beech as is the shelving. Noticeable, by contrast with the previous library, are the plastic holders filled to the ends of the bookcases, each holding a periodical–a space saver in a small library. At Chester-le-Street the problem of giving publicity space for local activities was solved, sadly, by sellotaping posters to the ends of island bookcases, while pamphlet material had pushed out the facility of a desk at standing height for the registration of new readers.

Annfield Plain was interesting as a conversion but far from pleasing. A local committee had stubbornly refused one offer by the County of a new branch on a far more suitable site, insisting on the retention of a shabby 1908 Carnegie building, which is $\frac{3}{4}$ mile from the town centre. Whilst improvements have been achieved at a cost of £21,000 (a greater degree of openness, some carpeting, new counter etc) the wall surfaces have not been properly smoothed down and blemishes grin through most noticeably. The large square workroom/staff room has been left in its old form, neither space being maximised nor any apparent betterment being offered to the staff.

Chilton, a small but neat library bravely fights the constant threat and disheartening results of vandalism, the scars being visible externally.

In the main road, near shops, a school and opposite a converted building now used as a Community Association and Youth Club, it is obviously in a sound position for good use. The problem, prticularly in winter, is that being glass-fronted its lights are the only clearly visible ones in this main street. Youngsters from the housing estate (which stretches back from the rear of the library) try to use the library as a playground until the Youth Club opens at 7 pm. With no provision for a library attendant, the young lady Branch Librarian does manfully trying to keep control, but any miscreants whom she expels then turn all the library lights off as they go, as the switches are accessible in the main entrance hall–surely a point which has to be borne in mind by architects and librarians when they are planning libraries in a problem area. Even so, the library having been open for more than two years at the time of the visit, one could have expected a rectification before then of this oversight, either by relocating or making the switches key-operating.

It is understandable that the average daily issue of 300–400 is not higher, in spite of the good site, when adult users have little

Authority	County of Durham
Designation	Chester-le-Street Branch
Date of opening	January 1973
Population served	36,000
Name of Architect	J L Parnaby, RIBA, County Architect
Name of Librarian	R N Dixon, FLA
Special features:	
a) site	Corner site on main shopping near market; sloping site
b) architecture	Traditional brick
c) function	Serving local area with mobile and two part-time branches
Mechanical Services:	
a) heating	Gas-fired low pressure hot water
b) ventilation	Natural
c) lighting	Fluorescent strip
d) acoustics	Carpeted; acoustic tiled ceiling
e) other	—
Areas: in square metres	
a) lending	247
b) reference	in (a)
c) reading	—
d) special activities	—
e) children	73
f) control	in (g)
g) library staff admin.	83
h) exhibitions	in (i)
i) lecture hall	47
j) circulation	in (g)
k) services	in (g)
l) lavatories	in (g)
m) stack	in (g)
Total area:	450
Book volumes:	
a) adult lending	22,082
b) adult reference	896
c) children	5,597
d) stack	4,400
e) other	—
Total:	32,975
Costs in £ p:	
a) site	14,700
b) building	38,195
c) furniture & fittings	7,000
Total Cost (ex fees):	£59,895
Cost per square metre:	£133

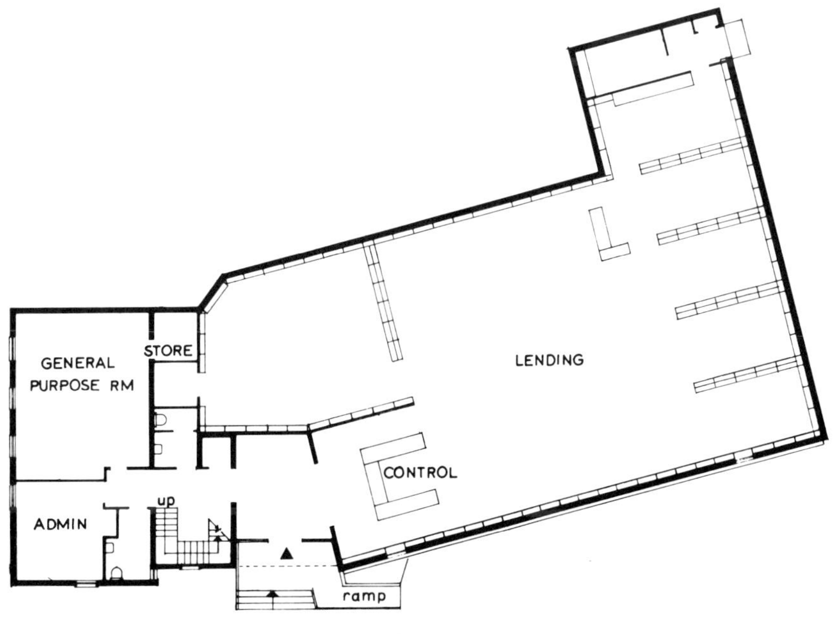

GROUND FLOOR

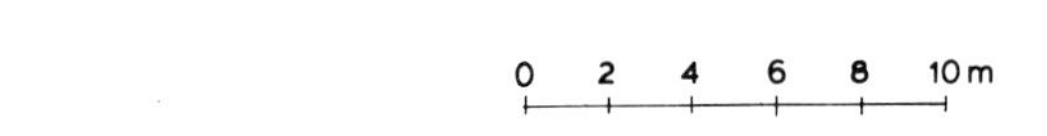

desire to come to the library at troublesome times and have even less wish to allow their well-behaved children to make the visit alone. The building is bright, attractively decorated in pale pink and grey and the bold magenta carpet looks and wears well. Large windows facing the south and west are, unfortunately, not provided with blinds nor curtains which would add to the decor as well as keeping the temperature reasonable on hot days.

A neat touch, where oversight from the counter into the children's area is vital, is the tough glass panelling between the low bookcases, for otherwise any gaps left between the cases would have provided yet more playground activity.

Spennymoor is not only the largest of those seen but is by far the most striking in design. It has been built as a District HQ library responsible for eight branches and four mobile libraries. The population of the town is 35,000, (most working in light industry) and the main road library site is close to a Health Centre and to a Recreation Centre as well as to the pedestrianised shopping precinct. It has good use for its 52 hours per week of opening, with annual issues of over 200,000. It is an irregularly shaped, light brick building with a glass and aluminium entrance; the exterior and interior doors are offset to prevent as much draught as possible from blowing directly on to the staff manning the counter which faces it—perhaps in peak periods this may prove to be a little too close. This counter, designed in chocolate colour and white, serves both adult and child readers, with the screen which partly separates the latter being most usual—dark wood strip vertically with large glass lozenge-shaped panels which allow good oversight into the carpeted areas, as well as glimpses of attractive displays. The

varying use of wood is a delight, the rich fluted mahogany is complemented by brown carpet which together set off the light oak of the bookcases.

The irregular contours of the building are noticed more from the interior, and are appreciated as the wide-angled corners allow floor-to-ceiling fenestration and good views outwards. Accident prevention is provided by the plant troughs across their whole width. As with the earlier or recently built branches, the large convector panels had been covered with Sundela or pegboard for display purposes, so there is much to catch the reader's eye. Circulation and browsing areas seem quite adequate.

The surface of the ceiling is irregular too—rough coated to assist the acoustic qualities—its angles fit in with the several substantial rooflights and are not at all displeasing. Over the counter there is a false ceiling, acoustically tiled, fitted with recessed fluorescent lighting but with six tungsten downlights, intended to highlight Browne issue trays and charging area, but not seeming to be as effective as hoped for.

The separated 'General Purposes' room has a separate entrance to an area which allows 40 seats and provides a toilet, but not kitchen facilities. The walls have display panelling fitted. Chairs are of the polypropylene variety in orange and black which on a vinyl tiled floor could be noisy. The garage for mobile library and transport also has its own entrance. This is a library which suggests careful thought and good co-operation between architect and librarian, with consequential benefit having been achieved.

HW

(Photographs and plans not available for these libraries)

Authority	County of Durham
Designation	South Moor Branch
Date of opening	December 1974
Population served	10,000
Name of Architect	J L Parnaby, RIBA, County Architect
Name of Librarian	R N Dixon, FLA
Special features:	
a) site	Within residential estate adjacent to boys club/play group centre
b) architecture	Traditional
c) function	Serving housing estate
Mechanical Services:	
a) heating	Oil-fired; convector fan assisted
b) ventilation	Natural
c) lighting	Fluorescent strip
d) acoustics	Carpeted
e) other	—
Areas: in square metres	
a) lending	98
b) reference	in (a)
c) reading	—
d) special activities	—
e) children	32
f) control	
g) library staff admin.	
h) exhibitions	
i) lecture hall	
j) circulation	45
k) services	
l) lavatories	
m) stack	
Total area:	175
Book volumes:	
a) adult lending	6,670
b) adult reference	186
c) children	3,700
d) stack	2,644
e) other	—
Total:	13,200
Costs in £ p:	
a) site	1,200
b) building	28,600
c) furniture & fittings	5,500
Total Cost (ex fees):	£35,300
Cost per square metre:	£201

Authority	County of Durham
Designation	Chilton Branch
Date of opening	December 1973
Population served	10,000
Name of Architect	J L Parnaby, RIBA, County Architect
Name of Librarian	R N Dixon, FLA
Special features:	
a) site	Main road site near shops and community association and school
b) architecture	Traditional
c) function	Serving local area
Mechanical Services:	
a) heating	Oil-fired; convectors fan assisted and radiators
b) ventilation	Natural
c) lighting	Fluorescent strip
d) acoustics	Carpeted; acoustic tiled ceilings
e) other	—
Areas: in square metres	
a) lending	84
b) reference	in (a)
c) reading	—
d) special activities	—
e) children	27
f) control	
g) library staff admin.	
h) exhibitions	
i) lecture hall	
j) circulation	29
k) services	
l) lavatories	
m) stack	
Total area:	140
Book volumes:	
a) adult lending	7,390
b) adult reference	160
c) children	2,960
d) stack	1,750
e) other	—
Total:	12,260
Costs in £ p:	
a) site	350
b) building	23,552
c) furniture & fittings	4,100
Total Cost (ex fees):	£28,002
Cost per square metre:	£200

Authority	County of Durham
Designation	Spennymoor Branch
Date of opening	March 1974
Population served	30,000
Name of Architect	J L Parnaby, RIBA, County Architect
Name of Librarian	R N Dixon, FLA
Special features:	
a) site	Main road site, near health centre and recreation centre and shopping pedestrianised precinct
b) architecture	—
c) function	District headquarters for seven full-time, one part-time and four mobile libraries
Mechanical Services:	
a) heating	Gas-fired low pressure hot water
b) ventilation	Natural
c) lighting	Fluorescent strips; down lights tungsten
d) acoustics	Carpeted in main areas; acoustic tiled ceiling
e) other	—
Areas: in square metres	
a) lending	165
b) reference	in (a)
c) reading	—
d) special activities	—
e) children	45
f) control	in (g)
g) library staff admin.	92
h) exhibitions	in (i)
i) lecture hall	38
j) circulation	
k) services	in (g)
l) lavatories	
m) stack	—
Total area:	340
Book volumes:	
a) adult lending	14,984
b) adult reference	344
c) children	3,835
d) stack	3,268
e) other	—
Total:	22,431
Costs in £ p:	
a) site	5,000
b) building	45,000
c) furniture & fittings	9,300
Total Cost (ex fees):	£59,300
Cost per square metre:	£174

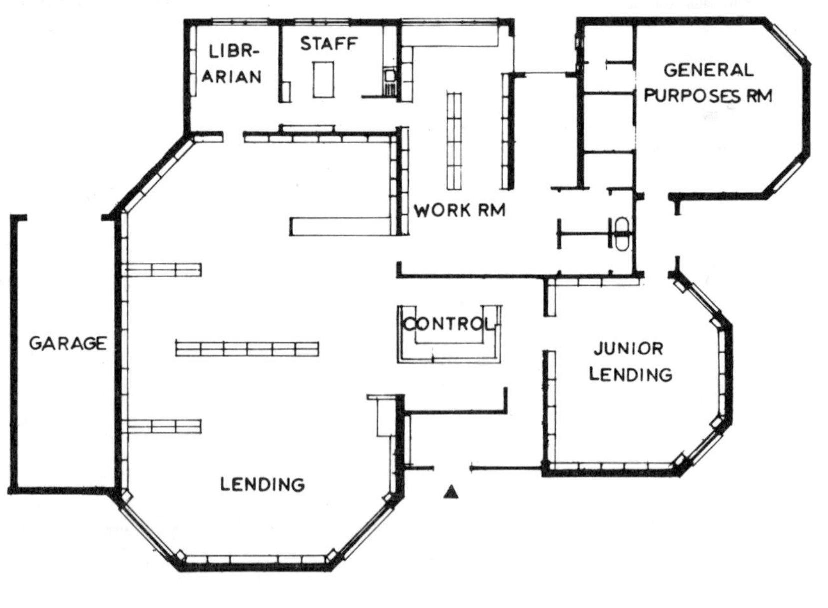

GROUND FLOOR

Essex County Council:
(formerly Southend-on-Sea County Borough) Shoeburyness:
(formerly Thurrock Urban District) Corringham

Shoeburyness This is a very small, but interesting, Southend Branch Library in that it shares common access with a Community Hall with which it is integrated in the same building. Together with shops these are in a pedestrian precinct at the focal point of a new estate of some 1,600 dwellings some being built by the local authority and the remainder privately. The total catchment area however is reckoned at 7,000. An old peoples' home and a pub are included in the complex and there are local schools nearby; all are served by a bus route into Southend's town centre some five miles away.

The view of the buildings from the car park, which is at the rear, looks forbidding; the series of inter-linked single-storey octagonal shapes of fired brickwork present something of a 'fortress' image; but within the precinct, the frontage is lightened and, happily, boldly announces its identity.

At the time of our visit, near midday, the hall (which even with such close proximity is not under library control) was a-bustle with young children while mothers waited to collect them: to the right the library with a few borrowers, presented a more sedate atmosphere. But if at other times it has some of the same activity, its 1,500 ft^2 (140 m^2) could soon prove to be too small. Perhaps as it has been open only a few months, use is not yet high.

Though small, the furnishing is of good quality, with Flotex carpeting while the warm sapele woodwork contrasts well against the dappled light facing brick walls and narrow floor-to-ceiling windows. The limited natural light virtually requires full-time artificial fluorescent lighting; heating which is fed from mechanical convectors, thermostatically controlled, is from district supply, the cost being recharged to the Libraries Department.

The Community Hall facilities comprise a main hall for 200 people, a stage, dressing (or meeting) rooms, kitchen, toilets, etc.

Corringham This branch is included although it was opened a few weeks before the period covered by this review. It had not been notified to us until recently but it was decided to visit and print because anything from Thurrock well deserves to be considered.

Corringham, which is in East Thurrock, had a Branch Library but, with considerable development of the area, it has reached 15,000 population and is still rising. A new shopping centre was built, but this was a mile or so away from the old Branch Library. Many of the residents work at the oil refineries, the docks at Tilbury or at one of the light industrial firms in the vicinity; this town is also conveniently situated for commuting to London or Southend.

The library has a well planned and quite generously sized site, giving a single ground floor area of nearly 500 m^2 and this is no more than a few yards away from essential shops. It has a wide frontage of rustic textured brown brick, well announced as a library in large white letters and with a generous breadth of glass and hardwood doors and windows for the entrance, which is

well canopied. It is good to see hardwood used for doors as this wears so much better than painted softwood which always becomes tatty with wear.

One proceeds through a smaller display area than one would expect, leading into a wide and deep open-plan library with excellent natural lighting. The walls are of brick and blockwork with windows framed in aluminium while the ceiling, which is low over the counter and the children's area is higher in the adult circulation sections by a series of pitched roofs with exposed pine boarding, supported by an intriguing series of laminated timber columns and beams which give a warm and friendly look to the whole space. The fluorescent lighting is fixed to the exposed timber trusses at the base intersections and the light reflecting off the warm timber colour, in turn produces a pleasing effect. The flooring is of vinyl tiles laid in a well thought-out four-colour pattern in order to link and define the main public areas. Though well maintained and attractive colourwise, the problems of cleaning vinyl tiles are now so generally recognised that it is surprising to come across a library using this finish when so many cheap carpets are available, and, in any case, produce a warmer and quieter atmosphere. The decision to have electric underfloor heating may have influenced this.

The children's area has a good outlook through several wide floor-to-ceiling windows and space provision here is very favourable, being nearly 80% of that allocated to adult lending.

GKVT   HW

Authority	Essex County Council, formerly Southend-on-Sea County Borough
Designation	Shoeburyness Branch
Date of opening	October 1974
Population served	4,000
Name of Architect	N P Astins, RIBA, succeeded by R Horswell, DipArch, RIBA, Borough Architect; J Breavington, RIBA, Original Design; D Cracknell, MSAAT, Project Assistant
Name of Librarian	L Helliwell, FLA
Special features:	
a) site	In pedestrianised shopping precinct which includes old peoples' home; library linked with community hall
b) architecture	Interlinked octagonal shapes; load-bearing brick construction
c) function	Community service
Mechanical Services:	
a) heating	Gas-fired low pressure hot water
b) ventilation	Natural
c) lighting	Fluorescent strip
d) acoustics	Carpeted
e) other	—
Areas: in square metres	
a) lending	88
b) reference	} in (a)
c) reading	
d) special activities	—
e) children	in (a)
f) control	7
g) library staff admin.	23
h) exhibitions	—
i) lecture hall	—
j) circulation	7
k) services	in community hall
l) lavatories	6
m) stack	7
Total area:	138
Book volumes:	
a) adult lending	}
b) adult reference	
c) children	} 8,000
d) stack	
e) other	}
Total:	8,000
Costs in £ p:	
a) site	—
b) building	} 18,508 Library only
c) furniture & fittings	} 3,891
Total Cost (ex fees):	£22,399
Cost per square metre:	£162

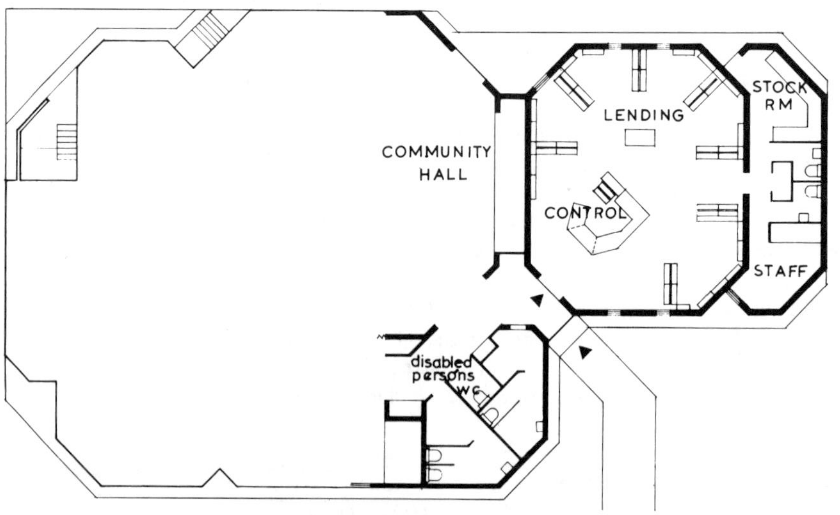

GROUND FLOOR

Authority	Essex County Council, formerly Thurrock Borough Council
Designation	Corringham Branch Library
Date of opening	November, 1972
Population served	15,000
Name of Architect	D C Vane, RIBA, Borough Architect; J Penwarden, RIBA, Job Architect
Name of Librarian	D A Wickham, FLA
Special features:	
a) site	At termination of shopping precinct overlooking open area
b) architecture	Timber laminated columns and beams; facing brickwork cavity walls
c) function	Branch to serve western area
Mechanical Services:	
a) heating	Electrical underfloor; wall thermostats
b) ventilation	Natural
c) lighting	Modular fluorescent
d) acoustics	White fissured ceiling tiles
e) other	—
Areas: in square metres	
a) lending	⎫ 212
b) reference	⎭
c) reading	—
d) special activities	—
e) children	80
f) control	108
g) library staff admin.	23
h) exhibitions	—
i) lecture hall	—
j) circulation	26
k) services	5
l) lavatories	10
m) stack	28
Total area:	492
Book volumes:	
a) adult lending	10,500
b) adult reference	1,000
c) children	4,500
d) stack	—
e) other	gr
Total:	16,000
Costs in £ p:	
a) site	N/A
b) building	39,902
c) furniture & fittings	5,706
Total Cost (ex fees):	£45,608
Cost per square metre:	£92

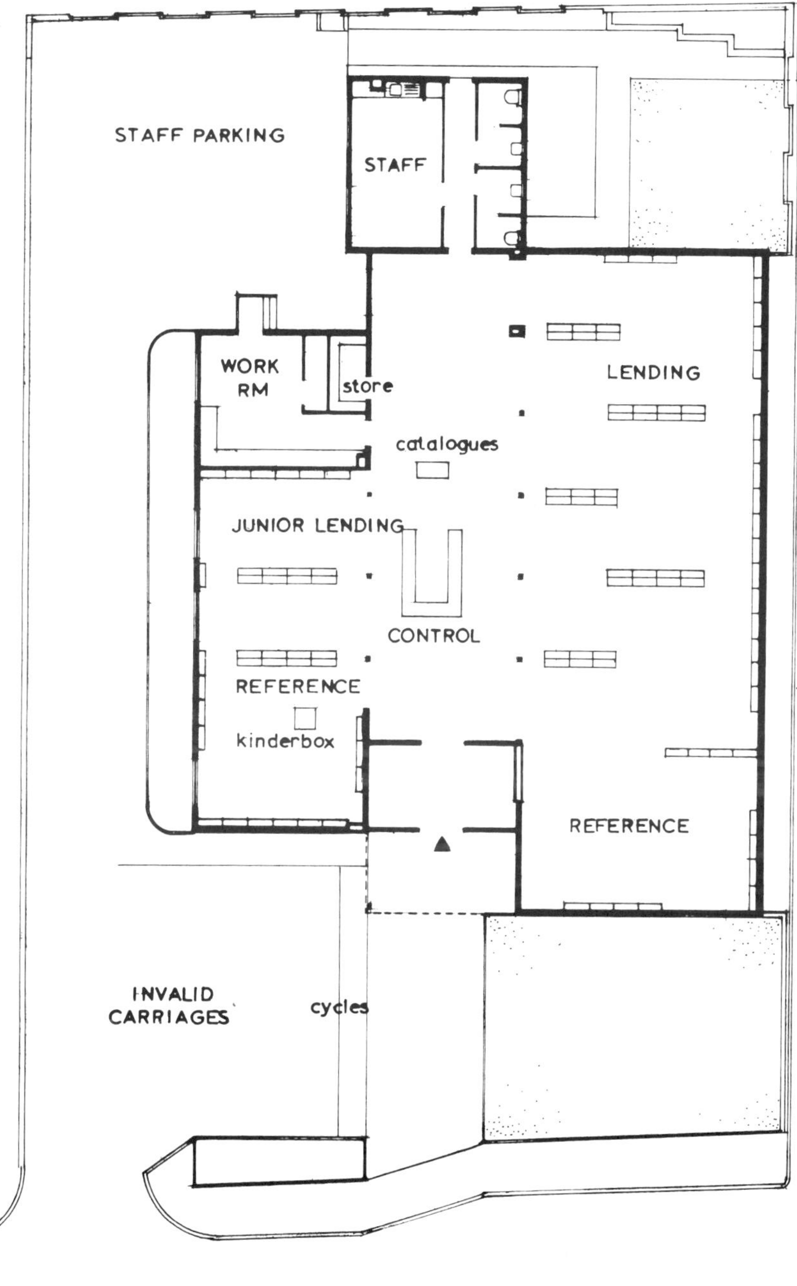

GROUND FLOOR

Corringham

Hampshire County Council:
Farnborough, Fleet, Yateley, Fareham, Waterlooville and Stubbington

Rushmoor District Central Library, Farnborough Farnborough forms parts of a now almost continuous urban area crossing county boundaries and including Camberley, Frimley, Aldershot and Farnham. It is thirty miles from London along the M3. Although by far the biggest and most important single feature of the town is the enormous Royal Aircraft Establishment, there is also much light industry. The fast train service to Waterloo Station inevitably encourages many London commuters to live here. Development of the town centre is everywhere apparent, with very large blocks of shops and supermarkets rising to the north of the new library, temporary roadworks lacing the whole area. It is, certainly for the present, very unfortunate for the library that its site lies amidst all this chaos and the approach could hardly be more unwelcoming than it was when we saw it, though the eventual completion of the overall planning intention should very much transform this situation.

The contrast between the library entrance and the very well signposted, wide and inviting entrance to the neighbouring new sports and recreation centre is marked, for due partly no doubt to the adoption of a SCOLA Mark II system, the library has a really rather obscure, narrow and quite unassertive front door, without even a canopy to draw attention to it. The restriction of the road also forces the entrance steps and wheelchair ramp into a totally inadequate space for such a major building. It is surely possible that these drawbacks will in some way be remedied when the planning improvements are completed (maybe before this book is published).

Viewed externally the architecture of the building is rather neutral, expressing the plain rectangular plan on two floors. The first floor is faced with rather pleasant crisp white precast-concrete panels with projecting ribs and narrow slot windows at intervals. This is above a curtain-walled base of windows with grey metal panels, under and between, in galvanised steel frames on a dark brick plinth. Some of the paintwork on the panels already looks much the worse for wear and will prove a continuing maintenance problem. A large entrance porch with big mats and a space for prams, with notice boards on one wall, leads into a low entrance and exhibition gallery.

Immediately upon entering the library one cannot fail to respond more appreciatively, for beyond the low entrance with a carefully designed counter facing it, the centre of the building rises through two storeys to a high-ceilinged rectangular space with clerestory windows on all sides surrounded by galleries. At a glance one takes in the form of the building and much of the planning. Lending services are all on this floor with a Children's Department to the right beyond the counter and with Reference Library, a Music Library, offices and staff rooms at first floor level.

Exhibitions have a long open space allocated to the left of the entrance area and this can, when desired, be used in the evenings for meetings. Largely for this reason lavatories are provided immediately to the right of the entrance. It seems unfortunate, however, that no provision has been made for any facilities for refreshments in connection with the meetings room functions,

though a little-used store which opens off the space could have provided convenient accommodation for this purpose. Close to the main entrance doors a coin-operated Xerox 422 copying machine offers a very useful service.

The design of the Lending Library counter appears to satisfy the needs of the workload and the staff's requirements, despite the fact that it is, if anything, a little smaller than that at Fleet (book issues c. 420,000 per annum as compared with Farnborough's 600,000). There seems ample space for trolleys and plenty of counter length to accommodate the Browne-system issue trays. It seems more likely that the Fleet counter is too large.

We do not regret, repeatedly, to find in so many new library buildings what can only be thought a distinct want of lively imagination in the planning of children's libraries. A separate department has been provided here, but beyond the presence of a number of diminutive chairs there is, unaccountably where so many matters of design and decor have been well handled, none of the feeling of warmth, of the kind of attractiveness to make a special appeal to children. It is over-formal, even severe in a dull way; the display facilities, of such major importance in a children's library, are surprisingly inadequate. No doubt some changes in location, during the planning stages, are partly to blame. Three recessed study carrels used now as enclosed listening cubicles are, it seems, an unavoidable residue of earlier planning intentions which originally sited reference services in this part of the building.

A stair in the high, open, centre section of the Lending Library leads directly to the Reference Library gallery. It is somewhat disappointing to find that the natural lighting here is very limited, for though there are many rooflights they are of a curious form which looks large enough at ceiling level but rapidly diminishes to a very small opening at the top. This undoubtedly overcomes problems of glare but cuts down useful light to such an extent that artificial lighting is needed to supplement it.

Plenty of seating is provided at this level, with a range of desk carrels for the use of language instruction and other cassettes. Adjoining this area, an enclosed room at present used for the music collection is designed eventually to become a music and gramophone record library. Two sizable listening rooms at present used as stores seem a useful idea but are without special acoustic treatment—there must be a doubt about the possibility of disturbance to the whole library. It is understood that the issue of gramophone records would be from the main counter.

A large reserve stack accommodating some 12,000 volumes occupies the west side of the building. The staff offices and staff room open off a narrow gallery overlooking the central well facing south. The staff room has a separate small kitchen and is of very reasonable size for the staff of 17. In summer, ventilation seems to be distinctly less than adequate and the building, we were told, tends to get unpleasantly hot. The internal well takes on a conservatory-like quality, for there is no means of shading the high-level windows. The largely uncompartmented ground-floor space, with this central well opening on to the upper levels,

Farnborough

Authority	Hampshire County Council
Designation	Rushmoor Central Library and District HQ, formerly Farnborough
Date of opening	December 1973
Population served	50,000
Name of Architect	H Benson Ansell, CBE, TD, RIBA, FRSA
Name of Librarian	R R Lawson, FLA
Special features:	
a) site	Adjacent to shopping precinct in town centre
b) architecture	Steel frame with pre-cast concrete floors; Scola standardised building system
c) function	Main library service to town and surrounding areas
Mechanical Services:	
a) heating	Gas-fired to low pressure hot water radiators
b) ventilation	Natural
c) lighting	Fluorescent strip behind translucent panels
d) acoustics	Carpeted
e) other	—
Areas: in square metres	
a) lending	465
b) reference	280
c) reading	in (b)
d) special activities	70
e) children	232
f) control	in (a)
g) library staff admin.	78
h) exhibitions	93
i) lecture hall	—
j) circulation	315
k) services	in (j)
l) lavatories	in (j)
m) stack	352
Total area:	1,885
Book volumes:	
a) adult lending	30,000
b) adult reference	4,000
c) children	6,500
d) stack	12,000
e) other	—
Total:	52,500
Costs in £ p:	
a) site	—
b) building	147,524
c) furniture & fittings	20,000
Total Cost (ex fees):	£167,524
Cost per square metre:	£89

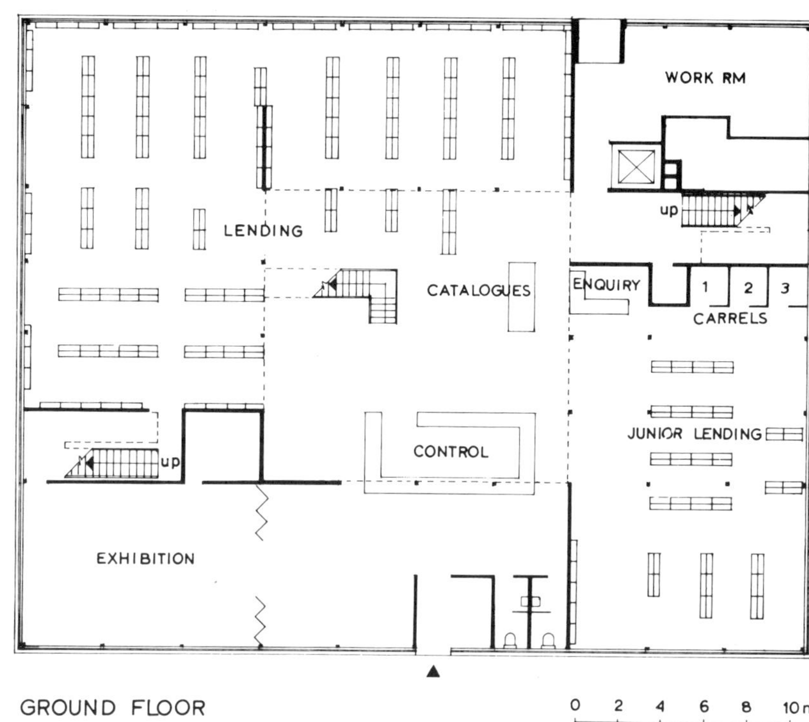

GROUND FLOOR

0 2 4 6 8 10m

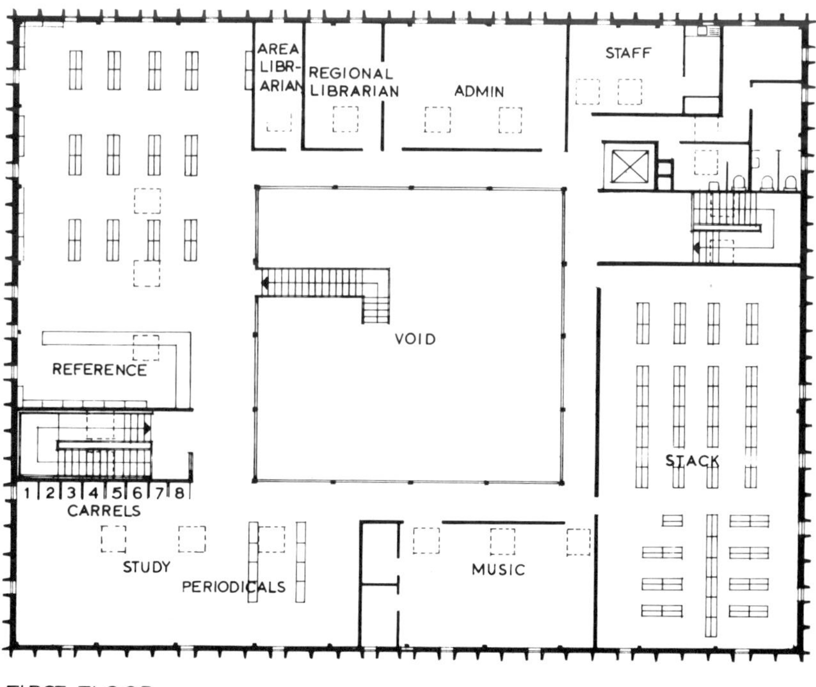

FIRST FLOOR

one of the most striking features of the building aesthetically, must have presented problems in making fire-escape arrangements, although smoke detectors are installed throughout the building.

Hart District Central Library, Fleet Hampshire's new library in Fleet is fortunate in having an ideal site in this town of about 28,000 people. It lies some way back from the main shopping street from which it is directly entered, with good space for car parking. The site is shared with a community centre which has a large public hall, meetings facilities and an old peoples' welfare centre. Beyond is a large and pleasant park.

Approaching the library from the main street, Fleet Street, one's attention is drawn to a covered way beneath the first floor link between the community centre and library. This leads to the main entrance to the public halls: signposting to the library entrance is not very clear. The doors into the library are actually on the side facing Fleet Street but, at present, tucked away behind a large Victorian house which used to serve as the library. The planning intention is that this will be demolished to make way for a double-sided shopping arcade with pedestrian access, with the front doors of the library directly at the end in clear view. When the intended plan has eventually been carried out, it is to be hoped that rather better signposting and altogether more emphasis on the library's presence will be provided, perhaps with a canopy for an enlarged entrance.

Why are so many of our new libraries so self-effacing, so reluctant to declare their importance to the community? It is really not fair of us to load the burden of this heartfelt question on to Fleet, where there is a most evident explanation for its temporary low-profile entrance and approaches. But too many other pages of this book say just the same and so do many in the earlier *New library buildings* volumes. We risk abuse as the most blatant of would-be advertisers. 'You must shout', we say, like the equivocal TV commercial; 'Simply an honest face is *not* good enough'.

Fleet's is one of those many new libraries overtaken by local government reorganisation. In 1960, the UDC decided to proceed with a scheme for a complete Civic Centre comprising new offices, Council Chamber, Assembly Hall, Library, shopping precinct and car parks. The library, however, has become a headquarters for the Hart District of the county. The revised brief called for comprehensive planning of the library and the assembly hall so that both buildings could be used as one. To achieve this the bridge link at first floor level, already referred to, and close to it two committee-sized rooms for joint use, were introduced. Services were also jointly provided.

Library accommodation is on two floors with the Lending and Children's sections at ground level and Reference at first floor level. The staff areas, incorporating a parking and loading space for the District's Mobile Library, lie at the south-west end of the building on both floors. The floors are connected by a staircase, fully enclosed, though with generously glazed screens, and at the other end of the library a lift. There is not the open visual connection between the floors, such as forms an attractive

feature of the same authority's Farnborough library. Problems of fire risk are, however, reduced—an interesting comparison.

The Lending Library, which has large windows on both sides, is extensive enough to necessitate permanent artificial lighting. The Children's section has the most attractive corner, with windows on two sides and with no major division between it and the general lending library. An unusually large counter area is generous enough to accommodate three or four staff, with plenty of space for book trolleys and for movement generally. This has its advantages when the library is busy and heavily staffed but may not be so satisfactory when one or two staff have to attend to the whole area.

The Reference Library is as large as the Lending and much better lighted by numerous rooflights which are concealed by plastic laylights flush with and integrated into the Treetex Glacier mineral fibre tiles of the ceiling. Fluorescent lights are placed in the rooflight opening above the diffuser, so that it is hard to tell whether one is enjoying natural or artificial light. This is a most satisfactory feature and produces a cheerful atmosphere more evident here than in the Lending Library.

The design of the external walls on this floor leads to an attractive arrangement of windows, leaving recesses between. It is a pity that more use has not been made of these for desks, seats or other forms of furnishing which could, with imagination, have provided a very lively and interesting feature of the building.

Staff are well provided for, with an attractive staff room in the sunny south-west corner, well and comfortably furnished and with excellent facilities. The only slight disappointment is that the lockers, which could very easily have been incorporated into the bays in the external walls are, instead, of rather workaday appearance in steel which detracts somewhat from the room's quality. The Librarian's office, opening directly to the Reference Library, has been provided with an escape route on to the stair at this end of the building, which leads down to a staff entrance through which books are also delivered and off which access is gained to the workroom in which the good natural lighting from a sloping rooflight at one side is supplemented by small slit windows which provide pleasant openings to the outside world. The rooflight does, in summer, apparently generate a good deal of solar heat, which has to be countered by using blinds. Remploy rolling stacks are placed against the inside wall of the workroom which has reserve stock accommodation for some 7,000 books.

In view of the fact that this library acts as the District Headquarters for Hart District which runs a mobile library van, the lack of proper loading bay provision, or even a canopy covering the staff and deliveries' entrance, is surprising.

Yateley Branch and School Library This new library is the third to be opened within a year in the Hart District Council area, following the new Central Library in Fleet (qv) and converted premises at Odiham in August (not separately considered here). Opened in October 1974, this branch provides not only a basic

Authority	County of Hampshire
Designation	Fleet Library (Hart District Library HQ)
Date of opening	January 1974
Population served	28,000
Name of Architect	Evans and Roberts (Winchester) in conjunction with County Architect
Name of Librarian	R R Lawson, FLA
Special features:	
a) site	Set back from main road
b) architecture	To blend with adjacent civic halls
c) function	Serving the community of Fleet
Mechanical Services:	
a) heating	Oil-fired low pressure water from civic halls
b) ventilation	Natural
c) lighting	Recessed fluorescent strip
d) acoustics	Acoustic tiled ceilings
e) other	—
Areas: in square metres	
a) lending	515
b) reference	93
c) reading	46
d) special activities	—
e) children	186
f) control	72
g) library staff admin.	93
h) exhibitions	—
i) lecture hall	—
j) circulation	54
k) services	36
l) lavatories	36
m) stack	54
Total area:	1,185
Book volumes:	
a) adult lending	40,282
b) adult reference	2,588
c) children	14,832
d) stack	7,196
e) other	Language cassettes
Total:	64,898
Costs in £ p:	
a) site	—
b) building	119,748
c) furniture & fittings	14,000
Total Cost (ex fees):	£133,748
Cost per square metre:	£113

public library service for the area, but serves as the library of Yateley Comprehensive School, which it directly adjoins. This is a large school, with over 1,800 pupils and some 200 staff. Joint library provision with the new school was first broached in 1968 and represents a new venture for the County Library service, with the Branch Librarian, who is on the County Library staff, being also responsible for the School Library service.

Yateley is an expanded village (pop 20,000), very widely scattered, in attractive countryside. The village centre with its shops, church and pubs is about ¾ mile from the school and library. Until the new building was opened, Yateley was served by a mobile library and then by a temporary service point in the village hall. The present site is immediately adjacent to a complex which includes a community centre as well as the school and its swimming pool, available to the public at weekends. The centre houses adult education and other meetings facilities, as well as the offices of the local district council. It appears to be intensively used, so that the apparent separation of the site from the village centre is less of a drawback than at first suggests.

Open until 7 pm three nights a week, the new library is busy for a branch of this size, with book issues of about 200,000 a year, a third of which are to children. At lunchtimes the chidren swarm in and it becomes very much the school's library.

Yateley is quite evidently an area with a preponderance of young families in the large new housing estates, but enterprising arrangements are made to bring coachloads of old people to the library for regular visits. Tea and biscuits are provided by sixth-formers from the school, who make themselves responsible for looking after the old people on their way to and from their home.

From the road, the library is rather self-effacing and is set amidst a positive muddle of service roads, car parks and wire fences. These detract from the pleasant impression made by the surrounding school playing-fields. The form adopted for the building consists of two superimposed pentagons offset one above the other. Clerestory lights round the centre pentagon give good daylighting. The outer spaces, beyond the raised centre pentagon roof, accommodate various functions ancillary to those of the main library room: a reference section, Children's Library, staff workroom, entrance hall and school study room for use by children working in the library on projects. The exterior, in heather-brown brickwork, has a series of slit windows in the low block with white plastic weather boarding above, the fascia of the pentagon being in a similar material. A cobbled strip divides the building from the adjoining paths, car park and grassed areas. Entrance is by means of a small, oddly-shaped lobby, with pin-boarding for notices, and involving a slight change in ground level which necessitates some steps and an awkwardly placed steep ramp for wheelchairs. The large entrance canopy seems poorly detailed and untidy.

The main library, under the inner pentagon, has the counter in the centre, also of pentagonal shape. It is too small and cramped, but supervision is excellent. The Children's Library is at the same level but beneath the lower ceiling, whilst the

reference section is at a raised level, also under the low roof. Structurally the roof is supported on a deep central beam with other beams radiating to the corners of the pentagon and to the centres of each side. The steel beams are exposed and painted and the ceiling lined with Parana pine, with a strip of the same timber in short vertical lengths beneath the high-level windows. This latter looks rather insubstantial, an applied cosmetic treatment. Walls are finished sensibly in vinyl wall covering and the floor has blue nylon carpeting. Doors are faced with a cheap mahogany, frames are of Parana pine and yet another timber is used for the ends of the bookcases and the counter. The result is over-fussy.

The staff workroom, with space for some reserve stock material, is a well lighted room with strip windows overlooking and overlooked from the entrance and car park. No separate staff restroom is provided and a corner of the workroom therefore has to suffice for this purpose, a surprising arrangement which is not satisfactory. There are no curtains, so that staff not only have no privacy within the building but no protection from teasing children or prying eyes outside. A poorly designed kitchen corner with a curious sink, more appropriate for a laboratory, does nothing to modify the impression that staff needs have been too little considered. When the building was first opened no staff lavatory was included, the staff being apparently expected to use the facilities in the neighbouring Community Centre. An intended store has now been converted for this purpose so that, whilst the lavatory problem is now solved, presumably the building is short on storage.

There are other surprises. Amongst these are a long flat bench with no back, set immediately across the face of a large ground-length window, a surely dangerous position. Also a damp proof course which has been bridged, by an apparently afterthought ramping of the tarmac of the exterior path, seemingly to give trolley or wheelchair access to a rear escape door.

We thought the services of this library and their relationship to the school and the social fabric of the village most enterprising. It achieved a very pleasant, welcoming air and a feeling of enthusiasm for what it had to offer, but we were surprised at the apparent lack of detailed consideration given to solving practical problems.

LHS   GKVT

Fareham Visiting new libraries during the last four years there has, understandably, been a wide range of initial impressions gained from each building as one approached it. Some immediately indicate a 'winner'; some a conundrum, others a feeling of further mediocrity. Fareham, visited in midsummer 1975 was, at that time, unique in its situation at the focal point within a midstream of development which was going on with speed and determination, even on a Saturday morning. But reaching this focal point by car posed some problems in the town's strict one-way system, but it was accomplished by stopping on a double yellow line and awaiting the approach of a policeman—an understanding one, willing to help, happily! So, going *through* a car park, then winding slowly along a narrow

Authority	County of Hampshire
Designation	Yateley Public and School Library
Date of opening	October 1974
Population served	20,000
Name of Architect	Stansfield Smith
Name of Librarian	R R Lawson, FLA
Special features:	
a) site	Within complex of school, community centre (adult education) and swimming pool
b) architecture	Steel-framed pentagon
c) function	Service to public and to staff and pupils, within school
Mechanical Services:	
a) heating	Electric underfloor
b) ventilation	Natural
c) lighting	Fluorescent strip
d) acoustics	Carpeted
e) other	—
Areas: in square metres	
a) lending	
b) reference	} 372
c) reading	
d) special activities	36
e) children	in (a)
f) control	—
g) library staff admin.	36
h) exhibitions	—
i) lecture hall	—
j) circulation	10
k) services	5
l) lavatories	5
m) stack	—
Total area:	464
Book volumes:	
a) adult lending	12,125
b) adult reference	300
c) children	8,380
d) stack	573
e) other	—
Total:	21,378
Costs in £ p:	
a) site	—
b) building	60,400
c) furniture & fittings	5,250
Total Cost (ex fees):	£65,650
Cost per square metre:	£142

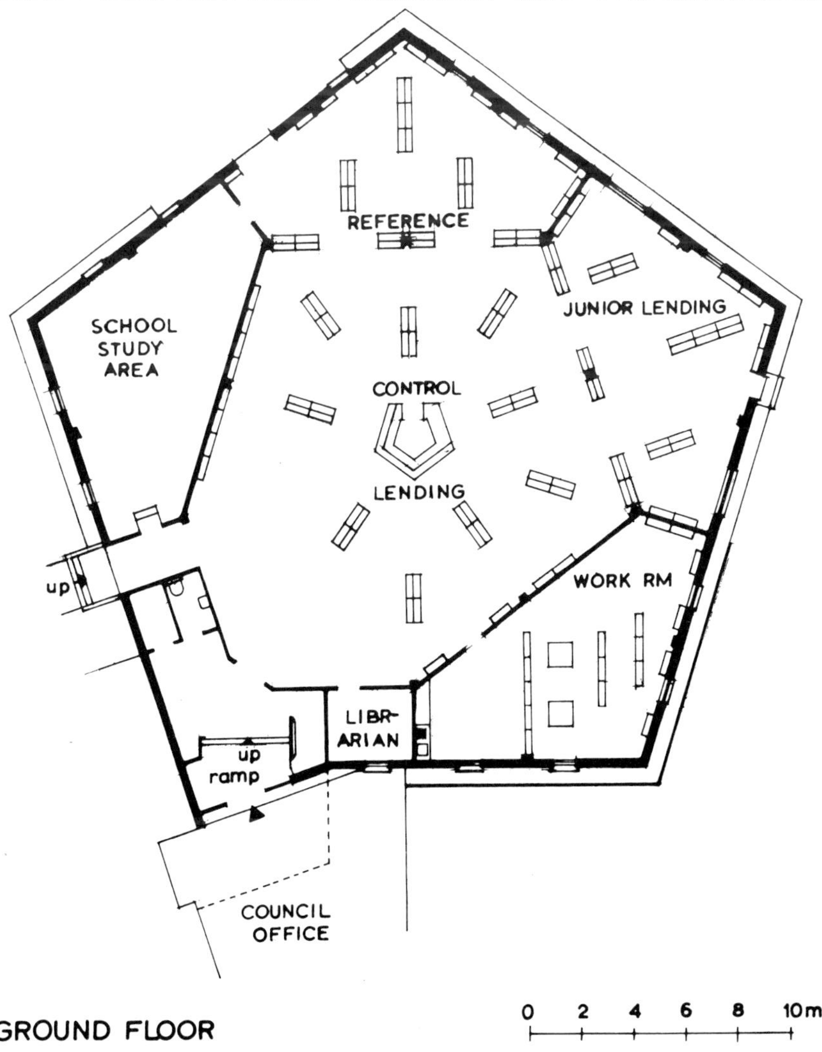

GROUND FLOOR

temporary roadway, it was possible to park behind a large complex within the construction, (part of it to be a Health Centre it was afterwards learned). Then by walking through a narrow passageway one emerged into an open area where a bulldozer was busily a-scooping, while ahead lay the library—although not identifiable as such at that distance. No doubt it will all be clearer and simpler when the development is completed, for the library is excellently located within the shopping precinct, an administrative complex and with a multi-storey car park at the rear.

This library is a three-storeyed building with a front elevation unusual in the building materials used—a variety of brick and of window patterns, (picture windows at ground level contrasting with the fifteen narrow vertical windows at an upper floor). Zinc, wood and grey plastic form a range of materials which are immediately noticeable. Within the entrance the use of rough, poorly finished wood in strips, sparsely painted light blue, provided a shock. Although the building has not been open long, the exterior (particularly the woodwork) is weathering badly due, it was stated, to the salt from the sea and the frequent gales and rain which had been experienced during the preceding winter; this accounted no doubt for the rusting of the not-so-effective exterior sign. The availability of a Careers Office within the building was much more prominently proclaimed!

Inside the building, the adult Lending Library was oppressive—in part, no doubt, due to the time of day for this was nearly midday on a summer (average 4,000 issue) Saturday. But the low coffered ceiling, sprayed with asbestos fibre, seemed to bear down. The carpet (nylon) was wisely a cool blue-green. In spite of the picture windows, near-overall fluorescent lighting was on, and needed; some upper areas were tungsten lit 'to create a more intimate atmosphere'. An L-shaped Children's Library is also at this level, the dividing walls being of block with plaster board partitions. This produced a far less warm atmosphere although a brown carpet and the sapele woodwork mitigated this. Coloured hessian display panels above the wall cases carried samples of children's art which were illuminated by movable spotlights. The stated need to use some furniture from the old library building in this Children's Library is indeed unfortunate.

At first floor there is a 60–70 seater Reference Library, but the provision of flat tables is rather unimaginative; nevertheless they were being well used. A private study facility of eight carrels and four audio-visual booths was noticed. Exhibition and meeting rooms occupy the second floor, (although there was an exhibition of local art being erected in the Lending Library), with stock, workroom and staff accommodation at this level too. Heating is from the Health Centre (oil-fired, low pressure hot water) and there is some mechanical ventilation for the inner rooms.

This was a 'good in parts' building. Some of the 'not-so-good' was due to the fact that the resultant contractors had to take on the work at short notice in order to meet a deadline because the previous library just had to close on a fixed date. Having to construct and complete, we were told, within 12 months, provides a reason for the lack of quality workmanship, but one

is still left with the feeling that some of the finishes were so terribly skimped as not to have been acceptable.

Waterlooville In spite of the helpful provision of a sketch map, this library was difficult to find when driving up the A3 after making the other Hampshire visits: even an enquiry from a local person sent me in the wrong direction! Three traversings of the main street did not show up any 'Library' directional sign; happily, in a side road a milkman directed me to a large car park to the rear of a shopping precinct dominated by a sombre, almost forbidding building—three storeys of red brick, topped by another which is lead covered, while that is capped by a bulky lead-covered turret. The locals call it 'Colditz' I was told—but in Waterlooville 'Colditz' has a pub next door! The library is of framed reinforced concrete construction faced externally with brown hand-made brick.

The entrance to the library is within the precinct, which is itself pleasing, with raised plant beds, seats and lighting columns for good illumination in the winter. Only one set of doors to the library entrance, and another question produced an equally frank answer—'freezing in winter', especially at peak times when the control area cannot cope with the crush'! The greenhouse shaped glass roof to this hall must also give extremes of temperature. A large display case has in fact been moved to a second storey landing to give maximum circulation space. An attractive first impression though, with plants and blue paving bricks visible through the tinted glass walls. The sole counter (for all issuing) has a light oak wood fascia with hessian panels, down almost to head height; downlighters give supplementary assistance over the discharging sections. Glass partitions to the front and back of a workroom set behind this counter give staff supervision over the 'Popular' library, which has full carpeting, wood strip ceiling (with glass fibre behind), wall-to-wall fluorescent strip lighting on tracking; shelving here and throughout is LDE.

The Accessions/Workroom lies beyond, where deliveries come straight in through a separate entrance, lift access to upper floors being adjacent. Immediately above this area is the Reserve stock room (rolling stacks) while the main area at this level is the Children's Library with separate activities room. Glass partitioning provides a very spacious homework and study area and children's reference collection. A most attractive feature here (and above in the main Reference Library too) is a bank of four 6 × 5 ft glass display cases well illuminated and tastefully arranged with objects and related books.

Above is the main non-fiction stock which leads into a Local History Section and the Main Reference and study area (approx 3,000 vols). Two carrels, large enough to accommodate wheelchaired persons, project out beyond the main elevation producing, when viewed from the outside, unnecessary excrescences, windowed but with their lead covering merely looking dark and hideous. Another depressing feature, this time internally is the emulsioned brickwork on the narrow public staircases which would be more in keeping with poorer tenement housing blocks, not leading out of carpeted areas. Admittedly it

Authority	County of Hampshire
Designation	Fareham District Library
Date of opening	July 1973
Population served	75,000
Name of Architect	Benson Ansell, CBE, TD, RIBA, County Architect in collaboration with Taylor Woodrow
Name of Librarian	R R Lawson, FLA
Special features:	
a) site	Adjacent to shopping precinct and multi-storey car park
b) architecture	—
c) function	Serving large town and surrounding areas; controls branches
Mechanical Services:	
a) heating	Oil-fired low pressure hot water; shared with health centre
b) ventilation	Natural
c) lighting	Fluorescent strip some tungsten and spotlights
d) acoustics	Carpeted; coffered ceiling; asbestos fibred
e) other	—
Areas: in square metres	
a) lending	577
b) reference	475
c) reading	—
d) special activities	—
e) children	242
f) control	—
g) library staff admin.	198
h) exhibitions	94
i) lecture hall	—
j) circulation	42
k) services	—
l) lavatories	32
m) stack	365
Total area:	2,439
Book volumes:	
a) adult lending	60,136
b) adult reference	8,368
c) children	21,667
d) stack	31,835
e) other	Linguaphone
Total:	122,006
Costs in £ p:	
a) site	—
b) building	294,017
c) furniture & fittings	26,000
Total Cost (ex fees):	£320,017
Cost per square metre:	£131

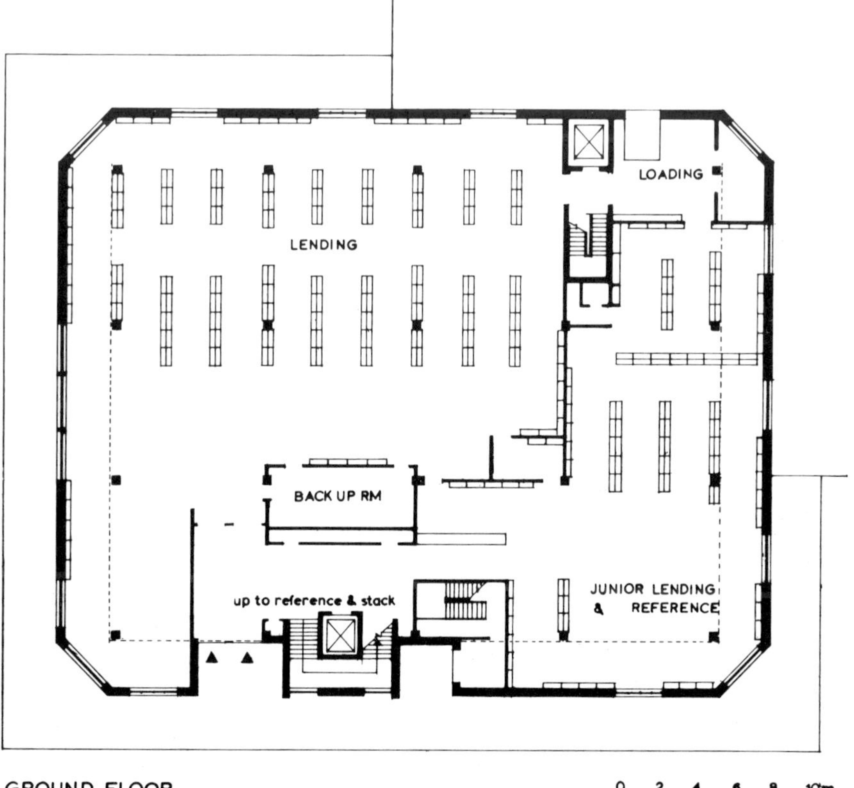

GROUND FLOOR

Authority	County of Hampshire
Designation	Waterlooville Branch Library
Date of opening	June 1973
Population served	36,000
Name of Architect	Benson Ansell, CBE, TD, RIBA, County Architect
Name of Librarian	R R Lawson, FLA
Special features:	
a) site	Limited, costly site in rear of shopping precinct
b) architecture	Framed reinforced concrete faced with hand-made brick; upper storeys clad in pseudo-lead
c) function	Branch service to large population
Mechanical Services:	
a) heating	Oil-fired; warm air
b) ventilation	Natural
c) lighting	Fluorescent strip; variable track
d) acoustics	Carpeted; softwood slatted ceilings with glass fibre
e) other	—
Areas: in square metres	
a) lending	356
b) reference	132
c) reading	55
d) special activities	22
e) children	164
f) control	20
g) library staff admin.	62
h) exhibitions	—
i) lecture hall	—
j) circulation	118
k) services	—
l) lavatories	26
m) stack	159
Total area:	1,114
Book volumes:	
a) adult lending	44,926
b) adult reference	1,561
c) children	17,763
d) stack	17,889
e) other	34
Total:	82,173
Costs in £ p:	
a) site	13,500
b) building	125,880
c) furniture & fittings	11,250
Total Cost (ex fees):	£150,630
Cost per square metre:	£135

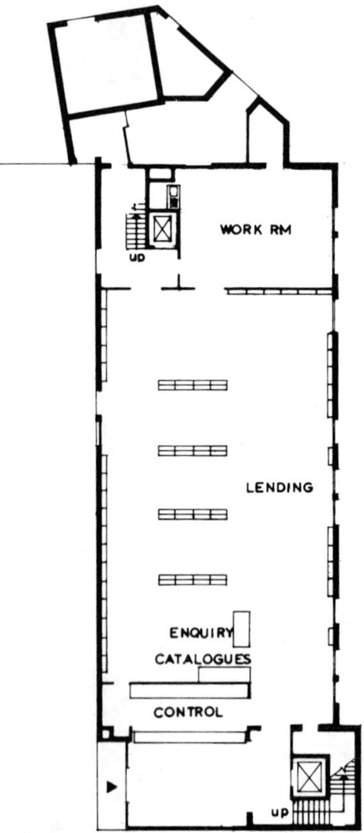

GROUND FLOOR

0 2 4 6 8 10m

was stated that the site, being ideal, was costly and this may
have needed special economies; supporting this is the claim that
a multi-storey building was required because of the limited size
of the site (certainly there is a distinct lack of depth) and that the
top floor had to be entirely allocated to the Social Services
Department, because the planned exhibition/meeting room was
ruled out for financial reasons–and perhaps the income from this
tenant is helpful!

Stubbington (pop 15,000) has a fairly high proportion of retired
people, while employment is mainly gained from Service
establishments at Lee-on-Solent and Hillhead or in Fareham or
Gosport. This library, which is a branch under the immediate
control of Fareham, opened in March 1974, has peak issues of
1,200 and a daily average of 700. Situated pleasantly in
parkland and facing tennis courts it is visible from the road
junction where shops and a pub are located. A round red brick
building of, perhaps, 80 ft diameter, its exterior is broken up by
protruding 'cogs', ample window space and with blue panels and
plinth below; each cog accommodates internally, a settee or
study table. The roof is pitched and is lined with wood strip

culminating in a central, circular wooden 'cap' with eight down
spotlights. Main lighting is by fluorescent, in parallel with the
wood strip.

The glass entrance itself is not very impressive, the fascia and
ceiling woodwork being of poor quality, but it leads into a more
pleasing interior, revealed by the low shelving. It is dominated by
a circular counter behind which (partitioned off) are the work
and staff areas occupying one whole quadrant of the circle. Wall
surfaces are exposed brick, with display panels in fair quantity.
Blue carpeting throughout and the underfloor heating (although
as often indicated, tiring to the feet) help to combat the low
temperatures in winter, but extremes in summer are also
experienced.

Reminiscent of Callington Library in Cornwall (see *New
Library Buildings 1974 issue,* pp 82–3), there is not the same
quality of materials but perhaps Callington's superiority was due
to part use by a comprehensive school–Education departments
are not usually so tight on funds!

HW

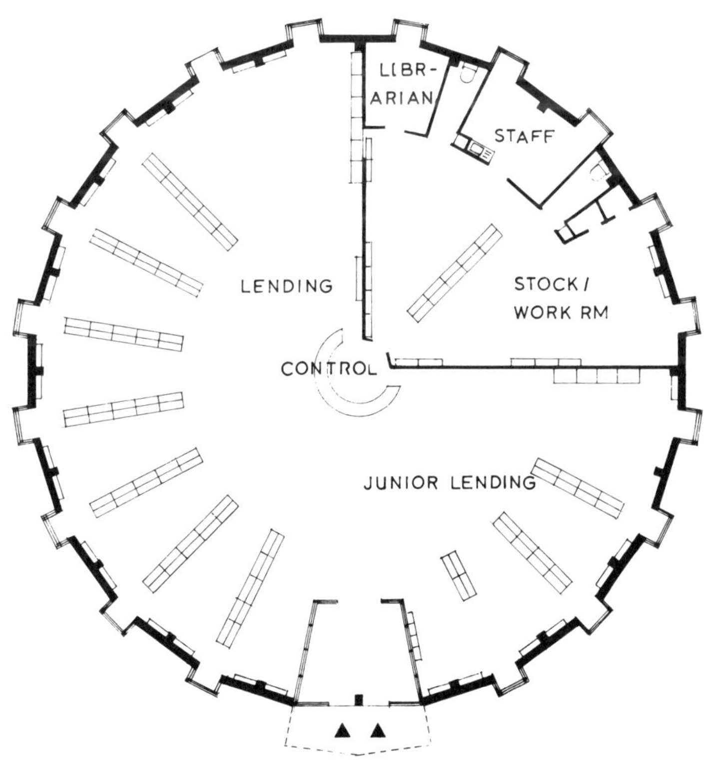

GROUND FLOOR

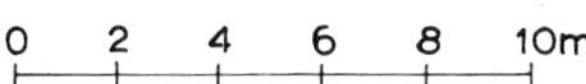

Stubbington
(No photograph or
statistics available)

Humberside County Council:
(formerly City and County of Kingston upon Hull) Ings:
(formerly East Riding County Council) Hornsea:
(formerly Lindsey and Holland County Council) Crowle and Messingham

Ings This is a library which was originally conceived in the early 1950's because of the considerable housing development in East Hull; but from that time the library service has had to be restricted to a part-time one located in a primary school in the vicinity. Now with a catchment population of 22,000, which includes the villages of Wawne and Brandsholme (nearly three miles away) a full-time library has become vital. Residents of those villages usually shop in East Hull on Saturdays and a bus service for this is provided.

This 6,000 ft² library serves as a district library and controls six branches including the book selection for them. Its position is good, being within a shopping precinct and with reasonable car parking; it is at the heart of substantial housing, with a council estate to the east and owner-occupied property to the west. Surprisingly, far less library use comes from the much larger council estate, although there is encouraging response by teenagers from that area.

It is an open-plan building with a slightly pitched ceiling of varnished wood strip. It is light and airy but concern was expressed by the Librarian at the way the tip-over windows can be opened by youngsters who have been caught passing books through to 'confederates' outside. The lack of good oversight from the control counter is also frustrating to the staff as the 'L'-shaped entrance hall is regularly vandalised when displays and exhibitions are mounted. Another unpopular feature is the underfloor heating which has proved very tiring for the staff.

The building gives an impression of incompleteness—certainly some furniture and equipment due 18 months ago (prior to local government reorganisation) had still not been delivered at the time of the visit, so that the workroom and offices were still not able to operate efficiently, and some 30 feet of wall space was without a single picture. That end of the building is devoted to a reference area deliberately left windowless 'to assist uninterrupted concentration', it was stated.

With the claim that this serves as a district library controlling six branches a greater capability could have been expected in respect of book stock, reference and information provision, facilities for extention activities etc. Limited to ground floor only, this does not compare well with library buildings visited and successfully operating a district responsibility.

Hornsea This is yet another scheme overtaken by the events of reorganisation, opening at the end of 1974, thus well into the life of the new Authority. Planned for a population of 10,000 this seaside town is swollen with holidaymakers during the summer, although in the heat of 1975 few of these took the opportunity to use the library. The resident population includes many commuters to Hull, which is less than 20 miles away and to Beverley or Bridlington, each about 15 miles distant. The flourishing Hornsea pottery industry caters for several hundred while in the outlying areas work is mainly agricultural.
Under reorganisation Hornsea is now but one of 96 libraries in the Humberside system, of which nearly two-thirds are north of the Humber.

The building is striking, modern and perhaps not to everyone's taste as the general character of the town is much older. The architectural scheme was mainly the work of an American exchange student located at East Riding County. Restricted to the size of the site on which a cinema formerly stood, it is a pity that some of the open space land to the rear (reached by a wide gravel path at the side of the library giving access also to a golf course beyond) could not have been obtained. The library thus needs to be on two floors with the exhibition and meeting rooms at the upper level and the Adult and Children's Lending and Reference services at ground floor.

Sad it must have been for the East Riding County Librarian, at the time of the commencing of building the library, to learn that the site had revealed on the demolition of the cinema an eight foot depth below ground level, hitherto unknown, which the contractor had energetically filled in with hard core; it was then deemed too late to reclaim that space for much needed basement storage. It could even have allowed space for, or by exchange with a meeting room, staff accommodation, which strangely is now non-existent. The only kitchen is part of a small room off the main exhibition/meeting room which, if hired by a society, could put that 'out of bounds' for full use by the staff as is normally required.

The contours of the building are far removed from the all-too-familiar box type, as the oriel windows buttress out, slate clad, from the reddish brickwork while, at the side, recessed picture windows with interior cills, on which stand plants, attract the eye. The entrance hall is limited, with almost the entire floor area (approx 15 ft × 5 ft) covered with coconut matting; the woodwork gives the first glimpse of a monotonous use of coral shade paintwork which continues throughout, and seems hardly to harmonise with the plum-coloured carpeting.

The new reader seems well catered for by a purpose-built one-off counter with readers' adviser's desk at the 'In' arm. Moderate space is provided to the side of that point for reference use and study (which pleasingly includes about 300 volumes of local history). Proceeding into the library it becomes crowded as it caters for a total stock of 22,000. The suspended ceiling at low height accentuates this feeling.

The Children's Section at the end is on a raised level and has a mini-'amphitheatre' of five raised carpeted steps in rectangular form for story hours etc. This can be curtained off and a range of eight down-spotlights can be used to effect. The walls were, at the time of the visit, hung with examples of local children's art. At one side of this feature is a guard rail to prevent children from the drop, while at the other is a long horse-shoe ramp for wheelchaired children; adjacent to this is a store room with roll-shuttering for deliveries, which, one felt, might be used for handicapped children to save their negotiating the length of the adult department to reach this ramp, as the one control counter at the entrance regulates all issues. The amount of shelving to cater for a children's issue of 150/200 per day seemed sparse as was the floor space when class visits are encouraged.

The first floor is reached by stairs from the entrance (or by lift for the handicapped) and, at the time of this visit, it had both rooms fully committed to a local art society's exhibition. Only the public toilets and a store cupboard remain on this floor. This brought to the fore the question of the best allocation of space within a building of limited area.

The demand from enthusiastic society members for exhibition and meeting areas needs to be met but the feeling must be that the prime need is for adequate space for main library use. This requires expansion of some sort, be it adjacent premises as soon as possible or—and this did not seem an impossibility, even if car access to the open space and golf course via the path at the side of the library were vital—to extend laterally at first floor level *over* that path, thus allowing car access to continue to the rear areas. Difficulties no doubt—not least the additional cost and possible planning doubts—but what a gain! With such extension there could be substantial areas for the Children's Library and its activities (much favoured at first floor level in several London libraries), as well as separate staff kitchen, restroom accommodation and a workroom. Reference and reading areas might also go to the raised level, which would indeed be quieter away from the bustle of the counter area. But do not let this detract from the value of the vastly improved library service that this new building has brought to a somewhat isolated community.

Crowle This is yet another library linked with a Health Centre and in this case there is a joint entrance. They serve a population of about 3,000, many being engaged in agricultural work (corn dollies were on display in the library) but others are employed in a potato and pea factory. There is a comprehensive school for 350 pupils and a junior school whose pupils use the library during its 29 hours of opening each week.

One's immediate impression is of a smaller area than expected and a feeling of being crowded. This would have been worsened but for the room height in the main area but there is a narrow concrete-slab mezzanine situated along the front wall which is reached by a wood-tread spiral staircase at the far corner of the room. The purpose is to provide three study sections and double seating in the window spaces.

The natural brick walls, vari-coloured, blend with the light brown carpet and there is plenty of colour from the books and displays. The counter with glass-fronted displays and the wood fittings are of West African mahogany.

Discussion with the local librarian revealed a disappointment with regard to the positioning of a staircase to the upper floor for an intended dental clinic as, in the form it finally took (in spite of strong representations made by the County Librarian) it cuts off considerable library space which had obviously been planned for Children's Library use. There was however still room for a medium sized workroom and reserve stock area on four rolling stacks.

Messingham seems a heavy building particularly when viewed from the side road where the roof 'cleavage' design (seen also at Sutton-on-Sea) here runs parallel, and not at right angles, to the frontage. With completely tiled roof too, the few windows fail to alleviate the solid look of the building.

This village is in a rural area six miles south of Scunthorpe and the library serves a population of about 2,000. The library is also related to a health centre and old peoples' dwellings and all have a common heating system.

HW

Authority	County of Humberside formerly City and County of Kingston upon Hull
Designation	Ings District Library
Date of opening	January 1974
Population served	20,000
Name of Architect	A R Peadon, BArch, RIBA, MRTPI, County Architect
Name of Librarian	D J Bryant, FLA
Special features:	
a) site	Within shopping centre on main ring road
b) architecture	Traditional
c) function	District library also controlling branches in East Hull
Mechanical Services:	
a) heating	Electric underfloor
b) ventilation	Natural
c) lighting	Fluorescent strip
d) acoustics	—
e) other	—
Areas: in square metres	
a) lending	
b) reference	} 160
c) reading	
d) special activities	11
e) children	77
f) control	in (a)
g) library staff admin.	86
h) exhibitions	28
i) lecture hall	—
j) circulation	15
k) services	in (g)
l) lavatories	18
m) stack	—
Total area:	395
Book volumes:	
a) adult lending	7,138
b) adult reference	295
c) children	4,969
d) stack	150
e) other	255 gr
Total:	12,807
Costs in £ p:	
a) site	2,600
b) building	43,000
c) furniture & fittings	8,000
Total Cost (ex fees):	£53,600
Cost per square metre:	£136

Authority	County of Humberside formerly County of East Riding
Designation	Hornsea Branch
Date of opening	December 1974
Population served	15,000
Name of Architect	A R Peadon, BArch, RIBA, MRTPI, County Architect; B G Shore, RIBA, Job Architect
Name of Librarian	R G Roberts, DMS, FLA, FIM Ent
Special features:	
a) site	Corner site, sloping up to rear; former cinema in main shopping street
b) architecture	ASC system; rationalised traditional construction
c) function	Serving whole catchment area
Mechanical Services:	
a) heating	Gas-fired low pressure hot water; radiators and fan convectors
b) ventilation	Natural for most areas
c) lighting	Fluorescent mainly; tungsten downlighters and spots
d) acoustics	Suspended mineral fibre ceiling tiles
e) other	—
Areas: in square metres	
a) lending	137
b) reference	56
c) reading	in (a)
d) special activities	13
e) children	68
f) control	6
g) library staff admin.	4
h) exhibitions	45
i) lecture hall	65
j) circulation	85
k) services	29
l) lavatories	9
m) stack	71
Total area:	598
Book volumes:	
a) adult lending	15,709
b) adult reference	702
c) children	4,227
d) stack	—
e) other	—
Total:	20,638
Costs in £ p:	
a) site	4,750
b) building	85,000
c) furniture & fittings	6,600
Total Cost (ex fees):	£96,350
Cost per square metre:	£162

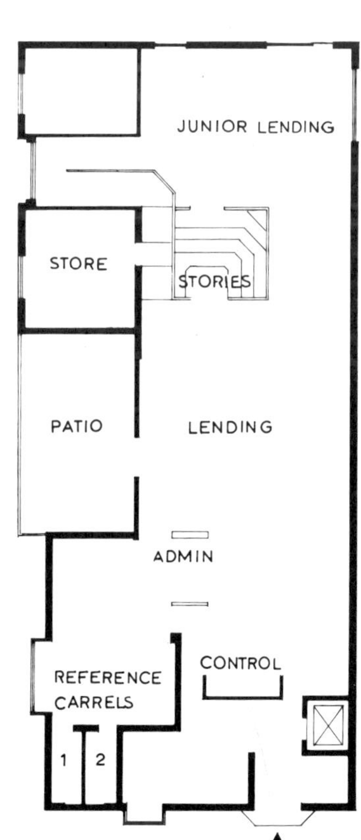

GROUND FLOOR

Authority	County of Humberside formerly Lindsey and Holland
Designation	Crowle Branch Library
Date of opening	July 1973
Population served	3,100
Name of Architect	A R I Aitken, RIBA, County Architect
Name of Librarian	E H Roberts, FLA
Special features:	
a) site	Corner site near main shopping and market square
b) architecture	Mainly brick construction
c) function	Serving village and surrounding rural area
Mechanical Services:	
a) heating	Oil-fired with fan boost
b) ventilation	Natural
c) lighting	Mainly fluorescent strip
d) acoustics	Carpeting; textured ceiling
e) other	—
Areas: in square metres	
a) lending	64
b) reference	29
c) reading	in (a)
d) special activities	—
e) children	13
f) control	10
g) library staff admin.	23
h) exhibitions	—
i) lecture hall	—
j) circulation	7
k) services	7
l) lavatories	2
m) stack	—
Total area:	155
Book volumes:	
a) adult lending	4,100
b) adult reference	220
c) children	1,650
d) stack	940
e) other	—
Total:	6,910
Costs in £ p:	
a) site	—
b) building	—
c) furniture & fittings	—
Total Cost (ex fees):	—
Cost per square metre:	—

Authority	County of Humberside formerly Lindsey and Holland
Designation	Messingham Branch Library
Date of opening	October 1974
Population served	2,225
Name of Architect	A R I Aitken, RIBA, County Architect
Name of Librarian	E H W Roberts, FLA
Special features:	
a) site	Near main road and adjacent to shops
b) architecture	Brick; sunken central roof section
c) function	Serving locality
Mechanical Services:	
a) heating	Central unit for health centre; old peoples' dwellings and library
b) ventilation	Natural
c) lighting	Fluorescent strip
d) acoustics	Carpeted
e) other	—
Areas: in square metres	
a) lending	50
b) reference	in (c)
c) reading	30
d) special activities	—
e) children	17
f) control	7
g) library staff admin.	14
h) exhibitions	1
i) lecture hall	—
j) circulation	5
k) services	2
l) lavatories	2
m) stack	2
Total area:	130
Book volumes:	
a) adult lending	3,500
b) adult reference	210
c) children	1,100
d) stack	620
e) other	—
Total:	5,430
Costs in £ p:	
a) site	Not known
b) building	14,400
c) furniture & fittings	2,800
Total Cost (ex fees):	£17,200
Cost per square metre:	£132

Kent County Council:
Faversham, Sandwich and Seal

These libraries offer an interesting cross section of building from small village libraries to a medium-sized central library.

Faversham is a small town of about 15,000 population close to the Medway towns of Rochester and Chatham set in rich agricultural land. It is close enough to London for morning commuters and has a predominantly middle class population with many retired people, to whom such a quiet town naturally appeals. Set close to the shopping centre the library enjoys a corner site twice the size of the building, so that it has been possible to place it between an enclosed grassed courtyard on one side and a largely paved garden with heathers and other attractive planting on the other side. This, together with a generous forecourt and roadway in front and with several car parking spaces behind ensures that the library is in a pleasant setting though the surrounding property is undistinguished.

The architecture has been kept in a low key, with brick walls and a flat roof on two levels, the Lending Library being higher than the surrounding Children's and Reference Libraries and staff accommodation. The garden walls surrounding the enclosed courts run up to form end walls which hide the roof.

Inside, the furniture layout in the Lending Library is unimaginatively arranged and the serried ranks of bookcases give an oppressively dense appearance, particularly as the bookshelving is too high to see over. Clerestory windows run right round the higher room producing good natural lighting and allowing sunlight to enter. Predictably this does make the library too hot in summer as there is no air conditioning, but it is certainly a welcome feature in other seasons. Finishes are sympathetic, timber shelving, concrete block walls, woodwool slab ceiling with perforated steel beams and, throughout, a rather dark purple nylon carpet.

The counter is, as so often found, rather muddled in conception with much cross circulation, but in fairness to the designers the way in which it now functions is different from when the brief was written. The location of the staff room and Librarian's office immediately behind the counter is sensible and works well but the placing of the workroom at the furthermost end, dictated by the goods entrance position, is rather remote. With $5\frac{1}{2}$ staff there are times when counter staff need reinforcement to deal with the heavy demand and in these circumstances it is helpful if staff areas are grouped together to allow flexibility in the use of staff. Staff workrooms can be dreary places and this one was apparently just such a one at first, but a large window was introduced later which makes it more cheerful—though the use of obscured glass means that one can never look out.

A useful entrance exhibition hall serves as a draught lobby or for prams, with plenty of pin-boarding and good display cases; lively exhibits provided by the County Museum's staff add a happy note.

By far the happiest idea in the building is the use of enclosed courtyards to provide a tranquil outlook on an otherwise dull site. This helps excuse many of the small design shortcomings eg the lack of a proper postbox resulting in small children opening the flap to make cheeky remarks to the poor librarian in her room or to drop rubbish. In a number of places insufficient thought has been given to service pipes which wander across floor to ceiling, window strips at low level, and bookshelving fixed to glazed partitions, which are very unsatisfactory. The library is, however, justifiably popular as issues of 230,000 per annum testify.

Sandwich Of all the places that we visited in Kent, Sandwich is outstandingly the most charming. A closed-in medieval town of 5,000 people on the Stour, close to the coast, the classic old English country town clusters around its church. Market Street has a fine collection of old styles of architecture, very vernacular, very varied and quietly distinguished so that the library's colourlessly Neo-Georgian façade intrudes as an anachronism, as unimaginative and alien as a rather poor bank. The libary site is wedged into the street between old buildings and, in fact, in the wall of the Lending Library an old mullioned stone window has been left as a sad reminder of the past, embedded in a very undistinguished new building.

The Adult Library opens out after passing through the hall with its stairs up to the Priory Room on the first floor, a blank featureless unlovely room unwanted by the public since there are already four alternative meeting places in this small town. The poor librarians huddle behind a side counter without so much as a rooflight to let in a ray of sunlight. From this a door leads to the workroom which looks on to the street, a pleasant working space but little used.

The main Lending Library is light and airy but white plastic tiles, poorly maintained, are a poor substitute for carpet, which not only deadens sound but is much easier to keep clean. This, in turn, leads to the narrow Reference Library with good views into a charming garden courtyard at the rear, into which readers will eventually be able to proceed on sunny days; eventually, and not now, because there are openings on to adjoining gardens and no security.

Children have to put up with a narrow slip of room with lower ceiling which opens off the side of the Lending department but which makes few concessions to its young readers, being conceived as a book storage area just like the Adult area, rather than a warm friendly welcoming area, full of fun, that it should have been. Libraries are more than book dispensing points, a fact that has not been remotely grasped by the designers of this building.

Seal Far the smallest of the libraries visited in Kent is at Seal, a village of about 3,000, close to Sevenoaks. This is a very middle class commuter area and it is therefore surprising to find that the library, which is attractive and well run, as well as immaculately cleaned and polished, is somewhat under-used, the one full-time and one part-time librarian issuing only 30,600 books in a year. Sited on the main road, on a corner with its own small car park, the building is very evident with its rather villagey character which is due largely to the pitched roof over the lending room. A covered way extends along the car park side but unexpectedly does not continue to the front door which leads, however, to a lobby with business-like quarry tiled floor and doormat. This lobby is just big enough for a pram but it is a nuisance that a step has been introduced which must make it difficult for pram-pushers and well nigh impossible for disabled readers to enter.

The counter is 'U'-shaped with a large glazed screen to the lobby and clearly marked doors lead to the 'In' side and from the 'Out' side. This has been well thought out with ample space for the Browne issue cards, and shelves and pigeon holes for storage. The ceiling over this area, which also contains part of the non-fiction stock and room for the Librarian's desk, is low but the main library area which opens out beyond the counter is a very tall handsome space with a laminated timber framed roof and pine boarded ceiling. The walls are in part plastered and painted but with some facing brick and with high-level windows in the triangular gables. Lighting has been well managed with concealed fluorescent tubes illuminating the warm coloured ceiling. Shelving is purpose designed and fixed with warm air heating ducts incorporated in the base. Only five shelves are used which has the advantage that no books are placed too low down for comfort.

The only real fault is the use of plastic floor tiles instead of the usual carpet. This material is very hard to keep clean although here, a devoted cleaner maintains it in virtually new condition. This is however only by dint of persistent hard work which may not always be so freely available.

The Librarian is particularly pleased with the daylighting which imparts a very friendly atmosphere throughout whilst avoiding glare in summer and admitting plenty of low winter sun. The small Librarian's room with its sink and cooker is used also to house additional books. This room is only top lighted owing to the lightness of the site which did not allow any windows on this side.

A library of considerable character has been created here at the centre of village life but perhaps the presence of other bigger, better stocked libraries within a very few miles of the largely car-owning population may account for its light use.

GKVT   HW

Authority	County of Kent
Designation	Faversham Branch
Date of opening	February 1973
Population served	15,000
Name of Architect	L Mason Apps and Partners in collaboration with Eric Hains, RIBA, County Architect
Name of Librarian	D Harrison, MA, FLA
Special features:	
a) site	On bus route near shopping centre
b) architecture	Steel frame; yellow stock bricks
c) function	Serving locality
Mechanical Services:	
a) heating	Gas-fired
b) ventilation	Natural
c) lighting	Fluorescent strip
d) acoustics	Carpeted; wood wool ceiling
e) other	—
Areas: in square metres	
a) lending	234
b) reference	72
c) reading	—
d) special activities	—
e) children	82
f) control	—
g) library staff admin.	72
h) exhibitions	72
i) lecture hall	—
j) circulation	in (h)
k) services	18
l) lavatories	10
m) stack	—
Total area:	560
Book volumes:	
a) adult lending	16,000
b) adult reference	3,000
c) children	4,000
d) stack	2,000
e) other	—
Total:	25,000
Costs in £ p:	
a) site	—
b) building	60,000
c) furniture & fittings	1,500
Total Cost (ex fees):	61,500
Cost per square metre:	£110

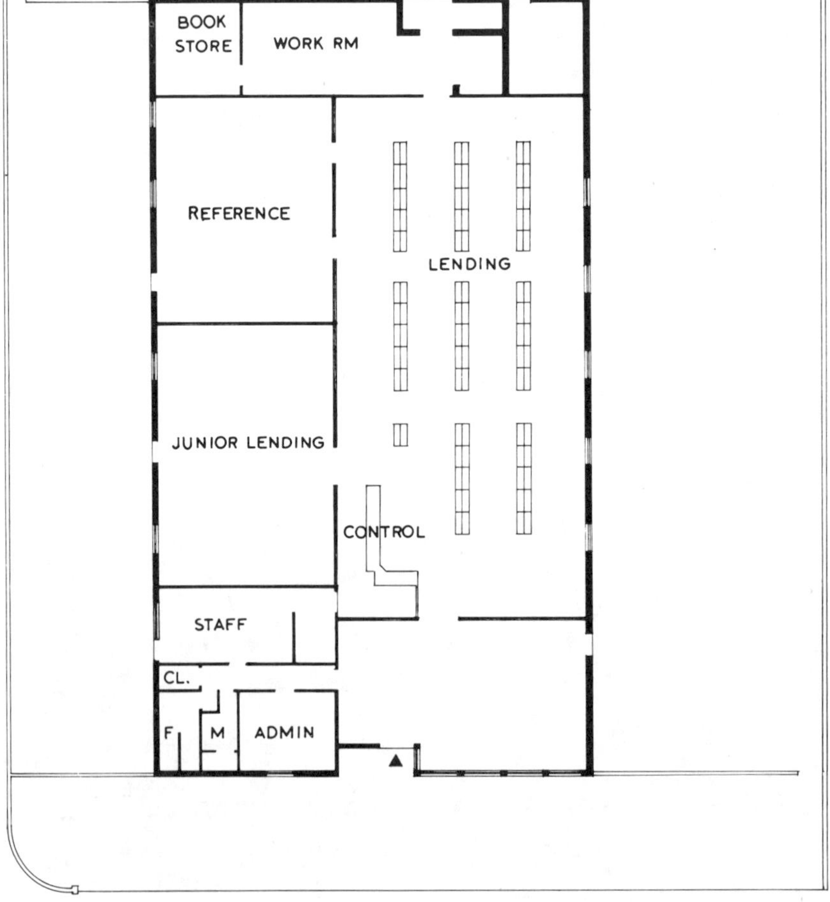

GROUND FLOOR

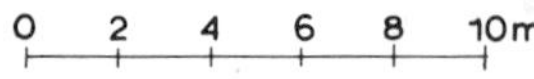

Authority	County of Kent
Designation	Seal Branch Library
Date of opening	February 1973
Population served	2,000
Name of Architect	Eric Hains, RIBA, County Architect, E R Lane, Project Architect
Name of Librarian	D Harrison, MA, FLA
Special features:	
a) site	Corner site on A25; conservation area
b) architecture	Traditional
c) function	Serving locality
Mechanical Services:	
a) heating	Gas-fired warm air
b) ventilation	Natural
c) lighting	Fluorescent strip concealed in main area
d) acoustics	—
e) other	—
Areas: in square metres	
a) lending	
b) reference	
c) reading	94
d) special activities	
e) children	
f) control	
g) library staff admin.	33
h) exhibitions	—
i) lecture hall	—
j) circulation	6
k) services	7
l) lavatories	
m) stack	—
Total area:	140
Book volumes:	
a) adult lending	
b) adult reference	5,000
c) children	
d) stack	
e) other	—
Total:	5,000
Costs in £ p:	
a) site	—
b) building	18,700
c) furniture & fittings	500
Total Cost (ex fees):	£19,200
Cost per square metre:	£137

Lancashire County Council:
Shadsworth, Leyland, Livesey, Wheatley Lane and other libraries

The present Lancashire Authority, following local government reorganisation, covers the area of 18 former Authorities and has consequently inherited a number of libraries planned under the earlier arrangements. At the same time some libraries planned by the former Lancashire County have now been passed over to new autonomous Authorities.

Shadsworth library is one of the former; originally planned by Blackburn County Borough this library is now under Lancashire jurisdiction. Shadsworth is a new industrial estate with new housing nearby on the eastern edge of Blackburn. The building in which the library is housed is part of a large complex consisting of a comprehensive school and community centre with swimming pool, squash and badminton courts and gymnasium with coffee and licensed bars and generous car parking areas—all set in a large area of playing fields on the windy uplands above the town.

This has proved, in social terms, a great success, for the Centre is intensively used, the library alone being open no less than 64 hours every week, more than any other library in the County. The Centre is not only popular with the local community but draws a wider public attracted by the variety of activities offered and the ease of parking.

It is the more disappointing to find that the library has been poorly housed (evidently as an afterthought) on the ground floor of one of the school blocks. The entrance is shared with that of a number of classrooms which makes the lobby intolerably noisy on many occasions during the day. As there is a similar lobby on the far side of the library noise is suffered from two quarters, not to mention the audible thumping of squash balls against another shared wall.

The planning has had to be fitted around structures, staircases and external walls determined by the design of the school above and this has led to unfortunate shortcomings, particularly the lack of supervision of a section of the library invisible from the desk. The desk itself is a totally misconceived piece of detailed design with functional requirements ignored, or botched, leading to much discomfort and extra work for an already overworked, understrength staff.

Three carrels are provided, with earphones connected to audio equipment installed in the desk. Since this is operated by the staff, it needed to be efficiently designed so that the delicate equipment could be easily used. However, it is housed in awkward cupboards and equipment needs pulling out and propping up to be used. The carrels have louvred openings to the library so that they suffer from the noise and general disturbance in the busy library.

The staff room, with workroom attached, is totally internal with neither natural light, ventilation nor fire-escape, which does not comply either with health or safety regulations. This is now to be modified, but the lack of proper architectural consideration in the first place which characterises this library is a cautionary tale—a pity in a building which is so successful in social terms, for it would be hard to find a library which 'earns' its keep' more

convincingly. Ceilings are oppressively low, though the acoustic tiles together with carpeted floor help to mitigate the outside noise. Signposting is virtually non-existent but perhaps the community soon learn where the library is.

The contrast between the slipshod design of Shadsworth and the general run of libraries in the County is marked. With the experience of many new libraries behind them in the last few years and plans for about 75 new ones in the future the Authority has had to give thought to how such a large building programme can be met.

Nelson Another new building inherited by Lancashire is the new central library at Nelson, designed by the local Borough Engineer and Surveyor. The town is a valley community of about 35,000, and the new library is built on the site of the old market hall which was burnt down, and is in a quiet position near to a large new central area development.

The building consists of three elements, clearly seen in the photograph: a two-storey entrance block, leading to a simple 'hole in square' behind, onto which a single-storey workroom and staff block is added. The ground floor contains Lending and Children's Library, on the first floor is a reference library, exhibition space, and lecture room, with adjacent store and toilets. The simple concept of a library planned around a central void is excellent in terms of flexibility and change. However, here there is an awkward relationship between the position of the control counter and the stairs to the upper floor, and the drawings show a different staircase to that built.

The building is a simple 46 × 22 metre two-storey reinforced concrete structure, with external walls faced with Westmorland stone. The south, east, and west walls have large full height windows, and there is also a large area of rooflight over the central void, with a suspended translucent ceiling of unusual design. This overglazing is emphasised in the meeting room, where both long walls are fully glazed, making the room difficult to black out, and making a room which is unpopular with many people because of its 'goldfish bowl' effect. Surprisingly, with so much glass, there were no complaints about excessive cold, overheating, or glare. Cork and carpet form the main floor finishes, and there are acoustic tiles on the ceiling.

Summarised, this is a thoroughly workmanlike library, which works well within its own limited terms; mundane in design, but excellent in workmanship; a follower rather than a leader. Nelson has 'a tradition of belonging', and local people are obviously proud of and satisfied with their new library.

Apart from purpose-built libraries such as that at Nelson, and others like Shadsworth, inherited from other bodies, the County identified six main types of requirement and to meet these have developed a range of virtually standard solutions.

Four types are variations on a standard design produced by the County Architect. The simplest of these, type 1, consists of a square library cell with rectangular staff–workroom, kitchen, lavatory and store totalling 186 m². Type 2 is similar but on a slightly larger scale totalling 260 m². Type 3 is similar to type 2 but adds a children's room and is about 325 m², whilst type 4 has additional rooms for study or reference. A meeting room with external entrance and a door to the staff corridor enable the staff lavatories to be available to the public.

These four types are of similar design and materials, based on the Onward Mark 1 system with an added glazed porch.

It is worth looking at this series of designs in some detail for they are of far-reaching significance in the Lancashire system. When first planned it was estimated that fifteen type 1, thirteen type 2, eight type 3 and sixteen type 4 would be required. In the period under consideration the County have completed type 2 libraries at Livesey, Bolton-le-Sands, Blackrod, Heydock and Ormsden. (The last three now fall in the areas of other new Authorities under reorganisation). Type 4 libraries have been built at Leyland and Golbourne (now in Wigan). A series of other new libraries on these lines are in the programme for the future.

The basic shape adopted for these standard designs is a square for the public area with rectangular rooms added as required. These additional areas are neatly integrated in the design and are in no sense tacked on. The main square library room has a roof which consists of a gently sloping ceiling of flat pyramidal form with a very steep and tall pyramid at the centre, fully glazed.

Leyland library differs from the standard since it has been planned to serve as a temporary service point until such time as the new town centre has been planned. Since this will probably involve the construction of a new and larger purpose-built building the present structure has been designed to be adapted to another use at a later date with the glass pyramid being replaced by smaller fibreglass rooflight pyramids.

The outer walls of the whole building are built in an attractive pale grey artificial stone-faced concrete block. Internal walls are of finely finished concrete block, left undecorated. The windows run from floor to ceiling, in some cases large plates of Spectrofloat anti-sun glass with a band of etched lines to warn people against walking into it or with timber sills at the usual level and opening lights for ventilation.

A broad block design band of dark stained timber provides an emphatic cap to the buildings whilst additional interest is given by a hexagonal glass box porch with glazed roof like a very elegant greenhouse. The form of the building is generally simple, and neutral so that it fits rather well into diverse architectural backgrounds.

Internally the sloping ceiling with glass pyramid is very dramatic and produces a fine interior. The detailing of the ceiling of plastic boarding is crisp and incorporates strips of fluorescent light which follow round the four sides of the square. There are however problems with the glazed pyramid, which is very hard to clean owing to the height inside and the slope of the glass, whilst the large expanse of glass facing in all directions lets in far too much glare and sunlight and lets out too much heat. The

libraries are thus hot in summer and cold and draughty in winter once the electric underfloor heating has lost most of its initial overnight heat.

Livesey Here, efforts have been made to improve conditions by fitting a row of horizontal louvres or sunbreakers around the sunny sides of the pyramids and this has greatly helped with glare and solar heat but does nothing to reduce the heat loss.

During a later visit to Ford library, inherited by Sefton from Lancashire with local government reorganisation, we were told that temperatures in that building had varied between 110°F in summer and 46°F in winter. An attempt has been made there to mitigate these extremes by replacing most of the glazing with aluminium faced polystyrene boarding painted white externally to reflect sun, though it remains to be seen whether this will meet with much success.

In these days of increasing concern about energy conservation this design unfortunately begins to look very extravagant especially as the very high level of 3.2 m (10 ft 6 in) has been adopted from which the sloping ceiling springs. There is no practical reason why this should not be considerably reduced for the sloping roof and pyramid produce a great impression of height in themselves. Artificial lighting levels are very high and in practice the librarians seldom have more than half the lights switched on. Natural light is, of course, excellent.

The entrance porch is large enough for a number of prams to be left under cover but lacks any provision for notices, opening times board, post box or any of the obvious features which the porch should accommodate. The fully glazed form makes this a very cold area despite electric floor heating. A huge mat is provided in the link.

The control desk is a standard unit made in 1,200 mm-long units of hardwood and black metal framing well studied and convenient in use. In Livesey library the placing has posed some problems. It was originally intended that this should be beneath the pyramid but it was found in practice to be too cold a position so that the whole unit has now been moved nearer to the door where it serves equally well, but this position exposes the back of the desk and the librarians to public view.

Generally insufficient provision is made for pin-up boards so that an accumulation of notices appear on walls and glazing fixed by Sellotape, an untidy substitute. For colour the library relies on the natural materials, pale grey concrete block and white plastic ceiling, and hardwood bookshelving on black steel framing but the strong orange-coloured carpet tiles provide a welcome warmth to the colour scheme. The shelving, by Scot Smith, is in welded black steel with hardwood shelves, a neat system giving about 65 mm shelf adjustment increments. The tier guides are particularly well thought out being easily interchangeable black fascias which hook into pockets in the framework giving positive alignment and levelling. However rising costs now look like making these units too expensive for future use.

Staff accommodation is more spartan than the library, with plastic tile floors and the rest area in a corner of the workroom off which opens a kitchenette, a lavatory without any lobby and a meter-room and store. The kitchen is well equipped with rather more cupboards than strictly necessary.

Whilst admiring the principle of a standardised solution it is felt that insufficient thought has been given to the solution of some of the practical problems particularly those affecting heating, insulation and maintenance. These points will no doubt be improved upon in later buildings and it is to be hoped that the very pleasant appearance will not suffer in the process. The buildings are attractive, though they could afford to be more intimate in scale.

In very small communities, mainly rural, or semi-rural suburbs, the library is sometimes combined with a clinic, both being operated for strictly limited times. These are based on Vic Hallam prefabricated timber units. Other neighbourhoods however, whilst requiring library service, do so on a more temporary basis, because the neighbourhoods themselves are undergoing, or will undergo, radical change, such as slum clearance followed by rebuilding in other forms, not so far determined. For these cases Terrapin Reska 'skip' libraries, on temporary cheap foundations, are being used. The buildings are of standard form with the long prefabricated sections fitted together on site and a timber skirt around to finish the job.

Wheatley Lane library, near Nelson, is one of three of the Library/Clinic buildings built in a scattered village of about 1,200 people, the others being Foolridge and Trawden near Colne.

The library and clinic share a common entrance hall with large mat, notice boards, hat and umbrella stands. A wheelchair users' lavatory and a small kitchen open off this hall and a staff lavatory with lobby off the kitchen. The library itself is very small with a one-man counter backed by a workroom. Bookshelving is provided for a stack of about 4,000 volumes in fairly tight spacing.

Natural daylighting is through a large window (with venetian blind) which also provides a view, high level windows at the back and three small rooflights. The workroom seems very wasteful of space in this tiny building and one wonders if it is really necessary at all for little work on books is involved beyond packing and unpacking cases delivered from the divisional library, so that a large deep cupboard would have sufficed to keep things tidy. The front of the building gives no view into the library since the workroom is on this side. A display of books is placed in the window but this in turn hampers the use of the room. If the library were to have been planned as a single room, arrangements could have been made very easily to provide for both display and a view into the building. In smaller buildings of this nature the avoidance of wasted space calls for much ingenuity and thought so that the public can enjoy the maximum possible space consistent with efficiency.

The County are to be commended for tackling an obviously enormous programme of library building with imagination and energy but more detailed development of the main library types is necessary if mistakes—all too evident in the present buildings—are to be avoided.

GKVT

Nelson Central Library
(No statistics available)

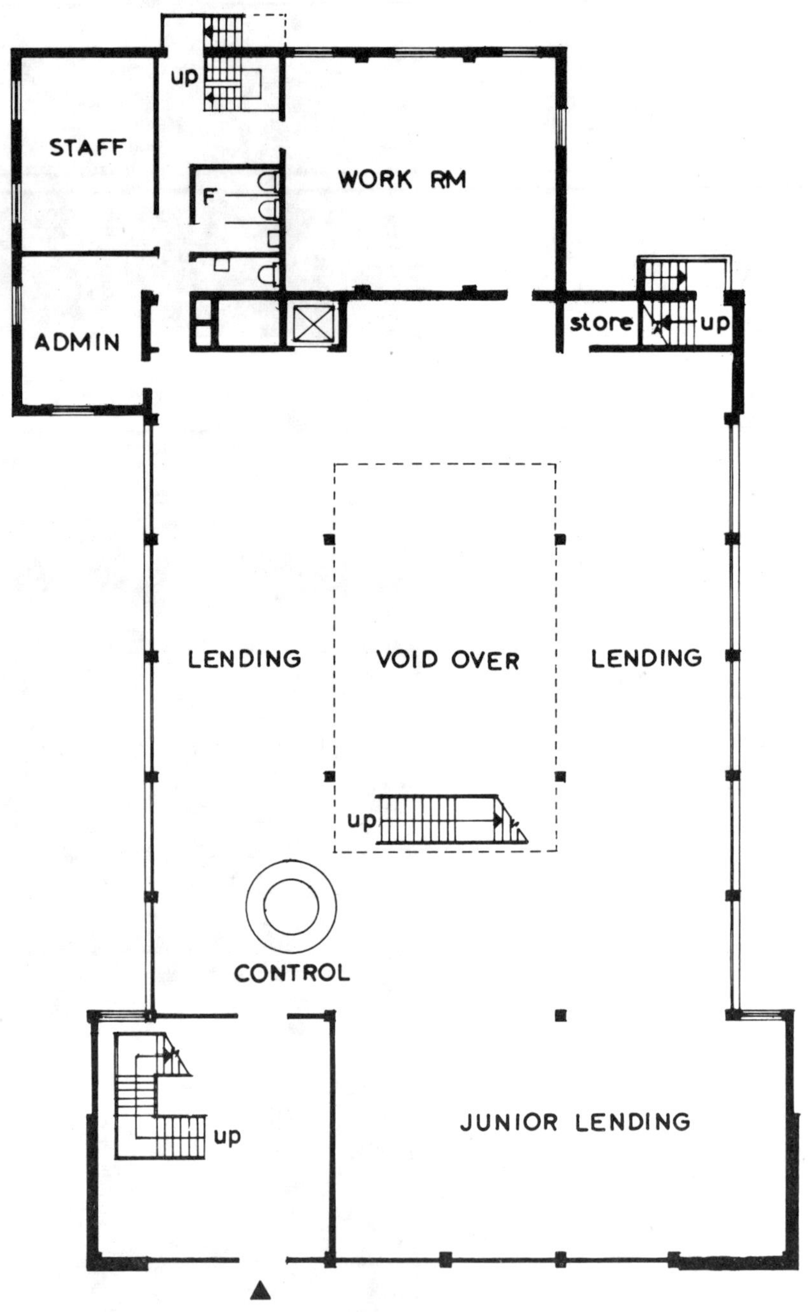

GROUND FLOOR

Authority	Lancashire County Council
Designation	Leyland Library
Date of opening	November 1974
Population served	23,690
Name of Architect	Roger Booth, DipArch, RIBA, FRSA, County Architect, Brian Hartley, RIBA, Principal Designer
Name of Librarian	Alan Longworth, FLA
Special features:	
a) site	Adjacent to local authority offices and shopping centre
b) architecture	Onward Mark 1 system plus glazed porch
c) function	Public Library
Mechanical Services:	
a) heating	Electric underfloor
b) ventilation	Natural
c) lighting	Fluorescent with supplementary tungsten (300–500 lux)
d) acoustics	Carpet
e) other	—
Areas: in square metres	
a) lending	194
b) reference	49
c) reading	—
d) special activities	—
e) children	50
f) control	in (a)
g) library staff admin.	60
h) exhibitions	in (a)
i) lecture hall	38
j) circulation	47
k) services	4
l) lavatories	8
m) stack	in (g)
Total area:	442
Book volumes:	
a) adult lending	28,000
b) adult reference	600
c) children	8,500
d) stack	4,500
e) other	—
Total:	41,600
Costs in £ p:	
a) site	7,000
b) building	57,440
c) furniture & fittings	5,000
Total Cost (ex fees):	£69,440
Cost per square metre:	£140

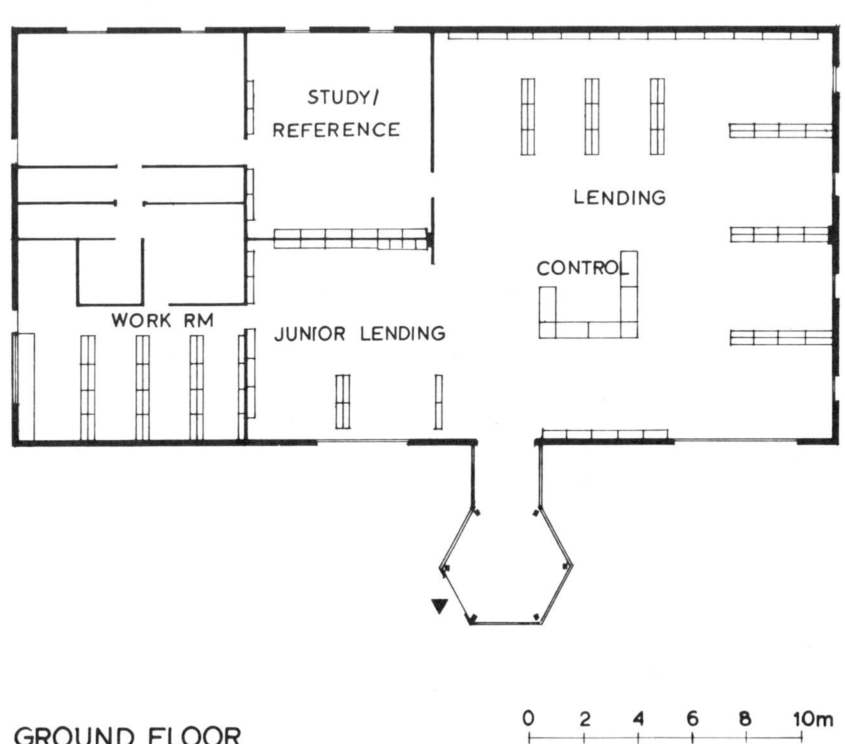

GROUND FLOOR

Authority	Lancashire County Council
Designation	Livesey Library
Date of opening	July 1973
Population served	6,400
Name of Architect	Roger Booth, DipArch, RIBA, FRSA, County Architect, B Hartley, RIBA, Principal Designer
Name of Librarian	Alan Longworth, FLA
Special features:	
a) site	Corner site adjacent to clinic and school
b) architecture	Onward Mark 1 system plus glazed porch
c) function	Public Library
Mechanical Services:	
a) heating	Electric underfloor
b) ventilation	Natural
c) lighting	Fluorescent 300–500 lux with supplementary tungsten
d) acoustics	Carpet
e) other	—
Areas: in square metres	
a) lending	199
b) reference	—
c) reading	—
d) special activities	—
e) children	—
f) control	in (a)
g) library staff admin.	37
h) exhibitions	—
i) lecture hall	—
j) circulation	22
k) services	—
l) lavatories	3
m) stack	—
Total area:	261
Book volumes:	
a) adult lending	13,500
b) adult reference	200
c) children	4,000
d) stack	300
e) other	None
Total:	18,000
Costs in £ p:	
a) site	630
b) building	34,331
c) furniture & fittings	3,710
Total Cost (ex fees):	£38,041
Cost per square metre:	£145

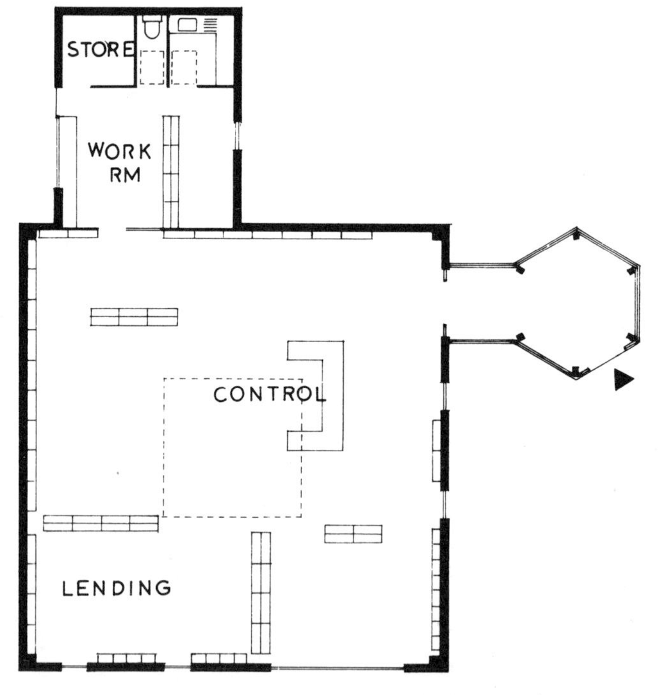

GROUND FLOOR

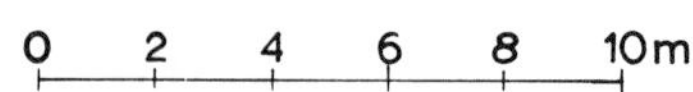

Authority	Lancashire County Council
Designation	Branch Library, Wheatley Close, Nelson
Date of opening	October 1974
Population served	1,000
Name of Architect	Charles B Pearson Son & Partners
Name of Librarian	Alan Longworth, FLA
Special features:	
a) site	Corner site in residential area next to old peoples' housing
b) architecture	Vic Hallam Derwent structure type B
c) function	Branch Library combined with health clinic
Mechanical Services:	
a) heating	Electric underfloor plus fan heaters
b) ventilation	Natural
c) lighting	Fluorescent
d) acoustics	—
e) other	—
Areas: in square metres	
a) lending	30
b) reference	—
c) reading	—
d) special activities	—
e) children	—
f) control	—
g) library staff admin.	7
h) exhibitions	—
i) lecture hall	—
j) circulation	Shared
k) services	—
l) lavatories	Shared
m) stack	—
Total area:	48
Book volumes:	
a) adult lending	3,500
b) adult reference	50
c) children	900
d) stack	—
e) other	—
Total:	4,450
Costs in £ p:	
a) site	3,215
b) building	9,285
c) furniture & fittings	271
Total Cost (ex fees):	£12,771
Cost per square metre:	£209

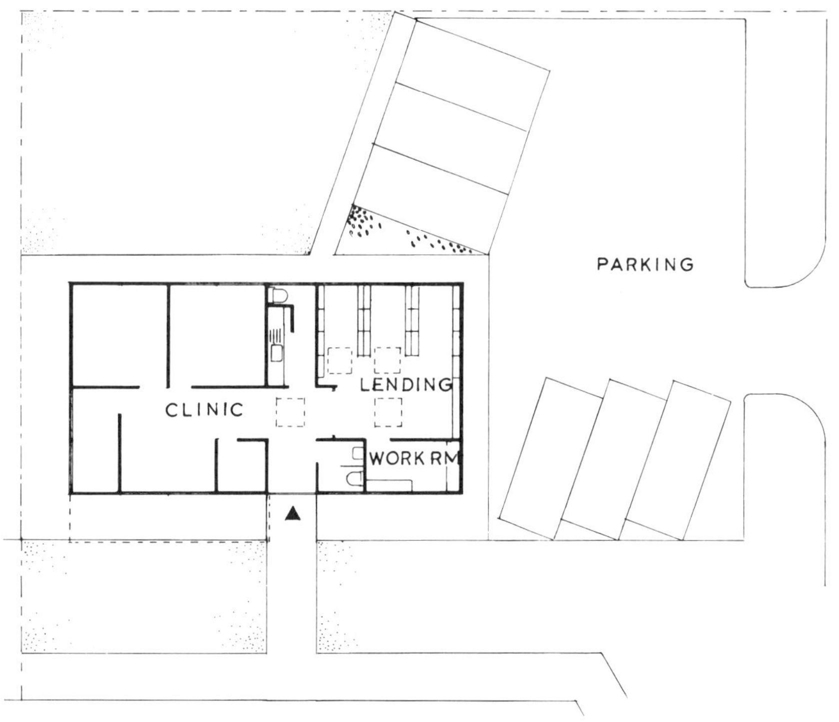

GROUND FLOOR

0 2 4 6 8 10m

Leicestershire County Council:
Wigston Magna, Birstall, (formerly Rutland County Council) Ketton and Ryhall

Wigston Magna The new district at Wigston Magna is on the southern outskirts of Leicester, serving about 35,000 people, and is also the major library resource for south-east Leicestershire, and the base for the team of librarians that serve the area.

The library faces onto a new dual carriageway by-pass, making a frontal approach rather hazardous. The main approach to the library appears to be from the shopping centre and car park to the rear of the building, and to reach the front entrance involves passing the staff entrance, and climbing a rather tortuous ramp or staircase to the front entrance at first floor level. Possibly this approach will be improved when the building work around is completed, but in any building the entrance should be clear, unmistakable, and approachable.

Once inside at first floor level, the main public areas are contained in one column-free space, 36 m. × 18 m., the only visual interruption being the lift shaft connecting down to the ground floor. The entrance, stairs, lift, control, and enquiry counters are off-centre, with the quieter group study area and study carrels at the other end. Windows are restricted on the south and west elevations, providing extensive wall space to shelve the fiction stock, non-fiction being in bays away from the walls. There is extensive glazing on the north elevation, where the study areas are situated, and on the east elevation, facing the bypass. The floor is carpeted throughout; walls are hessian-faced, and can act as display panels; there is a liberal range of seating, and extensive use of display and exhibition. This large open space offers a considerable degree of flexibility, which will meet most future needs of the library. Supervision is made easy, and the open space allows users to experience visually the full range of facilities and activities. Not surprisingly theft is not a problem, but the staff did speak of incidents of rowdy behaviour by young people.

The ground floor contains the Children's Library, reached by going to the main library on the first floor, and then down again. It is a generous space facing west, but with the study area in the central part of the building, away from the windows. Also there is a Citizen's Advice Bureau, tucked away off the lower staircase lobby, and although there needs to be some degree of confidentiality, it seems a pity that this was not in a screened position on the main floor. The main function of the ground floor is as a staff workroom, store and social area, and with a separate Team Base office, where the team of librarians serving the area have their own room, away from the clerical staff and library workroom.

Externally, the lower floor forms a brown brick base for the grey aluminium cladding and roofing of the main upper floor. The upper floor cladding, windows and roof are particularly well-detailed and articulated. A certain eclectism in design has for some time been a characteristic of Leicestershire schools, and this seems to be also apparent in the range of new libraries being built. Wigston Magna, despite certain reservations about access, provides an excellent space to meet the changing needs of the library, contained in a classically distinguished envelope.

Birstall is a northern suburb of Leicester, in the heart of the commuter belt, and the library serves an essentially middle-class catchment population of 15–20,000. The site is restricted, being formerly the corner of a school playground, but it is one of the best in Birstall, just 200 yards from a large supermarket. It is in a largely residential area, and the planners imposed restrictions on the development.

It is a very different building to its opposite number on the south-side of the City, Wigston Magna, accepting that Birstall is much more the typical branch library. Whereas Wigston appeared a large, open building, Birstall is very domestic in appearance and feeling. Basically it consists of two rectangular brick blocks placed at right-angles, with the upper floor cantilevering over the ground floor at front and rear.

The adult sections of the library are all on the ground floor, with only the Children's Library on the first floor. In the building generally windows are restricted in size, so providing considerable wall space for bookshelving, and so reducing the number of island units; and these have tended to be rather informally arranged, rather than in serried rows. The staircase to the Children's Library juts out in the middle of the room, so tending to reduce flexbility and movement. Coming directly from the openness of Wigston, the intimacy and low ceilings at Birstall proved slightly claustrophobic; but it should be said that this informal, intimate and domestic feeling is appreciated by the users, and the library is obviously easy to supervise at ground floor level.

The control desk faces you as you enter the building, and it connects directly with the workroom and staff area. There is a rear door and a second staircase that leads to a separate room on the first floor, used by the area team of librarians. The first floor also contains the Children's Library and activities area, a large area occupying almost as much space as the Adult Library below. Being separated from the rest of the library by a staircase and a door, it must make supervision difficult; or possibly easy, as you keep the space locked unless there are staff on duty there.

Architecturally there are several curious features about the library. Beams supporting the first floor seemed to be undersized, and appeared to have been reinforced. The ceiling height of the first floor is only 2.1 metres, which is low for a domestic, let alone a public, building; although such a low height could be appropriate to young children. Also the pivot windows on the first floor, as designed, seemed dangerous, and easy for children to climb out or fall out. Remedial work has been done on this.

Birstall is a very good example of the 'curate's egg'—good in parts. It fits well into the streetscape, and the massing and fenestration are well handled; the planning on the ground floor is good; and the domestic feeling, aided by carpet tiles on the floor and the extensive use of hessian covered pin-up on the walls, is very pleasant. There remain the curious construction faults and details, one of which, involving the use of a baffle behind ground floor clerestory windows, is too difficult to describe verbally. There remains one unrelated column on the first floor which

Authority	Leicestershire County Council
Designation	Wigston Magna Library
Date of opening	May 1974
Population served	35,000
Name of Architect	T Locke, DA(Glas), RIBA, County Architect
Name of Librarian	G E Smith, FLA
Special features:	
a) site	Restricted sloping site fronting dual carriage by-pass
b) architecture	Two-storey traditional construction, using acrylic finished bonded aluminium cladding panel to upper floor and sloping roof; Himley brown facing brick to lower floor
c) function	District library
Mechanical Services:	
a) heating	Gas-fired ducted warm air
b) ventilation	Extractor fans
c) lighting	Partially recessed diffused fluorescent panels, and ditto tungsten lighting. 'Litespan' track display fittings
d) acoustics	'Lay-in' grid suspended ceiling; carpeted floor
e) other	—
Areas: in square metres	
a) lending	
b) reference	} 530
c) reading	83
d) special activities	—
e) children	98
f) control	17
g) library staff admin.	158
h) exhibitions	—
i) lecture hall	—
j) circulation	79
k) services	29
l) lavatories	22
m) stack	51
n) citizens advice	20
Total area:	1,087
Book volumes:	
a) adult lending	17,153
b) adult reference	1,694
c) children	4,894
d) stack	18,798
e) other	285 records and cassettes
Total:	42,824
Costs in £ p:	
a) site	7,500
b) building	111,000
c) furniture & fittings	15,000
Total Cost (ex fees):	£133,500
Cost per square metre:	£123

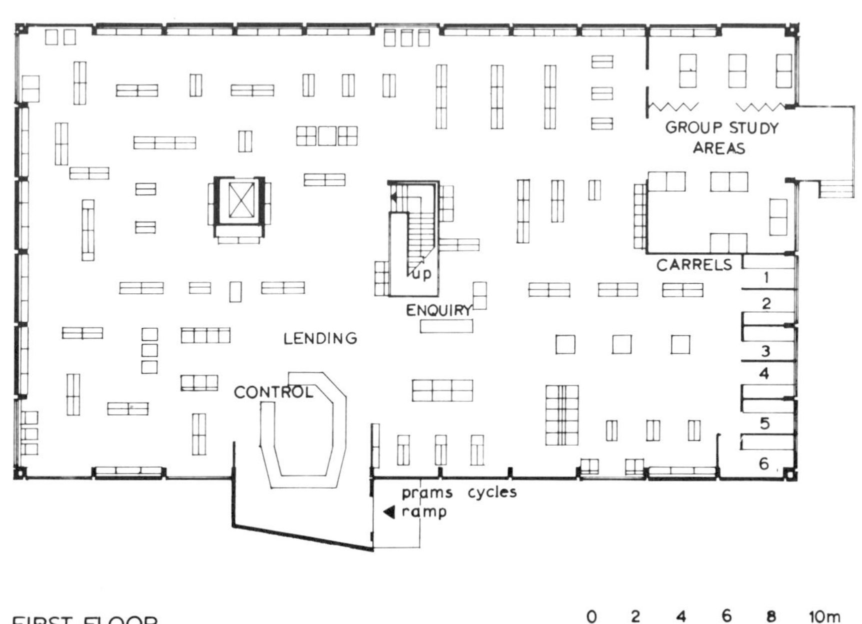

FIRST FLOOR

Authority	County of Leicestershire
Designation	Birstall Library
Date of opening	November 1974
Population served	13,000
Name of Architect	T A Locke, DA(Glas), RIBA
Name of Librarian	G E Smith, FLA
Special features:	
a) site	Part of primary school site, adjoining housing and car park; planning restrictions on frontage
b) architecture	Traditional; part steel frame cantilevered first floor
c) function	Main library in a group
Mechanical Services:	
a) heating	Gas-fired; fan assisted convectors
b) ventilation	Natural
c) lighting	Fluorescent strip
d) acoustics	Carpeted public areas; ceiling tiles
e) other	—
Areas: in square metres	
a) lending	156
b) reference	in (a)
c) reading	in (a)
d) special activities	50
e) children	80
f) control	12
g) library staff admin.	68
h) exhibitions	in (a)
i) lecture hall	—
j) circulation	56
k) services	16
l) lavatories	9
m) stack	—
Total area:	447
Book volumes:	
a) adult lending	9,100
b) adult reference	400
c) children	5,100
d) stack	10,600
e) other	500 gr; cass
Total:	25,700
Costs in £ p:	
a) site	—
b) building	43,750
c) furniture & fittings	7,500
Total Cost (ex fees):	51,250
Cost per square metre:	£97

(No photograph available)

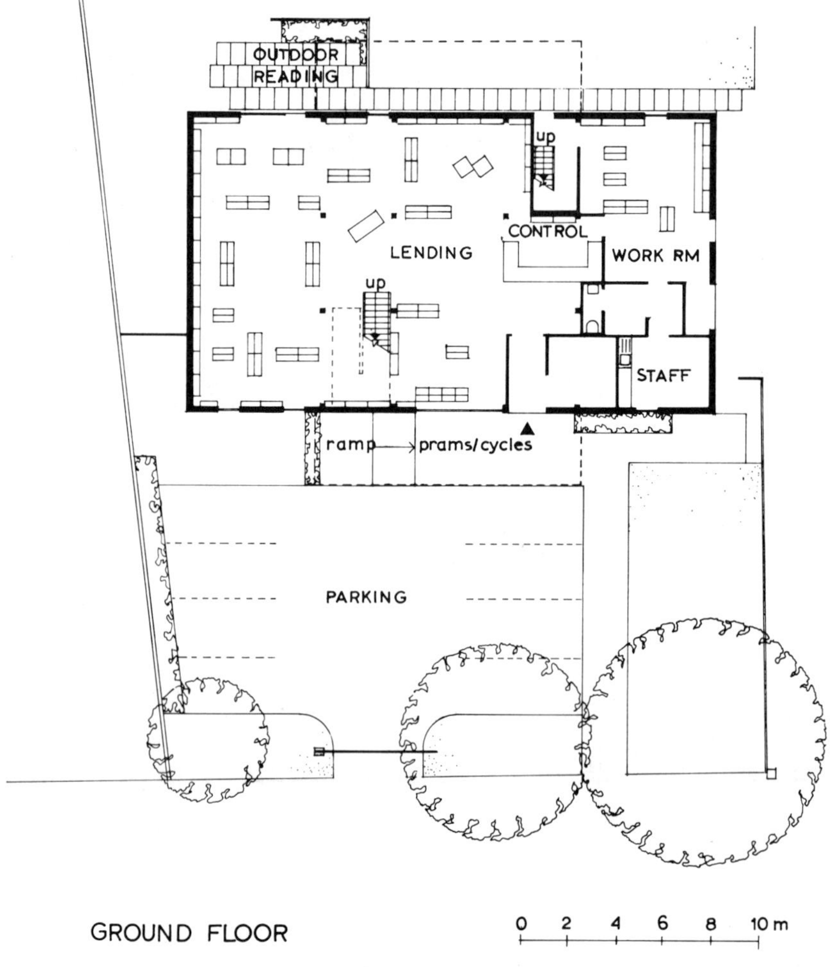

serves no apparent structural purpose. One of the architects is reported to have remarked 'B——r, I must have forgotten it was there'!

Having been very impressed by the then new County Library Headquarters for Rutland when I visited Oakham for the 1974 issue of this publication (see pp 42–45) a visit to these two new branches, which were being planned at that time, seemed well merited.

Ketton is a delightful village, the light stone houses and trees giving a warm impression of a truly 'picture' English village. The library building, which has been built of reused stone and local Colley Weston slate, blends into this picture, although the new school adjacent, while admittedly set back from the road, is not in the same mould. The surrounding area is agricultural although a nearby cement works employs several hundred local people.

The background history of the library is interesting, for previously it had been in a classroom of a Rutland School since Victorian times—and this still included an open coke stove! The new school in 1970 allowed this building to be demolished and the site developed attractively with lawns, trees and shrubs, ('Plant-a-tree-Year' encouraged local Councillors to be generous in this). At the moment the library only opens for 14 hours each week.

The project architect for this library was the same as for the County HQ which was so impressive; this interior is pleasant with its carpeting throughout, its mahogany woodwork and tungsten lighting in not unattractive shades, together with deep cream walls and white skirtings harmonising well. But in the viewer's opinion, the architect has lessened the character of the building by introducing a false ceiling of wood strip. Remembering the charm of the Buckinghamshire Library at Great Missenden (See 1974 issue pp 78–79) with its high roof-shaped ceiling of lovely wood caused a feeling of disappointment when viewing Ketton. Modern metal shelving adds further to the feeling of visual conflict but this may have been decided upon because of cost.

Heating is by off-peak electricity (in fact there is no gas in this village), and one wonders whether this would be really adequate in a really deep winter.

The glorious sunshine, the tree-lined approach to the village and the initial visual impact of the setting of the library had produced the feeling of high hope: yet as one drove away there was the feeling that the design of the interiors had not matched this—but apparently the library users are highly satisfied which is the main object of such an exercise.

Ryhall (population 1,300) is approached through a wonderful avenue of trees which leads into an open area which is graced with trees and shrubs. Some fifty yards to one side is the old parish hall and infants school. In the near distance and beyond, viewed from the rear of the library and its car park, is a new housing estate (mainly for workers in Stamford) whence come most of the library users. The rather small, rectangular low flat building has one full window to the left of the entrance and brickwork to the right, while the interior has block walls in beige and a cedar strip ceiling and tungsten lighting. This library is, at the moment, open only on two days per week and is controlled from Oakham. It is pleasing but, one felt, too small for ultimate use, particularly if wider facilities were to be offered for children.

NR   HW

Lincolnshire County Council:
(formerly Lindsey and Holland County Council) Crowland, Sutton-on-Sea, Welton, Cherry Willingham and Alford: (formerly Kesteven County Council) Washingborough

The new Lincolnshire has many libraries to report for the period under review, most planned by the former Lindsey and Holland Authority. The main ones are reported here but the new libraries which Lincolnshire planned at Crowle and Messingham were in 1974 transferred to Humberside on Local Government reorganisation and are reviewed under that Authority (page 137).

Crowland is a village of some 3,000 population in the south-west of the County between Peterborough and Wisbech. It has an antiquity, immediately noticed by a quite unique bridge, of three arms yet not more than 14 m. in diameter. The streams that it spanned have long since disappeared, but a life-size stone royal figure at the foot of one of the arms is still just recognisable as such. There is also a ruined 12th century abbey and, strikingly, the library which is of modern design, sits virtually in its lap; being across the end of a main street these two buildings, one set against the other, provide a surprising but pleasing visual impact.

The library is linked with the small police station and there is joint use of a car park. Octagonal in shape, this library (similar but larger than Shoeburyness) has its eight walls of purple-black brick separated by floor-to-ceiling windows of bronze solar glass which are fitted into tall rectangular steel columns. This allows ample viewing of the interior—and an enticing view it is! A wide, white canopied entrance leads in to a hall with display case and separate display boards with lower shelves for information material; beyond is the control counter with specially designed glass display frontage—a pattern to be seen repeated in Lincolnshire's other new branches. Special high density nylon carpet, claimed to be anti-stain, completely covers the floor and its mustard colour is a good foil for the natural Abura wood used for fitments and shelving. The ceiling is of Douglas fir-faced ply with recessed fluorescent lighting.

Pride and care of the library is evinced by the flowers on top of the wall cases, standing in relief against the dark brown facing brickwork, as are some framed paintings; red leather settees in the window alcoves add even further to the internal atmosphere. Staff and work areas to the rear of the counter are very adequate. The heating through convector heaters from an oil-fired boiler also serves the police station.

In contrast to other library buildings for small communities this may seem larger than basic requirements with a book stock of 8,000 volumes and only part-time opening—but it is a quality library of which the residents and the Council can be justifiably proud.

Sutton-on-Sea (population 2,500) is on the extreme east of the County, a few miles below Mablethorpe which is larger and better known. Here the library is much smaller and seems oddly sited some 200 yards from the beach and just beyond a large facing car park, hardly able to accommodate all the summertime day-trippers. Opposite is a telephone exchange and to the rear is open space on which more vehicles, including a coach were parked. Discussions later with the County Librarian revealed that the site was chosen to meet the proposed development plans which would provide executive-type buildings in this area but this, sadly for library use, has not materialised—at least not yet.

The design is unusual if not completely pleasing, although the trees, plants and shrubs at the frontage are welcome. The brickwork is dark but there are large glazed areas at the front and in the exposed side which leads to the private car park and goods entrance. Viewed from a short distance the front of the building appears to have a deep and wide cleavage in the centre of the steeply pitched roof (which rises from shelf height). This is however practical in that it allows windows in those sides for more natural lighting—artificial lighting being almost entirely provided by 24 adjustable spotlights. The nylon based carpet is red, the wall surfaces are of fair-faced brick and plaster, with a comparable ratio of matched boarding and plaster for the ceiling. The counter is of a similar display type mentioned already. This is a neat but not ideally sited library.

Welton (pop 3,500) lies about 8 miles north-east of Lincoln in a mainly agricultural area, but many of the residents work in the city. The library is a Spooner prefabricated construction with brick cladding to two walls. A Health Centre is attached to the library while village shopping facilities are nearby. Substantial car parking space has been provided.

The interior space has an area designated 'reference area' which is capable of segregating for meetings by use of a 'concertina' screen. For purely reference purposes, with such a small population, the space seems disproportionate—certainly as the Children's area is then within the Adult Lending Department.

The impression on entering is of lightness and colour: the floor-to-ceiling windows on the front and side elevations mean that artificial lighting needed only to be to minimum standards. Carpeting, curtains and furniture, together with bookstock, provide the colour. Counter design and workroom furniture units have been carefully thought out and the staff are appreciative of this.

This is a remarkably cheap building for the value obtained—under £11 per square foot in mid-1973 is quoted.

Cherry Willingham lies about five miles to the east of the city and has a higher population, approaching 6,000. It occupies a corner site in a precinct which also contains a Health Centre and shops, and has a good site area sufficient to have a grassed as well as a paved area frontage, with a number of bench seats provided. The entrance is well canopied to allow shelter for prams and has floor-to-ceiling windows (cedar framed) here and at the left hand frontage so the colourful interior is well advertised to those outside.

Similar provision is made here, as at Welton, with dual use for reference service and reading room but the extra overall area of approx 2,000 ft² (to Welton's 1,370) allows better Children's facilities. Wood strip ceiling and recessed lighting give a more finished air, with nice contrasting and attractive carpet to assist.

Alford (population 3,500) lies about 12 miles to the north-west of Skegness and the library is set in a conservation area. This restricted the design of the library which had to fit in with the environmental rehabilitation of the Market Place area based on former buildings which were removed in 1920. This demanded a two-storey construction and with only a relatively small readership to cater for, this caused the first floor accommodation to be allocated for a Dental Clinic.

It would not be expected therefore that the design of the library could be exciting and the residential shape and the uniform brickwork certainly do not make the building stand out as a library would wish to do. It is therefore surprising and disappointing that the attempt to announce the identity and purpose with the letters LIBRARY above the flush entrance are too small and nondescript to have any real effect–but perhaps in a small community its purpose soon becomes known.

A brave attempt has been made with the interior–plants and flowers on the low bookcases, display and the usual attractive Lincolnshire counter help in this. The bookcases are angled but circulation space is rather limited: in the Children's Section for instance chairs at a study table, when pulled out for use, overlap three shelves of books in the adjacent tier, while a kinderbox and floor cushions are too close to this study table to be comfortable.

Washingborough planned by the former Kesteven Authority is a real case of missed opportunity for much of the available site area has been quite ignored. Admittedly it had been expected that the neighbouring school would have extended but it didn't. Accordingly this Vic Hallam system-built structure was planted as near as possible to the former Mobile Library site.

The result is a tiny library set off-centre and to the rear of the site, the unused area, which is quite substantial, being used by the few cars which, at any one time visit the library. The interior is terribly cramped with far too little space for any circulation and virtually none for browsing or activities. The Libraco metal shelving is far from satisfactory as it has a 'whip' on it which is worrying.

HW

Authority	County Council of Lincolnshire
Designation	Crowland Branch Library
Date of opening	October 1974
Population served	3,000
Name of Architect	A R I Aitken, RIBA, County Architect, K Stevens, RIBA, Project Architect
Name of Librarian	E H W Roberts, FLA
Special features:	
a) site	Corner site with small police station near centre of village close to Crowland Abbey (12 cent)
b) architecture	Octagonal on reinforced concrete raft with supporting concrete ground beams. Steel framed; facing brickwork
c) function	Branch library for village and surrounding rural area
Mechanical Services:	
a) heating	Oil-fired boiler serving convector heaters
b) ventilation	Natural
c) lighting	20 Fluorescent tubes in ISORA Leaflite suspension ceiling fitting with 16 mercury discharge lamps recessed in ceiling panels
d) acoustics	Nylon carpeting
e) other	—
Areas: in square metres	
a) lending	84
b) reference	9
c) reading	in (b)
d) special activities	—
e) children	24
f) control	6
g) library staff admin.	22
h) exhibitions	18
i) lecture hall	—
j) circulation	—
k) services	5
l) lavatories	2
m) stack	—
Total area:	170
Book volumes:	
a) adult lending	4,790
b) adult reference	150
c) children	2,390
d) stack	850
e) other	—
Total:	8,180
Costs in £ p:	
a) site	1,250
b) building	33,308
c) furniture & fittings	4,000
Total Cost (ex fees):	£38,558
Cost per square metre:	£230

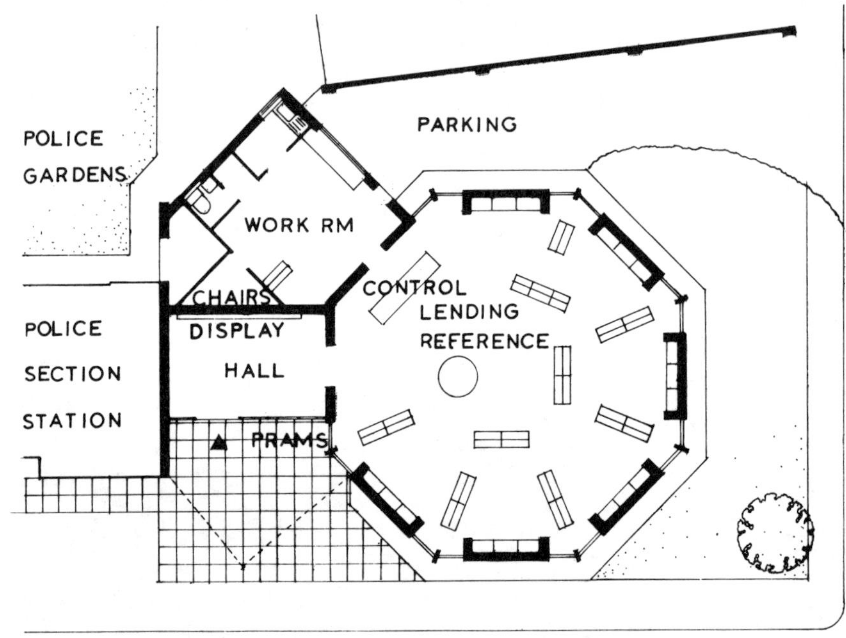

GROUND FLOOR

Authority	County of Lincolnshire (formerly Lindsey and Holland)
Designation	Sutton-on-Sea Branch Library
Date of opening	March 1974
Population served	2,500
Name of Architect	Maurice Palmer, DipArch, RIBA
Name of Librarian	E W Roberts, FLA
Special features:	
a) site	Near sea; set in area scheduled for executive type building
b) architecture	Traditional to blend with domestic character architecture
c) function	—
Mechanical Services:	
a) heating	Gas-fired supplying ducted warm air
b) ventilation	Natural
c) lighting	Tungsten variable spotlights and fluorescent strip
d) acoustics	Carpeting
e) other	—
Areas: in square metres	
a) lending	40
b) reference	19
c) reading	—
d) special activities	—
e) children	28
f) control	4
g) library staff admin.	14
h) exhibitions	—
i) lecture hall	—
j) circulation	11
k) services	4
l) lavatories	2
m) stack	—
Total area:	122
Book volumes:	
a) adult lending	5,745
b) adult reference	200
c) children	2,536
d) stack	957
e) other	—
Total:	9,438
Costs in £ p:	
a) site	595
b) building	13,440
c) furniture & fittings	1,984
Total Cost (ex fees):	£16,019
Cost per square metre:	£131

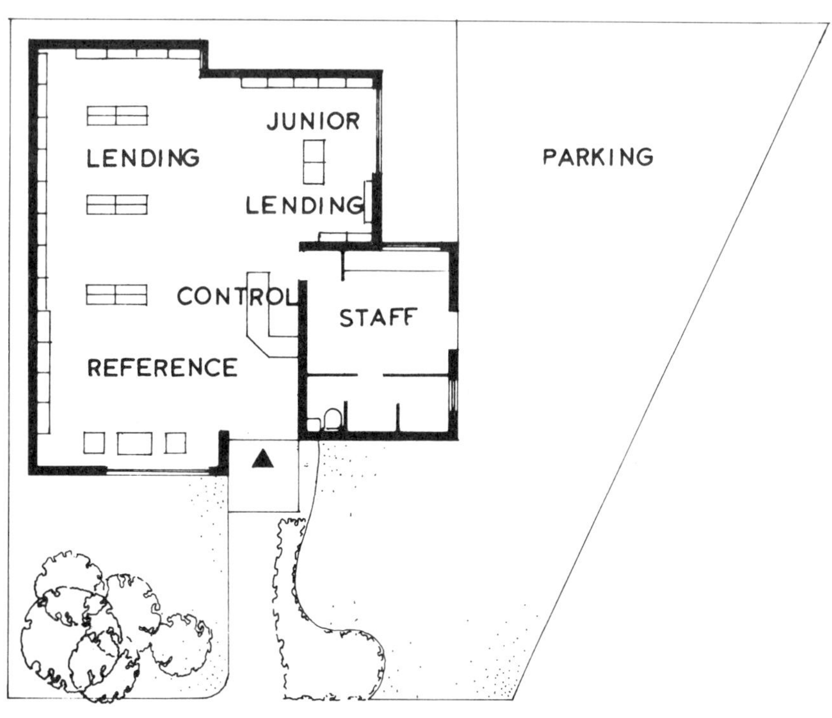

GROUND FLOOR

Authority	Lincolnshire County Council (formerly Lindsey and Holland)
Designation	Welton Branch Library
Date of opening	June 1973
Population served	3,500
Name of Architect	A R I Aitken, RIBA, County Architect, N A Pearson, RIBA, Job Architect
Name of Librarian	E H W Roberts, FLA
Special features:	
a) site	Centre of village, with Health Centre, near shops
b) architecture	Spooner pre-fabricated with brick cladding
c) function	Serving locality
Mechanical Services:	
a) heating	Underfloor electric
b) ventilation	Natural
c) lighting	Fluorescent strip
d) acoustics	Carpeted
e) other	—
Areas: in square metres	
a) lending	83
b) reference	28
c) reading	in (a)
d) special activities	—
e) children	in (a)
f) control	—
g) library staff admin.	14
h) exhibitions	—
i) lecture hall	—
j) circulation	—
k) services	—
l) lavatories	—
m) stack	—
Total area:	125
Book volumes:	
a) adult lending	7,350
b) adult reference	250
c) children	2,400
d) stack	900
e) other	—
Total:	10,900
Costs in £ p:	
a) site	300
b) building	12,000
c) furniture & fittings	2,150
Total Cost (ex fees):	£14,450
Cost per square metre:	£116

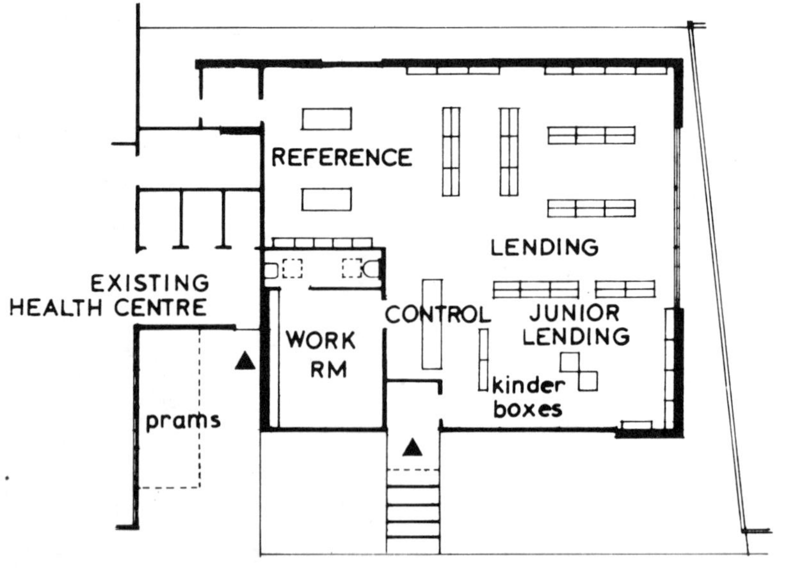

GROUND FLOOR

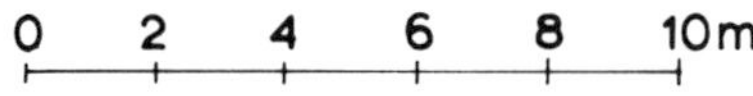

Authority	Lincolnshire County Council (formerly Lindsey and Holland)
Designation	Cherry Willingham Branch
Date of opening	February 1973
Population served	5,300
Name of Architect	A R I Aitken, RIBA, County Architect, N A Pearson, RIBA, Job Architect
Name of Librarian	E H W Roberts, FLA
Special features:	
a) site	Corner site with Health Centre and near shops
b) architecture	Traditional: rustic brick
c) function	Serving locality
Mechanical Services:	
a) heating	Gas-fired warm air
b) ventilation	Natural
c) lighting	Fluorescent strip, some tungsten
d) acoustics	Carpeted
e) other	—
Areas: in square metres	
a) lending	67
b) reference	26
c) reading	—
d) special activities	in (b)
e) children	42
f) control	7
g) library staff admin.	16
h) exhibitions	—
i) lecture hall	—
j) circulation	9
k) services	7
l) lavatories	5
m) stack	—
Total area:	179
Book volumes:	
a) adult lending	10,876
b) adult reference	in (a)
c) children	3,706
d) stack	—
e) other	—
Total:	14,582
Costs in £ p:	
a) site	1,538
b) building	—
c) furniture & fittings	—
Total Cost (ex fees):	—
Cost per square metre:	—

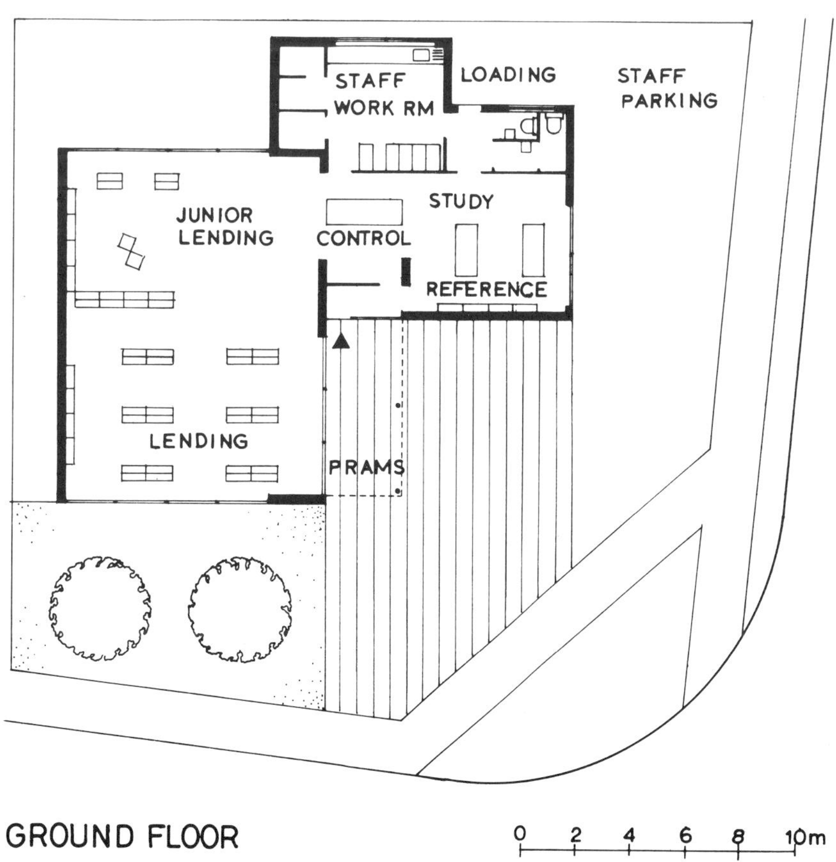

GROUND FLOOR

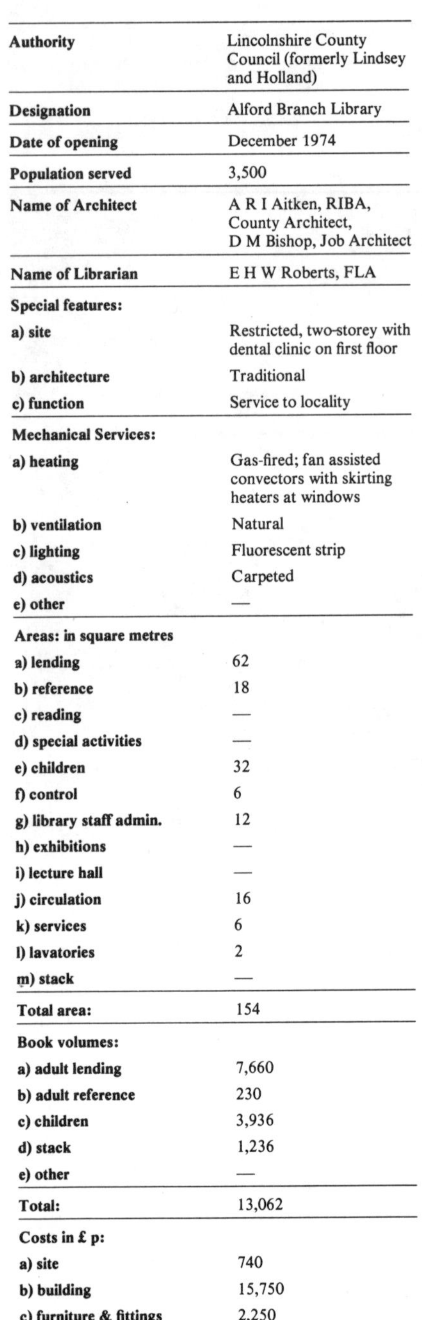

Authority	Lincolnshire County Council (formerly Lindsey and Holland)
Designation	Alford Branch Library
Date of opening	December 1974
Population served	3,500
Name of Architect	A R I Aitken, RIBA, County Architect, D M Bishop, Job Architect
Name of Librarian	E H W Roberts, FLA
Special features:	
a) site	Restricted, two-storey with dental clinic on first floor
b) architecture	Traditional
c) function	Service to locality
Mechanical Services:	
a) heating	Gas-fired; fan assisted convectors with skirting heaters at windows
b) ventilation	Natural
c) lighting	Fluorescent strip
d) acoustics	Carpeted
e) other	—
Areas: in square metres	
a) lending	62
b) reference	18
c) reading	—
d) special activities	—
e) children	32
f) control	6
g) library staff admin.	12
h) exhibitions	—
i) lecture hall	—
j) circulation	16
k) services	6
l) lavatories	2
m) stack	—
Total area:	154
Book volumes:	
a) adult lending	7,660
b) adult reference	230
c) children	3,936
d) stack	1,236
e) other	—
Total:	13,062
Costs in £ p:	
a) site	740
b) building	15,750
c) furniture & fittings	2,250
Total Cost (ex fees):	£18,740
Cost per square metre:	£115

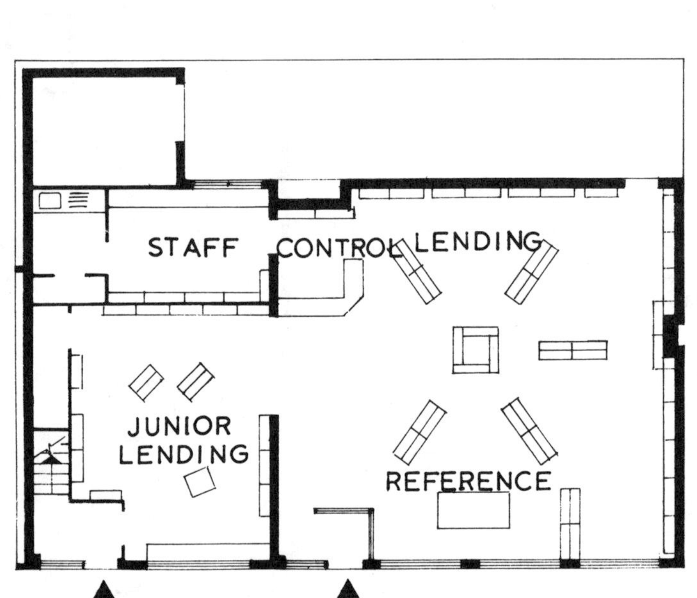

GROUND FLOOR

Washingborough
No photograph available

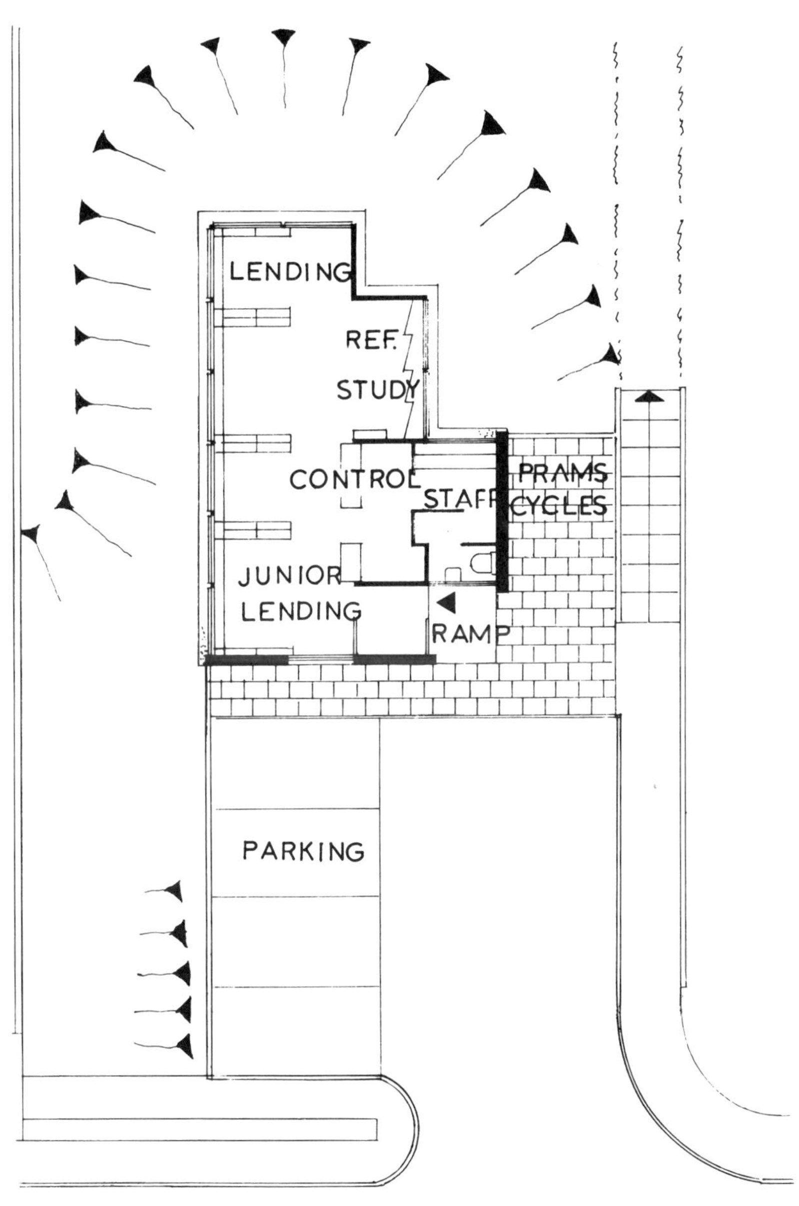

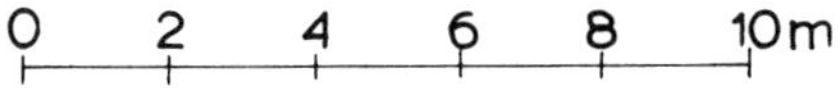

Manchester District Council (formerly City of Manchester): Abraham Moss Centre, Crumpsall District Library

The Abraham Moss Centre in the Crumpsall district of
N. Manchester is one of the most ambitious and far seeing
community buildings to have been built in this country in recent
years, and one that has surely equal significance for the future.

Four factors gave rise to the development of this massive
scheme which was named after a former Lord Mayor of the city
and distinguished local figure. The city required a new College
of Further Education, a new High School, a district library to
replace an old and outdated library close by and a recreation
centre. In a bold and imaginative mood it was decided to bring
all these functions together on the same site and to add various
other communal elements to it to produce a major community
complex where old and young could meet for academic and
entertainment purposes, sport and social events under one roof,
or series of roofs.

A 32 acre site was found in Cresent Road, Cheetham, formerly
allotments and a tip. The building occupies no less than $8\frac{1}{2}$
acres.

Designed by the City Arcitect and erected by the Direct Works
Department at a cost of some $£2\frac{1}{2}$ m. The buildings, mostly two-
and three-storeys are in CLASP construction, steel-framed and
clad externally in white precast concrete with some blue brindled
bricks.

The huge building is of incomprehensibly complex form
wandering over the great site, with a network of access ways,
beautifully laid out and imaginatively landscaped. Signposting is
generally clear and the visitor has little difficulty on arrival in
finding his way to the various elements of the development.
However this immediately throws up one of the fundamental
problems for the library, that of approachability.

The very scale of the building seen from the entrances to the site
is daunting: a long access road must be negotiated before one
even arrives at the entrance to the main pedestrian ways. It is all
rather remote from the public road and though well indicated
there is just the uncomfortable feeling on first approach that one
may have misunderstood or made a mistake, that perhaps one
has no business there after all. It would have been so much
better if it could have been so arranged that the building touched
the road, that the pedestrian circulation system linked direct
with the public footpath, that the whole building were made to
be very obviously a public open access building, which it is
certainly intended to be.

Once inside everything is at once easier; it is apparent that this is
where the public life of the community centres, children with
bathing towels mingle with old people on their way to their club,
somewhere a disco is heard and crowds of teenagers head
purposefully for the sound, library visitors with armfuls of books
encounter judo wrestlers on their way to a class. During the day
the schools are naturally predominant, but always the building
seethes with people and throbs with life.

At the very heart of all this activity, like a pivot, is the library,
not a separate unit but with its three elements on different floors,
Children's Area on ground level, the Lending Library on the first
floor and the Reference Library on the second floor. This
arrangement reflects the progression from bustle and informality
in the Children's Area, where the library overlooks one of the
main pedestrian roads and is next to a crèche approached off a
busy internal corridor, to the top floor Reference Library which
is at the end of a corridor and not overlooked, a relatively quiet
corner. The Lending Library is in an intermediate position with
busy corridors on two sides, arguably too much overlooked
through the glass screens to the corridor.

It is slightly questionable whether the arrangement on three
floors is ideal, particularly as there is no internal communication
purely for staff. Any journey from one department to another
involves going out into the corridor then through doors to the
stairs and back into the next corridor. The divisions are
obviously necessary in such a large building to limit the danger
of fire but these do cut the library into three slices.

The Junior Library is totally separate with its own small office
and children's lavatories, with a reserve stockroom. The
arrangement of bookcases is rather formal and restrictive with
four shelf-high units with hardwood faced ends and neat
canopies above children's eye-level. As so often in children's
libraries it is the lack of a sense of fun that is particularly sad. To
design a children's library without in any way playing down to
children but at the same time giving it character appropriate to
them is to walk a tightrope. It is so much easier to settle, as
has been done here, for a scaled-down adult library and leave it
at that.

The restraints of the rigid structural system are very apparent in
the building and the feeling of building in Lego or Meccano is
hard to accept. The steel framework makes it rather difficult to
damp down the sounds of heavy tramping feet in corridors and
it is a noisy building.

The Lending Library is more interesting for it has been possible
to introduce a central section where the library is of double
height, lit by rooflights high above. The Reference Library
surrounds this internal well and looks down into it albeit through
glazed screens. The feeling of space in both departments is vital,
for elsewhere ceilings are sensibly low and such large areas of
unrelieved flat ceiling can be oppressive.

Walls are lined with pine boarding which imparts a warm
colouring, picked up in the timber ends of the bookcases and
enhanced by the totally carpeted floor. Ceilings are of acoustic
absorbent tiles in metal framing with a simple, unobtrusive and
efficient layout of fluorescent lighting.

In one respect, however, this library suffers, as do so many
others which adopt the deep plan with minimal external wall:
they are hopelessly stuffy, and in summer unbearably hot, since
the chances of obtaining any cross ventilation virtually nil. This
complaint is met with quite sickening regularity in new libraries.
Admittedly air conditioning is generally out of the question on
financial grounds, but if this is the case, resort must be had to
natural ventilation, and this becomes a basic design

consideration influencing plan form and the whole architecture solution.

Counters are well designed, very efficient and functional, and we particularly liked the arrangement whereby trolleys for returned books are housed beneath the counter. Furniture and fittings generally have been well considered and there are many interesting ideas worthy of study.

The accommodation is completed by an Audio Visual Aid Resources Room and a large separate study room off the Reference Library. Staff have a workroom at Lending Library level with Librarian's office and staff locker room with WC's but unfortunately no separate staff room.

This is a bold experiment and it would be interesting to know how the public react to it. Certainly when this reviewer visited the building on a wet cold evening in January it was exceedingly busy but of the visitors young people seemed to form the majority. It would indeed be unfortunate if, as one rather suspects, middle-aged or elderly library users were to be put off by the remoteness of the building complex or by the obvious predominance of the young. However the links with school and college are vitally important and the opportunities for people pursuing a wide variety of occupations to become involved in the library as a by-product must be an exciting prospect for the librarian. This is a new slant on setting the library 'in the market place'.

GKVT   GT

Authority	Manchester City Council
Designation	Crumpsall District Library, Abraham Moss Centre
Date of opening	July 1974
Population served	35,000
Name of Architect	S G Besant Roberts, DipArch, RIBA, ADF(Man)
Name of Librarian	Isadore Wallman, FLA
Special features:	
a) site	Part of complex including school, college of further education, adult education centre, leisure centre, old people's and youth club
b) architecture	Clasp system
c) function	District Library
Mechanical Services:	
a) heating	Natural convection and forced warm air
b) ventilation	Natural
c) lighting	Fluorescent 400 lux
d) acoustics	—
e) other	—
Areas: in square metres	
a) lending	—
b) reference	—
c) reading	—
d) special activities	—
e) children	—
f) control	
g) library staff admin.	—
h) exhibitions	—
i) lecture hall	—
j) circulation	—
k) services	—
l) lavatories	—
m) stack	—
Total area:	1,869
Book volumes:	
a) adult lending	38,785
b) adult reference	2,224
c) children	10,278
d) stack	—
e) other	Records 3,198, cassettes 1,445, framed prints 233
Total:	56,163
Costs in £ p:	
a) site	—
b) building	157,722
c) furniture & fittings	28,212
Total Cost (ex fees):	£185,934
Cost per square metre:	£99

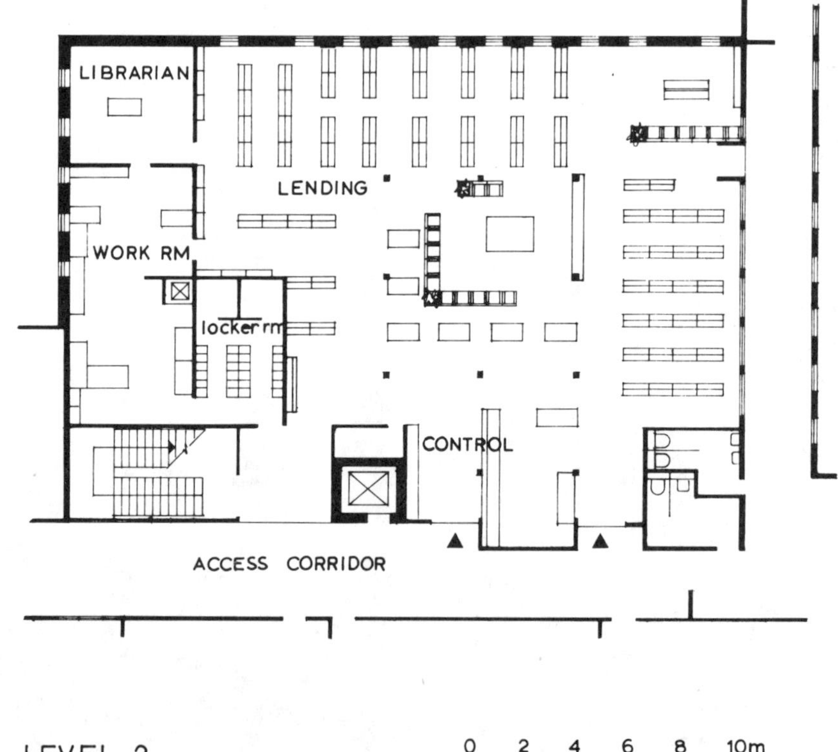

Photographs by courtesy of Manchester City Council

Northamptonshire County Council: Desborough

Desborough is a small town of 6,000 population (due to grow to 9,000 by about 1990), located on the A6 road between Kettering and Market Harborough. The library is situated on a slight curve of the road near the centre of the town, but with through traffic being diverted on a new by-pass, the area will be relatively traffic-free. An old peoples' home has been built adjacent to the new library.

The plan basically comprises three square spaces with internally exposed monopitch roofs, around a central exhibition space and control counter. Staff, work and store areas are in a low block to the rear, the store designed to take part of the county stock. The Meeting Room can be used separately, reached from the entrance lobby, which is a slightly constricted space.

The main library is a square room, with continuous windows on the east and south walls, the south-facing windows protected from glare by deep overhanging roof eaves. There is a continuous upholstered bench seat under the windows, with grilles beneath supplying warm air from the electric night storage heaters. Exposed monopitch timber roof trusses span north to south, with a large north-facing rooflight. The trusses are stained, and their soffit provides a fixing for fluorescent light fittings, which run at right angles to the shelves. The librarian spoke of a slight problem of supervision, but this could easily be solved by switching round some of the shelves. Off the library is a low 'inglenook' room for reading periodicals; with a continuous perimeter seat, its intimacy and snugness makes it a very pleasant place for a quiet read – or snooze! A simple vocabulary of finishes are used throughout internally: painted brickwork, stained timber, and carpeted floors.

Desborough Library, despite or because of its small scale, has all the qualities of fine architecture: a simple plan, and an evolution of interesting spaces through the building; it is well related to its site, with appropriately simple landscaping around the building; and with excellent use of materials and detailing, both internally and externally. It has that quality of unpretentious rightness associated with Japanese and Danish architecture, which is the highest praise; and if this reviewer was asked to award prizes, Desborough Library would be a strong candidate. It is also an example of the fine work being done quietly in the provinces, away from the often suspect spotlight of the glossy magazines.

NR

Authority	Northamptonshire County Council
Designation	Desborough Library
Date of opening	February 1974
Population served	6,000
Name of Architect	County Architect's Department
Name of Librarian	R Wright FLA
Special features:	
a) site	Main road frontage
b) architecture	—
c) function	Library purposes plus display area/exhibition room/lecture room
Mechanical Services:	
a) heating	Electric storage heaters
b) ventilation	—
c) lighting	Fluorescent
d) acoustics	—
e) other	—
Areas: in square metres	
a) lending	126
b) reference	16
c) reading	—
d) special activities	—
e) children	38
f) control	—
g) library staff admin.	6
h) exhibitions	25
i) lecture hall	—
j) circulation	56
k) local colln.	2
l) staff room	16
m) stack	39
Total area:	324
Book volumes:	
a) adult lending	7,100
b) adult reference	77
c) children	4,100
d) stack	4,050
e) other	40
Total:	15,367
Costs in £ p:	
a) site	4,450
b) building	32,109
c) furniture & fittings	2,432
Total Cost (ex fees):	£38,991
Cost per square metre:	£120

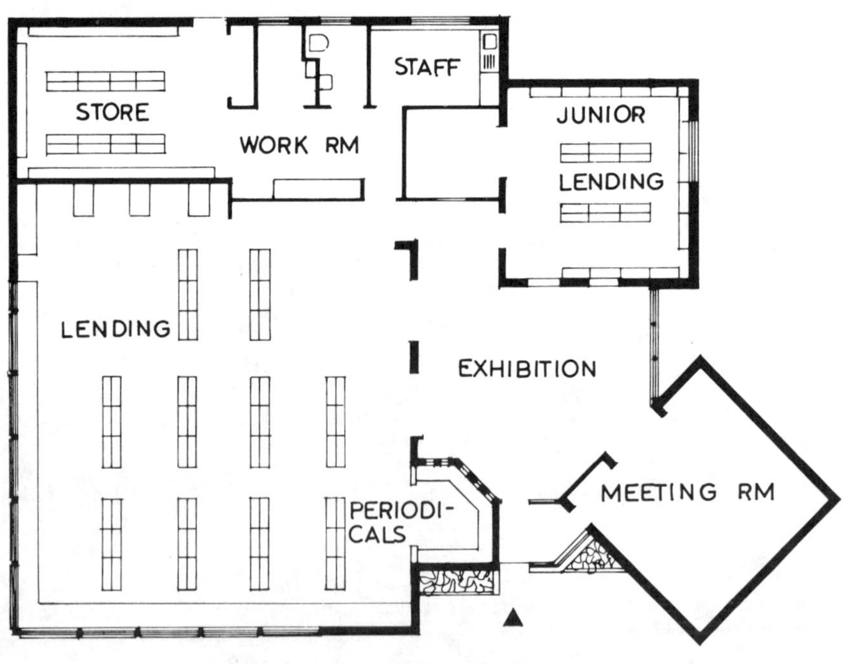

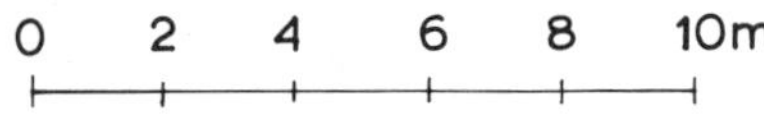

GROUND FLOOR

North Yorkshire County Council (formerly North Riding County Council): Ayton

The library is in the centre of a pleasant village about $4\frac{1}{2}$ miles west of Scarborough and is obviously very popular with the local inhabitants. An attractive free standing building, chunky in local stone: the only possible objection to its site is that it is on a busy tourist route. The locals say, however, that this traffic is periodic and does not affect the library at all.

The building invites; surrounded by car parking, it has a most attractive entrance with a clear notice of hours of opening (movable letters behind glass) and the notice even includes the name of the librarian-in-charge. A shatterproof lighting pillar serves not only to guide after dark but to make the exterior of the building even more charming.

The porch is generous and serves as a display area and through the swing doors (which seem noisy) one comes to a conventional oblong room. Although fully carpeted, the interior does not attract as much as the exterior. One has the feeling that the librarians are trying to make the building do too much. The shelving appears to crowd it somewhat and, to my mind, the provision of reading space for reference work (and much of this is merely homework) appears excessive. Perhaps this is a comment on librarianship and not architecture, and therefore out of place in this critique.

Heating is by blown air through ducts and the Propane oil tank is camouflaged at the side of the building. In the Children's Library, which serves also for story hours, are some rather cute little chairs for use with Kinder boxes. The emphasis on work with children is very strong.

To me the great disappointment of the building is the very low standard of wood and metalwork around the doors and windows. This would be less noticeable if it were in a cheaper and less attractive building.

GT

Authority	North Yorkshire County
Designation	Ayton Branch Library
Date of opening	August 1973
Population served	2,500
Name of Architect	D J Lane, RIBA, Project Architect, J Brian Jackson, MCD, BArch, FRTPI, Principal Architect
Name of Librarian	D M Hudson, FLA, County Librarian
Special features:	
a) site	—
b) architecture	—
c) function	—
Mechanical Services:	
a) heating	Propane gas warm air
b) ventilation	—
c) lighting	Recessed fluorescene
d) acoustics	Ceiling tiles, carpet tiled floor
e) other	—
Areas: in square metres	
a) lending	—
b) reference	—
c) reading	—
d) special activities	—
e) children	—
f) control	—
g) library staff admin.	—
h) exhibitions	—
i) lecture hall	
j) circulation	—
k) services	—
l) lavatories	—
m) stack	—
Total area:	140
Book volumes:	
a) adult lending	5,990
b) adult reference	170
c) children	2,210
d) stack	230
e) other	—
Total:	8,600
Costs in £ p:	
a) site	1,400
b) building / c) furniture & fittings	16,800
Total Cost (ex fees):	£18,200
Cost per square metre:	£120

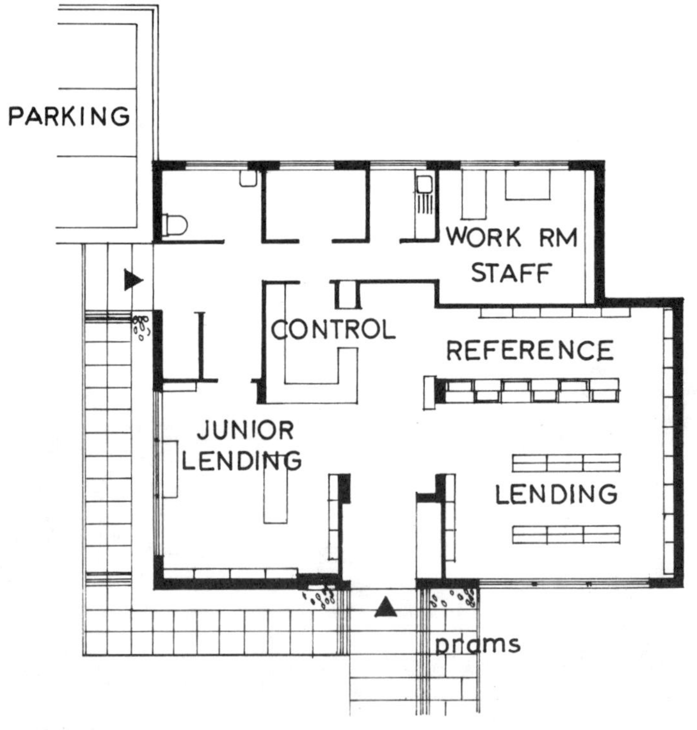

GROUND FLOOR

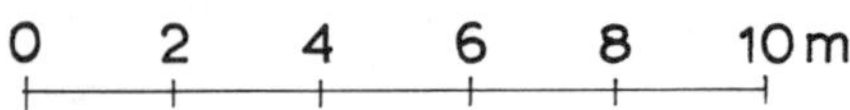

Rotherham District Council:
Mowbray Gardens: (formerly Rotherham Borough Council)
Kiveton Park:
(formerly West Riding County Council)

Mowbray Gardens Library (strictly the Percy Wright Branch Library) replaces one previously in a nearby school and serves a fairly small estate, not far from the centre of Rotherham. Its clientele, past and future, is somewhat limited by the confluence of two major roads; I make this point because it is a very generous library for the number it actually serves.

The single room library is an octagon of just over 200 m², joined by a common entrance hall to a small swimming-bath. The buildings are nicely balanced but the large car park is at the rear; consequently those parking cars almost invariably walk across the grass surround to reach the front of the building. There is a large paved area in front of the building, leading on to the main road which has no apparent purpose.

Inside the library room the effect is quite breathtaking. Large wooden supports to the octagonal roof give an effect rather like a series of prows of Viking ships. There is a tremendous impression of room and light, the colour of the wood being the dominant feature. Inside the roof, recessed fluorescent lights make a striking pattern but they must be permanently switched on because the clerestory windows below the octagon roof bring in light which is not very helpful to those using the wall shelving. Adjustable spots on tracks along the roof add emphasis but do not give sufficient general lighting. The areas of glass in the roof provide some light and, as usual, considerable heat from the sun, for which the small extractors do not really compensate. Heating is by gas-fired hot water pipes embedded in the concrete floor. Effective enough, but one wonders what happens if the pipes ever need servicing.

Symmetrical, full-length windows occupy three of the eight sides (the entrance door forming a fourth) and the cheerfulness of the library is enhanced by paintings standing on top of the wall shelving and by displays around the room. The counter faces the entrance but an odd feature is that the Children's Library surrounds it, hemmed in by free standing bookcases forming half a circle. This is, of course, ideal for supervision for this small library but the other side of the coin is that behind these cases the area is completely unsupervisable. It also means that the staff have an unnecessarily long walk when shelving books.

The size of the library is generous for an estimated population of 8,000 and the purpose-made wooden shelving is to a lower height than would normally be fitted; more books could have been accommodated in the room but are obviously not needed. The staff room is adequate enough with a window on to the car park but the woodwork and finishes here are of a surprisingly low standard compared with that of the public areas. The skylight over the staff room has had to be reinforced by bars because of nocturnal visitors.

An unusal point is that the common approachway to the baths, floored in vinyl, produces very considerable noise when classes of schoolchildren pour into the baths for there seems to be no way of keeping this noise out of the library. The common foyer has a very pleasant shadow-sculpture mural based on alphabetical themes. There is a very small display window at the front of the building but it is behind the grassed area and is not very cleverly placed.

Generous for the public it has to serve, and beautifully made inside! That one feels it is rather expensive for its purpose perhaps shows the low standards to which we have become accustomed.

Kiveton Park is a great contrast to Mowbray Gardens. It is on the main shopping street of a straggling village newly embedded into the Rotherham Metropolitan District but looking naturally to Worksop or Sheffield for its big town shopping. It was the last library put up by the then West Riding County and is pretty spartan.

Providing nearly 300 m² of public space, it is constructed with reinforced concrete floor, load-bearing brick walls and a flat timber roof. Despite the picture window at the front there is a claustrophobic effect from the utilitarian shape and the unimaginative repetition of small windows along the walls. The children's section of the open plan library, divided by columns, can be separated by folding vinyl screens which recess into a case. The walls and plywood ceiling are painted white and the library area is completely carpeted.

There is plenty of space within the room and comparatively little shelving; the whole library looks what it is, a standard production unit. The best features are some well-thought-out fitted furniture in the reference area, including a built-in map case. It is a busy library and one of the difficulties of increasing the amount of shelving is in the matching of additional shelving to that provided by the now defunct Authority. There is a large workroom/staff room and a good range of discs and cassettes on special stands. Prints for loan are used extensively to brighten up the area and every effort has been made to overcome the very bleak architectural concept.

GT

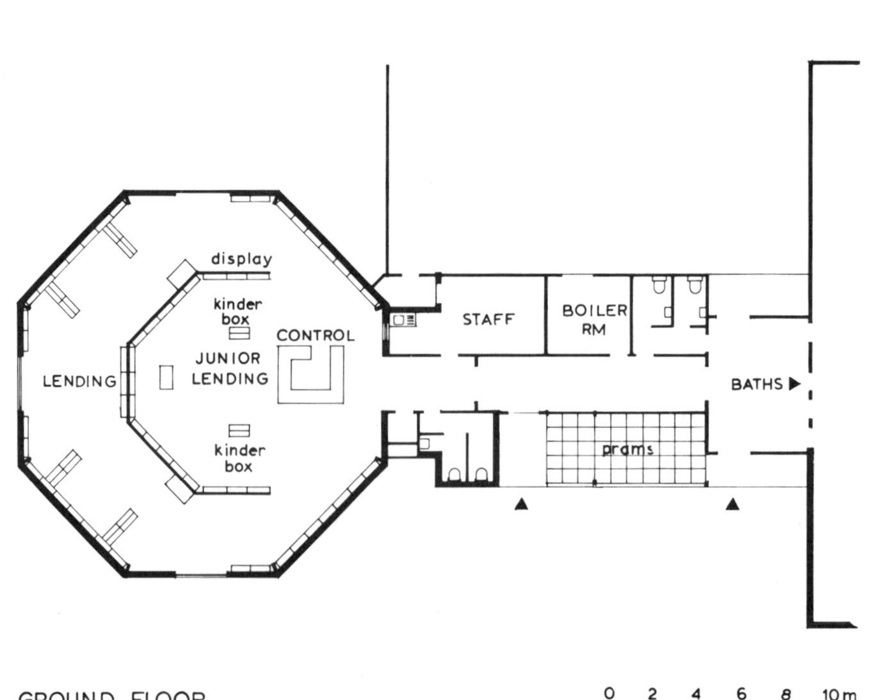

Authority	Metropolitan District of Rotherham
Designation	Percy Wright Branch Library, Mowbray Gardens
Date of opening	December 1973
Population served	8,000
Name of Architect	D Knox, DipArch, DipCD, MRTPI, ARIBA, Borough Architect
Name of Librarian	L G Lovell, FLA (now Director, Manchester)
Special features:	
a) site	Acute triangular site adjoining main road
b) architecture	Timber frame
c) function	—
Mechanical Services:	
a) heating	Gas-fired hot water with pipes embedded in floor
b) ventilation	2 extractor fans
c) lighting	Fluorescent diffused
d) acoustics	—
e) other	Shares entrance foyer and public lavatories with adjacent swimming bath
Areas: in square metres	
a) lending	
b) reference	
c) reading	
d) special activities	210
e) children	
f) control	
g) library staff admin.	—
h) exhibitions	—
i) lecture hall	—
j) circulation	—
k) services	—
l) lavatories	—
m) stack	—
Total area:	300
Book volumes:	
a) adult lending	5,700
b) adult reference	50
c) children	3,300
d) stack	250
e) other	—
Total:	9,300
Costs in £ p:	
a) site	—
b) building	34,365
c) furniture & fittings	3,989
Total Cost (ex fees):	£38,354
Cost per square metre:	£182

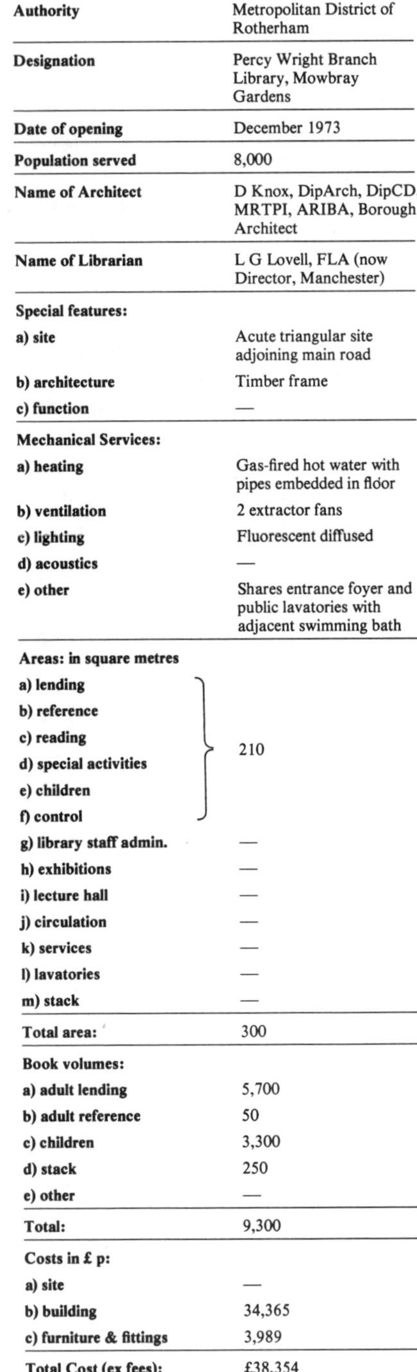

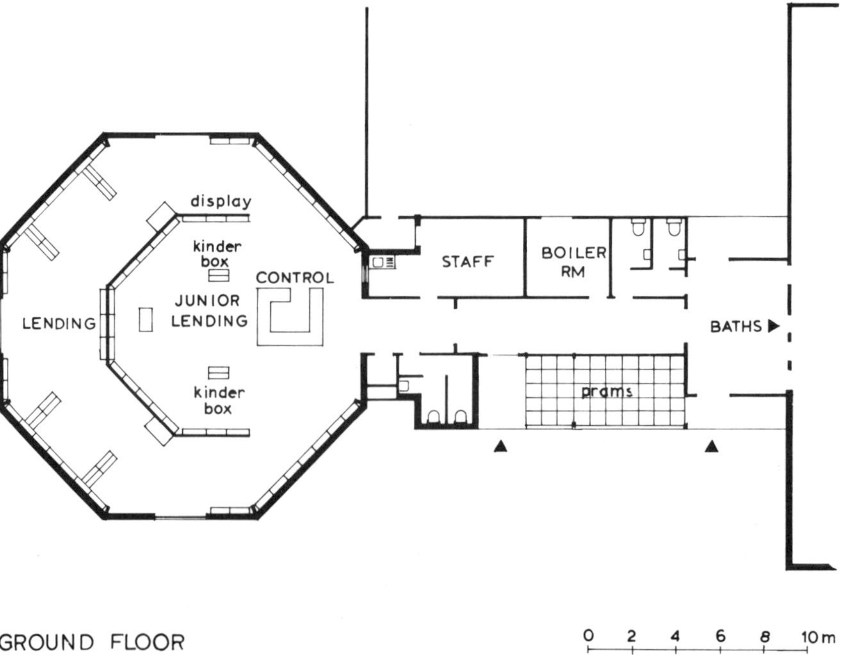

GROUND FLOOR

Authority	Metropolitan District of Rotherham (formerly County of West Riding
Designation	Kiveton Park Branch Library
Date of opening	January 1974
Population served	7,000
Name of Architect	K C Evans, DipArch, ARIBA, Former County Architect
Name of Librarian	W J Morison, FLA, FLAI, Former County Librarian
Special features:	
a) site	—
b) architecture	Reinforced concrete floor, load bearing brick walls, flat timber roof
c) function	—
Mechanical Services:	
a) heating	Electric underfloor
b) ventilation	—
c) lighting	Roof lights and fluorescent
d) acoustics	—
e) other	—
Areas: in square metres	
a) lending	—
b) reference	—
c) reading	—
d) special activities	—
e) children	—
f) control	—
g) library staff admin.	—
h) exhibitions	—
i) lecture hall	—
j) circulation	—
k) services	—
l) lavatories	—
m) stack	—
Total area:	316
Book volumes:	
a) adult lending	8,700
b) adult reference	800
c) children	4,600
d) stack	600
e) other	Records 500, cassettes 60, pictures 100
Total:	15,360
Costs in £ p:	
a) site	—
b) building	31,762
c) furniture & fittings	—
Total Cost (ex fees):	31,762 plus fittings (unknown)
Cost per square metre:	£100 plus fittings

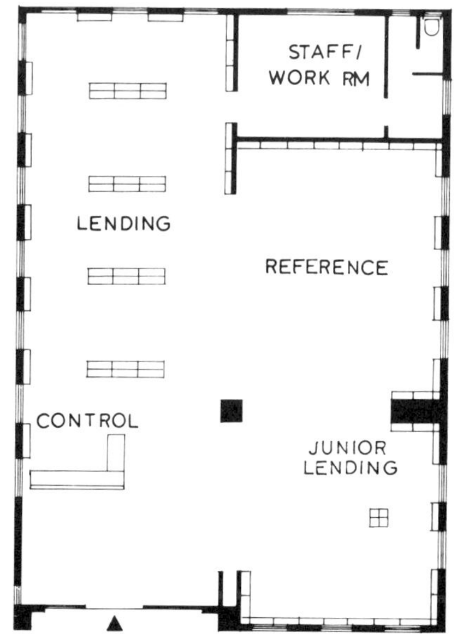

GROUND FLOOR

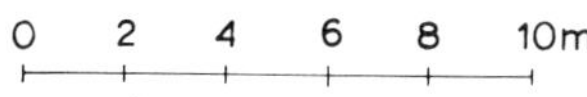

Salop County Council:
Market Drayton and Oswestry

Market Drayton, the Draitune of Domesday Book, is in the heart of the rural Shropshire, Cheshire, Staffordshire plain. A market town since the charter granted in 1245 it sits compactly on its small hill over the River Tern, a gridiron of narrow streets with a Butter cross, and half timbered buildings. Its most famous son, Clive of India, went to the grammar school where his desk can still be seen. It was therefore a nice touch to call the new building the Clive Library, a link with the past in a town conscious and proud of its history.

The relationship of the library to the town could scarcely be better, for it is situated at the centre of gravity of the town on market day, Wednesday, when the surrounding population pours into the town, greatly increasing the normal population of 7,500. Apart from a large sausage factory there is little industry in the town which relies mostly on its close relationship with the country for employment.

The library, open 40 hours per week is very busy and popular, manned by a librarian, with one full- and one part-time assistant and an additional Saturday helper. Part of a new and large SCOLA system-built complex, which also includes a Health Centre and clinic and magistrates court and is backed by a large public car park, the library faces on to Cheshire Street where the market is held on the wide pavement. Library and Court entrances face each other beneath a wide archway leading from the street to the car park.

Out of sight behind the single storey staff wing of the library, a service courtyard gives access for van deliveries from other county libraries. Market Drayton is a satellite of Whitchurch Area Library, some 10 miles away to the north-west, though it is busier than its parent building, issuing about 125,000 volumes a year.

The building complex as a whole is rather large in scale for the small town, despite attempts to break up the mass by modelling and the archway mentioned above. A porch from the covered pedestrian way, fitted with a business-like mat, leads into an open area with plenty of pin-board for display. The counter is rather a long way off at the centre of the library. This space is used for local history displays or travelling exhibitions arranged by either the County service or local societies.

The local Council have provided a telephone link to their own offices for use by members of the public wishing to make enquiries about Council services. This telephone is fitted with an acoustic hood and is situated immediately inside the entrance. In practice this has been unsatisfactory, for people telephoning can be heard in the library—to their embarrassment and that of other library users.

The counter takes the form, at present, of two desks, and a new purpose-designed counter is awaited. Since issue is by the photocharge method there is comparatively little clutter at this point, as noted in the review of Oswestry Library. The placing of the staff enclosure at the junction of the two arms of the L-shaped room, one arm of which is the Children's Library and the other the Adult's section, allows good supervision.

The informality of the layout helps in the establishment of a warm friendly atmosphere in the library which owes much to its being at the centre of the life of the close knit community. Individual readers are recognised and treated as such by the staff, something that is more difficult to achieve in large communities.

The almost intimate character of the library is enhanced by the choice of a yellow carpet, curtains to the long lines of windows and the comfortable informal furniture. The ceiling is of white painted slag wood acoustic panels and walls are finished with either bright coloured paint or patterned wallpapers, producing an almost domestic feeling of considerable charm.

A delightful idea is the slightly dropped oval canopy in the Children's area finished in brown hessian which incorporates a curtain track with brown curtains that can be drawn to form an oval, cosy 'tent' for story hours for younger readers. Lighting in this enclosure is by a ring of glass shaped tungsten lights with flexes draped from a centre ceiling rose, forming a decorative 'Chinese hat' pattern which shows up well against the brown ceiling. The fact that this area is in the library, not segregated or hidden, is appealing.

For quiet study, a row of six semi-carrel desks with individual lights is tucked away in a corner out of sight of the counter. This is popular with schoolchildren and though it might elsewhere have proved an open invitation to misbehaviour and vandalism this has not been the case here. Such problems seldom arise, though there is no lack of high spirits on the part of children using the library. It is noticeable how much better rural communities treat their buildings than their counterparts in large urban situations.

Local history material is kept in locked glass-fronted showcases and there is also a fine display of brass market grain measures and standard weights of special interest.

Timber bookshelving is by Reska and there are matching canopies. Tier guiding is rather casual with cardboard, rather crudely lettered labels stuck on to canopies. There are a number of neat solutions to this problem which fit in well with the canopy design costing comparatively little but giving a much more professional appearance. A gramophone record browser box is sited close to the readers' adviser's desk.

Staff quarters are very small but quite adequate for such a small staff. A workroom with an outside door to the service yard fitted with workbench and Remploy shelving leads direct to the tiny staff room with cooking facilities. Stores for cleaner and librarians and men's and women's lavatories open off a short corridor from the counter area to the workroom.

In addition to Oswestry and Market Drayton Libraries reported here, the County have, in the same period, converted a Victorian primary school building in Church Street, at minimal cost, to serve as a library. Limitations of time precluded this being visited.

Authority	Salop County Council
Designation	The Clive Library, Market Drayton
Date of opening	January 1974
Population served	7,089
Name of Architect	John V Bunker, RIBA, County Architect, W A Clarke, RIBA, Job Architect
Name of Librarian	G Dickens, ALA
Special features:	
a) site	Part of health centre, magistrates court complex adjacent to market
b) architecture	System built "scola"
c) function	Public Library
Mechanical Services:	
a) heating	Gas-fired warm air
b) ventilation	Natural
c) lighting	Fluorescent and tungsten
d) acoustics	Carpets; acoustic panel ceiling
e) other	—
Areas: in square metres	
a) lending	130
b) reference	In lending
c) reading	37
d) special activities	—
e) children	45
f) control	10
g) library staff admin.	33
h) exhibitions	15
i) lecture hall	—
j) circulation	28
k) services	—
l) lavatories	8
m) stack	—
Total area:	306
Book volumes:	
a) adult lending	4,732
b) adult reference	378
c) children	1,652
d) stack	251
e) other	448 gramophone records
Total:	7,013 vol
Costs in £ p:	
a) site	—
b) building	32,844
c) furniture & fittings	4,450
Total Cost (ex fees):	£37,294
Cost per square metre:	£126

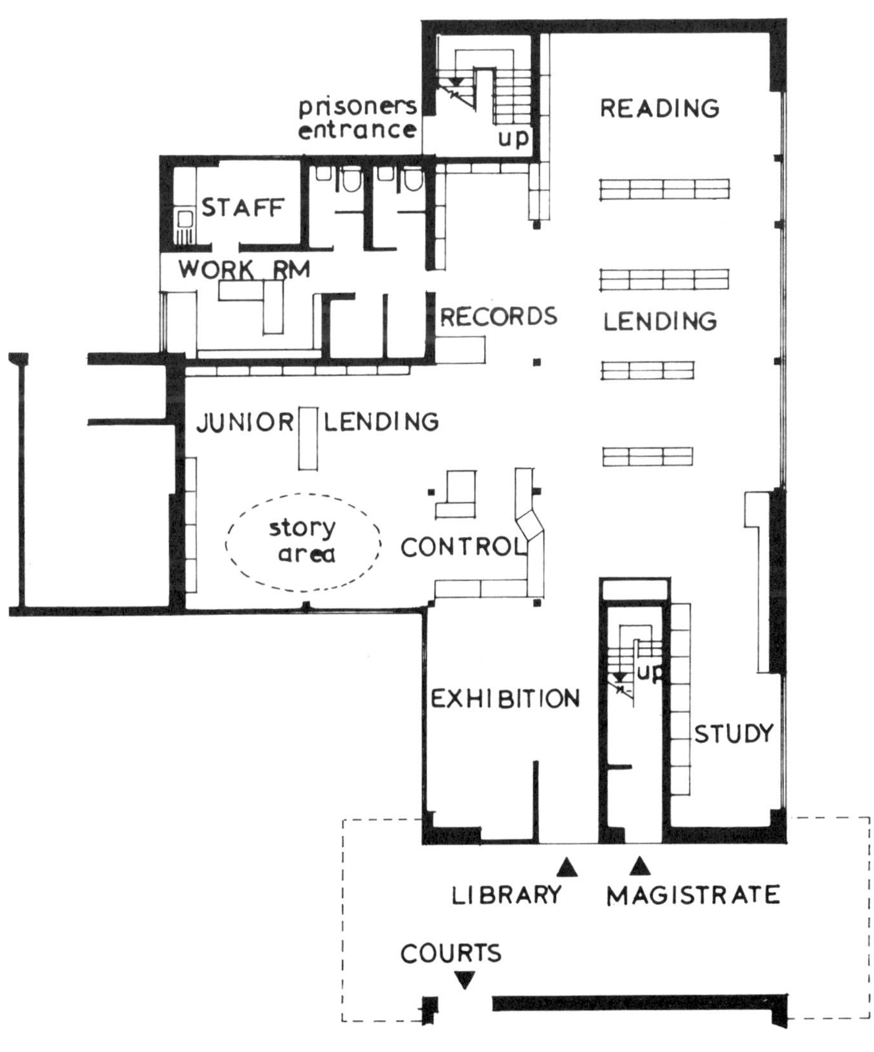

Oswestry Set in the delightful scenery of the Welsh border country the little market town of Oswestry, with its population of about 12,000, is an important rural centre. The library serves a population of perhaps 30,000 including regular visitors to the town for shopping and market.

Tucked away up the hill from the main shopping area but only a minute or two's walk from the market the library occupies a building which is thought to have started life as a mill. This has been modernised and a new wing added in an imaginative scheme by the County Architect. The small lane onto which the library faces has been carefully landscaped after removal of old derelict buildings and now forms a very pleasant approach to the library with small scale planting and paving. A car park for library users accommodates 14 cars and there is room for the mobile library vehicle to drive into the covered garage and beyond to a washing area.

The old part of the building is a simple gabled building with decorated door and window openings, well proportioned vernacular architecture. Unfortunately the new building, bold and simple though it is, does not live up to its parent building. The large, grim, almost windowless box with red brick at first floor over a purple brick base presents an unsympathetic and unwelcoming exterior.

However, the delightful design and detailing of the interior somewhat makes up for these shortcomings. Planned on several interconnecting levels, with skilfully placed openings linking the various rooms with intriguing views, the whole library unfolds as one walks round in a most satisfying manner. The small coir matted lobby leads to a reception area where the Librarian, sitting at a low desk, contrives to run the issue and book-return single handed without the usual paraphenalia of a counter. This is made possible by the use of camera issue system which does away with the usual trays of cards and allows a feeling of considerable informality to prevail. A pleasant feature of the desk area is that the lively books and pamphlets, produced by the County on aspects of rural local history, are on sale, thus adding interest.

From the reception area stairs lead down to the large workroom, with its doors beyond, direct to the mobile library garage. There is considerable storage space for books for stocking the mobile. The workroom is large enough to facilitate the considerable volume of book movement to and from other libraries in the authority, linked by a sophisticated and efficient Telex inter-library loan system. A book hoist serves all floors. The building acts as Area HQ for North West Salop with five satellite branches to be served besides the mobile, which itself accounts for nearly half of the 200,000 books issued each year. It is heartening to find that the staff in the workroom have a large window on to the garden in front of the library from which people coming to the library can be seen. Too often staff are hidden away in dark internal rooms without any view.

At the same level as the reception desk, through an archway, the original library has been rearranged to form a large adult lending room with tall side windows to the high ceiling at the sides of the room. A dropped centre section of ceiling, pine boarded and with recessed fluorescent lights, makes for a more intimate atmosphere than would have been possible if the high ceiling had been used throughout, whilst the tall windows give good natural daylighting. Shelves line the walls leaving the centre clear. The colours are cheerful with a yellow carpet and orange hessian pin-boards for display material.

Further lending stock and reference material together with partly limited access rolling stock containing local history material is to be found at a mezzanine level in the extension building. Because of its position, so close to Wales, the library also houses a substantial collection of Welsh language books. This large room has a floor-to-ceiling window with a view to the Welsh hills over the roofs of the town. It is well lighted from two rows of rooflights running right across the room in the pine boarded ceiling. These are of complex interesting shape with concealed fluorescent lighting. Within this large airy room is a further mezzanine balcony on which gramophone records and books on music are to be found. The view from this eyrie through the main room and out to the distant hills is dramatic and exciting. The mezzanine which is at the level of the first floor of the old building leads on through to the staff accommodation on the way to the Children's Library up steps at the highest level.

In addition to the Librarian's office, staff room and so on, there is a small lobby with display cases containing a fascinating collection of brass market scales and weights and other material of local interest. The staff room which is far too small for the needs of the staff of four professionals and three part-time librarians with additional Saturday helpers and van driver, is dark and gloomy in contrast with the cheerful public areas.

Only in a place where behaviour is as good as Oswestry could the Children's Library have been planned in such a remote corner, out of view of the desk, seldom manned. Here there is apparently little trouble. A cosy stepped pit for story hours is hidden behind a bookcase, a delightful idea for younger readers.

A separate staircase from the street leads to the overlarge, rather forbidding meeting room which is understandably little used as it has neither lavatory nor refreshment facilities. Fortunately a number of alternative rooms are available in the town.

Despite the unprepossessing exterior the warm, friendly, informal atmosphere of the interior ensures it popularity. A note of discord is, however, struck by the collection of unsightly unco-ordinated furniture–inherited, no doubt, from the original building.

GKVT

Authority	Salop County Council
Designation	Oswestry Library
Date of opening	September 1973
Population served	12,000
Name of Architect	John Bunker, DipArch, RIBA, County Architect, Peter Parker Jones, RIBA, Job Architect
Name of Librarian	—
Special features:	
a) site	Restricted urban site
b) architecture	Loadbearing brick, RC floors
c) function	Public library extension
Mechanical Services:	
a) heating	Gas-fired low pressure hot water radiators and fan convector
b) ventilation	Natural
c) lighting	Fluorescent, tungsten spotlights
d) acoustics	Carpet
e) other	—
Areas: in square metres	
a) lending	198
b) reference	18
c) reading	30
d) special activities	—
e) children	56
f) control	32
g) library staff admin.	72
h) exhibitions	13
i) lecture hall	60
j) circulation	24
k) services	13
l) lavatories	10
m) stack	—
Total area:	526
Book volumes:	
a) adult lending	10,998
b) adult reference	2,000
c) children	7,198
d) stack	—
e) other	—
Total:	20,196
Costs in £ p:	
a) site	—
b) building	45,559
c) furniture & fittings	6,660
Total Cost (ex fees):	£52,219
Cost per square metre:	Not applicable, part of cost is conversion

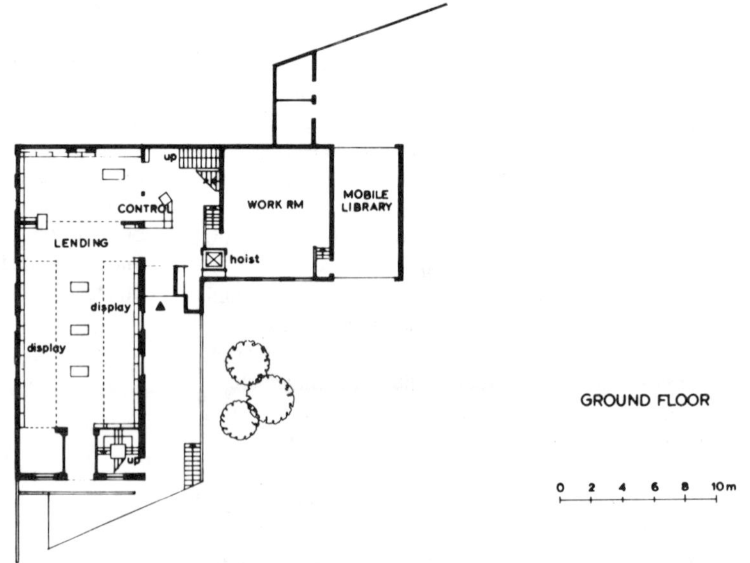

Sefton District Council: Birkdale

Birkdale is virtually a suburb of Southport on the Lancashire coast at the northern end of the long Borough of Sefton which also includes Formby, Bootle and Crosby. The main road linking these towns passes the new library which is a hundred yards or so from a minor local shopping parade. Though there is no particularly apparent reason for the choice of site (other than the availability of a number of run-down properties), in practice it has proved to be well situated. A good car park has been provided and there is space for about 15 cars.

It is unfortunate that the pleasant landscaping scheme by the architect, with paving and cobbles as well as shrubs and seats on the grass, has not been started. The area around the library is very untidy and scruffy and does not do justice to a pleasant and intelligently designed building. This consists of a large Lending Library room, uninterrupted by any columns, with splayed sections of wall with windows between and a rectangular block behind containing Children's Library, staff rooms, store and public toilets approached from outside at the rear of the library.

The entrance lobby is spacious and has glazed walls to outside and to the library, with a ribbed matted floor and large pin-boards for notices. A large canopy outside provides pram parking areas, in clear view from the counter. The interesting counters works well and is a good example of the result of close co-operation between the architect and libraries at briefing stage, working well and providing ample space for staff to move around. The catalogues are all placed facing inwards to staff and not accessible to the public, a policy followed consistently in Sefton. Lighting in the library is all controlled from the counter, a convenient arrangement. Visibility of the whole library with its low bookcases on wheels is excellent.

The room is very spacious and has ample room for growth of the stock. Daylighting is from the side windows only, with no rooflighting. Permanent artificial lighting is accepted and the building is well insulated and consciously designed to conserve energy; the double glass screens and the front provide good views whilst at the same time preventing excessive heat loss.

The small odd-shaped Reference Room is difficult to furnish but is so little used that this has not been found critical. A small stock of quick-reference material and four semi-carrel desks provide all that is necessary for the limited reference demand— probably because the central library in Southport is not too distant.

The arrangement of window recesses with their lower ceiling height makes for pleasant areas for quiet browsing; the reader can tuck himself away beneath the windows on a seat out of the circulation area. The seats are unfortunately not very comfortable and a little draughty since the budget did not run to double glazing.

The least satisfactory feature of the library is the rather distracting ceiling. This is finished in corrugated white enamelled aluminium sheeting, with very peculiar recesses lined in brown painted timber, which promise at first sight to be roof-lights but are in fact only patternmaking, varying the otherwise uninterrupted ceiling. There is a certain amount of twinkle from the shiny material but a plain acoustic tile would have provided a more restful atmosphere and more acoustic absorption. The powerful pattern formed by the brown, black, orange and beige tiles is quite sufficient in itself, the patterned ceiling merely making the room fussy. The artificial lighting, mainly by fluorescent tubes without diffusers, can be varied by the use of a line of tungsten, swivel spotlights.

Bookshelving is by Remploy in Abura hardwood with top and bottom rails to the bookcases painted black. The lowest of the five wall shelves is at a sensible height above the floor which runs through beneath to the wall giving a very neat appearance. The centre bookcases, all on wheels, allow considerable flexibility in arrangement but are rather too heavy to wheel when full.

Between the Adult Library and Children's Library two large double-sided glass display cases allow good vision into the latter but it is rather remote from the counter which makes supervision and advice on book selection difficult. The cases do give excellent opportunities for arranging interesting exhibitions.

The Children's Library is designed to double in the evenings as a meeting room for local societies and the planning of the staff area permits this to be used with this small library as a suite with a small kitchen and toilets. This is a popular and sensible provision particularly as it can so easily be isolated from the main library by locking three doors. The store adjoining the Children's Library has been thoughtfully provided with a projection hatch so that films can be shown.

The staff room and workroom are both pleasant and have comforting views on to what one hopes, will one day be those pleasant garden areas intended by the architect.

Careful thought has been given to solving all the small functional and technical problems of the library so as to create at very reasonable cost, a warm, friendly and informal atmosphere for browsing and enjoying books.

Sefton are to be congratulated on a very good small library which will, however, only be able to fulfil its full promise when the landscaping is done and the tall notice board feature, intended by the architect to stand in the forecourt, has been erected and draws attention to the building. The 300,000 books issued each year are some indication of the building's popularity and potential.

GKVT

Authority	Metropolitan Borough of Sefton
Designation	Birkdale Branch Library
Date of opening	March 1974
Population served	12,000
Name of Architect	Ian M Hindle, RIBA, DipTP, Borough Architect B D Rothera, DiplArch(L'pool), DipCD(L'pool), RIBA
Name of Librarian	—
Special features:	
a) site	Main road close to shops
b) architecture	Brick walls; long span ply roof beams
c) function	Branch Library
Mechanical Services:	
a) heating	Gas
b) ventilation	Natural
c) lighting	Fluorescent
d) acoustics	Carpet
e) other	—
Areas: in square metres	
a) lending	327
b) reference	20
c) reading	In lending
d) special activities	—
e) children	49
f) control	20
g) library staff admin.	69
h) exhibitions	—
i) lecture hall	—
j) circulation	33
k) services	4
l) lavatories	40 public lav adjacent
m) stack	13
Total area:	575
Book volumes:	
a) adult lending	7,750
b) adult reference	350
c) children	1,700
d) stack	1,400
e) other	—
Total:	11,200
Costs in £ p:	
a) site	—
b) building	—
c) furniture & fittings	—
Total Cost (ex fees):	£62,825
Cost per square metre:	£98

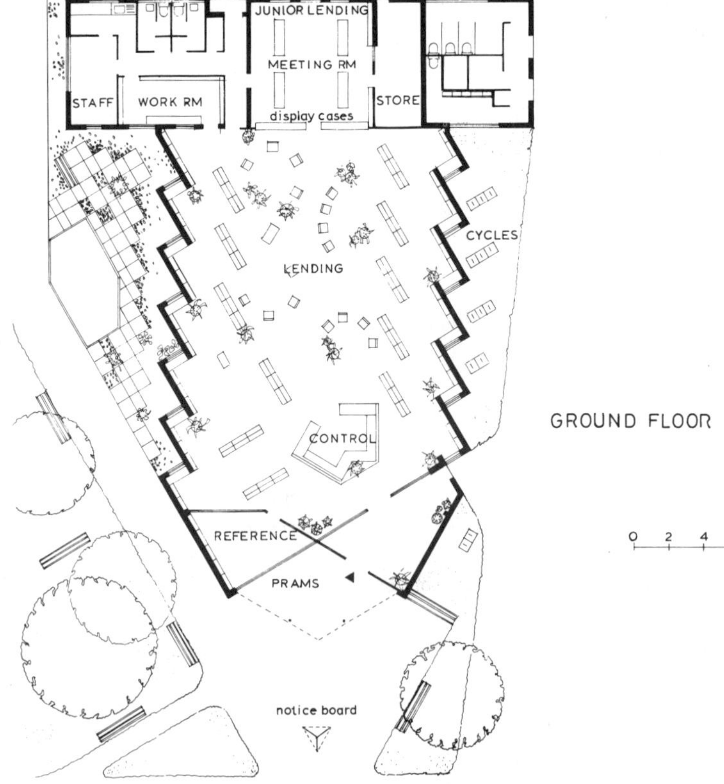

Sheffield District Council:
Totley

A small branch library, well under 400 m², to serve a population of 12,000 in a Sheffield suburb; situated just into the estate and just off a main road with shopping nearby. This sounds a boring situation but the result is quite charming.

The building is constructed of two single-storey octagonal rooms, the adult's being somewhat larger than the children's, with a linking control area. The Librarian reports that the size of rooms had to be reduced because of price rises, but the rooms feel open enough. Octagonal rooms are not new to libraries and small ones are often disastrous, but here we have a most successful example. The construction of the octagons is in the form of load-bearing brick panels which support the main steel domed roof: areas of patent glazing are incorporated to provide natural lighting. In fact half of the eight panels have their lower portion made of tinted glass and this is generally most successful, although, during certain periods in the winter there is apparently some light shining directly into the eyes of the staff working at the counter. There is no excessive heat from sunlight, a normal snag from this type of development, despite the fact that there are only quite tiny ventilating fans.

The entrance is into the link between the two octagons and, when turning into the Lending Library, the absolutely overwhelming impression is of the beauty of the carpet. It is not an expensive carpet nor does it feel particularly luxurious, being of Floatex nylon fibre without underlay. The attraction lies in its absolute plainness: the even, pleasant yellow is very attractive to an eye now well used to various twills and patterns. The first reaction is to presume that it is quite impractical but after two winters' use there is still no sign of wear upon it and it is apparently easy enough to clean.

The counters between the two octagons serve as a labour-saving control; there is a nominal work area between them and its window serves as an exhibition area into the entrance hall as well as being useful for supervision.

In the Children's Library there is a raised area with a screen, which recesses into the roof, for lectures, listening groups, story hours, films, etc. Attempts to use a small room for so many purposes normally run into difficulties; the difficulty here is that the bookshelving along the edge of the raised dais is bolted down and, I believe, a great deal of trouble to move; so story hours and so on have to take place despite this low fitment. Incidentally, the raised platform behind the shelving serves as a separate study area for children.

Many different factors help to make up the pleasing impression of this building: the very pleasant brick exterior, views over open country through the slit windows in the Lending Library, the patches of shrubbery around the car park, the dog hitching rail and even the exterior sign is neat and well thought out. A nice library.

GT

Authority	Metropolitan District of Sheffield
Designation	Totley Branch Library
Date of opening	February 1974
Population served	12,000
Name of Architect	Bernard F Warren, RIBA, FRTPI, City Planning Officer and Architect
Name of Librarian	John Bebbington, FLA (now retired)
Special features:	
a) site	Sloping from main road to estate, with car park on estate side
b) architecture	Two octagons of load-bearing brick panels which support main steel dome
c) function	Serving locality
Mechanical Services:	
a) heating	Gas-fired ducted warm air
b) ventilation	Natural
c) lighting	Fluorescent
d) acoustics	—
e) other	—
Areas: in square metres	
a) lending	
b) reference	164
c) reading	
d) special activities	—
e) children	114
f) control	18
g) library staff admin.	14
h) exhibitions	—
i) lecture hall	—
j) circulation	40
k) services	11
l) lavatories	9
m) stack	—
Total area:	370
Book volumes:	
a) adult lending	16,300
b) adult reference	150
c) children	7,900
d) stack	—
e) other	—
Total:	24,350
Costs in £ p:	
a) site	6,500
b) building	
c) furniture & fittings	43,660
Total Cost (ex fees):	50,160
Cost per square metre:	£135

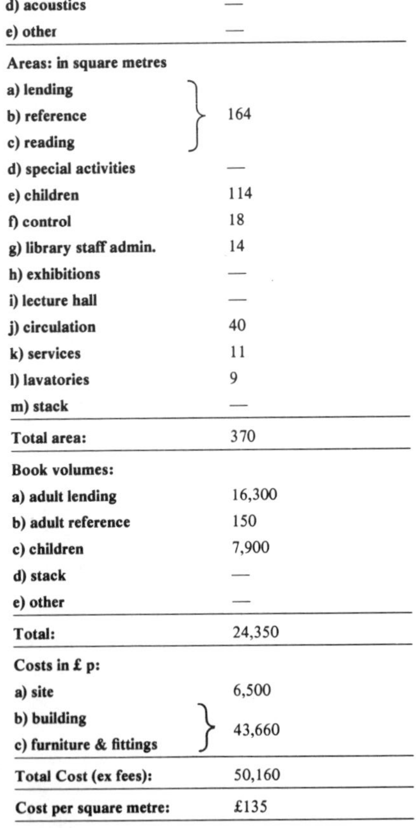

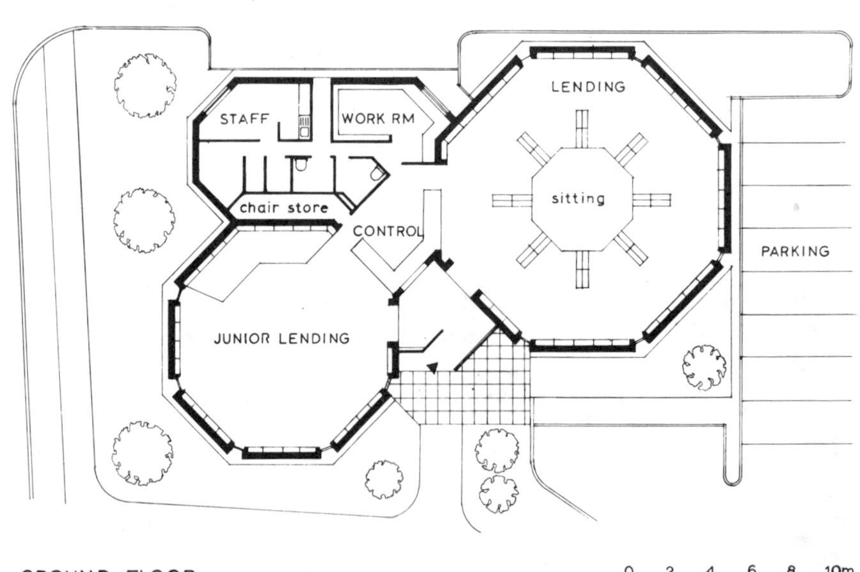

GROUND FLOOR

Somerset County Council: Wincanton

The Wincanton Library, opened in 1973, is a Somerset County Area Library providing a base for the service of a mobile library and three satellite village libraries. It serves a population of 5,200, about 3,000 of which are in Wincanton. The area is essentially rural, Wincanton having as its only industry a large dairy products factory.

In terms of architectural quality in the matter of appearance, inevitably the first interest of a visitor, this is an excellent library; the exterior, walled with a pleasant red brick and with a low pitched pyramidal roof, is characterful, convincingly of today but fully up to the standard of the town's many good old buildings and in sympathy with them: a thoroughly worthy addition to Wincanton. It is well-sited, just off High Street adjacent to a new and equally seemly Health Centre. The library has its own car park into which the Bookmobile garage opens from the library basement.

The entrance from a small covered porch opens into the one largish room which visually echoes the quality of the exterior. The colour of the room is good—the floor carpeted in a chequer-board pattern of Altrolux 90, in two shades of brownish-green, the ceiling of natural coloured wood (a lively design feature) and the whole dominated by the bright panorama of the books which, in their wall and free standing cases, dominate the view across the room. The Remploy chairs are black, as are the members of the shelf units. The issuing desk and a show-case for exhibitions are flanked by rather heavyweight side members which conflict with the colour and scale of the other furniture.

On the west side, under a sloping roof are the service and work rooms and a most amenable staff room. A staircase leads down to the bookmobile garage in the basement.

This library is the first to be designed by its architects and it would seem that their brief was insufficiently explicit in defining lighting requirements; or perhaps the architects were not, themselves, experienced public library users else they would not have designed the daylight and artficial lighting to satisfy aesthetic at the expense of functional requirements. The lay-lights near the walls, on all four sides, give good general distribution of light but they cannot be screened in really hot and direct-sun conditions so that librarians in their fixed positions at the issuing desk were 'roasted', until the lights over their heads were obscured. Also, as first designed, the library had no windows, on the supposition that enough illumination came from the lay-lights, but the librarians soon asked for windows in the walls to avoid the psychological effect of confinement. So two windows were installed, admitting some useful light and a view, but no ventilation, so a further alteration had to be made to provide opening lights. These windows were glazed to the floor, a somewhat popular architectural convention, adding nothing to illumination or view or ventilation, but providing a vulnerable area of glazing which is most easily soiled and least easily cleaned.

The book collection of 7,200 volumes which fills the shelves to capacity is kept up to date by the monthly supply of new books from the County Headquarters, an equivalent number of books being returned to HQ. Modest provision is made for exhibitions in one show-case and on a wall. The Librarian is responsible for the exhibitions and tries to make them of immediate local interest, and she also does her best to enliven the library with flowers.

There is no special provision for meetings but the side of the room by the entrance can easily be cleared and made available for meetings. Also children's story-telling groups can be fitted into the bay holding the children's collection, adequately screened acoustically to avoid interference with other library users.

To anyone who envisages even a small rural library as more than an efficient and amenable book-issuing establishment, which the Wincanton library certainly is, it is a pity that more space had not been provided for browsing and just sitting around—but nonetheless this is an attractive and well-planned library of which Wincanton can be proud.

EJC

Authority	Somerset County Council
Designation	Wincanton Area Library
Date of opening	June 1973
Population served	5,200
Name of Architect	Steel, Coleman & Davis of Taunton in collaboration with Somerset County Architect, Bernard C Adams
Name of Librarian	C R Eastwood, FLA
Special features:	
a) site	Frontage position as part of town centre development
b) architecture	System built incorporating Method Construction components
c) function	—
Mechanical Services:	
a) heating	Gas-fired
b) ventilation	Internal electric circulation fans
c) lighting	Tungsten and fluorescent, no specific level
d) acoustics	Carpeted throughout, Altrolux 90
e) other	—

Areas: in square metres	
a) lending	
b) reference	
c) reading	
d) special activities	
e) children	
f) control	
g) library staff admin.	204
h) exhibitions	
i) lecture hall	
j) circulation	
k) services	
l) lavatories	
m) stack	
Total area:	204
Book volumes:	
a) adult lending	
b) adult reference	
c) children	7,500
d) stack	
e) other	
Total:	7,500
Costs in £ p:	Not yet available
a) site	—
b) building	—
c) furniture & fittings	—
Total Cost (ex fees):	—
Cost per square metre:	—

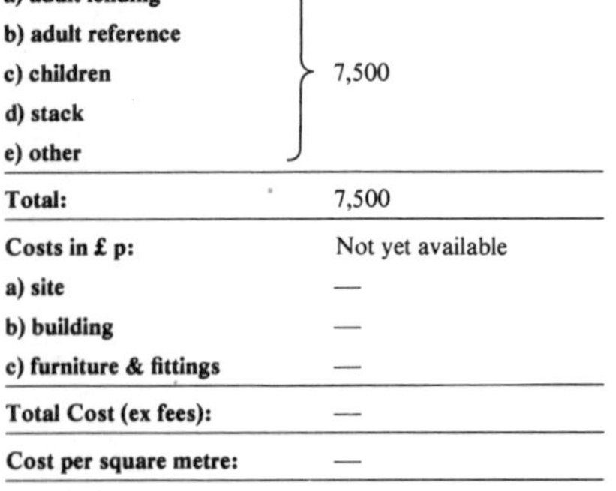

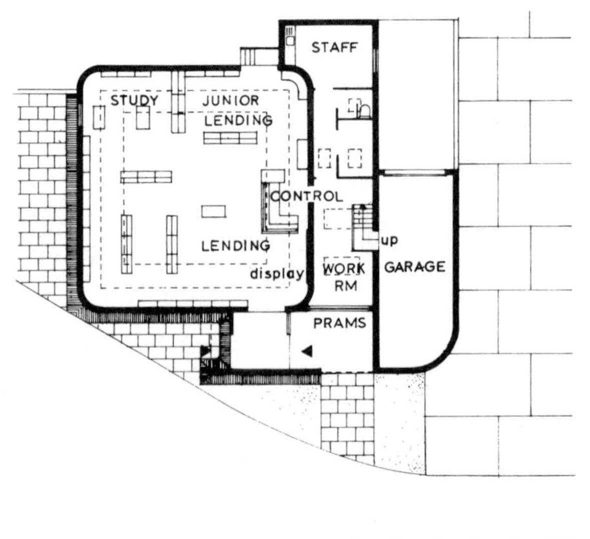

GROUND FLOOR

Suffolk County Council:
(formerly East Suffolk County Council) Eye:
(formerly West Suffolk County Council) Kedington

Eye is a small country town in the agricultural heart of East Anglia, typical of so many comparatively unspoilt little towns up and down the area. The main street, Lambeth Street, has islands of old buildings in a varied and interesting traditional setting. A large car park has been made, unobtrusively placed in the area behind the old houses, tucked away out of sight and it is here that the small, neat modern library has been sited, only a minute's walk from the shops and quite impossible to miss by anyone using a car. Landscaping around the building will eventually help it to settle more happily into the site, for at the moment it is a little raw looking, in a rather cheap brown brick.

The single-room library houses adults' and childrens' books with virtually no divisions beyond projecting bookcases forming six distinct bays. The Librarian's desk is in the centre, facing the door from the small lobby. It is a great pity that the original plans which envisaged a somewhat bigger building were pruned as the result of financial limitations, for this is certainly one of the busiest buildings that this reviewer has seen. Open for only $14\frac{1}{2}$ hours a week on three days, upwards of 800 books are issued each week by a Librarian stretched to her limits to cope. When visited there were no less than 20 readers in the tiny library. Much of the credit for this success undoubtedly goes to the Librarian who runs this and another library in a nearby village; she has been the Librarian for 10 years and knows all her readers well.

The natural daylighting from continuous clerestory windows, with four roof-lights in addition, has been a mixed blessing, for temperature builds up in the summer to as much as 106°F. A film has now been applied to all the windows to cut down sun penetration and it will be interesting to see if this is effective. A small Librarian's office, with sink and cooker and with lavatory off, completes the accommodation. This little room has no view out but since the Librarian has little time to use it this hardly matters.

Heating is from a huge night storage heater placed in the centre of the room, as obtrusive and ugly a device as it would be possible to imagine, which is the one really serious fault. This was again apparently an afterthought brought about by financial problems. Other details have luckily been solved with more thought, and the counter in particular is a good practical detail, neat and tidy. Returned books are put direct on to a trolley which stands by the desk; this is small enough to give the desired impression of informality which is such a feature of this library. Metal bookshelving is by Reska and with such a small stock (about 7,000 on shelves) no tier guiding is necessary beyond three signs indicating fiction, non-fiction and children's stock.

Kedington It would be hard to be as enthusiastic about Kedington library, for this is altogether different from the building at Eye. Kedington had the misfortune to have been swamped by the overspill housing, built by private enterprise, encouraged by the Greater London Council in the expansion of nearby Haverhill in this quiet corner of Suffolk. Kedington's share of the increase has taken its population from about 750 to around 2,000 now.

Presumably because the village has several rival centres (the sterile new neighbourhood-shopping arcades compete with the old centre grouped around the pub by the bridge over a small stream), a site on more neutral ground was chosen for the Community Centre. One is perhaps unduly suspicious of the idea of Community Centre since, traditionally, communities seem to choose and create their own centre, whether it be a pub, a church or church hall or even a library. To build one from scratch the Authority must be very sure of its purpose and its importance to the community. The fact that Brownies and Guides happen to meet next door on two evenings when the library is open hardly justifies its position, so isolated from the village. Here the Community Centre includes a public hall with small tea bar off the entrance hall, changing rooms for use with the adjoining playing field and the library. The site is in an open field several hundred yards off the main street, down a dusty gravelled lane which leads to a large gravelled and very unlovely car park which must be crossed to reach the building.

At first sight the building looks quite attractive with a big monopitch roof over the hall and low flat-roofed surrounding building, well composed architecturally, if rather too consciously modern. However, form follows function, we are told by the pioneers of modern architecture, so how does the library stand up to this test? A covered entrance way leads to the hall entrance, but the library door opens direct off this covered area; no lobby is provided, the Librarian freezes whenever the door opens and the gravel gets trodden straight in. Prams can be left outside under cover but the step up would make it difficult to wheel a pram inside even if there were a place for it to stand.

The library faces on to the grand car park, though an attempt has been made to plant some shrubs, which may improve the view but cannot obscure the bleakness of this prospect. This when there is, from the completely windowless changing room block, a fine view available over the playing fields and in to the beautiful valley beyond.

The single library room with its plastic tile floor, red painted steel beams and woodwool slab roof is a dark and dingy place as one could find in the village. Windows appear to have been placed solely with regard to their outside appearance; two thin vertical strips at one end, and a square window at the other giving totally inadequate natural lighting. No roof-lights are there to alleviate the gloom, but of course it is always possible to rely on artificial light as one would in a city basement. The shelving accommodates only 5,000 books with no possibility for any future expansion.

No office is provided for the Librarian whose book deliveries are often made when the library is shut. There is nowhere for the Librarian to put away untidy boxes, nowhere to make a cup of tea. This is about as poor an attempt at designing a library as it has been this reviewer's misfortune to find. The Librarian is so delighted to have a library at all that the shortcomings are largely excused, but it is such a pity when better design could so have improved her lot.

GKVT

Authority	East Suffolk County Council
Designation	Eye Library
Date of opening	November 1973
Population served	4,000
Name of Architect	H G Tuffley, RIBA; R A Hoggar
Name of Librarian	E F Ferry, FLA
Special features:	
a) site	Central site close to main street
b) architecture	Conventional brick faced; William Brown timber frame
c) function	Branch public library
Mechanical Services:	
a) heating	Multitherm electric warm air
b) ventilation	Natural
c) lighting	Fluorescent IEE standards
d) acoustics	Carpet
e) other	—
Areas: in square metres	
a) lending	42
b) reference	—
c) reading	—
d) special activities	—
e) children	—
f) control	—
g) library staff admin.	4
h) exhibitions	—
i) lecture hall	—
j) circulation	—
k) services	4
l) lavatories	—
m) stack	—
Total area:	50
Book volumes:	
a) adult lending	6,983
b) adult reference	70
c) children	1,828
d) stack	—
e) other	—
Total:	8,881
Costs in £ p:	
a) site	700
b) building	10,793.46
c) furniture & fittings	1,300 (included)
Total Cost (ex fees):	£12,793.46
Cost per square metre:	£255

(No plan available)

Sunderland District Council (formerly Borough of Sunderland): East Herrington and Ryhope

In 1967 the Borough of Sunderland took over the Rural District Libraries and East Herrington and Ryhope were two of the villages so absorbed. Lying south of Sunderland they are but three miles from each other; their new libraries are of the same style although the respective catchment populations of 20,000 and 10,000 vary the size of the two buildings.

East Herrington has a small and quite inadequate building at the south-western end of the village but to make it more accessible to the majority, a site was chosen in a more central situation. A little unhappily, this is fifty yards off the main traffic route with the building situated on the central grassed area of a road which has private residential property on the north side, occupied by persons working in Sunderland, Newcastle or Durham (GPO Savings HQ is in this area), while on the south side stands the 'front line' of the substantial council housing estate of Farringdon, whose occupants tend more to be employed in factories and docks. Discussion with the Librarian revealed that, in its way, the new library was helping to reduce the 'them and us' gap which had been noticeable; yet even at the time of the visit bollards still prevented cars having through access from one side to the other.

The building is on a sloping site which is narrow in width because of the circumstances mentioned; it is mainly a brick structure and of open-plan and design. Carpeted in blue and with insulated suspended ceiling it is acoustically good but natural light is not too satisfactory. Just three ceiling lights approximately 3 ft square are not sufficient, even with generous double-glazed side windows, to obviate fluorescents being used on all but the brightest days. Heating is by gas-fired low pressure hot water through skirting wall strips in the public areas.

Sensible thought has been shown with the Librarian's office, glazed, so as to allow oversight of the library but with venetian blinds should privacy be required (as for money counting, etc), which were in operation on arrival. Workroom and staff rest-room provisions are generous in space and the provision of kitchen unit, small cooker and refrigerator was noticeable. Car parking space is also provided for staff and public.

Wheelchair access to the library and toilets have been clearly provided yet there are neither directional signs to the library from the main road nor any 'Library' sign whatsoever on any elevation of the building—which seems a great pity when, as mentioned, the library is in a strategic position to foster harmony, particularly between the children of the adjacent areas.

Ryhope is more clearly a working-class population; many are pit workers in the areas around, although this village now has no mine still working. A general and a mental hospital are located at the eastern end, but professionals are mainly in-resident; if living outside the hospitals then it is usually in housing more towards Sunderland.

The library is on a very restricted site, one of the few such buildings, perhaps even the only one, to be situated between a miners' hall advertising 'bingo' sessions and a very dismal and elderly 'pub'. Efforts were made to acquire, in order of desirability, three other sites in preference to this but to no avail; so this building is on a steep 1:8 slope with yet another change of levels between front and rear. Wheelchairs have been well catered for by ramp access and with good space between bookcases.

The Director of the Library Service said, in discussion later at the Central Library, that the planning of these libraries and the discussions on the projects with the Council's architects had been, in some measure, affected by the greater priority given by the Council, at that period, to the speedy conversion of a disused railway station at Monkwearmouth to become a Transport Museum, under the Librarian's control (as was the Museum within the Central Library at that time). The 1300th anniversary of the monasteries of St Peter and St Paul and the connection with the Venerable Bede also required the active attentions of the library staff at this time. Accordingly the exteriors and interiors of the two libraries were, by and large, repeated e.g. building materials, carpeting, interior decoration, shelving. Surprisingly, this *earlier* library, which is about two-thirds the area of East Herrington, has fourteen ceiling roof-lights, providing a much higher natural light facility.

Staff at both libraries commented on the design of the counters which have cupboard space but no fitted drawers for completed readers application cards to form a borrowers' register, nor properly compartmentalized stationery storage. More time given to staff consultation at the planning stage could have prevented these disadvantages.

HW

Authority	Metropolitan District (formerly Borough) of Sunderland
Designation	East Herrington Branch
Date of opening	May 1974
Population served	20,000
Name of Architect	H C Bishop, DipArch, RIBA, Director of Architecture; T Vinter, RIBA, Group Architect
Name of Librarian	E W Kirtley, ALA
Special features:	
a) site	Restricted and sloping; bounded on two sides by estate traffic roads
b) architecture	Traditional
c) function	Serving large housing estates
Mechanical Services:	
a) heating	Gas-fired low pressure hot water
b) ventilation	Natural
c) lighting	Fluorescent with prismatic diffusers
d) acoustics	Carpeted; acoustic tiled ceiling
e) other	—
Areas: in square metres	
a) lending	
b) reference	187
c) reading	
d) special activities	—
e) children	in (a)
f) control	—
g) library staff admin.	49
h) exhibitions	—
i) lecture hall	—
j) circulation	17
k) services	in (g)
l) lavatories	
m) stack	—
Total area:	253
Book volumes:	
a) adult lending	16,262
b) adult reference	63
c) children	4,642
d) stack	—
e) other	—
Total:	20,967
Costs in £ p:	
a) site	—
b) building	47,000
c) furniture & fittings	4,960
Total Cost (ex fees):	£51,960
Cost per square metre:	£205

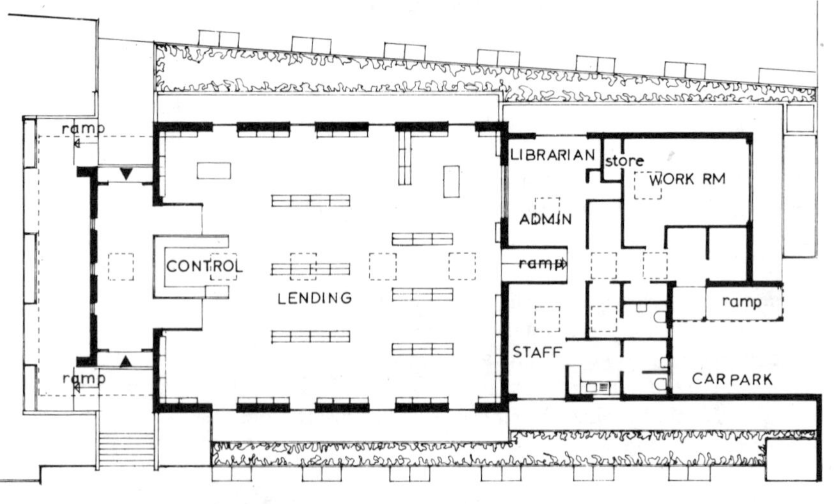

GROUND FLOOR

Authority	Metropolitan District (formerly Borough) of Sunderland
Designation	Ryhope Branch
Date of opening	May 1973
Population served	10,000
Name of Architect	H L Bishop, RIBA, DipArch, Director of Architecture; T Vinter, RIBA, Group Architect
Name of Librarian	E W Kirtley, ALA
Special features:	
a) site	Restricted and steeply sloping between miners hall and pub
b) architecture	Traditional
c) function	Serving locality
Mechanical Services:	
a) heating	Gas-fired low pressure hot water
b) ventilation	Natural
c) lighting	Fluorescent with diffusers; some recessed downlighters
d) acoustics	Carpeted; acoustic tiled ceiling
e) other	—
Areas: in square metres	
a) lending	
b) reference	132
c) reading	
d) special activities	—
e) children	in (a)
f) control	—
g) library staff admin.	53
h) exhibitions	—
i) lecture hall	—
j) circulation	in (a)
k) services	
l) lavatories	in (g)
m) stack	
Total area:	185
Book volumes:	
a) adult lending	14,186
b) adult reference	155
c) children	4,417
d) stack	—
e) other	—
Total:	18,758
Costs in £ p:	
a) site	2,000
b) building	27,418
c) furniture & fittings	2,468
Total Cost (ex fees):	£31,886
Cost per square metre:	£172

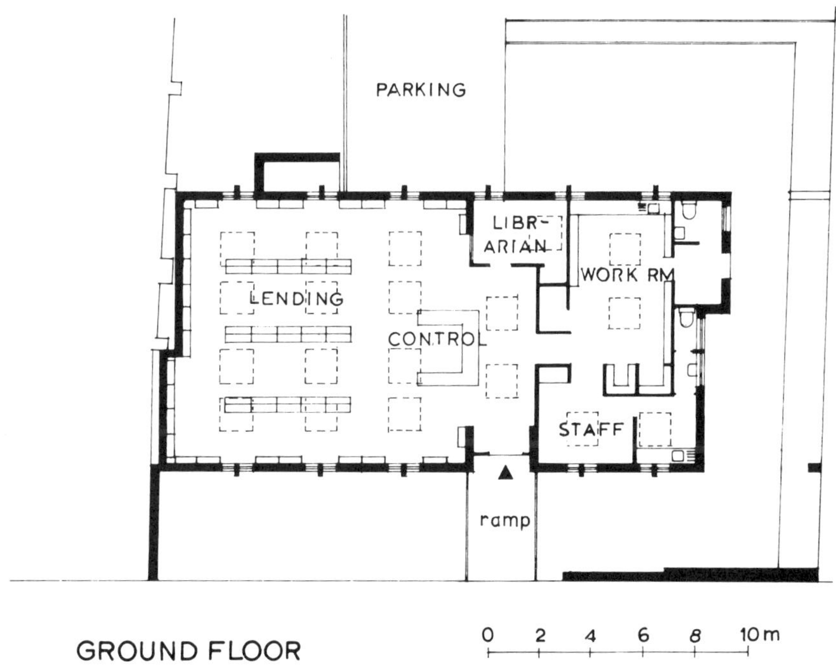

GROUND FLOOR

Surrey County Council:
Frimley Green and Oxted

Frimley Green This Surrey library was planned, as a modest-sized branch with a bookstock of about 12,000 volumes, to serve the immediate locality having a population of some 8,000. Frimley Green is on the eastern edge of a very large urban belt, continually growing in extent and density, stretching across county boundaries and running, virtually unbroken, from Camberley in the north, through Farnborough and Aldershot to Farnham in the south. It is interesting, therefore, to note that Hampshire's new Farnborough library (see p 125) is only four miles away.

The intention was that the site, set a little back from the main road junction in the centre of Frimley Green, would be shared by the library with a community centre and possibly a health centre to come later. External impressions are certainly favourable. There is good landscaping of the approaches and forecourt, with ample parking space, and the brick-built, single-storey building looks well placed and well proportioned, if a trifle heavy with some largish areas of unrelieved brick. The interior does nothing to diminish this first impression. The whole design has a pleasantly welcoming air about it, from its generously spaced entrance hall to the Adult and Children's Libraries and the reading/exhibition/meetings room which are its principal public areas.

There are good display facilities everywhere, apart from the particular opportunities offered by this latter room which, opening directly from the Adult Library, is planned with tables and comfortable chairs as a very pleasant reading/reference/periodicals room, serving also for special exhibition purposes and becoming easily available for meetings. Hinged partition panels provide access to an adjoining chair store, with kitchen and tea bar facilities beside it. The room can seat some fifty people comfortably and has its own direct entry provided. All this carefully planned and a model for a library of this size.

The overall layout is very simple. Stretching back centrally from the entrance hall and staff counter is the Adult Lending Library and to the left is the reading/meetings room; to the right the Children's Library. High clerestory windows give good natural light to the Adult Library and reading room. The appearance of these windows, just below ceiling-level, with a continuous band of dark brown wall fabric beneath, is very neat and visually satisfying. The shelving is of teak finish by Library Design and Engineering Ltd, and tier lettering is bold and clear. Floor coverings are in heavy-duty ribbed rubber in the entrance hall, vinyl in the Adult Library and carpet in the Children's Library and reading room. Heating is gas-fired with hot water radiators and blown air convector units. There is good and well arranged staff accommodation.

Which leaves the one criticism: it seemed very surprising to find the Children's Library almost entirely obscured from view of the staff at the counter. The separating partition—book-shelved on the children's side—between it and the counter is 5 ft high. In what is undeniably an open-plan layout, it certainly goes a good way towards providing a solid barrier between the children's area and the adults', but one would have thought the better

advantages would have resulted from using a form of screen which gave a visual link, at least at and above eye-level.

Of a total area of 250 m² (2,700 ft²), this is a well-planned and well-finished small library.

Oxted The population of Oxted is approximately 18,000 and this is obviously a substantially larger branch than the one previously discussed: in terms of the Surrey library service it is a medium-sized branch, intended to meet both the needs of the immediate locality and also the information and reference library needs for a wider area. It stocks about 42,000 books and has a Group mobile library service based on it.

Gresham Road, in which the library is sited, runs into the approach road to the forecourt of Oxted Station, passing the site of the former library building. The new library was designed on three floors on a sloping site, as an integral part of a block which includes the Oxted Health Centre and also the County Divisional Surveyor's Offices. Externally, its building elements balance well and give it an attractive quality, unmistakably a library, even from a distance. It is a concrete-framed structure with concrete floors and a flat timber-framed roof. Dark grey Sussex stock bricks have been used and a feature of considerable design emphasis is provided by the tall, vertically pivoted timber windows. These are in continuous bands, with slate sills, black concrete lintels and copings and black rendered columns. A projecting porch, of generous proportions, is raised, at the building's ground floor level, well above the pavement with access on one side by a flight of six steps and at the other by a ramp. Along the length of the street side it is fully glazed and big enough for prams to be left in it. Inside the library, the reception area is well finished, with plenty of pin-up display boards, some seats and flowers. Ribbed rubber flooring is used up to the staff counter, otherwise the library is all carpeted. Walls throughout the building are covered with vinyl coated papers in various designs.

The Adult Library, with rather remotely placed offices at the far end for the District Librarian and a typist, occupies the whole of the ground floor. It is a little unfortunate that the staff counter and the approach to it from the main entrance, have had to divide the shelved areas, thus causing a cross flow of movement to and from this substantial central desk which handles an annual book issue of some 273,000 books. Fiction has been shelved in the area to its right, as one faces it, and other stock, including reference material, is to the left. In this, by far the largest part of the Adult Library, two rows of island tiers are spaced towards the street side of the building and between them and the rear windows, running the length of the room, are rows of reference tables with desk chairs for 24 students. There are also attractive display units.

The Children's Library and the meetings room are on the first floor. A wall with central sliding partition enables the two areas to be used together when required. The meetings room, which will seat 50 people, has a separate stair entrance and a tea bar, as well as a chair store at one end. Off the entrance lobby to the meetings room, at the foot of this stair, are lavatories.

Authority	County of Surrey
Designation	Frimley Green Branch
Date of opening	February 1973
Population served	8,000
Name of Architect	Brewer Smith & Brewer in association with Raymond Ash, DipArch, RIBA, County Architect
Name of Librarian	Robert Ashby, FLA
Special features:	
a) site	Corner site in new development
b) architecture	Single storey; brick built
c) function	To serve immediate locality
Mechanical Services:	
a) heating	Gas-fired hot water radiators with blown air convectors
b) ventilation	Natural
c) lighting	Suspended fluorescent strip
d) acoustics	Suspended acoustic ceiling; carpeted
e) other	—
Areas: in square metres	
a) lending	70
b) reference	—
c) reading	—
d) special activities	—
e) children	28
f) control	24
g) library staff admin.	44
h) exhibitions	50
i) lecture hall	in (h)
j) circulation	16
k) services	18
l) lavatories	in (k)
m) stack	—
Total area:	250
Book volumes:	
a) adult lending	10,103
b) adult reference	258
c) children	3,367
d) stack	—
e) other	75 gr
Total:	13,803
Costs in £ p:	
a) site	6,444
b) building	35,662
c) furniture & fittings	2,000
Total Cost (ex fees):	£44,106
Cost per square metre:	—

The one distinctly unattractive feature of the building is the stair which runs opposite the ground-floor counter, up to the Children's Library on the first floor. It has, apparently as a matter of insistence for fire safety reasons, been rather massively walled-in and is ugly. Strangely enough, but partly because of this, the Children's Library is quite the least attractive part of this building. It is a pity that it had to be on the first floor. Even its display fittings are dull: the whole of the design has a heavy air about it. Children's book issues are dealt with at the counter below.

Opening off the shared car park behind the building, which has access along the side of the Health Centre, is a rear door at the library's lower ground floor level with a deliveries platform (surprisingly without a canopy to give weather protection for loading and offloading operations from the mobile library van and other vehicles).

To one side of this is a useful packing area and to the other a cleaners' store and then a comfortable staff rest room with kitchen and locker accommodation and cloakrooms. Beside a book hoist which comes down from the two main floors to this point is a reserve book store and a workroom, with another workroom immediately over it on the ground floor. This room is usefully behind the main Lending Library counter, the book hoist feeding all of these. One sees that this hoist is a carefully placed and vital link, but also gets the impression that work space is somewhat fragmented, especially with the administrative offices being at the further end of the building.

Lighting is by fluorescent panels flush with the ceilings, which are mainly of suspended acoustic tiling, and the carefully considered acoustics are further aided by the use of foam-backed carpeting. Heating is gas-fired. Shelving is by Terrapin Reska with teak end-panels and shelves.

With reservations about the Children's Library, this is also a well-finished and good-looking building.

LHS   GKVT

Oxted

Authority	County of Surrey
Designation	Oxted Branch
Date of opening	September 1972
Population served	18,000
Name of Architect	Hugh Pi and Associates in conjunction with Raymond Ash, DipArch, RIBA
Name of Librarian	Robert Ashby, FLA
Special features:	
a) site	Corner site with health centre in new development
b) architecture	Concrete frame and floor flat timber-framed roof
c) function	Serve immediate locality also group mobile library service
Mechanical Services:	
a) heating	Automatic gas-fired
b) ventilation	Natural
c) lighting	Fluorescent ceiling panels
d) acoustics	Carpeted; suspended acoustic-tiled ceiling
e) other	—
Areas: in square metres	
a) lending	354
b) reference	} in (a)
c) reading	
d) special activities	—
e) children	80
f) control	in (j)
g) library staff admin.	48
h) exhibitions	} 76
i) lecture hall	
j) circulation	} 177
k) services	
l) lavatories	
m) stack	25
Total area:	760
Book volumes:	
a) adult lending	30,873
b) adult reference	1,636
c) children	6,693
d) stack	—
e) other	425 gr
Total:	39,627
Costs in £ p:	
a) site	4,400
b) building	75,975
c) furniture & fittings	4,000
Total Cost (ex fees):	£84,375
Cost per square metre:	£105

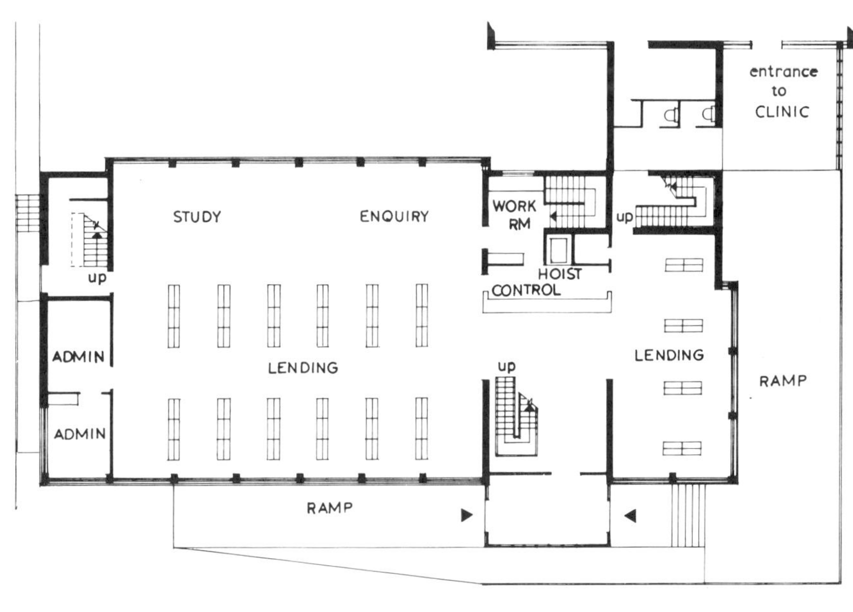

GROUND FLOOR

Tameside District Council:
(formerly Borough of Stalybridge) Ridge Hill:
(formerly Borough of Hyde and Hattersley) Hattersley

Ridge Hill Commissioned by the former Borough of Stalybridge this library falls within the new Metropolitan Borough of Tameside to the east of Manchester.

The library serves an area of comparatively nice housing with a population of about 5,000 and is situated in the centre of the estate with a row of shops, public house, church, post office grouped in a 'villagey atmosphere' on sharply rising ground above Stalybridge.

Built on a steep site the library is at road level on a podium of brick with a cantilevered concrete ground floor supporting red-brown, brindled brick walls with vertical strip windows. The simple rectangular building has splayed corners, each with a full-height window, and is capped with a copper-finished fascia and pitched roof finished with copper-faced felt.

Entrance is by a small lobby with doors leading to 'In' and 'Out' sides of the counter. Signs have not been provided to indicate the direction of flow and this leads to some confusion; no pin-up boards are provided so that sellotaped notices abound. The mat could have been larger with benefit of hindsight, perhaps even covering the whole lobby.

Inside, the library is a model of clarity and good straightforward planning. The counter which is very well-designed is spacious and functionally efficient, it divides the large room into Children's and Adults' Areas and supervision is excellent.

Finishes are good and well-detailed. Walls are plastered, the ceiling finished with Artex stippled plastic paint, the floor covering is green carpet tiles. The windows run from ceiling to top of hardwood skirting and are in black stained timber with opening hoppers and with venetian blinds on the sunny sides.

The use of slit windows enables runs of Reska shelving to be placed between them on external walls leaving the centre of the room spacious with only two rows of hardwood-ended Reska bookcases. To the west the elevated position gives splendid views over playing fields to faraway Manchester whilst the parking for 8 cars behind the library is so far beneath as to be quite unobtrusive. This gives a great sense of space in the library.

Slight emphasis is given to the counter by a drop in ceiling over this area which extends into the porch and houses the ventilator extract ducting.

The staff room serves as workroom and houses reserve stock whilst a small staff entrance lobby gives access to the staff lavatory. This area too is well-detailed and simple. The pleasant view to the south counteracts any slight disadvantage that might be thought to arise from the lack of a staff rest room. The staff is, in any event, perhaps too small to justify a separate room.

Heating is by radiant electrical elements in the ceiling boarding, invisible and effective, controlled by high and low limit thermostats and having the advantage of quick response to demand.

Landscaping is well handled but a little formal. Some tree and shrub planting could have helped.

All in all, this is an exemplary small library of quality in both design and finish not often seen; the practical problems have been solved apparently effortlessly—apart from the few criticisms of the entrance lobby.

Hattersley is a rather bleak overspill housing estate on high ground overlooking Greater Manchester. Intersected by broad, windy roads the estate has no apparent 'raison d'etre', for there is little industry and it becomes, in effect, a council built dormitory suburb.

In the centre of this dreary area an attempt has been made to create a community centre, including shops, council social services advice office, a youth club, coffee bar, flats and the library, built over car parking. No less than four Authorities were involved in this area before local government reorgnisation. The building as a whole is finished in a hard unsympathetic red brick with huge deep precast concrete plinths and fascias which are of crushing scale.

The centre is of a dense plan with an open courtyard on to which the offices, club and library face. No planting is provided and the hard surfaces produce an unsympathetic environment which seems to provoke vandalism. Already several library windows have airgun pellet holes to disfigure them and unrepaired they will encourage further damage.

A covered porch leads to a spacious entrance lobby and thence to the library. There is plenty of parking for prams but a lack of notice boards with sellotaped notices just as in the library entrance at Ridge Hill. The Pirelli rubber matting used for the floor appears not to do its job so that additional mats have had to be used.

The large library room is rather low with rows of roof-lights to supplement the four large windows. These unfortunately do not produce as much light as they should as they are rather deep slots, the sides of which are lined with hardwood faced plywood which absorbs most of the light. In windy weather the roof-lights rattle loudly. The windows are not large enough in relationship to the area of the room to light more than nearby areas. Furthermore they are not placed particularly well for taking full advantage of the limited views available; one faces a 13-storey block of flats and even the one facing the courtyard looks directly at the wall of an area of seating only 2 m away. The worst feature, however, is that a bar forming the bottom of opening hopper windows (complete with very ugly operating gear) occurs exactly at eye-level, making nonsense of any view. The windows are admittedly of thick plate glass but have window seats, without backrests, running in front of them; dubious for both comfort and safety.

Supervision from the counter is good but the design of the fitting is very poor, being made up of a number of units untidily assembled and fully open to view at the back (counters are notoriously difficult to keep tidy). Trays of readers' tickets slip

Authority	Tameside Metropolitan Borough formerly Borough of Stalybridge
Designation	Ridge Hill Branch Library
Date of opening	July 1974
Population served	4,000
Name of Architect	Messrs Turner and Benson (Stockport); A B Turner, RIBA, MRTPI, Project Architect
Name of Librarian	Frank W Roberts, ALA
Special features:	
a) site	Sloping steeply and restricted
b) architecture	Cantilevered reinforced concrete floor slab over recessed podium; load bearing brickwork above
c) function	Serving large housing estate
Mechanical Services:	
a) heating	Electrical elements in
b) ventilation	Natural
c) lighting	Mainly fluorescent strip
d) acoustics	Carpet tiles
e) other	—
Areas: in square metres	
a) lending	80
b) reference	—
c) reading	—
d) special activities	—
e) children	55
f) control	7
g) library staff admin.	15
h) exhibitions	—
i) lecture hall	—
j) circulation	—
k) services	3
l) lavatories	4
m) stack	11
Total area:	175
Book volumes:	
a) adult lending	6,700
b) adult reference	20
c) children	4,500
d) stack	—
e) other	—
Total:	11,220
Costs in £ p:	
a) site	400
b) building	32,716
c) furniture & fittings	1,635
Total Cost (ex fees):	£34,751
Cost per square metre:	£198

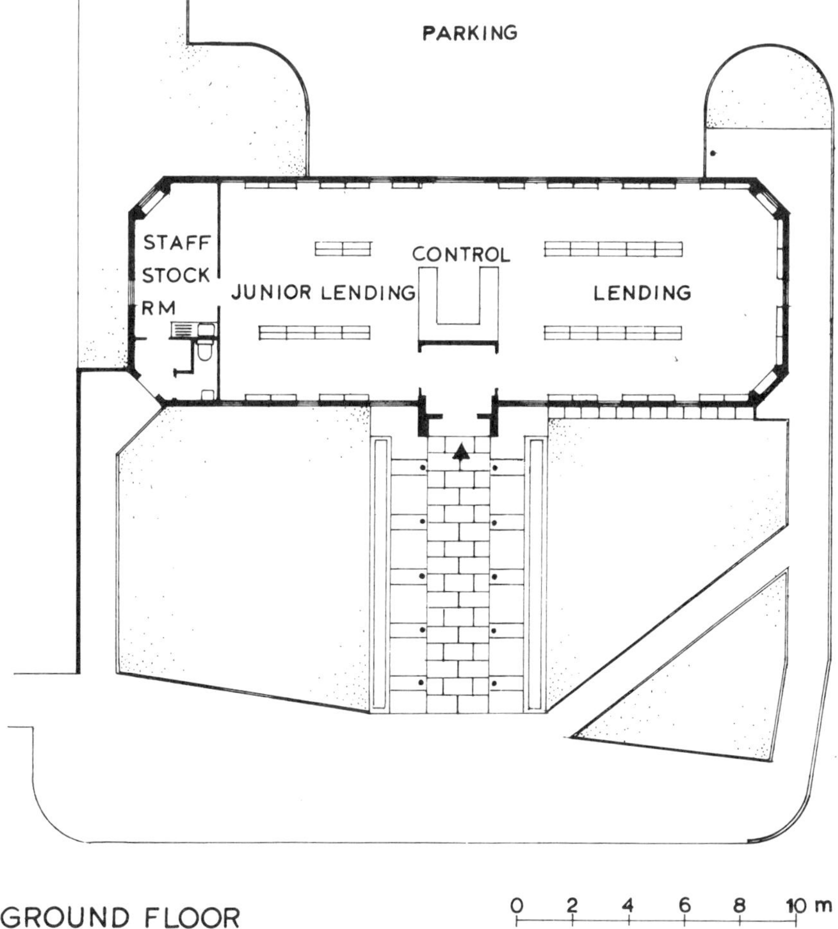

GROUND FLOOR

through between the counter and a shelf above it on which readers deposit their books so that cards become damaged.

The Reading Room which has only roof-lighting is largely out of view from the counter and use has had to be curtailed. Plans are being considered for using this for meetings but unfortunately the lavatories are only accessible through the workroom.

This workroom which has good roof-lighting has double doors to the goods yard, convenient for book deliveries but lacks any view and feels claustrophobic, whereas the pleasant staff room overlooks the square and has sensible provision for cooking and washing-up. Dustbins, surprisingly, are stored in the workroom!

Shelving is metal Reska with five shelf free-standing bookcases and six shelf wall units. The Children's Area has good display board provision.

GKVT

Authority	Tameside Metropolitan Borough formerly Cheshire County and Hyde
Designation	Hattersley Branch Library
Date of opening	January 1973
Population served	6,000
Name of Architect	W S Hattrell & Partners in collaboration with Edgar Taberner, RIBA, County Architect
Name of Librarian	S C Berriman, FLA
Special features:	
a) site	Elevated from, but access to main road; part of complex for youth, old people and community use; adjacent shopping precinct
b) architecture	Individual design
c) function	To serve a Manchester overspill
Mechanical Services:	
a) heating	District from community centre hot water pipes in skirting
b) ventilation	Natural
c) lighting	Fluorescent strip, some tungsten
d) acoustics	Carpet tiles and ceiling tiles
e) other	—
Areas: in square metres	
a) lending	170
b) reference	7
c) reading	in (b)
d) special activities	in (h)
e) children	46
f) control	11
g) library staff admin.	28
h) exhibitions	58
i) lecture hall	in (h)
j) circulation	30
k) services	50
l) lavatories	8
m) stack	—
Total area:	408
Book volumes:	
a) adult lending	14,306
d) special activities	220
c) children	6,150
d) stack	—
e) other	—
Total:	20,676
Costs in £ p:	
a) site	400
b) building	51,755
c) furniture & fittings	4,000
Total Cost (ex fees):	£56,155
Cost per square metre:	£138

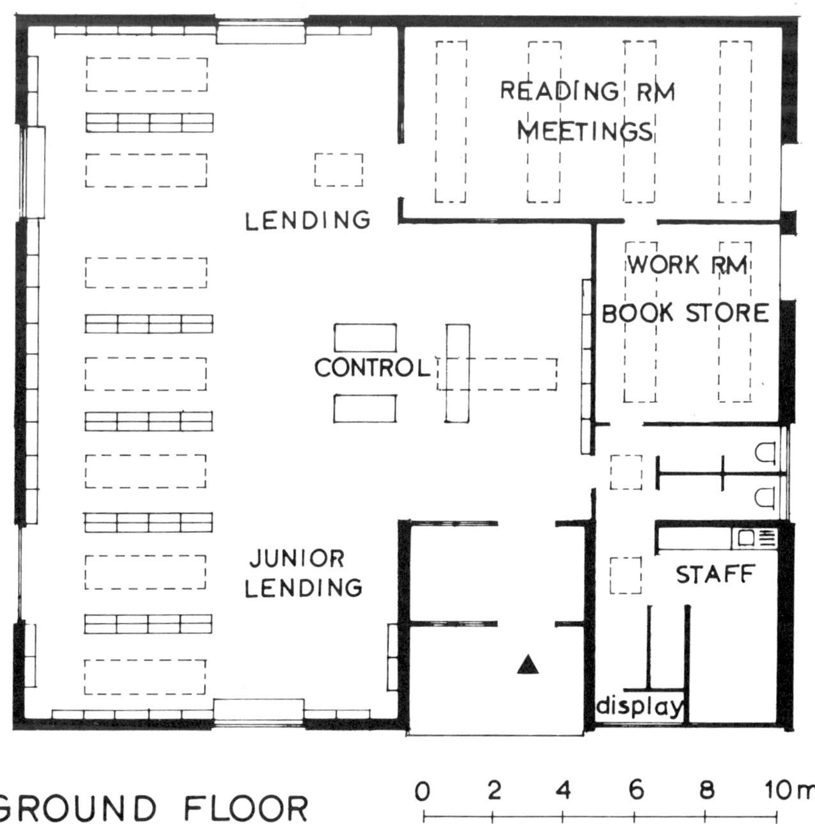

GROUND FLOOR

0   2   4   6   8   10m

West Sussex County Council:
Lancing, Petworth and the Witterings

Lancing The West Sussex County Council provides a library service consisting of thirteen large libraries, twenty-two smaller branches and area mobile services to meet the needs of the more dispersed rural communities. Until recently there were also a number of village centres but the last of these was closed in 1976.

Lancing is one of the system's larger libraries, serving North and South Lancing and Sompting, now together forming an unbroken built-up area of some size stretching east, as it does, to include about 90% of Shoreham Airport, the municipal airport for Brighton, Hove and Worthing. There is a good deal of light industry, which has grown in extent largely since 1965, as well as some agricultural/horticultural land. Lancing is said to pride itself on being 'the biggest village in England'. Its library certainly still has something of the feel, as well as the local involvement, of a village community centre. There is obviously very well fostered support for, and mutually productive co-operation with, many and varied local societies and organisations. The population of Lancing is rather more than 25,000.

Designed by the now recently retired County Architect, the new library was opened, on the site of a former hotel, in May 1974, beside an already established Health Centre, with which, in design, it achieves a close visual link. They are well placed in a central situation very near to the main shopping area, central post office and railway station. Immediately in front of the library is a large old ilex tree on which there is a preservation order. The book issue in the old building, on a site some way to the south of the present one, was 150,000 in its last working year. This increased very considerably to a first year's issue of 327,000 in the new library.

Externally it is, in design, a simple, unpretentious but good-looking building: two-storey, steel-framed and clad in a pleasing textured brick. It has a flat roof and timber windows. It shares with the Health Centre–though the two are not structurally connected in any way–a good car park at the rear, the access road to this separating the two buildings. All three new West Sussex buildings discussed here, shared some common planning features: small, well-planted forecourts with seats, good canopied entrances, good titling and prominently placed information boards with hours of opening well displayed. At crucial approach points and nearby road junctions, there was good guiding to the libraries. Shall we say, in general terms, that they declared their presence very well, obviously by careful intention. How often this is not the case!

Another system practice was evident in the part merging of adult and children's book stock in the open-plan lending libraries. Books for young children and children's stories were separately shelved in one area of the library but non-fiction, adult and junior, were merged. The Lancing library is well used by children; the increase in the junior issue in the new building was five-fold. Good contacts are maintained with its eight schools and with the College, though it was a little surprising to find no designated Children's Librarian on the staff, except at County Divisional level. There was, when I visited the library,

an interesting and substantial display in the children's corner in connection with a current conservation competition. Also giving further evidence of enthusiastic seizing of opportunity for good exploitation of display facilities were the special exhibition area on the first floor, to which a reference follows later, and the large, glazed external/internal faced display window beside the main entrance door, though there must be a slight reservation about the latter in terms of security or vandalism risks that must impose limits on the kind of material which could be displayed in it.

The Reference Library, on the first floor, is reached either by stair or by lift. Beside the latter on this floor are lavatory facilities furnished for the use of disabled people and accessible to wheelchairs, as are all public areas of the building. Much care, in this obligation, is obviously taken in all West Sussex buildings. The Branch Librarian, here, serves on the committee of the local society for the disabled.

The accompanying first floor plan shows the use, by means of an ingenious sliding, folding partition with a ceiling track 'points' provision, of what is basically a single rectangular, open-plan public space for Reference Library, exhibition area and activities room. The intentions are excellent on all three counts but one cannot help but recognise that such multi-purpose solutions of space problems are seldom, in practice, satisfactory. Good exhibition lay-outs inevitably clash with use of the same space for meetings and both clash with reference library/reading room requirements in such very close proximity as this. Enthusiasm to be able to provide a wide and attractive range of services and activities is so much to be welcomed and praised that it goes hard to feel the need to speak the cautionary word about discretion. But space for such a range cannot be had cheaply and on this floor, at least, there is just not enough room for all that has been envisaged.

There is a good staff workroom with first-class arrangement of long workbench under the windows, giving kneehole, kicking spaces alternating with carefully planned drawer and cupboard units and binning space. Opposite this is a useful run of wall shelving providing space, among other purposes, for some stock for a delivery service run in co-operation with the WRVS to housebound readers and old people's homes. There is also a Librarian's office and staff restroom and cloakroom provision on the first floor.

Interior design and furnishing is attractive and comfortable. Whilst there is a good deal of dependence on artificial lighting, windows have been placed with care. Ceilings are faced with good looking acoustic tiles and floors are carpeted throughout. The counter in the Lending Library is small–perhaps a little too limited in size, in its island position, for reserved books awaiting collection and other books set aside for various purposes. This library, however, uses the Plessey light-pen computerised issue system and so requires only small surface space for book issue and return procedures. As the sharply rising level of use shows, this is an attractive library to be in, good looking, lively and progressive.

Authority	West Sussex County Council
Designation	Lancing Branch Library
Date of opening	May 1974
Population served	25,050
Name of Architect	B Peters, DiplArch (Dist), ARIBA, Architect; Michael Strutt, Job Architect
Name of Librarian	W Huse, FLA
Special features:	
a) site	Flat with Ilex tree carrying preservation order
b) architecture	Two-storey; steel framed; brick clad; flat roof; timber windows
c) function	—
Mechanical Services:	
a) heating	Gas-fired low pressure hot water radiators
b) ventilation	Natural with mechanical in toilets
c) lighting	Natural and fluorescent
d) acoustics	No special
e) other	—
Areas: in square metres	
a) lending	170
b) reference	60
c) reading	see (b)
d) special activities	see (b)
e) children	see (a)
f) control	6
g) library staff admin.	45
h) exhibitions	see (b)
i) lecture hall	—
j) circulation	45
k) services	see (j)
l) lavatories	9
m) stack	—
Total area:	335
Book volumes:	
a) adult lending	19,750
b) adult reference	1,263
c) children	7,319
d) stack	—
e) other	—
Total:	28,332
Costs in £ p:	
a) site	—
b) building	54,186
c) furniture & fittings	1,765
Total Cost (ex fees):	£55,951
Cost per square metre:	£167

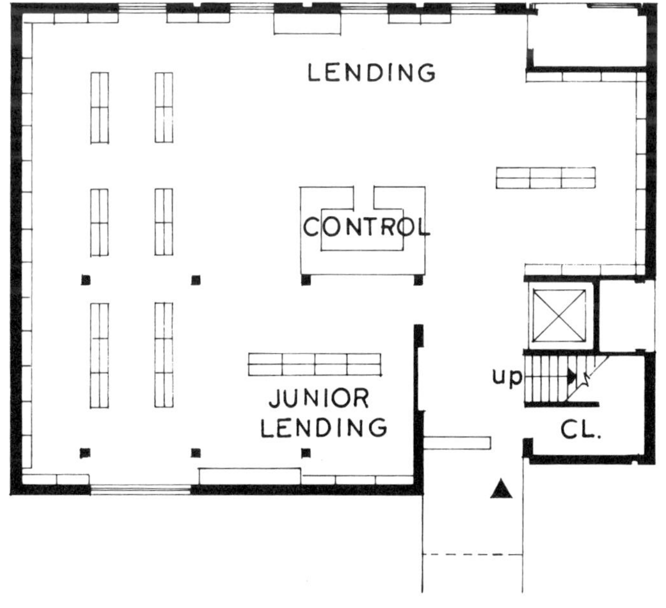

GROUND FLOOR

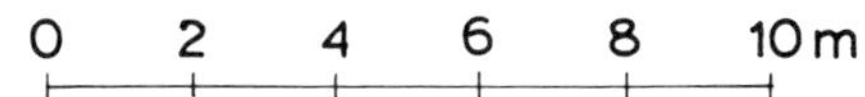

Petworth This is a much smaller library than the branch at Lancing. It serves a population of about 5,500 and is Petworth's first specially designed library; one which has been carefully planned by an Old Bosham firm of architects in association with the County Architect, to blend, as the brief required, with the unique townscape of Petworth. It lies in the conservation area of the town, with pedestrian access to the High Street, from which it is set back only a few yards. The approach to the building for vehicles is from its other side, on the edge of a quite extensive new housing development. There is a car park provided for library users and this may well prove valuable for mobile library purposes if the likely transfer of responsibility for this service from the Midhurst library, whose vehicle access is difficult, comes about in the near future. Book issues last year totalled 56,417.

Planned as a single floor area of 140 m² (1,500 ft²), the building is of load-bearing brick wall construction with a clay tiled pitched roof, half-hipped, in traditional local material. There is a small planted area around the library and the main entrance is canopied and provided with a ramp for wheelchair access. In accordance with the evident West Sussex practice there is an interest stimulating, internally-lit display case beside the entrance door.

Inside, one's immediate impressions are of a building neat, bright and attractive, perhaps dominated visually mostly by the diagonally set, light, strip pine ceiling. A slight 'domed' effect to the ceiling has been achieved by showing the roof slope in what becomes a surrounding shorter line of pine strips down to the wall-plate level. Immediately opposite the entrance, which is in the centre of one of the longer walls of the main rectangle, is the staff counter. The lay-out is open-plan to either side with the Children's Library to the right-hand as one enters, with the non-fiction and reference books to the left. In the former, recessed two steps deep in the floor, is a small well for informal story telling, carpeted as is the whole floor, in deep brown tiles.

The perimeter shelves are divided, in pairs of tiers, by thin slit windows. Natural light is also provided by three roof-light wells and reinforced by fluorescent strip lighting within simple box-diffusers, as well as by some spot-lights. The three light wells have, in use, presented problems. They were obviously causing undue heat loss and very evident and unwelcome draughts. The solution was to put on transparent coverings at ceiling-level. There are large windows at each end of the library, curtained to the ground.

Behind the staff counter is a small workroom/restroom with sink and cooker and, projecting further beyond the basic rectangle of the building, a neat, staff cloakroom and lavatory and a cleaner's store. There is a separate entrance door to this staff area.

Petworth is fortunate to have residents very active in their concern for its amenities and especially its heritage from the past. It has been proposed that the fine collection of local history material owned by the Petworth Society should be housed in the library and the County Council has given tentative approval to the consideration of an extension to the building to the rear of the present reference area.

The Witterings Roughly comparable in size to the Petworth Branch, this library serves an almost exactly equivalent population of round about 5,500. It is well sited in The Parade, East Wittering, behind shops and very central to the area it serves which is the coastal strip between Selsey Bill and Chichester Harbour, linking Bracklesham with East and West Wittering. For a number of years small collections of books for loan have been available from part-time libraries separately serving each of the Witterings but, with continuing population growth, these had become quite inadequate.

The building, by the County Architect, is set back a little way from the road and is of traditional load-bearing brickwork construction; one looks up for the expected flat roof but finds instead an interesting monopitch form adopted. Large windows give good natural light and, once more, satisfyingly declares its function.

Its plan is simple—a large rectangle placed endways on to the road and the entrance doors. The first of these leads into a small lobby with strip-matting set in a floor well, the door having a large letter-box adequate for books returned when the library is closed (a mound of them, in fact, when I was there). The inner entrance door opens to a small area screened ahead to the width of the lobby and separating it from the staff counter. This screen is glazed and ground-length but with a wide strip of timber, a good safety precaution, about a metre above ground. In this entrance corner of the library there is a well designed and face-lit notice board and small pamphlets rack, also a good, glazed display fitting in the forward corner of the window.

The counter is only 1.8 metres long, but designed specially for the Plessey computerised light-pen book issue system, with shelves on the wall behind it and a trolley for book shelving beside. There is an enquiries desk just beyond, within the main Lending Library area.

The first section of the open-plan library behind the street window is for children, and can be curtained off, by roller-track on the ceiling, to be used for talks and story hours. This should not interfere too much with use of the adult library since the reading area and reference books are at the far end of this quite long room. Good use is made in the adult library of island, castored display fittings and two-tier island book stacks, with perimeter shelving the length of one of the long walls. At the far end, the short wall is mainly a large, ground-length 'picture' window. One section of this is a fire exit, with panic bolt control, which perhaps introduces an element of concern at the security risk, though it is admittedly fully within sight of the staff counter. Placed in front of the window are two large six-seat tables. The other long wall has windows, again ground-length and curtain hung, as they all are. A door leads to a small enclosed garden with a piece of modern sculpture and seats for reading in the open-air. At the far end of the shelving on this wall, beyond the window, are reference books, near to the tables.

Authority	West Sussex County Council
Designation	Petworth Branch Library
Date of opening	January 1973
Population served	5,560
Name of Architect	Peter and Beryl Harrison, AADip, RIBA (Private Architects in collaboration with B Peters, DiplArch (Dist), RIBA, County Architect
Name of Librarian	W Hose, FLA
Special features:	
a) site	Elevated position in conservation area, near High Street
b) architecture	Traditional load bearing brick walls; local clay tiled pitched roof
c) function	Service to the locality
Mechanical Services:	
a) heating	Gas-fired ducted warm air
b) ventilation	Natural
c) lighting	Fluorescent strip
d) acoustics	Carpet tiles
e) other	—
Areas: in square metres	
a) lending	71
b) reference	25
c) reading	—
d) special activities	—
e) children	30
f) control	4
g) library staff admin.	6
h) exhibitions	—
i) lecture hall	—
j) circulation	—
k) services	—
l) lavatories	4
m) stack	—
Total area:	140
Book volumes:	
a) adult lending	7,200
b) adult reference	325
c) children	2,705
d) stack	—
e) other	—
Total:	10,230
Costs in £ p:	
a) site	5,509
b) building	15,952
c) furniture & fittings	1,982
Total Cost (ex fees):	£23,443
Cost per square metre:	£167

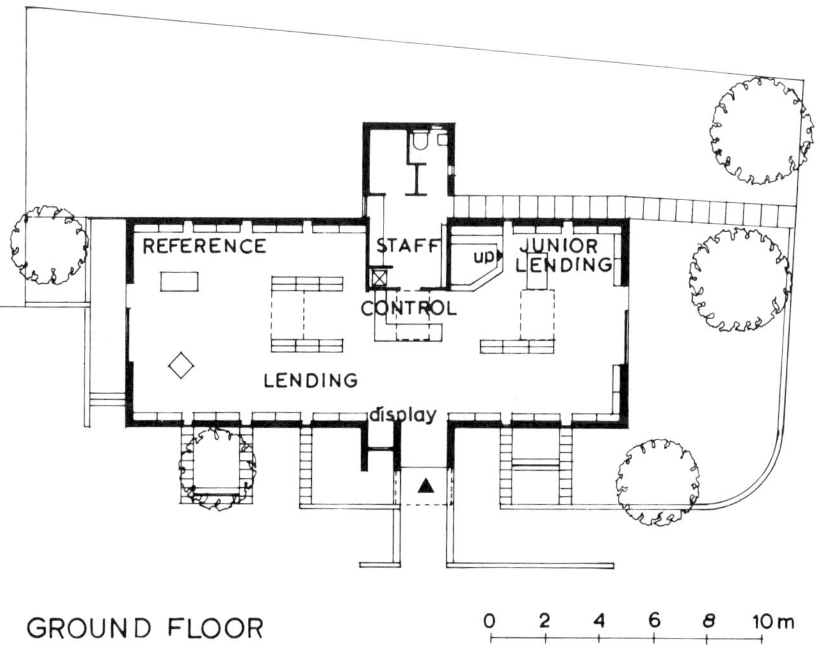

GROUND FLOOR

There is no natural lighting from the sloping roof. Diffusers, set flush in the acoustic ceiling tiles take parallel fluorescent light strips the length of the room. There are ventilators recessed above the ceiling, clearly audible as they moved in the sea breeze that was blowing. Heating is by off-peak electricity. The floor is fully carpeted.

With its own side entrance and approached internally from beside the staff counter is a block parallel with the main rectangle, containing staff accommodation and workroom, a lavatory equipped for wheelchair users, cleaner's room and chair store and boiler.

A most pleasant and comfortable little library in which details of design, generally, strike one as being very good, even to a small litter-bin under the entrance canopy.

LHS

The Witterings

Authority	West Sussex County Council
Designation	The Witterings Branch Library
Date of opening	November 1973
Population served	5,500
Name of Architect	B Peters, DiplArch (Dist), ARIBA, County Architect; J Groome, Job Architect
Name of Librarian	W Huse, FLA
Special features:	
a) site	Central position near shops
b) architecture	Load bearing brick with copper covered mono-pitched roof; Scola windows; doors ceiling
c) function	—
Mechanical Services:	
a) heating	Off-peak electric sealed highly insulated building
b) ventilation	Mechanical
c) lighting	Fluorescent, natural
d) acoustics	No special
e) other	—
Areas: in square metres	
a) lending	—
b) reference	146
c) reading	—
d) special activities	—
e) children	—
f) control	—
g) library staff admin.	9
h) exhibitions	—
i) lecture hall	—
j) circulation	—
k) services	7
l) lavatories	5
m) stack	—
Total area:	167
Book volumes:	
a) adult lending	9,095
b) adult reference	224
c) children	3,770
d) stack	—
e) other	—
Total:	13,089
Costs in £ p:	
a) site	—
b) building	21,579
c) furniture & fittings	7,209
Total Cost (ex fees):	£28,788
Cost per square metre:	£172

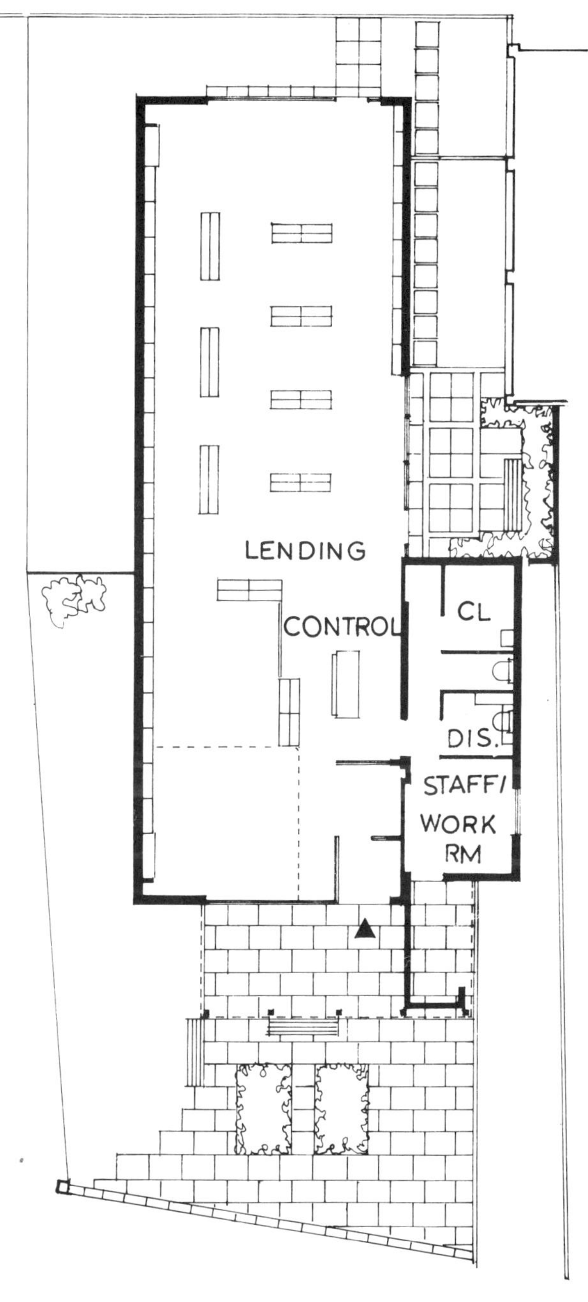

GROUND FLOOR

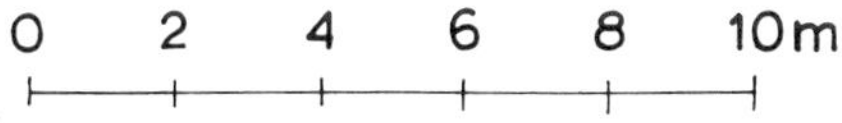

Wiltshire County Council:
Amesbury, Chippenham, Wroughton and (formerly Borough of Swindon) Moredon

Amesbury is a town of about 6,000–7,000 inhabitants. It has around it a number of large barracks and military camps on Salisbury Plain, swelling the population it serves to more than double that of the town itself. Readers from surrounding villages (served by a mobile library van running from Wilton) also visit Amesbury for shopping and tend to come to the new building. The site is quite conveniently placed at the end of one of its main streets though access to it is a little hazardous with busy roads to be crossed.

The need for the new library has been most emphatically demonstrated by the startling growth in the number of issues, from 6,200 books in the old library to 128,000 in the first twelve months of the new. During this period over 3,000 new readers joined. This is due to a number of factors which clearly include the attractions of this new building, but opening hours have been increased to 39 per week. It is interesting to note that, soon after the Public Libraries Act of 1919 led to the establishment of a County Library Service in Wiltshire, the first 'Village Library' for Amesbury, with 223 books, was opened for 2 hours a week. The present library contains an immediately accessible stock of over 22,000 books.

Amesbury House, a Georgian building which stood in matured, landscaped grounds was bought by the County Council and demolished to make way, initially, for road improvements. These left the present site available for a new building designed to accommodate both the library and a health centre to serve the town and surrounding area. The construction proceeded, basically in two phases, between 1968 and 1974, the library being opened on 30th August of that year.

An octagonal shape was chosen for the main open-plan area of the library, with a folded roof, rising slightly to an apex at the centre. The external walls of the octagon are faced in a traditional combination of materials seen in many old houses in the neighbourhood: a chequerboard pattern of stone and knapped flints set in mortar. In this case the panels of these materials are contained between the upright concrete columns at the angles of the octagon. A small, central view window is placed in each of the outward looking sides, with high-level windows above, following the triangular forms created by the roof's arched segments. Whether this combination of traditional style and modern shape and proportions is altogether visually satisfying, viewed externally, is arguable.

Blocks, of lower roof height, one containing an exhibition gallery and the other a workroom and reserve stack, staff room and lavatories, complete the accommodation, which is built on to the Heath Centre with an internal courtyard, accessible only from the library, between the two.

The approach to both is from a well laid out forecourt with a flight of steps up to a wide, covered platform linking both entrances. There is also a ramp for prams and wheelchairs. At the back of this covered way is the internal library courtyard but enclosing this is a rather unsightly screen of corrugated fibreglass sheeting. Although something is obviously necessary to prevent access to the courtyard from outside, and to provide shelter whilst letting light through, this does rather cheapen the look of the entrance area which is otherwise well-designed.

A small enclosed porch leads to the library 'In' and 'Out' doors, with a further door leading directly into the exhibition space which can be shut off from the library by means of a plastic fabric-faced and sliding, folding screen. This room, when not in use for exhibitions, obviously frequent and enterprising, is used as a meetings room for local societies and clubs; a small kitchen is attached, which is certainly of great benefit, but one wonders why a lavatory was not also provided. Normally the exhibition space opens directly into the large library area beyond the counter so that it is under supervision and the door to the lobby is kept locked.

An emphasis on the interests of children and their special needs is apparent throughout the main library, where one of the segments of the octagon is furnished for their use. In the main, the floor is finished with variegated Muhuhu hardwood blocks but in the children's section this changes to orange carpet. Large pin-up boards were full of the work of local schoolchildren and this lends an atmosphere of gaiety to the more sober areas of the library, for this decorative material can be seen above the free-standing bookcases which are only four shelves high, unlike the perimeter shelving in adult areas, of six shelves. For smaller children there is a life-size rag doll and other play figures. Reference material occupies another of the segments, with easy chairs and tables whilst in another, close to the counter, a large exhibition case only partly obscures the view into the courtyard. Doors to this are placed on either side of the case, with a canopy outside, and in fine weather readers sit in the sun. Children are apparently also encouraged to read outside and some games —chess was evident—are provided.

The counter is spacious and efficient but some confusion seems to arise about entry and exit. This is not as clearly guided as it might be, but since the doors only open in the direction of intended use, this is perhaps only a minor irritation. The provision of staff accommodation is as good as that for the public, with a business-like workroom with Remploy rolling-shelf reserve stacks to provide space for about 8,000 books. This area is mainly top-lit from domelights. The staff room is very satisfactory, well-furnished and with good facilities. Close by, off a short corridor, are staff lavatories of the same high standard of design and finish.

Heating, an oil-fired system, is shared with the Health Centre which, we were told, originally led to some difficulties since libraries seldom require to be as warm as doctors' consulting rooms, but provision for adjustment seems to have proved adequate.

This is, then, very much a family library and the staff have been able to generate an infectious air of enthusiasm which has altogether resulted in the quite spectacular growth in the library's use.

LHS   GKVT

Authority	County of Wiltshire
Designation	Amesbury Library
Date of opening	August 1974
Population served	6,000
Name of Architect	S Townrow, MBE, RIBA, County Architect; M Saunders, Job Architect
Name of Librarian	W F Hallworth, FLA, FRGS
Special features:	
a) site	Corner site
b) architecture	Steel portals to hall and copper roof
c) function	Service to town and surroundings
Mechanical Services:	
a) heating	Oil fired; fan assisted
b) ventilation	Natural
c) lighting	Mainly fluorescent plus tungsten
d) acoustics	'Dampa' aluminium slats to ceiling; flssured mimatone acoustic tiled generally
e) other	—
Areas: in square metres	
a) lending	140
b) reference	44
c) reading	—
d) special activities	—
e) children	44
f) control	in (a)
g) library staff admin.	23
h) exhibitions	
i) lecture hall	41
j) circulation	21
k) services	22
l) lavatories	10
m) stack	—
Total area:	345
Book volumes:	
a) adult lending	10,166
b) adult reference	1,513
c) children	2,955
d) stack	8,425
e) other	—
Total:	23,059
Costs in £ p:	
a) site	3,500
b) building	40,134
c) furniture & fittings	8,000
Total Cost (ex fees):	£51,634
Cost per square metre:	£149

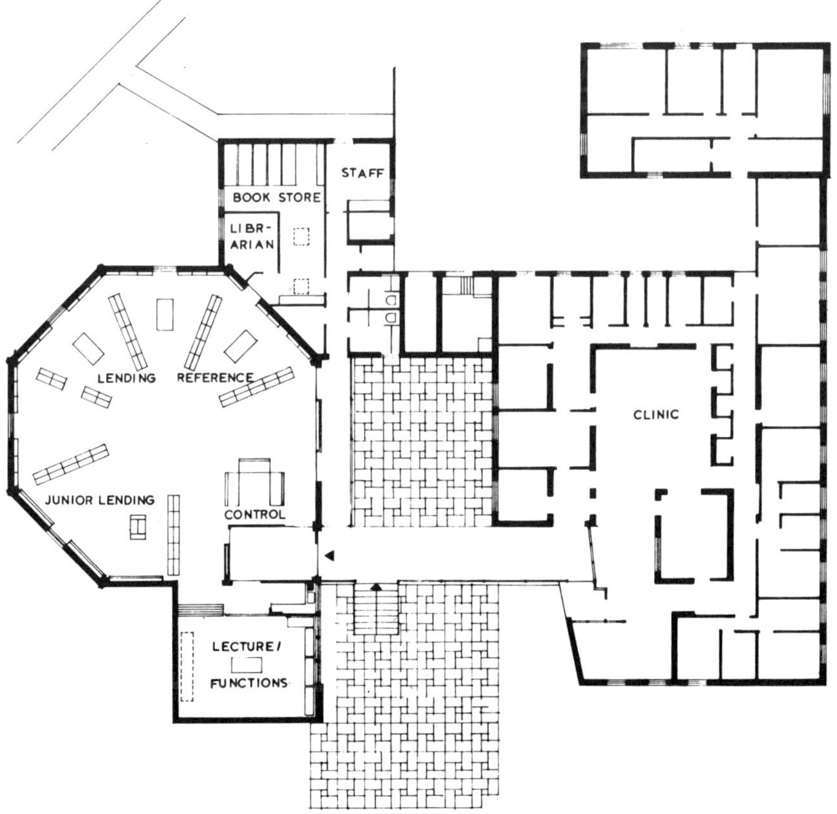
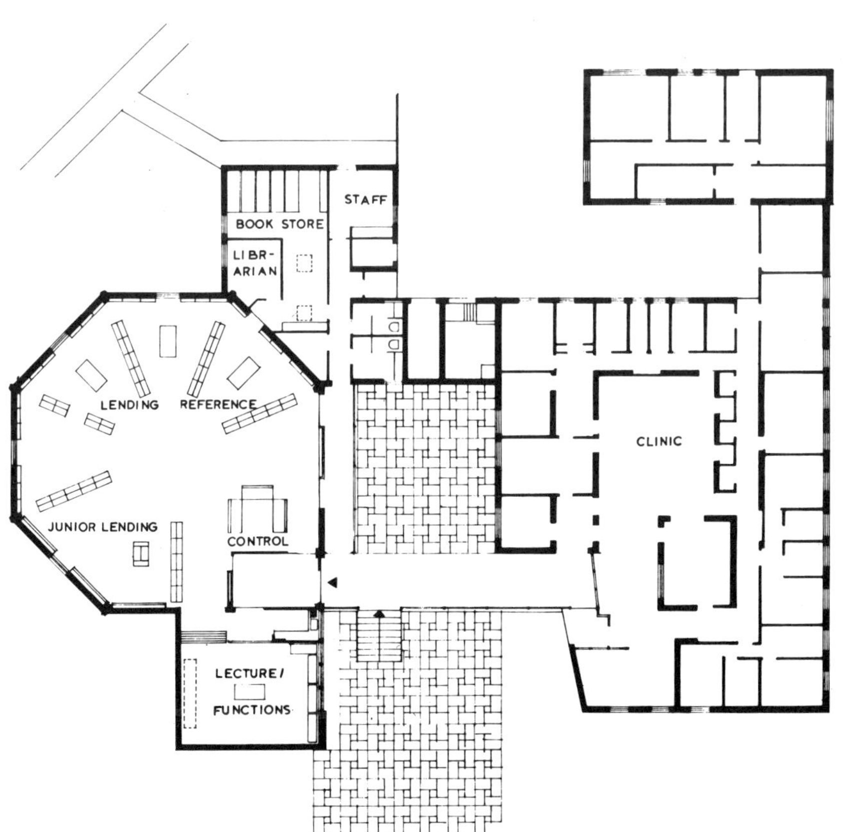

GROUND FLOOR

Chippenham is a typical West Country market town, and the new library serves it and the surrounding villages, a catchment population of about 30,000. It also serves as one of five divisional headquarters in the system. The two-storey library is built on a site purchased by the County Council in 1964, for a combined Library and Civil Defence Centre. Civil Defence policy changed, and with DES persuasion over loan sanction, the library was built as it is now, and not as a phased building, as originally planned.

Chippenham, like many similar country towns, is having considerable central area building development, and new road and car parking systems. The library site is in the central area, but on a side road, adjacent to a scheduled eighteenth-century building on the main road, also owned by the County. The County Librarian had hoped that the entrance to the library could have been on the main road, but the levels of the floors of the entrance to the new library will permit linking through to the old building in the future. Great care has been taken in designing the new library to make possible this physical link, but also in the visual link and streetscape. The entrance to the library carefully follows the roof line of the old building, whilst the main body of the library relates to the adjacent 1930's cinema. The lining-up of floors has necessitated a few steps up to the library entrance, which normally would have been avoided, but a ramp with handrail is provided for the disabled.

The site dictated a two-storey solution, and it also dictated some odd shaped areas at the rear of the building for work spaces and storage, not apparent from the smooth, classical street façade. Having been forced to separate the stock and services on to two floors, the obvious decision was to put the more popular and heavily used stock on the ground floor, together with the Children's Library, and large print books for the partially sighted. There is also a reception hall containing exhibition facilities, lounge seating, the control counter and the information section, with enquiry desk, catalogue, and telex. An interesting detail of the control counter is a series of sliding partitions between it and the workroom behind, where trolleys of returned books can be pushed through for later sorting–also the use of mirror glass, permitting concealed control from the workroom.

The first floor, approached by the main staircase or by lift, contains the remainder of the non-fiction stock, specialist periodicals, another enquiry desk, and two study areas, one of which converts easily and can be separated off as a meeting room: this also contains local history material, and Colonel E. P. Awdry's special collection of cricket books and periodicals.

There is a separate side entrance and staircase to the first floor meeting room, which together with its own toilets and kitchen, can operate separately out of library hours. There is also a lift for trolleys and the disabled, but it is not large enough for most wheelchairs; however the library have their own wheelchair for those in need, that does fit the lift! A photocopier and microfilm reader are provided, and the meeting room is equipped with sound and slide projectors, record player and cassette player. Reasonable bookstack areas exist, if rather oddly shaped to fit

the site restrictions, and divisional offices have been fitted into the upper floor work and storage area. Compact storage is fitted, a policy for all new libraries. There is a mobile library garage for future use, which now provides storage space for county stock. The staff restroom is well-sited above the entrance, but is separated from the staff toilets on the ground floor; more dubious in theory than in actual practise.

The structure consists of a steel frame, clad externally in precast concrete units, treated to expose the cornish granite aggregate. The surface texture and colour provide a muted contrast to the stonework of the adjoining building, to which the library is linked. Windows and external door frames are of aluminium to reduce maintenance costs, and for the same reason the main roof is faced with copper. When weathered this will contrast with the adjoining stone tiled roof. The general external treatment is restrained so that the new building will not dominate thossse adjoining; yet it has its own definite identity and character.

Internally, the steelwork, where exposed, has been encased in white concrete, surface treated to contrast with the fair-faced brick walls. The hardwood is Sapele, with contrasting areas of Parana pine panelling. The Frenger ceiling provides a constantly controlled temperature within the building, good acoustic balance, and a good overall level of illumination. Ceiling mounted hot-air heaters reduce the influx of cold-air into the main reception hall. The public areas of the library are carpeted throughout, and there are well chosen chairs, tables and fittings, care having been taken to blend colour and design to produce comfortable and informal surroundings, from which an efficient service can be given.

In Wiltshire all libraries are designed as 'one-off' and unique to their situation, but there is a co-ordination of fittings within the building. Their criteria for new library buildings are (a) Library to be in the right place; (b) Library to be stocked with the appropriate material; (c) Library to be informal and attractive; (d) Materials throughout to be easy to maintain; (e) Library should encourage staff to be public-orientated. The Library obviously matches up to these criteria and displays a close collaboration between librarian and architect, which has produced a building which functions well. Great care has been taken to design a building which is attractive within, and is sympathetic to its neighbours, and a contribution to the urban scene.

NR

Wroughton, three miles from Swindon, with a present population of about 7,500, has grown rapidly in recent years as a predominantly middle-class commuter area serving Swindon. Largely because of the enforced 'green belt' (if one can call it that) produced by the passage of the M4 motorway through the intervening country, Wroughton has not become just a Swindon suburb: it retains its identity as an expanded village.

The new library, replacing a small service point in a room in the Church Hall, is ideally sited in a new urban precinct which

Authority	County of Wiltshire
Designation	Chippenham Branch Library
Date of opening	June 1973
Population served	18,550 (up to 30,000)
Name of Architect	S Townrow, MBE, RIBA, County Architect; B G Hooper, MS, AAT, Assistant-in-Charge
Name of Librarian	Frederick Hallworth, FLA, FRGS
Special features:	
a) site	Restricted site opposite main bus station; adjacent to listed building
b) architecture	Traditional; steel frame; concrete panels; copper roofing; aluminium windows and doors
c) function	Serving town and surrounding villages
Mechanical Services:	
a) heating	Oil-fired; ceiling radiator panels
b) ventilation	Natural
c) lighting	Fluorescent strip in concealed panels
d) acoustics	Acoustic ceiling (Frenger); carpeted
e) other	—
Areas: in square metres	
a) lending	143
b) reference	145
c) reading	in (a and b)
d) special activities	—
e) children	60
f) control	54
g) library staff admin.	165
h) exhibitions	—
i) lecture hall	60
j) circulation	171
k) services	20
l) lavatories	32
m) stack	32 (garage)
Total area:	882
Book volumes:	
a) adult lending	25,400
b) adult reference	940
c) children	8,475
d) stack	13,773
e) other	692 (gr, cas)
Total:	49,280
Costs in £ p:	
a) site	29,332
b) building	86,287
c) furniture & fittings	12,000
Total Cost (ex fees):	£127,619
Cost per square metre:	£144

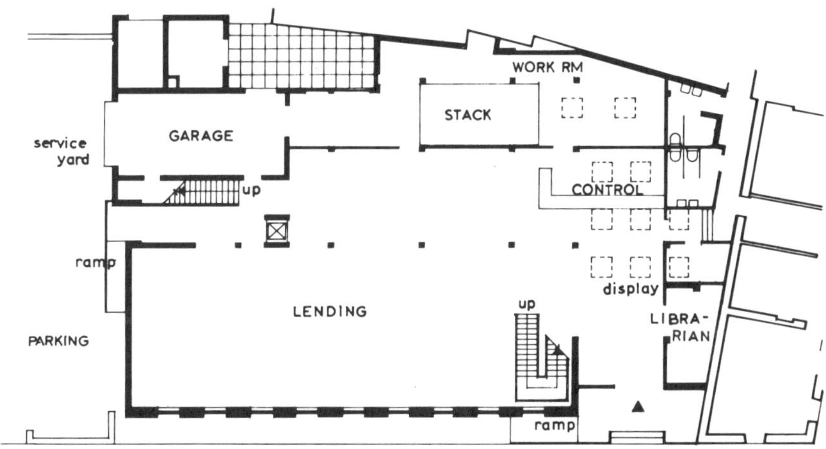

GROUND FLOOR

0 2 4 6 8 10m

Authority	County of Wiltshire
Designation	Wroughton Branch Library
Date of opening	November 1974
Population served	6,750
Name of Architect	S Townrow, MBE, RIBA, County Architect and Oxford Architects Partnership, G A Linfield; J A Holden, Job Architect
Name of Librarian	F Hallworth, FLA, FRGS
Special features:	
a) site	Corner site near shopping centre
b) architecture	Steel frame with red facing brick; bronze tinted glass in lantern roof and windows
c) function	Branch library in eastern division 3 miles from Swindon
Mechanical Services:	
a) heating	Oil-fired
b) ventilation	Natural
c) lighting	Fluorescent
d) acoustics	Insulated ceiling; carpeted floor
e) other	—
Areas: in square metres	
a) lending	180
b) reference	72
c) reading	—
d) special activities	—
e) children	90
f) control	in (a)
g) library staff admin.	77
h) exhibitions	54
i) lecture hall	in (h)
j) circulation	42
k) services	7
l) lavatories	18
m) stack	—
Total area:	540
Book volumes:	
a) adult lending	9,584
b) adult reference	170
c) children	5,498
d) stack	1,660
e) other	—
Total:	16,912
Costs in £ p:	
a) site	5,000
b) building	61,000
c) furniture & fittings	8,800
Total Cost (ex fees):	£74,800
Cost per square metre:	£138

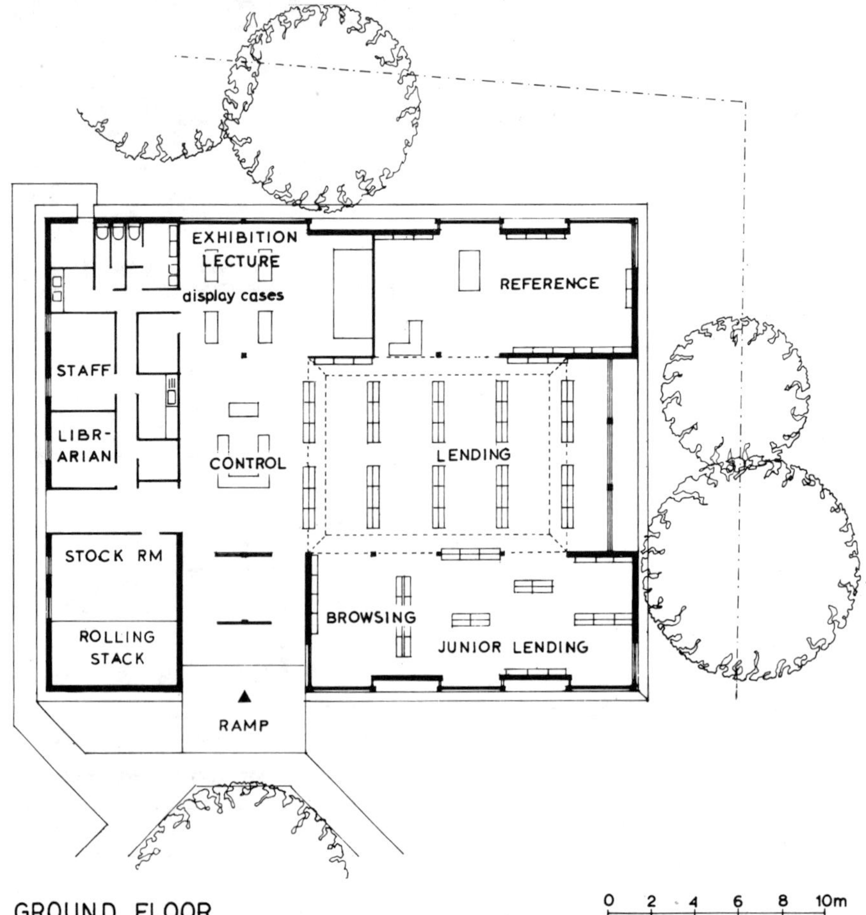

GROUND FLOOR

includes shopping and community centres and an adequate but inevitably stark and ugly parking space. For the library to be in the centre of so much special activity is excellent for readership.

The architect was Mr G. A. Linfield of the Oxford Architects Partnership who worked in co-operation with the Wiltshire County Architects and, of course, with the County Library and Museum Service which has excellent experience in briefing and in maintaining close contact with the architects on the job. Mr Linfield speaks warmly of the quality of the help which he received from Mr Peter Pickup of the Library and Museum Service, whose special job it is to assure full and continuous co-operation between the Department and the architects. The Oxford Architects Partnership was responsible for the general layout of the precinct and for the design of the shopping centre and other buildings.

Here, as elsewhere in Wiltshire, the County makes a notable contribution to the cultural, social and visual vitality of their *library* activity by including space for small, constantly changing exhibitions, generally of direct local interest.

The whole of the 4,000 ft^2 (372 m^2) of public area for loan, reference and children's collections is open without full visual separation. The exhibition room is similarly open to the rest of the library but can be closed off by folding doors for use as a meeting room. There is a separate entrance from outside for meetings which leads to the meeting room down a passage with cloaks pegs and access to the toilets and to the small kitchen—also for staff use.

The staff areas and stockroom are well placed and amply large and they are efficiently grouped together down the length of the east side. The entrance on this side, which is also the meeting room entrance, is wide enough for easy unloading from delivery vans which can back up against the door sill.

The library is good acoustically with insulated ceilings and close-carpeted floors and there is little external noise, the road passing the library being virtually free from noisy or heavy traffic. The walls of the library are white throughout, the colour, as is proper in a library, being provided by the bright variety of the books. One pleasing detail is the differentiation of the children's area by use of a softer (Heuga) carpet than in the rest of the library so that the children can sit comfortably on it. It has been found by experience that children's story telling groups can be held in the open library without more acoustic separation than is provided by the bookshelves.

The library as it is has sufficient space for enlargement of the collection to the maximum that is likely to be required by its catchment area, so that no provision has been made for structural enlargement either laterally or by addition of an extra storey.

The architects have avoided that gimmicky obsession of so many library designers of making all the windows stretch from floor-to-ceiling: here the windows are designed to give adequate daylight without subjecting the legs of all readers seated by the windows to total exposure and, as far as ground floor windows are concerned, extending the glazing only as far as the part that is both most easily dirtied and least easily cleaned.

Wiltshire is once more to be congratulated on an excellent new library.

Moredon Branch, opened in December 1973, but not reviewed at the time, is well worth record for its entirely satisfactory architectural qualities, sufficiently, and at the same time modestly, possessed of character to attract and hold attention in an area of mostly undistinguished suburban housing. The architects were A. W. Flack and K. Eade.

The library was designed and built by Swindon before their libraries became part of the Wiltshire service on 1st April 1974.

EJC

GROUND FLOOR

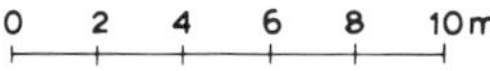

Wirral District Council (formerly Borough of Bebington): Bromborough and Heswall

There has been a noticeable tendency in the buildings reviewed in the present period for libraries to be combined with other public buildings eg clinics, schools, shopping centres.

Bromborough on the Mersey side of the Wirral peninsular is a growing town forming part of the now almost continuous urban area stretching from Birkenhead to Ellesmere Port. It nevertheless manages to preserve its identity, particularly in the centre, which has still the quality of a village, with a row of shops along one side of a large village green. It is on this open stretch of green that the library, combined in this case with a complex of halls and meeting rooms, is built.

Parking is provided close to the building and there are few restrictions on surrounding roads so that the public can park all round, while the entrance lobbies serving both halls and library become a public footpath to and from the shops. Space provision here is very generous, to cope with the crowds that can be generated if several activities take place at once.

There are almost palatial glazed tiled lavatories and a hexagonal cloakroom which can double as a small meetings room. Large and small public halls are provided, with a kitchen and servery block linking them, whilst two additional small exhibition and reading rooms adjoining the library double as extra meeting rooms. There are thus five rooms of various sizes, catering for all possible requirements from wedding receptions to concerts, from chess clubs to Womens Institute, with conditions of considerable sophistication and comfort. The cleaning staff, who are evidently proud of their building, keep it immaculate.

Firmly where it should be, at the centre of community life, the library is a natural place to drop into whilst shopping or before attending one of the numerous functions which the halls encourage.

Externally the building is of considerable complexity for most of the elements mentioned above are expressed individually in a rather sprawling composition lacking unity of architectural treatment. Rather too many shapes and finishes are in evidence. The form does however produce pleasant spaces between the halls and the library which have been landscaped, (since the photograph reproduced was taken), with an attractive heather and rock garden.

The library element is rectangular with a high roof rising above the lower blocks housing entrances, staff rooms, Reading and Exhibition rooms enabling clerestory windows to run continuously round all four sides, even above the large window walls. Walls are in a blue-purple brindled brick and the windows aluminium.

Internally a single open room houses Adult Lending and Reference as well as Children's Library with a lower area for children's study area. The counter divides adult and children's areas and is placed immediately inside the glass doors with clear direction signs. The sensible 'U'-shaped counter design encloses the staff in an area from which most of the library can be easily supervised. Alterations have had to be made to the original layout of the children's section, parts of which were out of sight, thus encouraging high spirits. Only in part of the adult reference section do the bookcases obscure vision in spite of the use of some lower bookcases.

Difficulty in achieving full supervision is one of the prices to be paid for fully-glazed walls in a library. The designer must weigh the relative merits of this approach, which puts the library on display from outside, against those of the opposite type of plan in which walls are used to house bookcases whilst keeping the centre more open.

In this case the full-glazed design seems to be justified though with some reservations about both the lack of openness in the room and problems of solar gain, glare and ventilation. Attempts are made to deal with these obvious drawbacks by providing curtains to all windows, which can be drawn at night to create a cosy atmosphere while making windows at high-level open by remote control to provide through ventilation. The fact that the only ventilation is at high-level does lead to stuffiness in summer and does not mitigate the solar gain sufficiently.

There remains the vexed question of insulation against heat loss. In fairness, concern over energy conservation is a subject which has only come to the fore in recent years, since this building was planned. Today rising fuel costs might well have dictated a different design approach and only time will tell whether this will lead to fundamentally different library design in the future.

The internal design follows in other respects standards of finish which seem to be almost universal, acoustic tile ceilings with fluorescent lighting, carpet tiled floors and the ubiquitous Reska fittings. Walls are finished in plastic paper or an attractive and practical striated plaster. A good deal of natural hardwood is used, in fascias under the clerestory windows, the counter doors. Black painted steel box columns stand clear of the side walls, getting slightly in the way but producing a strong sense of structure.

Staff have a pleasant room overlooking the entrance courtyard. It might have been kinder if their window had not been taken to the floor which leaves them rather exposed to public view. The workroom which is very small and crowded could have done with an external door for book delivery and a staff entrance. These rooms together with the Exhibition and Reading Rooms next to the library have supplementary roof-lights which ensure good natural light during the day.

Bromborough can be well satisfied with a lively and well-built library in just the right place. There is not doubt either as to its popularity or the fact that it is so readily accessible to the whole community, not just the car owning majority.

Heswall This prosperous little town lies on the south-west coast of the Wirral on high ground above the Dee estuary, straddling the main road from Chester to Hoylake at the end of the peninsular. Separated from the urban sprawl of Birkenhead by an area of beautiful wooded countryside, Heswall is a rather

Authority	Metropolitan Borough of Wirral formerly Borough of Bebington
Designation	Bromborough Library
Date of opening	July 1973
Population served	16,000
Name of Architect	T H McGrath, BEng, MSCA, FIMunE, Borough Engineer; J Brereton, RIBA
Name of Librarian	John Shepherd, FLA
Special features:	
a) site	In park adjacent to shopping street; part of complex including public halls and meeting rooms
b) architecture	Steel framed; glass and brick external walls
c) function	—
Mechanical Services:	
a) heating	Gas-fired central heating
b) ventilation	Natural
c) lighting	Mercury 30 lumens per sq ft
d) acoustics	—
e) other	—
Areas: in square metres	
a) lending	306
b) reference	—
c) reading	—
d) special activities	66
e) children	
f) control	in (a)
g) library staff admin.	
h) exhibitions	17
i) lecture hall	746
j) circulation	96
k) services	—
l) lavatories	4
m) stack	—
Total area:	1,235
Book volumes:	
a) adult lending	11,780
b) adult reference	1,200
c) children	4,020
d) stack	2,130
e) other	—
Total:	19,130
Costs in £ p:	
a) site	—
b) building	195,858
c) furniture & fittings	10,000
Total Cost (ex fees):	£208,000 including halls
Cost per square metre:	£168 including halls

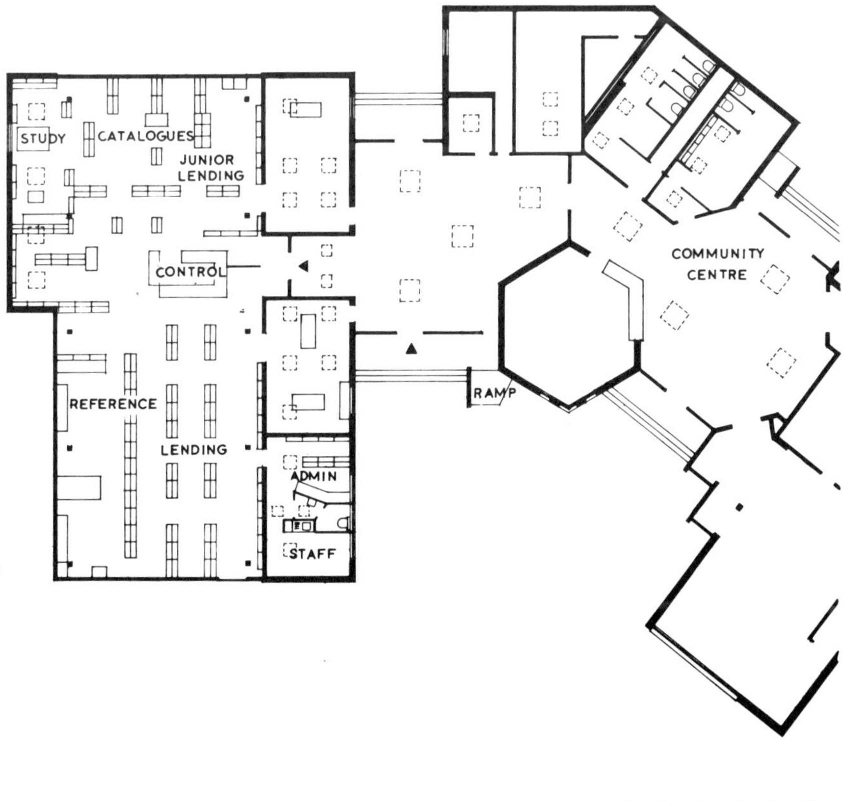

GROUND FLOOR

self-contained town of about 30,000. The main street is not particularly distinguished but has a quiet, varied country-town atmosphere with shops on both sides of the road. The site of the library and the adjacent Heswall Hall, both built at the same time and designed by the same firm, opens out around the town's bowling green.

After the enthusiastic report on Bebington Library, by the same architects, in the 1974 edition of this publication (pp 21–23) the visit to this building was keenly awaited.

In any modest town of Heswall's stamp it is a challenge to the architect to produce buildings which fit into the grain of the town, prominent but not dominant. In this case this has been achieved with great distinction as both buildings fit quietly into the scene as if they had always been there. As one approaches from Chester one senses before one actually sees the library where it should be—and there it is, at the centre of gravity, as it were. A simple rectangular two-storey building of brown brick with windows and intervening piers faceted, the bays sometimes projecting, sometimes recessing and complementary. The Hall, of very similar detail, lies beyond.

The landscaping is delightful with broad paved paths, good planting and clear directions and signs. A large car park which serves the whole town centre lies behind, well hidden, so that the buildings suffer no competition. A wide, deep, welcoming porch with draught lobby faces the road. One notices small thoughtful details, rings in the wall for tethering waiting dogs, good big display boards, umbrella stand, space to leave prams under cover, an outside litter bin, clear opening times board, all where they should be and solving problems without fuss. The draught lobby however is rather small and the Nuway mat not big enough to deal with the common problem of wet shoes.

Inside, the whole ground floor is one open room, comprising Lending and Children's Libraries with the counter close to the door. Straight ahead an immaculately detailed mosaic clad stair, with solid low walls and surmounted by a shiny chrome handrail, leads up to the first floor. The half landing is high enough to walk under so that surprisingly little space is lost.

The furniture layout with bookcases at the rear, following the lines of beams over, is not always exactly as originally planned by the architects. This is a pity, for supervision has thus been sacrificed here and there. For the most part, however, this layout has been intelligently thought out and relates well to the structure, to the lighting and to the windows which are a notable feature of the whole design.

The faceted window form is delightful, providing intriguing glimpses of the surrounding gardens. Sills on the ground floor are low and can be used as window seats or for display. No attempt is made to achieve natural lighting to more than the perimeter of the library, for the deep plan dictates permanent artificial light. Obvious economies in building and running costs stem from such a simple almost square plan form. Heat losses are reduced, planning flexibility increased, the proportion of costly outside wall in relation to the floor area reduced. The low cost of the building per square metre is ample proof of this, for the quality is excellent throughout.

At first floor level the Reference Library is on the sunny west corner, quiet because it is remote from the road. The ceiling height seems exactly right. Greater height, so often adopted, is quite unnecessary and leads to higher running costs. At the head of the windows the overhanging roof, with its upward splayed soffit, gives both excellent lighting and also shading when the sun is high in summer. It also gives a sense of protection.

The tea bar lobby can be used when the library is shut, by organisations hiring the Special Activities Room or Committee Room. This can be reached by a stair and door direct to the outside. Deeply splayed roof-lights produce ample natural lighting in this area. The staff room is quiet, domestic and sunny with the convenient kitchen corner accessible but out of sight behind a screen. The internal unlit store, on the first floor, is of somewhat dubious value and overlarge for its purpose. Part of this is supposed to be kept clear as a means of escape between Reference and Special Activities Rooms. There is a useful projection hatch into the latter. Complaints by the librarians about the lack of adequate provision for a workroom appear to stem from another change from the architects' intended furniture layout. This enclosed the area behind the counter with external delivery door, appearing adequate as originally planned but is, at present, reduced to a somewhat pokey, much smaller area. It was explained that as no book lift had been provided packages of books had to be humped up to the store and then down again after processing. Since the original layout does not show the store as a workroom this was evidently not intended as such. The plan reproduced here shows the architect's original intentions.

The staff of eleven, including four Saturday assistants, issue nearly 270,000 volumes a year which is some indication of the popularity of the building. This is in many ways an exemplary library for a town of this size (3,000 population). Cheshire County Council, under whose aegis this library was planned, must indeed have been sad to lose such a distinguished building to the Wirral District Council who run it.

GKVT

Authority	Metropolitan Borough of Wirral
Designation	Heswall Library
Date of opening	November 1974
Population served	30,000 (also served by two small branch libraries)
Name of Architect	Paterson, Macaulay and Owens
Name of Librarian	H H G Arthur, FLA, FRSA, MBIM
Special features:	
a) site	Adjacent to public hall of main shopping street
b) architecture	Load bearing brick part concrete frame
c) function	Public library
Mechanical Services:	
a) heating	Gas-fired; low pressure hot water cill line convectors
b) ventilation	Natural
c) lighting	Fluorescent with tungsten spots; 35 lumens per sq ft
d) acoustics	Carpet
e) other	—
Areas: in square metres	
a) lending	387
b) reference	103
c) reading	—
d) special activities	126
e) children	47
f) control	in (a)
g) library staff admin.	55
h) exhibitions	in (d)
i) lecture hall	—
j) circulation	37
k) services	—
l) lavatories	38
m) stack	—
Total area:	793
Book volumes:	
a) adult lending	15,000
b) adult reference	1,500
c) children	5,000
d) stack	—
e) other	—
Total:	21,500
Costs in £ p:	
a) site	—
b) building	94,320
c) furniture & fittings	10,290
Total Cost (ex fees):	£104,610
Cost per square metre:	£117

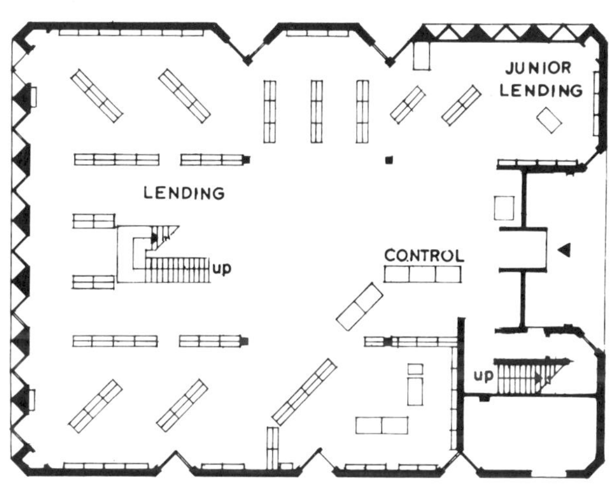

GROUND FLOOR

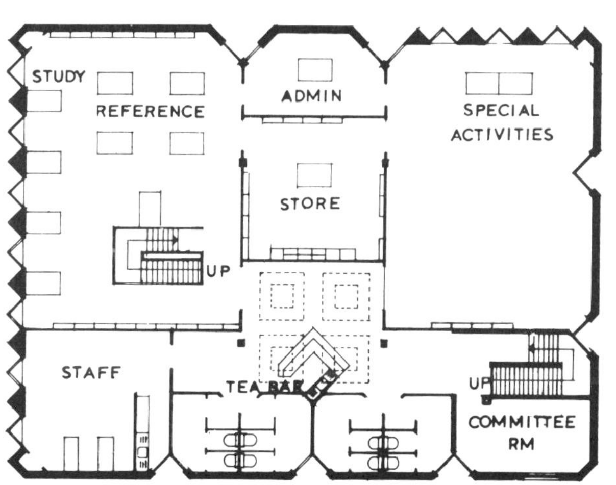

FIRST FLOOR

Highland Regional Council (formerly Ross and Cromarty County Council): Alness

Alness, situated on the Cromarty Firth was, until a few years ago, a village of about 1,000 people. Since the discovery of oil in the North Sea and the subsequent concentration of related activities in that area, and following the establishment of a large aluminium smelter a few miles away, Alness has grown six-fold; it may even be allowed to increase in the future to a population of 10–12,000. The average age of the population has dropped considerably and this, added to the new technology introduced to the area, has created a variety of quite different new demands on the library. There is, in addition, a high percentage of the population employed on shift-work which means that the use of the library is spread over the entire day.

The library is one element in a new leisure centre which provides one of the focal points of the community life. Apart from its normal functions the library is also, on occasions, used for other activities such as small exhibitions and lectures. The centre is sited beside the river in what was a children's playground; it forms one end of the main shopping street and stands at the junction of the old village with the new development–an ideal situation.

The library has pride of place at the front of the leisure centre at street level which is actually first floor level since the ground falls away steeply from the entrance. The library therefore has other parts of the leisure centre immediately underneath, as well as along one long and one short side. The initial approach is slightly disappointing as the design does not take full advantage of its prominent position in the street scene. A few glimpses of the interior would have positively stated the function of the building. Moving into the building, however, the immediate impression is one of an overall continuity of design generating a pleasant well-lit, relaxed atmosphere but with no visual link to the outside.

The library is planned within a long rectangle, the entrance being in one of the short sides, with the counter and staff workroom adjoining. The main library space is laid out with bookstacks generally around the perimeter on the walls, with the reading and reference areas in the centre, progressing in complexity of subject matter away from the entrance.

The building is in fair-faced white concrete blockwork with deep laminated timber beams supporting a timber lined roof. Continuous roof-lights and clerestory windows provide daylight washing down the two long walls. The floor is carpeted throughout and its design is well considered in relation to the various functions. The furniture has obviously been thought of as part of the total concept and complements the structure admirably. The book shelving is steel, assuring adequate strength, but timber trim has been added to enhance the visual effect.

A number of minor criticisms which do not detract from the overall success of the library must be mentioned. If the plan shape had been squarer then supervision would have been easier, the space more flexible and circulation reduced. The fixed plant trough in the centre of the floor also inhibits flexibility but adds a very welcome, softening touch. The noise attenuation between the library and other parts of the centre leaves a lot to be desired and rain drumming on the large roof-lights must be a further source of annoyance. There is no separate control of the library heating which is regulated to suit the centre as a whole; ventilation is by natural means and said by the staff to be inadequate on occasions.

On the whole the library is an excellent balance of functional requirements, fairly stringent economics and the limitations imposed by being part of the leisure centre. This is a first-class library interior in a fairly mediocre external skin.

AM

Authority	County of Ross and Cromarty
Designation	Alness Branch Library and Averon Leisure Centre
Date of opening	January 1973
Population served	6,000
Name of Architect	J Vaughan, RIBA, MRTPI, C Porteous, RIBA
Name of Librarian	Thomas M Gray, DPA, FLA
Special features:	
a) site	Sloping, with library on first floor level with entrance to street
b) architecture	Traditional; white fair faced concrete block walls (untreated)
c) function	Service to residential community and industrial workers
Mechanical Services:	
a) heating	Oil-fired; low pressure hot water
b) ventilation	Natural
c) lighting	Continuous fluorescent strip
d) acoustics	Carpet tiles
e) other	—
Areas: in square metres	
a) lending	150
b) reference	—
c) reading	—
d) special activities	—
e) children	35
f) control	7
g) library staff admin.	12
h) exhibitions	—
i) lecture hall	—
j) circulation	22
k) services	—
l) lavatories	in (g)
m) stack	—
Total area:	226
Book volumes:	
a) adult lending	5,890
b) adult reference	—
c) children	2,728
d) stack	—
e) other	354 gr
Total:	8,972
Costs in £ p:	
a) site	—
b) building	20,549
c) furniture & fittings	2,293
Total Cost (ex fees):	£22,842
Cost per square metre:	£103

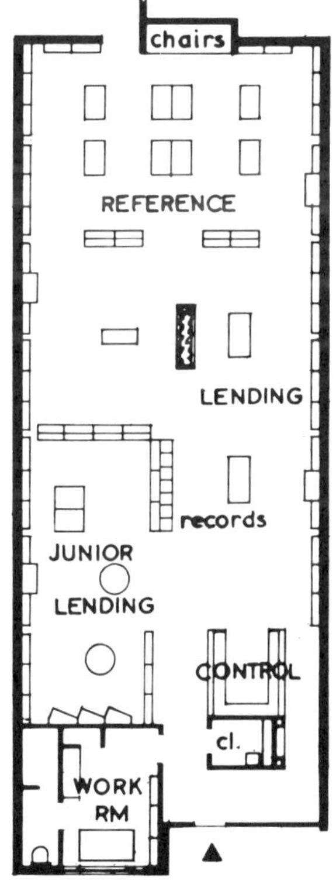

GROUND FLOOR

Clwyd County Council (formerly Flintshire County Council): Holywell (Treffynon)

Holywell is an attractive and historic town on the edge of the industrial coastal strip of what was formerly Flintwell. Many of the inhabitants are employed in the various industries associated with that coastal strip and the town is still tending to increase in population. An independent library service was operated by the Urban Council from 1905 until its transfer to the County Council in 1965 and this Branch Library replaces restricted library premises which had long outgrown their original purpose.

The new building is sited at the centre of the town, a few yards from the High Street and adjacent to a new swimming baths, a youth centre, Darby and Joan Club and a public park, all of which are jointly served by an extensive car park. The library could scarcely have been more conveniently placed.

The warm-coloured bricks used in the construction are appropriate in a town where Georgian domestic architecture is a permanent feature. The most striking characteristic of the exterior is the sculptural effect achieved by the projecting timber box beams which support the roof and between which the high-level windows are placed. An attractive example of exterior landscaping is provided by the forecourt which comprises a varied pattern of paving slabs, bricks on edge and stones set in mortar, with a circular paved area immediately in front of the entrance doors. Two fine elms on the site have been preserved to form a dignified background to the building as the main entrance is approached.

On entering this building the first impression is one of spaciousness. The foyer provides generous space for the display of posters and notices advertising local activities and organisations and these can be read without in any way impeding the flow of traffic in and out of the library. The temptation is not to hurry by but to linger to see what is going on in the town.

The focal point of the interior is the large control and information desk, backed by a wallpaper of arresting design. To the left are the Adult Lending and Reference Sections with the Children's Library on the right. At the rear of the control desk are the workroom, staff room, cleaners' store, etc. Facing the control desk are the Librarian's office and a general and well-lit display area which extends also into the Adult Lending Section. It is obvious that this valuable display area is well and intelligently used, not only for changing exhibitions but also for displaying pictures available in a picture lending scheme, established in the Delyn District under the auspices of the 'Quality of Life Experiment', and of course administered by the County Library.

The open-plan design of the library inevitably induces a sense of space. This can, however, so easily be confusing in a comparatively small area in that the different sections of the library are not always clearly indicated. In the present instance this drawback has been successfully avoided by placing Adult and Children's Sections on either side of the control desk with the Reference Section as a clearly defined projection from the Adult Section. The sensible height of the shelving units in the Adult and Children's Sections further contributes to the sense of space and the overall colour scheme of cream and varying shades of light brown provides a restful atmosphere which extends into the Reference Section. The latter has seating for 14, the high-level lighting being supplemented by the use of one wall as a large window, strong light being diffused by an off-white canvas blind. This section also houses the microfilm catalogue of the County Library's non-fiction stock.

The large and light workroom, easy of access to the loading bay, and the attractive staff room and the Librarian's office are all entirely in keeping with the high standard of the public area.

Natural lighting is provided by high-level windows between the beams, just failing to supply sufficient light on the fairly bright day on which the library was visited. Considerable use of artificial lighting would certainly be necessary on dull days. The entire public area, except the tiled foyer, is carpeted and this is wearing well, as indeed is all the interior decoration. Particularly pleasing is the neat lettering on the book units and also that indicating different sections of the library. This is bilingual throughout and, given this necessity, could as easily have appeared both ponderous and confusing. *Ffirthian,* or facts, is used for *non-fiction* in Welsh—surely a much more felicitous term!

In conclusion it is important to emphasise that this library is worth visiting as an essay in close co-operation between librarian and architect down to the most meticulous detail. This co-operation has produced a library which, besides being a delight to the eye of the reader, is clearly one in which the staff can, and do, enjoy working.

DGT

Authority	Clwyd County Council (formerly Flintshire)
Designation	Holywell (Treffynon) Branch Library
Date of opening	October 1974
Population served	10,000
Name of Architect	County Architect R W Harvey, ARIBA, General Contractor, Spooners (Hull) Ltd
Name of Librarian	Glyn Davies, FLA, FRSA, County Librarian
Special features:	
a) site	Restricted but central site adjacent to Youth Club, and baths; several large trees retained
b) architecture	Single storey of cavity wall construction; flat roof of timber supported on exposed timber box beams; high level windows between beams
c) function	To serve community
Mechanical Services:	
a) heating	Hot water radiators fed from adjacent Youth Club
b) ventilation	Natural
c) lighting	Mainly fluorescent strip
d) acoustics	Carpeted and exposed ceiling beams
e) other	—
Areas: in square metres	
a) lending	150
b) reference	
c) reading	50
d) special activities	—
e) children	96
f) control	26
g) library staff admin.	30
h) exhibitions	27
i) lecture hall	—
j) circulation	21
k) services	6
l) lavatories	7
m) stack	32
Total area:	445
Book volumes:	
a) adult lending	11,000
b) adult reference	650
c) children	5,500
d) stack	550
e) other	1,300
Total:	19,000
Costs in £ p:	
a) site	2,175
b) building	47,832
c) furniture & fittings	4,500
Total Cost (ex fees):	£54,507
Cost per square metre:	£122

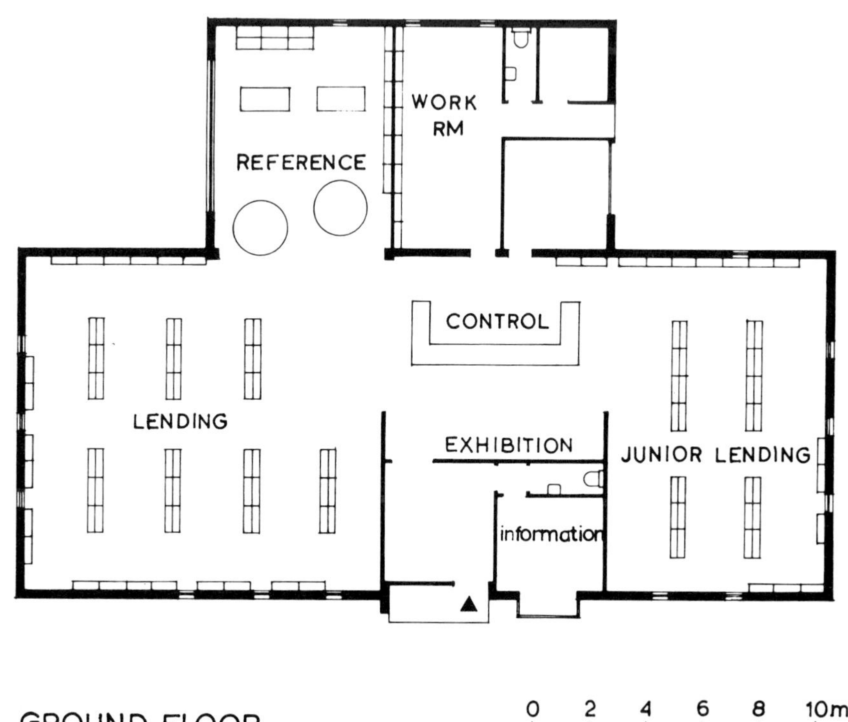

GROUND FLOOR

Gwynedd County Council:
Llangefni, Amlwch and (formerly Merioneth County Council) Tywyn

Llangefni is a pleasant and bustling market town of 4,000 inhabitants with one of the largest cattle markets in North Wales. It is the former shire town of Anglesey and is now the Headquarters of the Anglesey District of the new county of Gwynedd. The building under review was designed as a headquarters for the former Anglesey County Library with public departments serving as reading and reference libraries for the County as well as for Llangefni itself. Its present function as Area Library Headquarters for the Anglesey Area leaves its original purpose virtually unchanged.

This striking building of modern design stands on an open site in the centre of the town, almost surrounded by car parks and with the offices of the District Council and an electricity sub-station as its nearest neighbours. It is steel-framed and constructed of white breeze blocks, with metal cladding to the first floor and with a large concrete stair-well at one side. The materials were chosen with the sensible object of cutting down on subsequent maintenance. The site is sloping, providing an extensive lower ground floor at the rear of the building. Also at the rear of the building any monotony induced by the breeze blocks is broken by a balcony provided at, what here appears to be, first floor level. This balcony runs along one side of the building and part of another side and public access to it is gained from the Adult Lending Library.

On entering the building, however, the dominant feature is what can be best described as the counter complex. This is large, very well-planned in detail and totally avoids any feeling of barrier or enclosure.

All public departments are on the ground floor proper and the first impression given by the colour scheme of beige and dark brown, highlighted at intervals by wallpaper, is wholly favourable. The entrance hall is flanked on the left by an excellent and very well-lit exhibition area, which conforms to V. and A. standards of security and exhibition conditions, and is obviously extensively and intelligently used. There is access to public toilets from this area.

The Children's Library occupies the corresponding area to the right of the entrance. It consists of two distinct rooms, one of which was designed for story-hours and junior activities but now accommodates the non-fiction stock, the adjacent room having proved too small for the total stock. An interesting feature in the section serving the Children's Library is a wash basin and towels for those dirty hands!

The remainder of the ground floor is occupied by the Adult Lending and Reference Libraries. The former has angled windows to throw light along the shelving but this has, throughout, six shelves in height; with the bookcases too close together this gives a somewhat congested appearance which must indeed be awkward during busy periods. The department clearly serves a much larger area than Llangefni itself and it is unfortunate that it should be insufficiently large to display the bookstock necessary to satisfy the needs of its readers.

The Reference Library, with seating for eight, also appears to be on the small side but the accommodation is supplemented by three study carrels and a microfilm carrel. The stock is excellent and includes an extensive local history collection while, adjacent to the Reference Library, is an air-conditioned room for the storage of archives. Following the reorganisation of Local Government this material is being transferred to an Archives Department but the room will be put to good use for the storage of valuable local history material.

The lower ground floor at the rear of the building accommodates the Circulation Section and the Children's Librarian's office and stock room. It also provides access for loading in what is, in effect, a garage for three mobile libraries.

The first floor comprises the Accessions and Cataloguing Section, offices for the Area Librarian and his deputy, staff room and toilets, various storerooms and the stack. The latter is fitted with electrically operated sliding bookcases, designed to take 100,000 volumes which figure, it is anticipated, will meet the area's needs for the foreseeable future. Economical of space these sliding bookcases do carry the disadvantage that only one assistant can work in them at a time.

The favourable first impression of the public departments carries through to the staff work areas which are carpeted throughout and, including an almost opulent staff room, provide very pleasant working conditions.

A curious planning feature which has proved wholly unsuccessful is the provision of the three light wells idicated on the plan. Not only do these fail in their alleged purpose, in that extra lighting has had to be installed in the public departments, but they also produce areas of obscurity after darkness has fallen. In addition they transmit a great deal of noise from the staff working areas to the public departments.

Nevertheless this is an interesting and striking building which is well worth seeing. Its general appearance is pleasant and business-like and it includes many attractive and some original features. There has, however, been a general under-estimating of space in the public departments and, given the open site which was available, it would surely have been preferable to site the work areas on an extended lower ground floor, thus avoiding endless movement of books to and from the first floor. The total cost seems remarkably low and the building must be regarded as a commendable achievement for an Authority with a small population and low rateable value.

Amlwch is a rather undistinguished and scattered town with a population of 3,700. There is a fair amount of industry in the neighbourhood and this could ultimately lead to an increase in population.

The Branch Library replaces a single room used as a library in which no provision was made for children. Undoubtedly one of the most handsome buildings in the town, it is constructed of a combination of local granite and a mottled grey brick, with slate roofing. The agreeable colouring of this ensemble is

Authority	County of Gwynedd, Anglesey County Council
Designation	Anglesey Area Library Headquarters and Llangefni Branch Library
Date of opening	October 1973
Population served	4,000
Name of Architect	N Squire Johnson, ARIBA, AMTPI
Name of Librarian	G Thomas, BA, FLA
Special features:	
a) site	Open site, adjacent to Council offices
b) architecture	Steel-framed construction, breeze blocks with concrete stair well. Upper floor covered with metal cladding
c) function	Designed as County library headquarters
Mechanical Services:	
a) heating	Gas warm air
b) ventilation	Partial air-conditioning
c) lighting	Fluorescent and tungsten
d) acoustics	Carpeted
e) other	—
Areas: in square metres	
a) lending	84
b) reference	68
c) reading	—
d) special activities	—
e) children	54
f) control	—
g) library staff admin.	370
h) exhibitions	60
i) lecture hall	—
j) circulation	185
k) services	14
l) lavatories	35
m) stack	197
Total area:	1,236
Book volumes:	
a) adult lending	17,500
b) adult reference	4,500
c) children	5,500
d) stack	—
e) other Welsh	2,500
Total:	30,000
Costs in £ p:	
a) site	2,500
b) building	137,000
c) furniture & fittings	25,000
Total Cost (ex fees):	£164,500
Cost per square metre:	£133

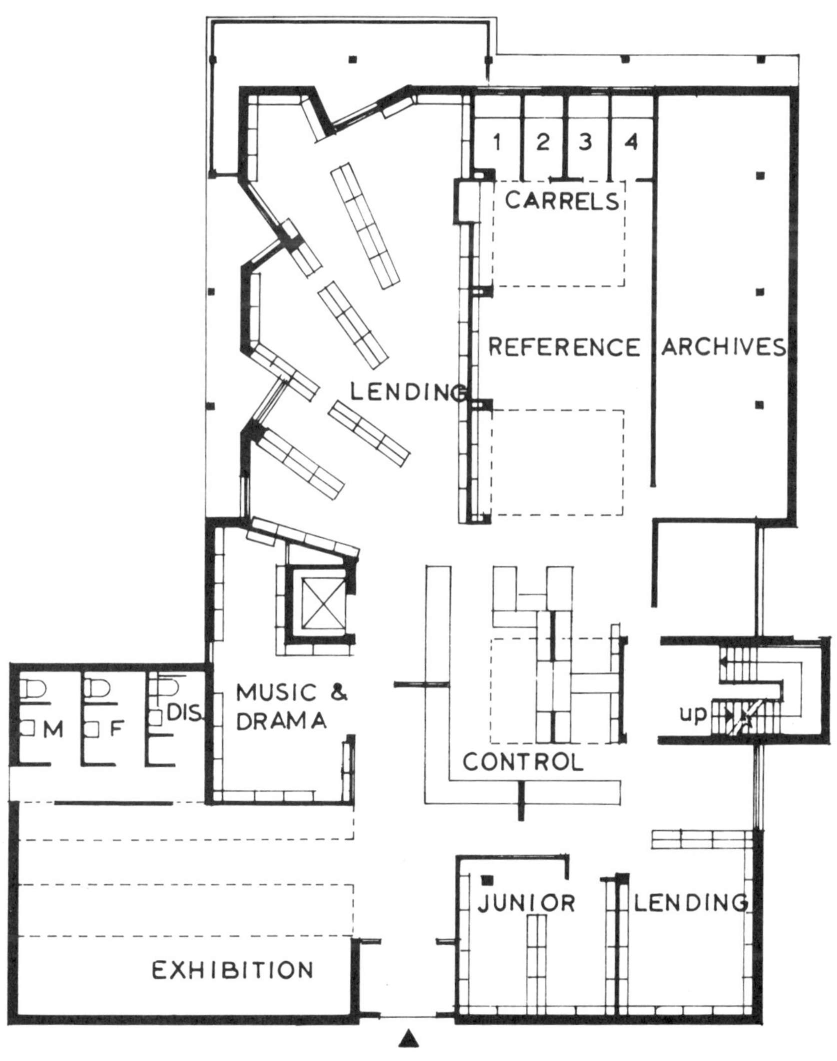

GROUND FLOOR

0 2 4 6 8 10m

Llangefni

unfortunately not apparent in the photograph. The building is set in a landscaped precinct of stone, cobbles and paving slabs with, at one end, a small grassed courtyard provided with seats. Windows are serrated, floor-to-ceiling, in order to light the bookcases which are set at the same angle. There is ample car parking adjacent to the site.

The interior, pleasantly decorated in cream with blue-green carpeting, would have benefited from a somewhat larger entrance area offering facilities for displaying notices and small exhibitions. Several small museum show-cases which are provided are too near the staff control desk and must be impossible to inspect during busy periods.

The disposition of shelving in the Adult and Children's Lending Sections is governed by the serrated windows. Given this arrangement the adult shelving appears a little congested but the two sections cope adequately with an annual issue of over 90,000, a figure which surely indicates considerable use from beyond Amlwch itself.

The Reference Room at the far end of the building has seating for six and a small but well-chosen selection of quick-reference books. It is lit by one large window, facing the grassed courtyard. The room is much used by older children for homework purposes and lack of oversight from the staff control desk brings its problems.

Apart from the shortcomings noted above this is an attractive small branch and, having regard to the materials used, has been built at surprisingly low cost.

Tywyn is a small resort on Cardigan Bay which attracts a considerable number of visitors during the summer months, a factor which has had to be taken into account in determining the scale of its library provision. The present Branch replaces a room in the adjacent offices of the former Urban District. The site is as central as could be desired—in the middle of the somewhat straggling community, a few yards from the main street and facing an extensive housing estate, with pleasant school playing fields at the rear. Adequate car parking is provided in the open space between the library and the housing estate.

The building material of the town is predominantly stone and this fact has determined the outward aspect of the library building. Reference to the plan and photographs will show how the façade is dominated by the massive stone panels, separated by floor-to-ceiling windows, which front half of the building whilst the remaining half is set back to produce a paved forecourt, decorated with concrete tubs of plants. This set-back portion fronts part of the Adult Section and the Children's Section, the former faced by a solid wall in slate-coloured brick whilst the latter is fronted by one large window supported by stone panels to match the other stonework of the building. Above the central Adult Section is a pitched slated roof with high-level windows beneath. The net effect of this design is totally to avoid the box-like exterior appearance of so many small libraries. It is a little unfortunate that side and rear walls

are faced with Canterbury spar chippings, in other words the pebble-dashing which is the curse of so much domestic building in North Wales.

The interior plan is simple—a display area, with separate Reference Room to the left, leads into the Adult Section which in turn extends into the clearly defined Children's Section. The tiled display area has, also, been given over to newspapers, an inheritance which proved impossible to discard. The inevitable untidiness of loose newspapers is, however, offset by the cheerful browser boxes of a small, but well-chosen, record collection.

The Adult and Children's Sections are both carpeted, sage-green predominating in a restful colour scheme. Circulation space and shelf-capacity appears large, given the population served, but this would doubtless not be the impression during the busier summer months. Natural lighting is excellent and this applies to all sections of the Branch.

The Children's Section is particularly attractive with its large window facing the road, a feature which gives a happy and inviting appearance to the building when seen from the outside and this must be especially so during hours of darkness. It is somewhat remote from the central desk and problems of oversight and control might also appear to apply in the separate Reference Section. I was assured that there was no problem in practice, a commentary on the superior behaviour of Welsh children!

The Reference Section seats 16 and, with its two large windows giving on to the roof, complements the outwardly welcoming impression of the Children's Section. Bearing in mind the close proximity of a housing estate, the object of the generous seating provision is to assist in solving that problem of escaping television which confronts so many schoolchildren today. It is good, therefore, to be able to report that the section is well-used for homework purposes. The combined store and office is a little stark but the amount of time which will be spent in it by staff cannot be very great.

It must be remembered that the Branch was built by the former Merioneth County Council, an Authority with a population of less than 40,000 and very limited financial resources. This delightful small library, provided at very low cost, will bear comparison with those to be found in much wealthier Authorities and is a credit to librarian and architect alike.

DGT

Authority	County Council of Gwynedd, Anglesey County Council
Designation	Amlwch Branch Library
Date of opening	March 1973
Population served	3,700
Name of Architect	N Squire Johnson, ARIBA, AMPTI
Name of Librarian	G Thomas, BA, FLA
Special features:	
a) site	Corner site within landscaped area
b) architecture	Local stone and matching brickwork
c) function	Serving locality and some surrounding areas
Mechanical Services:	
a) heating	Electric underfloor
b) ventilation	Natural
c) lighting	Concealed fluorescent
d) acoustics	Carpeted
e) other	—
Areas: in square metres	
a) lending	67
b) reference	20
c) reading	—
d) special activities	—
e) children	25
f) control	25
g) library staff admin.	14
h) exhibitions	8
i) lecture hall	—
j) circulation	—
k) services	1
l) lavatories	—
m) stack	2
Total area:	162
Book volumes:	
a) adult lending	6,250
b) adult reference	250
c) children	2,600
d) stack	—
e) other Welsh	1,900
Total:	11,000
Costs in £ p:	
a) site	—
b) building	15,000
c) furniture & fittings	2,000
Total Cost (ex fees):	£17,000
Cost per square metre:	£105

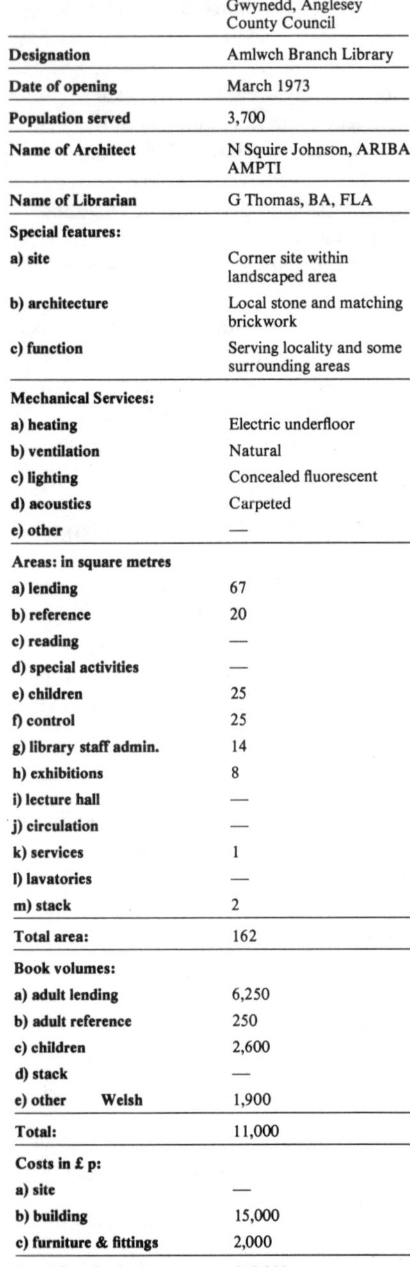

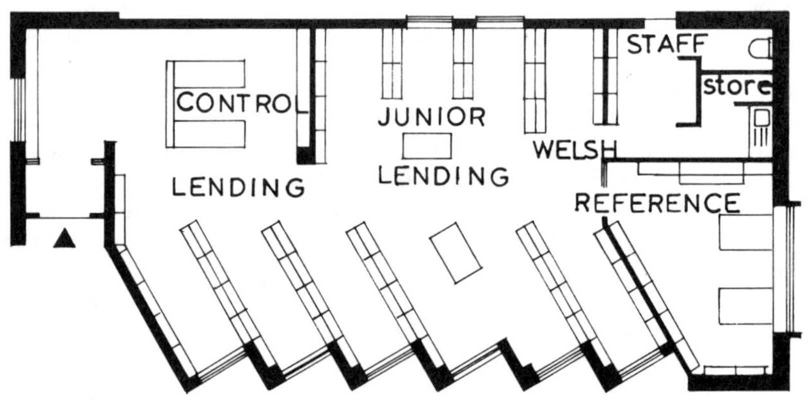

GROUND FLOOR

Authority	County of Gwynedd (formerly Merionethshire)
Designation	Tywyn Branch Library
Date of opening	January 1973
Population served	4,000
Name of Architect	N L Jones, LRIBA, County Architect, D M Jones, Job Architect
Name of Librarian	G Thomas, BA, FLA
Special features:	
a) site	Flat site, adjoining old UDC offices, central to town
b) architecture	Traditional construction; slated, pitched and felted flat roofs
c) function	—
Mechanical Services:	
a) heating	Electric off-peak storage heaters
b) ventilation	Natural
c) lighting	Mainly fluorescent tubes
d) acoustics	Ceiling tiles and carpeted floors
e) other	—
Areas: in square metres	
a) lending	88
b) reference	28
c) reading	—
d) special activities	—
e) children	27
f) control	—
g) library staff admin.	16
h) exhibitions	13
i) lecture hall	—
j) circulation	9
k) services	3
l) lavatories	3
m) stack	—
Total area:	187
Book volumes:	
a) adult lending	8,000
b) adult reference	500
c) children	2,000
d) stack	—
e) other Welsh	1,500
Total:	12,000
Costs in £ p:	
a) site	—
b) building	13,663
c) furniture & fittings	2,000
Total Cost (ex fees):	£15,663
Cost per square metre:	£84

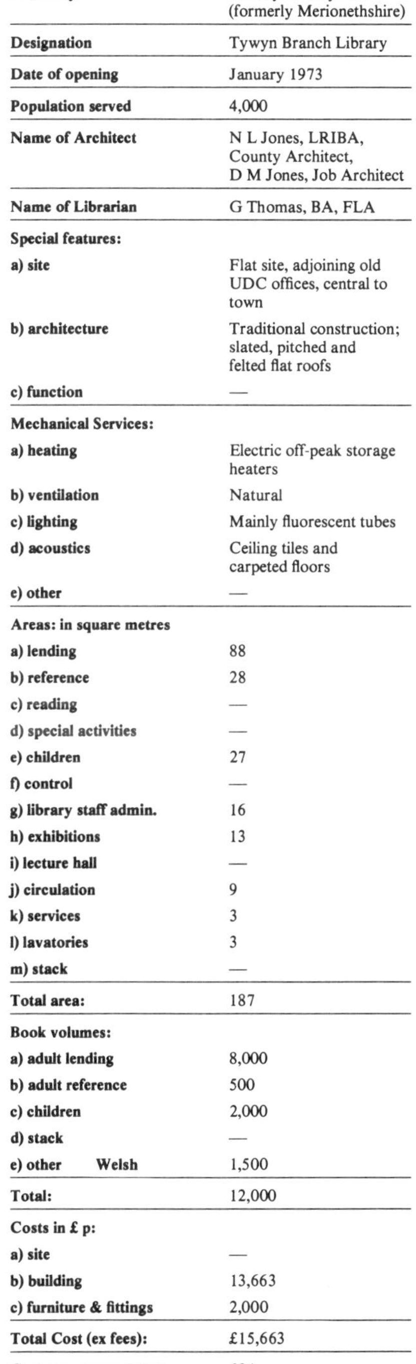

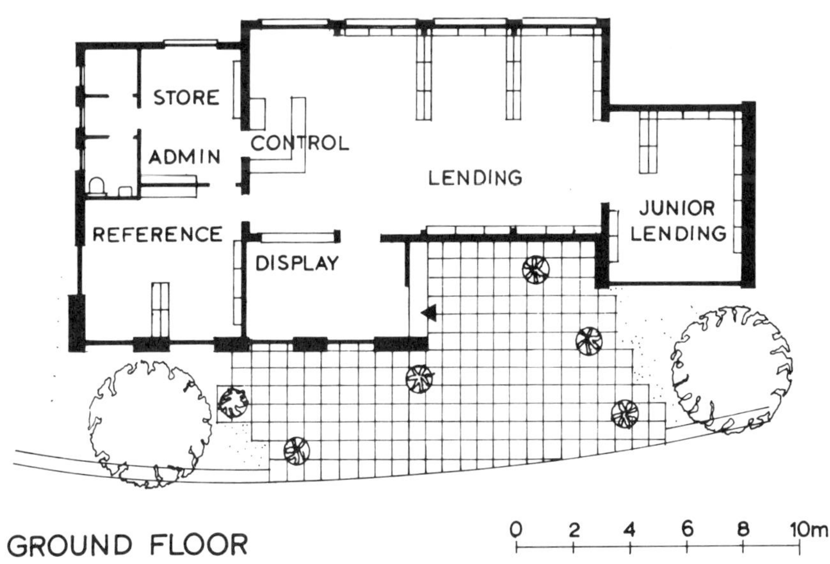

GROUND FLOOR

Northern Ireland, South Eastern Education and Library Board: Ballynahinch and Tullycarnet

Ballynahinch The library forms part of a new building which also houses a Health Centre, built adjacent to and backing on to an old bus station. This has necessarily created an area to the rear of the library which cannot have natural daylighting. The site, however, is a good one, being near the main street and at its junction with a fairly major county road. The building has been well integrated into the local scene and, although only completed in 1974, already looks as if it has always formed part of the environment.

The site slopes slightly (which internally is expressed by a raised floor level together with the provision of a Kinder Pit in the Children's Lending Library); a car park is sited in front and to one side of the building and, in practice, because of its triangular shape, does not detract as much from the building as would a more regimented type.

The building is of one storey, constructed of load-bearing walls finished in limestone chips with timber joists, and woodwool slabs with felt roof finish. It is approached by a paved terrace, with a pram shelter occupying an area adjacent to the entranceways to the Library and Health Centre. The double doors and a threshold almost level with the terrace permit access for wheelchair users. The reception counter is directly opposite the doorway, with the Children's Lending Library on the left, approached by a short flight of steps, the Kinder Pit forming part of this room. This section is gay with animal cut-outs and paintings on pinboard, and the glazing to the front is in different coloured glasses. No natural light other than that from four roof-lights is available due to the proximity of the bus station. It is perhaps surprising that direct access has not been provided from the reception to the Children's Library as, at present, quite a walk is entailed for the Librarian-in-charge wishing to make this journey.

The Lending Library is on the right-hand side of the entranceway, and contains a browsing area adjacent to the windows and a study area which is not visible from the control counter. The workroom is immediately behind the control counter, and provides facilities for servicing the mobile library. The staff room is behind this area, and is reasonably secluded. Toilet and cleaning accommodation is provided. It was intended at one time to have a folding partition erected in line with the end of the cleaners' room to cut off the study area with its separate entranceway, for use by visiting societies, but the old enemy 'cost' again reared its head.

The building is heated from an oil-fired boiler in the adjoining Health Centre, by means of cast iron skirting heating and fan convector heaters. Fluorescent lighting is ample throughout the building and it was noted that this followed a regular pattern with no particular reference to the stacks, thus causing certain areas to be less well-lit than others. No individual lights were noted over counters or tables, only over the Kinder Pit. The acoustics are good because of a floor almost fully covered in carpet tiles and an acoustically panelled ceiling.

This, then, is a small library, immaculately kept and maintained, colourful, airy, and a pleasure to enter and one which obviously serves the community well and appears to be just right for its purpose.

Tullycarnet The library occupies a separate building on an island site between a block of high-rise flats and avenues of terrace houses: this land is administered by the Northern Ireland Housing Executive. The site which is rather derelict at the moment will, it is understood, be landscaped suitably in the near future. The main approach from the major road nearest to the site is through a large car park which serves the various members of the community, including shoppers using an adjoining small shopping centre. Because of the lack of playground facilities in the neighbourhood, the car park tends to be used as a play area, and damage to the library (in the form of broken windows and panels) inevitably occurs. The architects chose an octagonal plan for the building, which is perhaps understandable in view of the island nature of the site. However as this slopes quite steeply it necessitates about thirty per cent of the octagonal drum being 'lost' in the slope, with not entirely happy results.

The building has two floors, the main library floor containing the entrance doorway, approached by stairs from the car park level or by ramped path from the diametrically opposite and higher roadway, particularly useful for wheelchair users. The lower or ground floor level, approached by a clearly visible staircase, contains the Music Library, exhibition room, kitchen and staff room, boilers, heating plant, oil tank storage, toilets and stores. An excellent point noted here is that the exhibition room with adjoining kitchen and toilets and entranceway at lower ground level, can be segregated for use by local societies or groups, even when the remainder of the library is not in use. Toilet accommodation is limited to this floor only and not readily accessible from the main floor.

Daylighting from the windows to the main floor area is very good, assisted by that from a centrally placed grouping of roof-lights over the staircase-well. The artificial lighting is not so happy, consisting as it does of fluorescent lighting running parallel to the main axis centred on the entrance doors, in contrast to the stacks which are mainly arranged radially. The fluorescent lighting is backed up by tungsten downlighters and spotlights over the reception counter, which create the necessary warmth and contrasts. The ground floor area is barely adequately lit, and it was noted generally that individual lighting was not provided at the carrels or reading desks.

Heating is by means of ducted hot air, emerging from floor level grilles below the windows, which is apparently fairly satisfactory in operation, although taking some time to bring the building to a comfortable temperature from a standing start in cold weather. The natural ventilation provided has proved adequate and satisfactory.

Acoustically this library is good despite the octagonal form's known propensity for causing trouble in this direction. Credit here must be given to the waffle slab ceiling and the use of carpet tiles on the floor in almost all areas. Noise from outside traffic did not pose a problem, although the glazing is single.

Authority	Northern Ireland South Eastern Education Library Board
Designation	Ballynahinch Library
Date of opening	March 1974
Population served	8,000
Name of Architect	D M Jones, DA, ARIBA, Down County Architect, G T Irvine, ARIBA, Job Architect
Name of Librarian	D H Welch, FLA
Special features:	
a) site	Slightly sloping in centre of town
b) architecture	Load-bearing walls
c) function	Civic amenity with Health Centre
Mechanical Services:	
a) heating	Skirting radiators and convectors
b) ventilation	Natural
c) lighting	Double fluorescent tubes
d) acoustics	Carpeting; acoustic panelled ceiling
e) other	—
Areas: in square metres	
a) lending	132
b) reference	—
c) reading	—
d) special activities	—
e) children	70
f) control	—
g) library staff admin.	—
h) exhibitions	—
i) lecture hall	—
j) circulation	—
k) services	} 43
l) lavatories	
m) stack	—
Total area:	245
Book volumes:	
a) adult lending	} 7,000
b) adult reference	
c) children	
d) stack	—
e) other	—
Total:	7,000
Costs in £ p:	
a) site	—
b) building	20,000
c) furniture & fittings	in (b)
Total Cost (ex fees):	£20,000
Cost per square metre:	£82

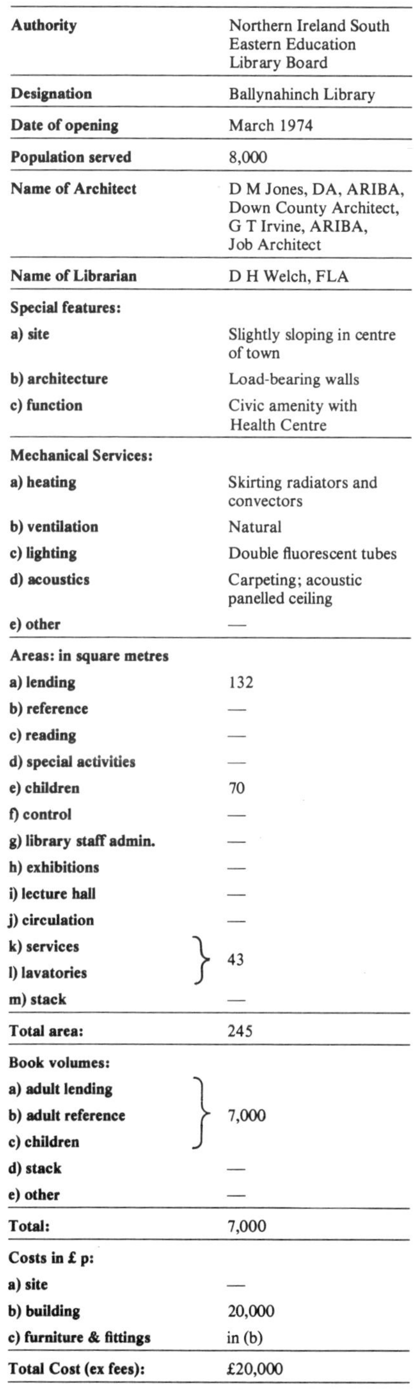

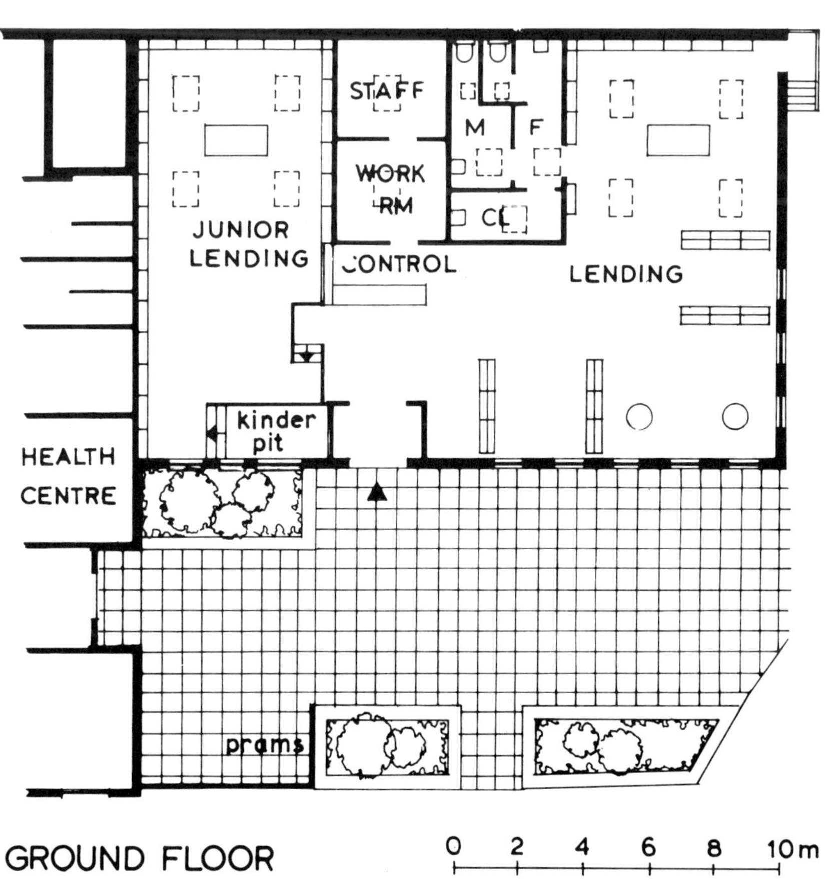

GROUND FLOOR

0 2 4 6 8 10 m

This, then, is a small, bright, airy, inviting library (with,
however, no visible sign outside denoting its function, nor with
any direction signs to it.) It is well thought of by staff and
readers alike, and that surely is 'half the battle'.

WCMcV

Authority	Northern Ireland South Eastern Education Library Board
Designation	Tullycarnet Library
Date of opening	July 1974
Population served	15,000
Name of Architect	D A Jones, DA, ARIBA, Down County Architect, R Press, ARIBA, Job Architect
Name of Librarian	D H Welch, FLA
Special features:	
a) site	Sloping on an island site in housing area
b) architecture	Octagonal form in precast concrete structural building, concrete floor and roof
c) function	Serving residential area of high density
Mechanical Services:	
a) heating	Ducted warm air
b) ventilation	Natural
c) lighting	Fluorescent strip
d) acoustics	Carpet tiles; rubber on stairs; coffered ceiling
e) other	—
Areas: in square metres	
a) lending	326
b) reference	101
c) reading	—
d) special activities	—
e) children	105
f) control	in (a)
g) library staff admin.	66
h) exhibitions	52
i) lecture hall	
j) circulation	—
k) services	—
l) lavatories	10
m) stack	—
Total area:	660
Book volumes:	
a) adult lending	
b) adult reference	13,000
c) children	
d) stack	4,000
e) other	—
Total:	17,000
Costs in £ p:	
a) site	—
b) building	60,000
c) furniture & fittings	in (b)
Total Cost (ex fees):	£60,000
Cost per square metre:	£91

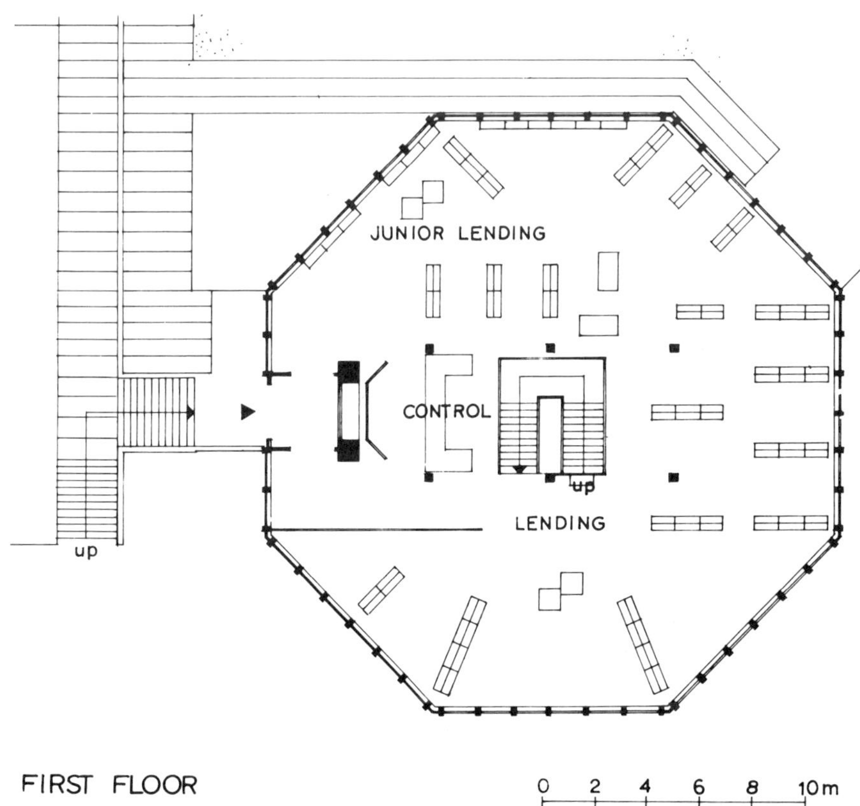

FIRST FLOOR

University of Aston

Aston is the last of the new university libraries to be reviewed–like Brunel, a technological university upgraded the short lived college of advanced technology. The library is designed for 4,200 students at present, but will eventually be enlarged to cater for up to 8,000 students. Aston University is sited near the centre of Birmingham, and from its general appearance 'just growed', with very little evidence of any planning or co-ordination; rather, visual chaos, with the new library a distinctive landmark in the confused central area of the university.

The problem for an architect in this situation is whether to merge into the surrounding mediocrity, or to assert some definite architectural personality. Sir Basil Spence's team have wisely taken the latter decision, and have produced a form that is like the other university libraries in being rectangular, but one that is not cubic. Rather, expressing the structural columns externally, with cantilevered carrels, prominent secondary escape staircase and recessed undercroft ground floor approach, has produced a distinctive, modulated building. It should be noted that the building as shown in the photograph is only the first stage; when completed it will be extended to the rear to double in size.

In studying the plans, it should be remembered that the entrance and main staircase, now at one end of the building, will eventually be in the centre of the completed library. The ground floor houses the entrance foyer, control, exhibition area, cloakroom, main and inter-library loan counters, catalogue and quick reference books, and the enquiry desk. The current periodicals area occupies one corner, with its own enquiry point. The administrative offices and staff areas extend around two sides of the building. The staircase to the upper floors leads off from the main circulation area, and there is a second staircase located in the staff area, which serves as a public staircase only between the reading floors 1 to 3. This provides staircases at both ends of the building, which also serve as emergency exits. UGC decreed only one lift, so it is generally used only for services, staff, and disabled users.

The three upper floors house books, periodicals and readers, stock being divided between floors on a faculty basis: Engineering on Floor 1, Science on Floor 2, and Social Sciences and Humanities on Floor 3. Reading tables and chairs are interspersed with blocks of shelving to produce an alcove effect and, incidentally, reduce traffic and noise. The long external walls are lined with open carrels, and each floor contains six lockable carrels, at the far end away from the main staircase. There is also a typing carrel and seminar room on each of floors 1 and 2, the central area of floor 3 being largely filled with air-conditioning plant. Audio-visual aids, photocopying and micro-reading rooms are located on the second floor. All stock is housed on open access, there being no closed bookstack.

The library was designed for staff service points at each floor, facing the main staircase, but present economic conditions do not permit these to be manned, so an internal telephone system connects these points with the central service and enquiry point on the ground floor.

Structurally, the Librarian's requirement for a clear and flexible space in the stack/reading areas has lead to a somewhat different solution from that of the other university libraries. A planning grid of 11.8 m.×5.4 m. has been used, and the structure placed beyond this. This has meant that on the perimeter of the building the columns protrude externally. These reinforced concrete columns, large in themselves, are clad in brickwork, so forming a very dominant feature of the facade. This use of brickwork, here used only decoratively, is architecturally suspect. The internal columns are divided into two, the space between forming service ducts, and the duct covers being faced with pin-up board.

No concrete is exposed externally, brickwork being also used as a facing material between the columns, with vertical metal slot windows adjacent to each column. Brickwork is also dominant internally, where it is used throughout, except in small offices and toilets, which are plastered or tiled. This red brickwork, with matching pointing, is of a very high standard of workmanship. Internal doors are ash veneered, set in hardwood frames, and are again also of a high standard. Generally the floor finish to library areas is carpet, vinyl in toilets, and ribbed rubber on the staircases. Ceilings are mainly 'Dampa' suspended metal with acoustic backing, and with continuous recessed fluorescent lighting at 1.8 m. centres, running the length of the building, and at right-angles to the bookshelves.

The building is air-conditioned throughout, and this raises certain doubts in 1976. The brief stage was about six years ago, in the days of relatively cheap power, when open and flexible planning was the obvious answer. From a library viewpoint this still holds, but now extremely expensive power and service makes it economically doubtful. In a building such as this, designed for full air-conditioning, it is very difficult to isolate areas, and so at times economise on running costs. This aspect should be seriously considered when now planning for the future. Again, the building is very efficient thermally, with its relatively short external walls in relation to the area of each floor, and small windows. However, this involves deep-planning and the reliance on artificial lighting, and so with the considerable increase in electricity costs has created problems. Note in this connection the treatment of windows at East Anglia University.

Aston University library is another variation on the UGC formula; well-planned, well-built, and again evidence of close collaboration between Librarian and architect, resulting in a building that is well liked by the staff and users.

NR

Authority	University of Aston in Birmingham
Designation	University Library
Date of opening	April 1975
Population served	4,700 students; 1,750 staff
Name of Architect	Sir Basil Spence, Glover and Ferguson
Name of Librarian	E N C Driver, MSc, FLA
Special features:	
a) site	Level site in centre of campus, with provision to double present area of library
b) architecture	Reinforced concrete structure with large spans, designed for maximum flexibility
c) function	—
Mechanical Services:	
a) heating	
b) ventilation	Full air-conditioning
c) lighting	Fluorescent throughout
d) acoustics	'Dampa' panels on ceilings
e) other	—
Areas: in square metres	
a) lending	—
b) reference	—
c) reading	—
d) special activities	—
e) children	—
f) control	—
g) library staff admin.	—
h) exhibitions	—
i) lecture hall	—
j) circulation	—
k) services	—
l) lavatories	—
m) stack	—
Total area:	6,800
Book volumes:	
a) adult lending	—
b) adult reference	—
c) children	—
d) stack	—
e) other	—
Total:	156,000, including bound periodicals
Costs in £ p:	
a) site	Not applicable
b) building	815,000
c) furniture & fittings	179,000
Total Cost (ex fees):	£994,000
Cost per square metre:	£146

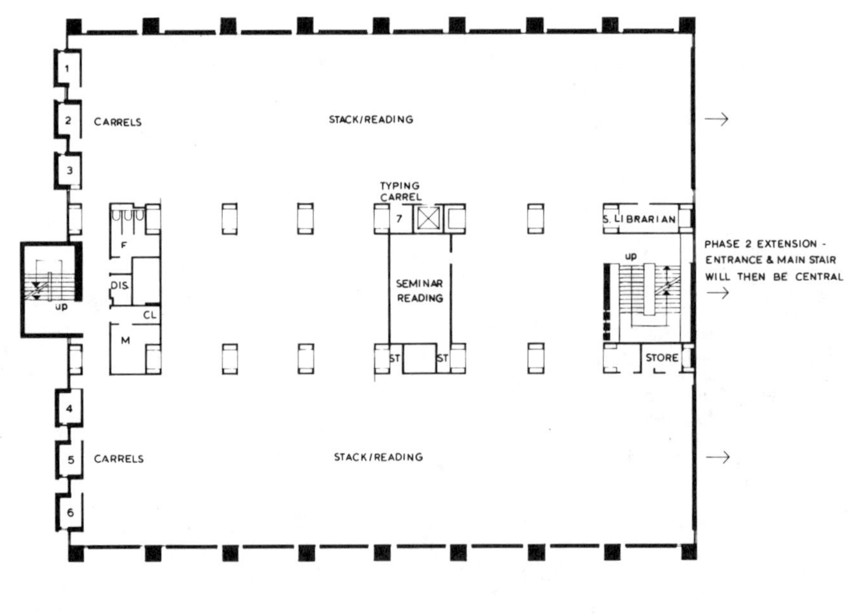

TYPICAL UPPER FLOOR

Brunel University

Five of the 1960s generation of new university libraries are reviewed here, all versions of a UGC formula which strictly controls cost and therefore area. Certain figures recur: 5,000 students, 1,000–1,200 seats, four-storey building. Of the five reviewed, Brunel and Nottingham were built in one phase, although both are capable of extension; East Anglia was built in two phases; Aston and Leicester will be.

Seen within a short period of time the pattern is so similar: the UGC formula, plus the lessons of American Universities seen through the gospel of Keyes Metcalf. The result is a rectangular cube, with the upper two floors comprising open bookstack and reading areas, and divided by subject or faculty grouping; short loans, reference and administration on the entrance floor. East Anglia is the exception, being six-storeys high, and entered from high-level walkways and, resulting from its two phases, the luxury of two lifts! One factor does seem to differentiate the libraries, especially when it comes to size and bookstock–the university's origins. Older established civic universities like Nottingham and Leicester, or the newly established and designated East Anglia, seem to fare better than those upgraded from the colleges of advanced technology, as are Aston and Brunel. What hope for mere polytechnics?

These introductory observations are a lead-in to Brunel's new library. Brunel University was granted its charter in 1966, having already within ten years been upgraded from technical college to college of advanced technology. Its proposed library was a victim of the Government's moratorium on university buildings in 1968, and was finally started in 1971, and completed in May, 1973. It was designed for the ultimate student number of 5,000, to be reached in the 1980s, accommodating more than 1,000 readers and 300,000 books.

The library is located in the centre of the university campus, and forms one of the group of buildings whose facilities serve the whole complex: central lecture theatres, refectories, computer building, shops and the administration building. All of these are placed on an east-to-west pedestrian way and the main library entrance abuts on to it. The library is capable of future extension to the rear at the service end.

The building is four-storeys high, and surmounted by a couple of huge funnels, housing the ventilation plant. Entrance is at first-floor level, up a wide flight of stairs from the pedestrian way but disabled users are issued with a key to the staff entrance at the rear. The entrance floor accommodates control desk, catalogues, short loan collection, exhibition space and the library administration. Toilets and cloakrooms are situated alongside the main entrance, the latter fitted with lockers operated electrically from the control desk. The upper two floors house Science and Technology on one floor and the Social Sciences on the other. All material related to these subjects is grouped on the appropriate floor; current periodicals in the centre, beyond rows of open access bookshelves are interspersed with groups for two, four and six readers. Lockable study carrels line one end of each floor and office accommodation is on the south-west corner of each floor, next to the lift, although a seminar room is substituted on the top floor. The lower ground floor is used for other teaching purposes and as an examination hall, until required by the library. One of the library's special features, on the second floor, is a section where students can select from a range of audio-visual materials, shelved like books and used and viewed on a range of equipment.

The building is almost square, being 6 bays by 5 bays, using a structural grid of 6.85 metres. The structure is of *in situ* reinforced concrete, with a cantilever on the perimeters while the external down-stand perimeter beams are brushed to show the aggregate. The brick panels are Staffordshire blue brindled bricks and these are generally used throughout the teaching blocks in the university. Windows are fixed in painted steel frames, with narrow vertical slits between the brick panels and a continuous clerestory forming a very distinctive feature of the façade. The entrance floor is recessed back to the line of columns and is completely glazed with fixed vertical window panels, the overhang above being used to avoid excessive glare.

Internally the space is subdivided by fairfaced concrete enclosures, containing the main stair and two escape stairs and two large ventilation ducts. However, the most prominent internal feature is a lightwell, running from above the control desk through the two reading floors to the roof. On the reading floors it is glazed, for fire and noise reasons, but it is successful in introducing a different quality of light into the heart of the building. The library partitions are fairfaced precast Lignacite block, with *in situ* concrete; all interior surfaces are thus formed from the material from which they are built, except the floor and ceiling. The interior is carpeted throughout in dark brown. The ceiling is rilled mineral insulation board in yellow and the chairs, tables and magazine racks were specially designed for the job by John Marshall of Marico Ltd.

The building is artificially ventilated, the floor-to-ceiling height being 3.00 m. with a 1.00 m. zone above the ceiling for trunking. This raises the most contentious issue concerning this library. Forced air-ventilation is definitely not air-conditioning, but of course is considerably cheaper to install and run. In this particular library it is argued that due to the 'sandwich' nature of the tuition courses, the summer term is least busy, unlike most universities, and there are very few people using the library during the summer holiday. This is a valid argument at present, but would not hold if the pattern of education changed; the conditions could become very uncomfortable if the library were crowded during a hot spell of weather. It raises the question too, whether, if the floor-to-ceiling height had been reduced and the 1.00 m. ceiling zone used more effectively as part of the room volume, the saving in cubic cost in the building would have provided the funds for full air-conditioning. In this respect it is worth studying the ceiling and air-conditioning solution at Nottingham University.

The general impression of the building is of a well-considered practical solution, centrally placed on the campus and its appearance reads what is expected of a university library. The rooftop 'funnels' are a rather heavy-handed tribute to Isambard Brunel, almost giving the feeling that a floor has been omitted that would have surrounded them. An opportunity seems to have been lost in lining the entrance façade with cloakrooms and toilets, for an open view into the library would have been much more welcoming. Small things irritate, like the shrinkage of heavily sectioned wood door frames not too securely fitted into *in situ* concrete walls, also yellow is not the most subtle colour for a ceiling. One is reminded of the superficial similarities between Brunel and Nottingham, but in cost per square metre Brunel is marginally more expensive. Yet for this reviewer Nottingham sets the standard for this generation of libraries, against which others should be judged.

NR

Authority	Brunel University
Designation	University Library
Date of opening	September 1973
Population served	Rising to 5,000 students
Name of Architect	Richard Sheppard, Robson, and Partners
Name of Librarian	Mr C E N Childs, BA(Oxon)
Special features:	
a) site	Central position in new university
b) architecture	4 storey rectangular brick clad concrete structure
c) function	University Library
Mechanical Services:	
a) heating	Plenum system
b) ventilation	Artificial ventilation
c) lighting	Fluorescent generally
d) acoustics	Mineral insulation board ceiling
e) other	Carpet throughout
Areas: in square metres	
a) lending	—
b) reference	—
c) reading	—
d) special activities	—
e) children	—
f) control	—
g) library staff admin.	—
h) exhibitions	—
i) lecture hall	—
j) circulation	—
k) services	—
l) lavatories	—
m) stack	—
Total area:	6,615
Book volumes:	
a) adult lending	—
b) adult reference	—
c) children	—
d) stack	—
e) other	—
Total:	max 300,000 volumes
Costs in £ p:	
a) site	—
b) building	532,682
c) furniture & fittings	150,000
Total Cost (ex fees):	£682,682
Cost per square metre:	£103

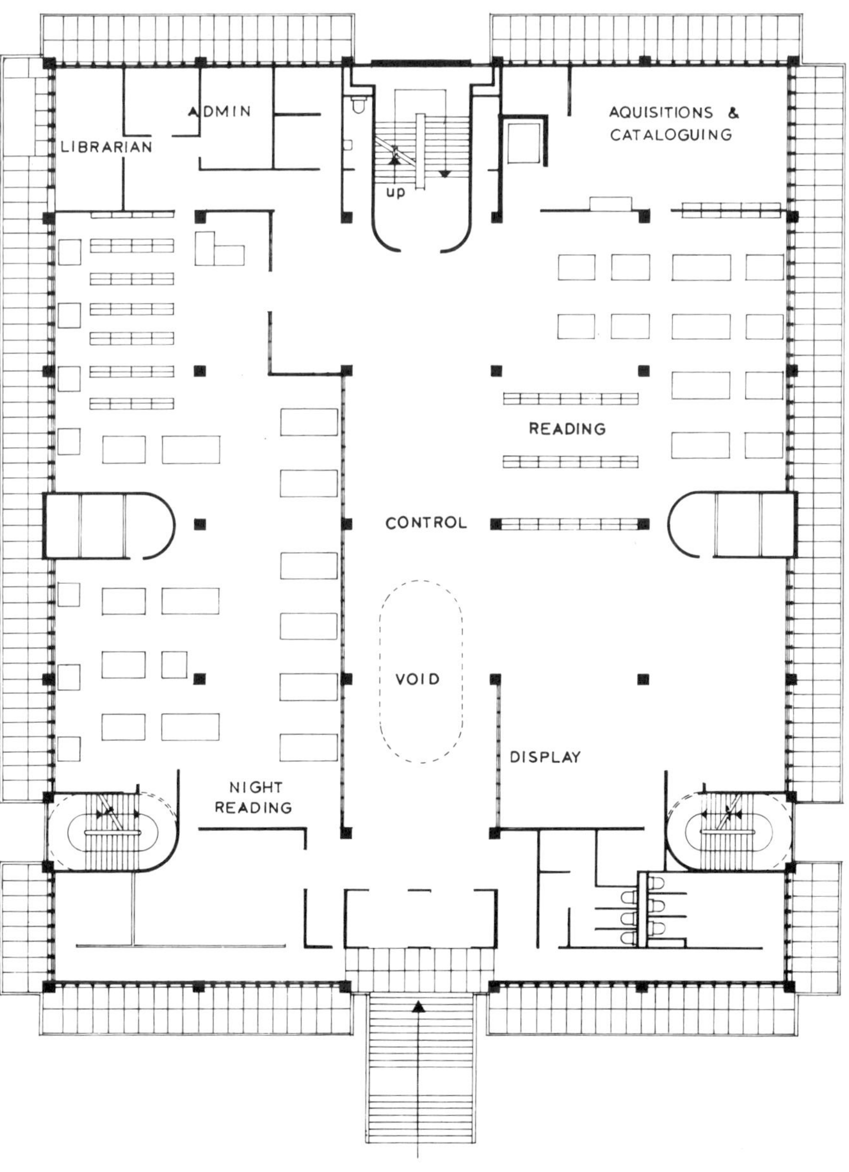

FIRST FLOOR

0 2 4 6 8 10m

University of Dublin

The University library was opened in 1973 and completed a significant phase in the relocation of the University from the centre of Dublin to a large new campus in the suburbs. This campus now accommodates some 10,000 students and the library, centrally situated, is a focal point of the complex. The present library is the first phase of a projected two-phase building, because financial exigencies required the postponement of the construction of the six-storey book stack. Consequently, the present use reflects a temporary organisation of spaces which will only be fully intelligible when the library is completed.

The library is carefully related to other buildings on the campus. It has direct access through an enclosed link from the Arts–Commerce Faculties building, and access by a covered way, which constitutes the main pedestrian spine in the campus, leading to the main entrance hall.

The campus is notable for its clear organisation and generous landscaping. The location of the building is most carefully considered in relation to the large ornamental lake. It makes a formal contribution to the setting which is appropriate to its use and to its symbolic significance in a university.

The building has a distinctive and assertive appearance. Nevertheless, its relationship in terms of circulation, scale, form and materials, is sensitively related to the already built Arts–Commerce block and the Administration building. This was achieved through fruitful liaison at the design stage with the architects responsible for the overall development and layout of the campus.

The key to such a successful relationship would seem to lie in the organisation of movement on the campus. Open arcades on the ground floor allow the main pedestrian spine to pursue its course through the building, and help reinforce the importance and connecting nature of the route. This link-feature is further emphasised by the fact that the direct enclosed walk from the Arts–Commerce block penetrates at first-floor level, thus allowing the library to operate as a natural extension and not just as a building alongside. In practice, the great majority of library users enter from this connection. The organisation of the building is simple, direct, and clear—at least in its design intentions.

The ground floor was intended to be primarily an exhibition and conference area, conceived on a grand scale, leading to a first-floor control which gave access to the bibliographical area on that floor, and a very large reading area on the upper floor. These activities had direct connection with the six-storey book stack.

Inevitably, with the delay to the building of the book stack, the plan had to be reorganised. It is a tribute to the flexibility of the building that this reorganisation was achieved initially without losing the powerful quality of space which has been created in the building.

The fortunes of the library since then have changed, and in what must be typical of many library buildings, the demands on space and limits on budget have led to major changes in the organisation and use of the building.

The second phase plan has faded, and is no longer expected to be undertaken during the next decade. In effect this means that temporary uses must be regarded as permanent, and the problems of using the library spaces in the most efficient way have had to be tackled, with considerable impact on the building form.

The library is heavily over-used. In an effort to respond to demand for reading space, every available corner has been furnished with tables, minimally spaced to accommodate a maximum of students. Any building would suffer from such overcrowding, and this library is no exception.

The ground floor, designed for exhibition and conference use, has now been incorporated as part of the library. Due to difficulties in gaining access through the first-floor control, it has been set up as a separate library for multiple copies with an unsupervised reading area but the fine Ballybrew limestone is hardly an appropriate surface for this use.

The spacious entrance areas have been sacrificed to an untidy clutter of coat-racks. The effect is to destroy, very nearly, the formal qualities of the entrance, though the reasons are all too understandable.

The first floor is filled with the bibliographical area and temporary bookstacks. The control desk was found to be too cramped in its original location and has been relocated to give greater flexibility for the staff.

In the vast reading area on the second floor, an attempt has been made to create relatively small areas, by curtaining and periodicals stacks. However, the effect of thousands of tightly packed reading spaces is demoralising, and has been described in a moment of anger as an 'educational pig-trough'. Further efforts at humanising the space with furniture, screening and planting could be effective without losing the splendid openness at ceiling-level.

The above describes briefly the present situation. Consequent upon the decision to defer the second phase, it is intended to encroach upon the open areas under the building to provide at least some extra space for the immediate future. Such a decision was clearly not anticipated in the initial design; it is merciful at least that the original architects have been reappointed to undertake the job. This conversion will doubtless cause innumerable headaches, practical as well as aesthetic. It can be seen that over a three-year period, the fortunes of the library have undergone remarkable shifts. It is to the credit of the architects that so much has happened without destroying the original concept altogether; but in this there must be a lesson for the future. The first phase of a building conceived on a grand scale has now become the main library facility for the foreseeable future. The central question seems to be: could this have been anticipated in any way when the brief was being drawn up?

Ballybrew limestone is used in a diamond-sawn finish on the walls of the entrance hall and conference/exhibition rooms and as a paving in the entrance hall. Split-faced limestone is used externally on the two lower floors. The reading room is glazed on all four sides and solar shading is provided on the south, west and east elevations by precast concrete louvres. The plant space over the second floor is clad in precast concrete blocks. Internally, walls are finished with spray-painted chipboard panels on breeze block walls, with the panels removable, providing access to service ducts and facilitating reuse at Phase II. Ribbed rubber is used on staircases and concourse areas, and carpet tiles in reading room areas. Handrails and entrance furniture are finished in stainless steel.

All concrete is exposed: columns are precast, floors *in situ* coffers. Light fittings are incorporated in the coffers and air diffusers in the columns.

The building will eventually be fully air-conditioned and an early decision was made to isolate all the horizontal distribution in one space above the second floor so that future additions and adjustment to services can be made with a minimum disturbance to Phase I. Vertical distribution is downwards at each structural column which incorporates three ducts, one service each floor.

PMcG

Authority	University College, Dublin
Designation	The University Library
Date of opening	January 1973
Population served	Up to 10,000 students and staff
Name of Architect	Sir Basil Spence, Glover and Ferguson, J Hardie Glover, OBE, ARSA, FRIBA, FRIAS and Andrew Merrylees, DipTP, ARIBA, ARIAS
Name of Librarian	Miss E Power, MA, FLA succeeded by H Heaney
Special features:	
a) site	New University campus
b) architecture	Precast columns with ducts, *in situ* core coffer floor, solar shading by precast concrete louvres
c) function	Central library for whole University
Mechanical Services:	
a) heating	Fully air-conditioned system
b) ventilation	
c) lighting	Fluorescent. Provision for 500–600 lux on horizontal plane
d) acoustics	Carpet tiles in reading areas
e) other	Service lift
Areas: in square metres	
a) lending	—
b) reference	—
c) reading	—
d) special activities	—
e) children	—
f) control	—
g) library staff admin.	—
h) exhibitions	—
i) lecture hall	—
j) circulation	—
k) services	—
l) lavatories	—
m) stack	—
Total area:	11,234
Book volumes:	
a) adult lending	—
b) adult reference	—
c) children	—
d) stack	—
e) other	—
Total:	700,000 (completed)
Costs in £ p:	
a) site	14,005
b) building	765,077
c) furniture & fittings	not available
Total Cost (ex fees):	£779,082
Cost per square metre:	£69

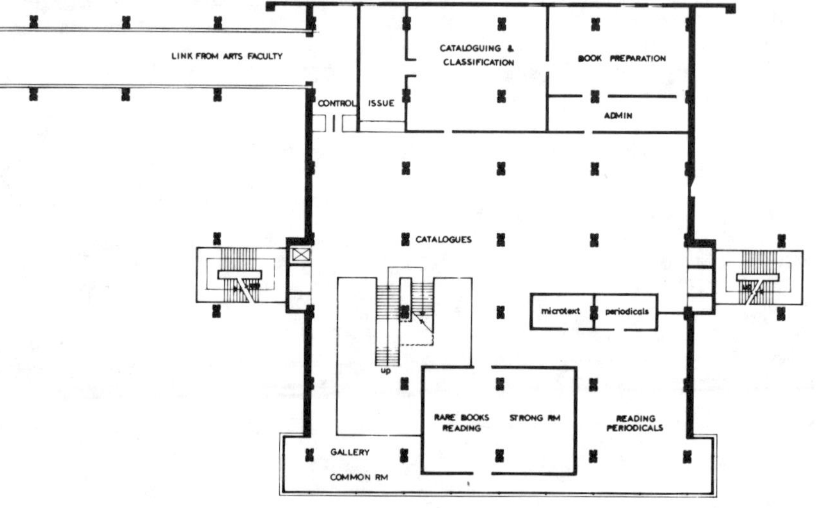

University of East Anglia

East Anglia was one of the seven new universities created in the early 1960s. Denys Lasdun was appointed consultant architect in 1962, and the original development envisaged an ultimate student population of 6,000. Other qualities envisaged were 'a sense of place'; a university that is compact and 'urban', and a place where activities merge and the individual can sense his identity with the whole.

The site of the University is about two miles to the west of the centre of Norwich; a south-facing slope rising 70 feet from the River Yare and with extensive views to the open country. The architect planned pedestrian and vehicle segregation, utilising the slope of the land and using a series of elevated walkways to bring all buildings within five minutes walking disance of the centre. The academic structure comprises a number of schools of study, numbering 300–600 students, forming a continuous building or 'teaching wall' that runs across the the north part of the site. It 'protects' two rows of linked 'pyramids' of student residences, one wrapping around two sides of the library and the other facing it. The library is considered the heart of the University and, together with a lecture theatre complex, is sited with the main group of social facilities: dining and common rooms, students' union, shops and an adjacent Music Centre.

The library was planned in two stages, the first completed in 1968 and the second one in September, 1974. Denys Lasdun designed the complete building, but after relinquishing his position as architectural consultant to the University in 1968 at the completion of stage 1, was succeeded by Bernard Fielden, who supervised the completion of the second stage. The completed library is designed to serve about 5,000 students and 600 staff and is capable of accommodating about 435,000 volumes and 1,334 seats. Recent UGC recommendations suggest a reduction in standards, implying that the present University library buildings will have to accommodate more students and bookstock. Asked about a future large increase in student numbers, the Librarian stated that there was site available to double the size of the building. However, the very fixed form of the building, unlike the 'demountable' precast façade at Nottingham, suggests that this expansion would be very difficult to achieve.

Seen from the 'teaching wall' and the student residences, the six-storey library stands out and above them, but when in the 'main square' of the social areas, a somewhat tortuous route leads to the entrance of the library, situated in the extreme north-east corner of the building. The entrance from the elevated walkway is at the third-floor level above the surrounding ground level. This approach at third-floor level has defined the library as a six-storey sandwich, with the administration and servicing occupying the two central floors and separating Arts and Humanities subjects on the upper two floors from Science subjects on the lower two.

The entrance floor comprises an entrance 'concourse', housing space for casual reading and exhibitions and off which there is a restricted loan collection, audio-visual area, and main stairs and lifts to the other floors. The level above, i.e. the fourth floor, comprises the catalogue, bibliographical and reference areas, cataloguing and processing, and the library and administrative staff offices. Both these floors are expressed on the façade with a different pattern of elevational treatment, in itself reasonable, but somewhat unconvincing, as it appears to produce a series of unusable and inaccessible balconies. Above and below these middle administrative levels are two floors, each devoted to bookstack and study areas.

The bookstack and study floors comprise a rectangle 8×4 modules, each module being based on the structural grid unit of 6.85 m. square (recognised better as that most favoured library grid of 22 ft 6 in.). Just three of the 32 modules on each floor comprise the service core, including open staircase, two enclosed escape stairs, two lifts side by side (so useful, and perhaps one of the benefits of two-stage construction), and toilets. Construction allows the bookstacks to be placed anywhere on these floors but they are largely concentrated in the centre of the floors, with seating near the windows. Study carrels are mainly concentrated on the east and west ends of each floor, with the external concrete structural bays forming a slightly more private study space than the large study tables.

The structure consists of reinforced concrete floor slabs, 300 mm thick, supported on a 6.85 m. grid of 500 mm columns. On the external walls, columns give way to deep precast concrete structural 'fins' at 3.43 m. centres, which define the carrel and study ares externally. These 'fins' support horizontal precast spandrel and window transom panels. All floor slabs are designed for loading of 200 lb/ft^2 or 10 kN/m^2.

The decision was made to allow maximum daylight penetration through large windows on all façades, and the use of largely natural ventilation, using pivoted windows, and horizontal louvres in the high-level transom panels.

Natural ventilation is backed up with mechanical plenum ventilation throughout the central part of the building, using a system of ceiling ducts and air diffusers and extractors, to achieve a controlled humidity of 55%. These two lighting and ventilation decisions must now be producing dividends in reducing the effect of the phenomenal increases in heating and lighting cost—although this could not have been anticipated at briefing stage. The design of the windows, using the deep structural fins, and a recessed transom window (see photograph), has reduced glare and allowed deeper penetration of natural light. In positions more exposed to direct sunlight, vertical louvres are used in the reading areas and curtain on the administrative floors. From experience gained in stage 1 of construction it was decided in stage 2 to omit opening windows and to use only the louvres in the transom panels. Lighting in the reading and stack areas comprise rows of fluorescent semi-recessed fittings at 4 ft 6 in. or 1.35 m. centres running parallel with the bookstacks. As the bookstacks are likely to be fixed at this close spacing it seems a sensible decision to position light fittings parallel to the stacks. More economy in operating costs is achieved by having each row of stack lighting individually controlled from a ceiling pull-switch with a central over-rider. A varying intensity of lighting can be achieved in the reading areas through the use of controlled switches. The lighting system is designed to produce a maximum intensity of 30 lumens at table top level. Heating comes from convection type heaters around the perimeter of the building, with zoned temperature control, the north-east faced being zoned to a higher temperature.

The central stack areas have suspended ceilings at 8 ft 2 in. or 2.5 m. height, using acoustic felt-backed aluminium tiles; reading and office areas have plastic foam ceiling tiles at a ceiling height of 9 ft 2 in. or 2.8 m. height. Walls internally are either fair-faced concrete or emulsion painted plaster on brickwork. The public and staff areas are all carpeted. Doors are veneered with Columbian pine and the reading tables are beech with linoleum tops. Generally these finishes give a warm and relaxed atmosphere and rely on colour accent coming from red chairs, books and people.

The library appears to be appreciated and well-used by both readers and staff, who find it a quiet and restful place. The solid construction and absorbent finishes have made for quiet conditions and yet the semi-open staircase and lifts allow for easy vertical access, without noticeable floor-to-floor noise penetration.

The compact arrangement of catalogue, offices and reference area, around the vertical core, and on one of the central floors, works well for library staff, book service and readers. In theory it would seem that users of the Science library would have to go up from the entrance level to the main catalogue and advice area before going down to their reading area; but this is covered by putting advice and a partial catalogue in that area. The problems of enclosed escape stairs, commented upon at Nottingham University Library, are solved here with two enclosed staircases leading direct to the open-air at ground floor level. On the upper levels there are magnificent views out over the student 'pyramids' to the open country but at the lower levels one is aware, despite some pleasant mature trees, of looking out onto what Mr Lasdun rather tastefully describes as 'undercrofts', which in more common parlance would be termed service yards and dustbin stores!

The library is a comfortable and pleasant environment in which to study and work; it is easily serviced and can be rated as one of the more successful buildings in a University where the vision of the original conception has not always been translated into good practical architecture.

NR

Authority	University of East Anglia
Designation	University Library
Date of opening	Stage 1: September 1968; Stage 2: September 1974
Population served	4,780 students + 600 staff
Name of Architect	Stage 1: Denys Lasdun & Partners Stage 2: Fielden and Mawson
Name of Librarian	Mr W L Guttsman, MSc(Econ)
Special features:	
a) site	Central; but library approached from elevated walkways
b) architecture	6-storey exposed precast concrete structure
c) function	Central library for university
Mechanical Services:	
a) heating	Mechanical plenum ventilation in central areas, and perimeter
b) ventilation	convector heating
c) lighting	Fluorescent semi-recessed fittings generally
d) acoustics	Absorbent lined metal ceiling tiles
e) other	Carpeted floors generally
Areas: in square metres	
a) lending	—
b) reference	—
c) reading	—
d) special activities	—
e) children	—
f) control	—
g) library staff admin.	—
h) exhibitions	—
i) lecture hall	—
j) circulation	—
k) services	—
l) lavatories	—
m) stack	—
Total area:	10,326
Book volumes:	
a) adult lending	—
b) adult reference	—
c) children	—
d) stack	—
e) other	—
Total:	435,000

Costs in £ p:	Stage 1	Stage 2
a) site	—	—
b) building	366,741	331,983
c) furniture & fittings	122,096	87,500
Total Cost (ex fees):	£488,837	£419,483
Cost per square metre:	£75	£104

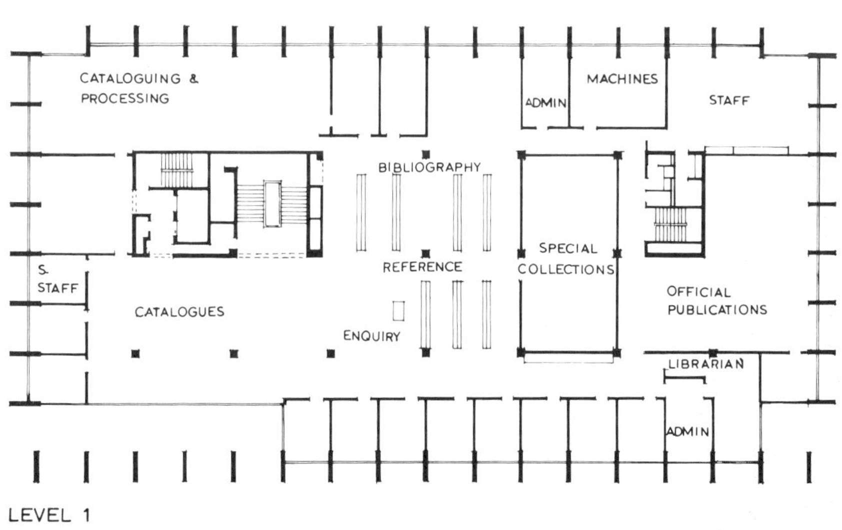

LEVEL 1

0 2 4 6 8 10m

University of Leicester

From the outside this is a most attractive building, square, solid, shining and balanced. Inside it shows every sign of having been very well thought out with accord between architect and librarian; it contains some highly original and effective construction ideas and in all, ought to have been a great success had it not been spoiled by arbitrary action arising from last minute economies. More of those later.

The five floors (including the lower ground floor) are all 40 m. square arranged in a traditional 'functional' way but with the possibility that other systems of library organisation can be accommodated in the future. The library services are planned on a linear basis alongside a central core so that the building can be extended by up to two further stages at the rear. The first of the economies cut off one of the five bays of its length, but as it had been decided that the book stock of 420,000 still had to be accommodated, the reader seating had to be reduced from 1200 to 800. This means that the stacks protrude into areas which were planned as reader seating and there is unfortunately, especially in the upper floors, a feeling of overcrowding. How infuriating this must be to the librarian who had worked it out so efficiently.

The structure consists of hollow *in situ* concrete columns and beams with precast double T floor units. The air-conditioning ducts are in fact the beams themselves and the hollow structural members. The architects claim that this has resulted in cost, as well as the obvious space, savings. The beams and walls however give an overwhelming feeling of grey shuttered concrete and together with the rather too 'functional' electric fittings, give an unfortunate impression of 'cheap and nasty'.

The most striking feature is undoubtedly the shiny glass covering which is, in fact, a true skin standing free of the building within, which is a concrete structure with little more than slit windows. The advantage of this is that there is virtually a layer of air-insulation immediately inside the glass skin. Although the windows are narrow they do give to those using the perimeter reading seats a small opportunity to see out.

On its own this is a very attractive building indeed but it stands almost touching a protected Victorian building and close to the Engineering and Attenborough buildings, themselves famous as examples of 'imaginative architecture'. From a distance the effect is odd although the library, especially when lit at night, can hold its own.

The side of the library near to the Victorian building has a sloping glass roof over the narrow gap here tall climbing plants are being encouraged to grow. The reason for this is obscure because they cannot be seen except by diligent explorers and will certainly do little for the readers. In fact the attraction of the building is confined to its two open sides; the rear has metal sheeting to allow for future expansion and this is hardly an attractive addition. The access to the rear is oddly arranged but this was probably another by-product of the economy measures.

The entrance is very inviting with its centralising canopy, revolving doors, dirt collecting mats and a case deposit area (not in use at the moment) before the positively manned controls. Beyond this, one comes to a 15 m. long issue desk, the great length being planned to cater for the two future lateral expansion stages. All ground-floor reader/staff service points are behind the issue desk with the exception of a square reference desk on the other side of the entrance. The rest of the ground floor is taken up with general reference and bibliography stacking, catalogues and (temporarily one imagines) an office area.

The upper floors contain runs of rather tight (1300 mm. centres) stacks with single perimeter reader seats, the rest of the reader seating being contained along the line of the core. There are 13 carrels—by no means enough and very claustrophobic: the only piece of the original planning which can be seriously condemned.

The lower ground floor contains the periodical stacks and reading room together with the technical service areas. A feature has been made of the proximity of the periodicals to the staff who control them, but it is hard to see why.

On all except the ground floor there are informal reading areas, glass enclosed, within the cores. Exhibition areas on the staircase landings add to the interest and everywhere one has the feeling that the library is in busy and happy use.

The most amusing features are the three lakes on the roof. Although they cannot be seen from ground level, people interested in the building will certainly come up to see them. Apparently the purposes are to give some thermal insulation, to provide reservoirs for the air-conditioning system and, perhaps incidentally, to provide a roof which will not leak because it never dries out. Air-conditioning units stand between the lakes—nothing if not original, and, from comments received so far, effective in operation.

It is a pity therefore that the overall effect of the library is ruined by the economies which have restricted the length of the library and have forced the Librarian to use furniture belonging to the numerous small libraries which this library has replaced. Chairs, tables, even the ground-floor stacks, for example, are not only of different materials, heights and colours but they detract from the functional efficiency. This, together with the mass of grey concrete everywhere and the rather dreary colour scheme, does ruin the inside appearance.

Although the excellent ideas of both Librarian and Architect have been somewhat spoiled by economies this is a library which any University Librarian who is going to build must visit. What a pleasure it would have been to visit it if it had been completed as was originally planned.

GT

Authority	University of Leicester
Designation	University Library
Date of opening	September 1975 (work completed December 1974)
Population served	Staff 550, students 4,000
Name of Architect	Castle, Park, Dean, Hook
Name of Librarian	D G F Walker, MA, LLB
Special features:	
a) site	Fill-in space between very different buildings of campus
b) architecture	Concrete faced with solar heat reflecting glass: lakes on roof
c) function	1st stage of University library
Mechanical Services:	
a) heating	Air-conditioning; ducts form support beams for structure
b) ventilation	
c) lighting	Fluorescent — very little natural light
d) acoustics	Felt floor tiles
e) other	Roof lakes also act as thermal stabilizers
Areas: in square metres	
a) lending	
b) reference	2,012
c) reading	
d) special activities	248
e) children	—
f) control	350
g) library staff admin.	1,148
h) exhibitions	5
i) lecture hall	—
j) circulation	—
k) services	—
l) lavatories	59
m) stack	3,620
Total area:	7,442
Book volumes:	
a) adult lending	570,000
b) adult reference	—
c) children	—
d) stack	—
e) other	—
Total:	570,000
Costs in £ p:	
a) site (external works)	72,000
b) building	852,900
c) furniture & fittings	
Total Cost (ex fees):	£924,900
Cost per square metre:	£116 (ex site)

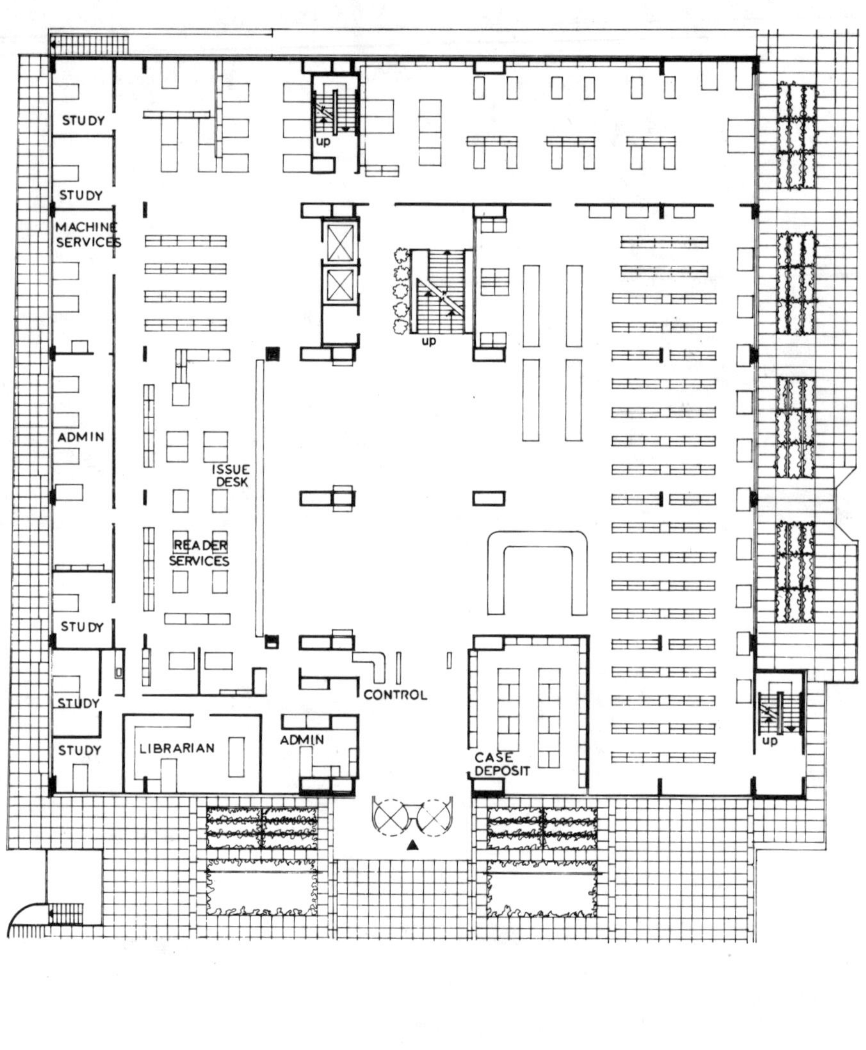

GROUND FLOOR

0   2   4   6   8   10m

University of Nottingham

The new library serves staff, research students and undergraduates in the Faculties of Arts and Social Sciences and accommodates the Sub-Department of Manuscripts, and the Library Photographic Unit. There are separate libraries elsewhere for the Faculties of Pure and Applied Science, Law, Music, and Medicine. The University Librarian is situated at the new library, which therefore acts as the 'central library' of the system. It was designed for a student population of 5,000, providing 1,200 seats, and a book capacity of 542,000 volumes.

The site was designated by the University in 1969, and it lies between the Faculty of Social Sciences and the School of Education and close to the Faculty of Art; it is also on the route between the halls of residence and the centre of the University. The site is almost at the highest point of the campus and is surrounded by mature trees, but with view southwards. The building is located to the south of the site and is capable of lateral expansion in two stages to the north, without disturbing the fine pattern of trees. The slope of the site from north to south-west has enabled a neat separation of users' entrance on the east side at level two, and the service and staff entrance on the west side of level one.

The Librarian and Architect visited university and college libraries in the United States, and this convinced them that the library must be deep-planned and air-conditioned, which allowed the degree of flexibility needed; conversely flexibility in this context implies deep planning. The logical outcome of this is a building which is a simple rectangular cube, four storeys high, and with a low wall-to-floor ratio concentrates money internally, rather than on the exterior.

The briefing period was obviously a very productive one, and from it came an admirable list of aims, or what are termed 'Qualities' against which the final building can be matched.

Agreement with the University was reached on ten desired qualities the library should possess. They were aimed to produce a building that was flexible, compact, extendible, varied, organised, accessible, comfortable, constant in environment, indicative of its function and secure. The brief also stated 'no undue windows' in reading areas, but asked for continuous glazing on the entrance level, so as to take account of the beautiful setting and to advertise the library within. The library was also to be open-planned as far as possible and to be a 'welcoming' and 'friendly' building.

Approaching the main entrance of the library the building has something of the simplicity and repose associated with 'classical' buildings. The vocabulary is a simple one of two upper storeys of reading and book areas, clad in neatly detailed precast concrete panels, with dark vertical slit windows; this above a ground or entrance floor 'piano nobile', completely glazed and recessed back 2.5 m. from the walls above, with a balcony terrace running around the building. On the southern side there is a lower level, glazed, but partly hidden by the landscaped grass mound. One curious external feature is the glazed cut-off on each corner of the upper levels which weakens the corner visually, but internally provides an informal corner where users can relax and fully appreciate the views around.

Entering on the west side of level two the principal elements are all obvious: catalogue, reference, bibliographical area, issue desk undergraduates' short loan collection, and the coffee and smoking area. There is a generous milling area between the entrance and the issue desk, justified in its friendly welcome to the library. The library administration area is behind the issue desk, largely open-plan and separated from the public areas only by the issue counter, which has not given rise to any security problems.

Above the entrance floor level there are two floors of open access bookstacks and reading spaces; one for Arts, and one for Social Science. Both are similar in layout, and each have space for 187,000 books and 480 readers. Each reading floor has a continuous row of open and closed carrels on the perimeter, for sound functional and structural reasons, and the bookstacks are laid out in compact groups, with sufficient cross aisles to facilitate easy access, and break up the mass of shelves. Desks and carrels are interspersed, and frequent coat-hanging units are provided—coats and bags being allowed into the reading areas. There is an advice area near the main stair, and groups of easy chairs and generous planting tubs break up any latent formality. The service and stair cores are to one side of the building, and presumably will be in a more central position when the library is expanded in future. The main stair is not completely enclosed, and presumably as this does not constitute a completely safe fire-escape, an additional escape stair has been built on the outside of the building.

The lower floor houses the manuscript collection, special collections, closed bookstack, muniment store, non-book materials room, and conference room. Also at this level is the service entrance, binding preparation and general storage, the photographic unit, and mechanical and ventilation plant rooms.

The reinforced concrete structure consists of a column grid of 6.75 m. 8 bays long by 6 bays wide, and the structural system employs the efficient principle of cantilevering the reinforced concrete floor slab beyond the outer columns, sufficient to allow the open and closed carrels that line the outer walls; this also emphasises the glazed 'piano nobile' at level two. The building is clad at upper levels by light coloured precast concrete panels, designed so that they can be removed from the façade and reused on the future extensions to the building.

The internal environment of a deep-planned building necessitates the provision of constant, even illumination, humidity and temperature control. Heating from the University district heating system is converted to the right temperature by heat exchangers at the library, then to the heater batteries of the air-conditioning system which operate from plant in the core of the building. The skilful integration of heating, ventilation, and lighting has led to an ingenious ceiling solution. The wasted 'dead' space above the usual flat suspended ceiling has been used to form toughened or sculpted panels, fitted between the structure and services. This gives additional height and volume to the reading and book areas; adds to the sculptural effect of the space; has a greater sound absorbent effect and diffuses the light, so that louvres on the fluorescent tubes are unnecessary, thus making the tubes more efficient in use. As an economy measure, 50% of the fluorescent tubes have been removed, but in most areas 35 Lumens lighting levels are achieved at table-top height.

Internal finishes have been carefully selected for their ease of maintenance, and the decision was taken not to use any plaster or other wet work, except tiling in toilet areas. Walls are either teak veneer, fair-faced brickwork, hessian covered pin-board or vinyl covered concrete; floors are covered throughout with carpet tiles, except in service and toilet areas. Most tables and fittings are custom built, usually teak veneer, of very high standard of design and workmanship. The interchangeable units forming the issue desk are particularly interesting. The Librarian admitted to one argument with his architect, he wanting red chairs throughout, similar to those in his office; but the architect insisted on a more neutral colour–justifiably.

The close collaboration of librarian client and architect is evident throughout the building and everywhere there is the feeling that the right considered decisions have been taken. It says a great deal for the quality of the building that the most contentious aspects concern the 2.5 m. set-back at the entrance level and the generous entrance space; both decisions can be justified qualitatively, rather than on the purely quantitative grounds that a few more square metres could have been used for some other purpose.

The overriding impression is of quiet, warmth and comfort, coupled with immaculate detailing and workmanship. 'Immaculate' is perhaps the most descriptive word, and it is interesting that such an open and 'socially attractive' building should produce such socially responsible behaviour from its young users. No mention here of vandalism, in fact just the opposite; a definite feeling of pride and affection for the building by both staff and users. This is a library that in its brief, practical design and immaculate workmanship, should be studied by anyone contemplating the design of a new library.

NR

Authority	University of Nottingham
Designation	Arts and Social Sciences Library
Date of opening	September 1972
Population served	5,000 students
Name of Architect	Faulkner-Brown, Hendy, Watkinson, Stonor
Name of Librarian	Mr R S Smith, BA, PhD, FLA
Special features:	
a) site	Centre of University, and close to faculties served
b) architecture	4 storey precast concrete clad reinforced concrete
c) function	Serving Faculties of Arts and Social Sciences
Mechanical Services:	
a) heating	District heating feeds heat exchangers in building
b) ventilation	Conditioned air-circulating system
c) lighting	Fluorescent lighting generally
d) acoustics	Specially detailed suspended acoustic trough ceiling
e) other	Carpet tiles generally
Areas: in square metres	
a) lending	—
b) reference	—
c) reading	—
d) special activities	—
e) children	—
f) control	—
g) library staff admin.	—
h) exhibitions	—
i) lecture hall	—
j) circulation	—
k) services	—
l) lavatories	—
m) stack	—
Total area:	10,035
Book volumes:	
a) adult lending	—
b) adult reference	—
c) children	—
d) stack	—
e) other	—
Total:	542,000
Costs in £ p:	
a) site	—
b) building	806,000
c) furniture & fittings	190,000
Total Cost (ex fees):	£996,000
Cost per square metre:	£99

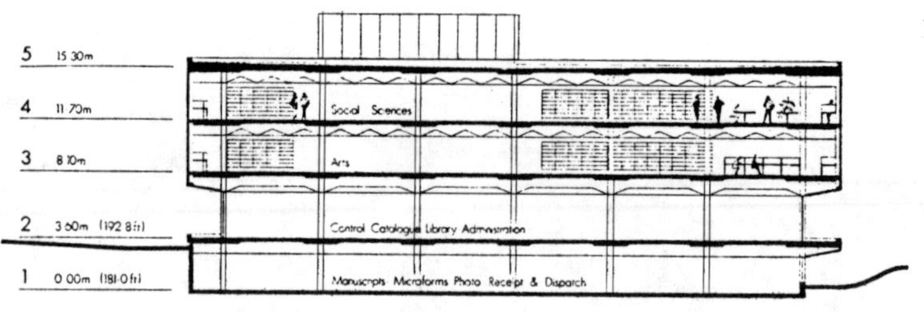

North South Section

191

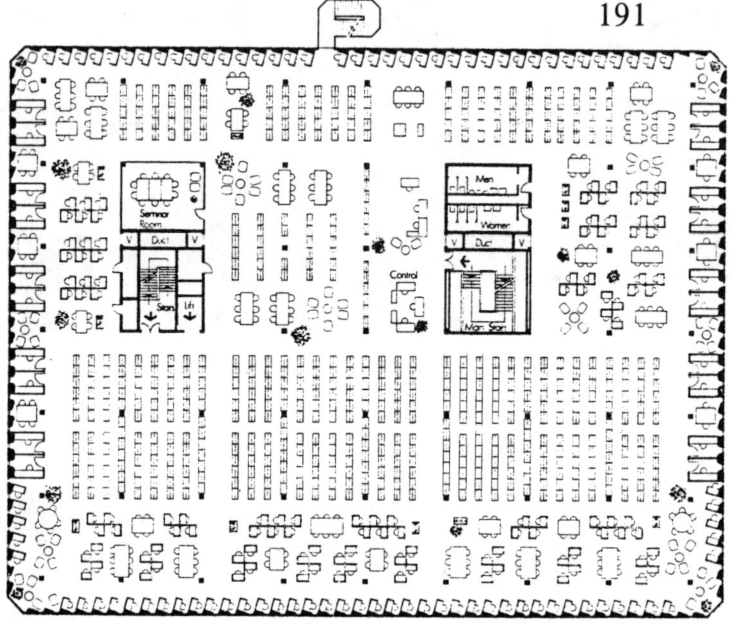

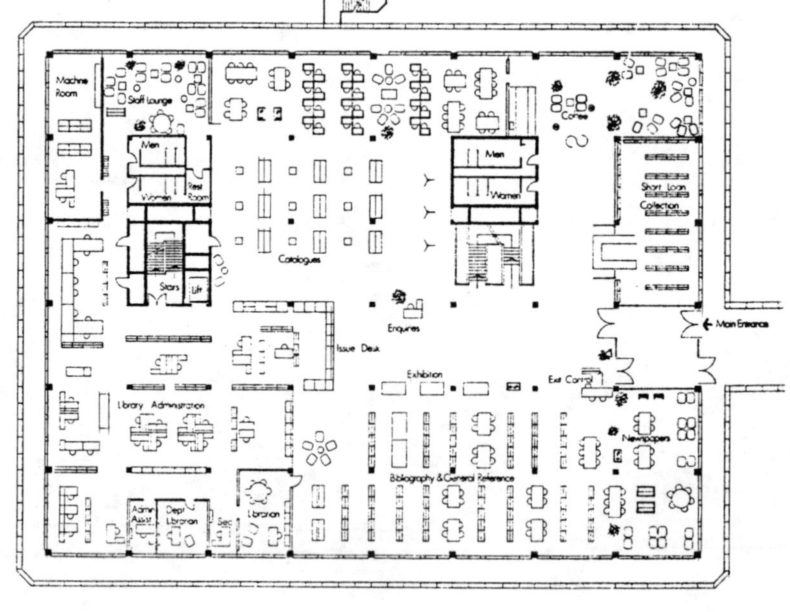

Scale 1 : 500

Humberside County Council (formerly City and County of Kingston-upon-Hull): Hull Nautical College

The strategic position of Kingston-upon-Hull as a key port in the North-East of England and particularly as a centre for the fishing industry, makes it logical for it to be the centre for nautical information, training and education. Although there has been a college for this specialist purpose for many years, it was only recently allocated, within that City's development plan, a strategic site in the City Centre for a purpose-built multi-storey building. This allowed space to be provided on the third floor for library purposes; the scope is not only for nautical, technical and commercial information for the 200 full-time students of Nautical Science and Fishing but to help local industries and even the public at large (yachting and other leisure pursuits). It plays a substantial part in the HULTIS scheme of co-operation which operates from the Central Library.

The substantial stock of books and periodicals is supplemented by several thousand pamphlets and cuttings particularly relevant to research and development of the fishing industry. Study carrels as well as study places are included in the plan, as well as rooms for microfilm reading and for seminars and tutorials.

The visit was made early morning during a period when students were on vacation and this unfortunately prevented the library being viewed while in use. The emptiness perhaps emphasised the 'chill' felt by the concrete pillars and waffled ceiling, the metal shelving, tiled floor and curtainless windows, which form a complete run round the three external walls; banks of strip fluorescents, though effective, do not alleviate this feeling. The aspect is pleasant and later in the day, no doubt, the sun would give a warmth (though perhaps at times during the year a heat) to the room. Venetian blinds have, however, been fitted to prevent glare. Convector heating is situated under the windows and there is a fresh air plenum input.

Perhaps there was a 'tight' budget for this project; maybe those connected with this industry are accustomed to rather spartan work-conditions but comparing with the College of Furniture in a similar type building (see 1974 issue pp 116–117) browsing areas, settees, carpeted floor and some decoratively papered walls create a warmer, welcoming atmosphere.

HW

Authority	Humberside County Council
Designation	Hull Nautical College Library
Date of opening	January 1973
Population served	300 approx (at a time)
Name of Architect	A R Peadon, BArch, RIBA, MRTPI
Name of Librarian	John H Witty
Special features:	
a) site	Third floor of college which is on main thoroughfare in city centre
b) architecture	White concrete blocks, curtain walling with solar control glass and mosaic features
c) function	Training fishermen to BSc(Fishery) and to master; also part-time leisure pursuits
Mechanical Services:	
a) heating	Free air convectors on perimeter wall
b) ventilation	Fresh air plenum
c) lighting	Fluorescent strip
d) acoustics	Coffered ceiling
e) other	—
Areas: in square metres	
a) lending	
b) reference	
c) reading	168
d) special activities	
e) children	—
f) control	—
g) library staff admin.	15
h) exhibitions	—
i) lecture hall	—
j) circulation	—
k) services	—
l) lavatories	—
m) stack	—
Total area:	183
Book volumes:	
a) adult lending	4,700
b) adult reference	300
c) children	—
d) stack	Plans, charts, (1,000) periodicals
e) other	—
Total:	6,000
Costs in £ p:	
a) site	
b) building	Part of college building
c) furniture & fittings	
Total Cost (ex fees):	—
Cost per square metre:	—

London Borough of Kingston-upon-Thames: Kingston College of Further Education

Kingston College of Further Education, situated in the centre of Kingston has a total student population of nearly 5,000, about 800 of whom are full-time. A wide variety of subjects is covered with full-time and part-time courses at 'O' and 'A' levels of GCE, ONC and HND standard. Many of the students are on day or block release training schemes sponsored by their employers in industry, and some adult training courses are offered.

The College building, a large 11-storey block includes a wide range of different types of accommodation on similar floors. From the outside there is nothing to indicate that the library is on the fifth floor whilst inside the means of access is somewhat confused, for the building has entrance halls at both ends, each with a bank of lifts. However, the library is only accessible from one end. No doubt students soon get used to the vagaries of the system, but careful signposting could have minimised the difficulties.

The library is entered off the staircase through the lift lobby at the north end of the building. Racks are provided for bags and briefcases to be left outside the library as a precaution against pilfering of books, which here is a major problem. The U-shaped counter, designed by the Librarian and Architect working very closely together, functions very efficiently. All the drawers, cupboards and pigeon-holes have been designed for specific purposes with considerable precision and the service can run without the minor irritations and annoyances caused by lack of attention to detail, so often encountered in the design of such fittings. As the building is of a deep-plan with windows set about 16 m. apart these serve more for views than daylighting; as a result, permanent artificial lighting is necessary at the centre of the library. Venetian blinds are installed to mitigate the effects of the sun on the south-west side, whilst curtains help to soften the appearance of the cold north-east facing windows. Though no air-conditioning is provided there does not appear to be any great problem of heat gain and the opposing lines of opening windows seem to allow enough cross ventilation to deal with hot summer conditions. Acoustic tile ceilings, together with the nylon looped pile carpeting, produce a pleasantly quiet environment.

The stock is of 25,000 volumes, issues running at about 160 per day with seldom more than 3,000 out on loan. Only about 1,500 of the total student population are enrolled as members of the library, perhaps reflecting the practical nature of many of the courses and the relative youth of the bulk of the student body, not yet fully accustomed to making the fullest use of the excellent facilities offered. The principal function of the library is reference and 90 seats are provided at rather spartan-looking four-seater desks.

The bookstacks of standard Reska metal shelving are at centres slightly wider than is strictly necessary, so placed as to conform to the spacing of columns and window mullions whose intervals are determined by other considerations. Book sequences are so arranged as to include oversize stock within the main runs, which leads to a slightly wider spacing than usual for the six shelves and a rather empty appearance. In a library of this nature, however, it was considered that the importance of maintaining an unbroken sequence was paramount. Periodicals are displayed on sloping perspex shelves. Not all the back numbers of the 200 magazines can be kept, although there is a store for selected material.

The Careers Advice area takes the form of a comfortably furnished room, off the main seating area, with an adjacent office in which interviews with advisers take place. Specially designed pin-boarded bays and stands for the large mass of careers leaflets and posters surround the room in which students are encouraged to browse. The relaxed atmosphere and informality is totally appropriate for students engaged in considering this most important stage in their lives.

Audio visual aids have proliferated in recent years and the librarian is faced with a formidable array of material to store, catalogue and make available for study in such a way as to ensure that the software is not liable to damage. The audio visual library is equipped with slides, records, sound and TV cassettes, film strip and loops, tapes and mixed media kits. A 'Stripdex' catalogue on the counter lists all the materials held in stock from which the choice may be made. Students must study in the 'Individual Learning Centre', a room fitted with earphones and television, both live and with video cassettes, all controlled by the Librarian from the media hardware in the Audio Visual Preview Room. College staff may use this room to examine available material and even to prepare material for lectures, such as dictating and recording commentaries for slide sequences. Staff may borrow audio visual materials for lectures but this facility is not available to students. This section of the library is of considerable interest and although still, to some extent, at the experimental stage is popular with both staff and students. Techniques have had to be evolved for storage, cataloguing and showing materials in these media which are beyond the range of many libraries.

It will be interesting to see how knowledge gained in handling such materials will be applied when it comes to building a new library, in due course, in a situation where much greater freedom exists, without the stifling constraints imposed by an already existing building. The present library is well organised, brisk and efficient and it is to be hoped that when a new one is built the opportunity will be taken to add elements to make it more human and with a less impersonal working environment.

GKVT

Authority	Royal Borough of Kingston-upon-Thames
Designation	Kingston College of Further Education
Date of opening	September 1973
Population served	5,200
Name of Architect	J H Lomas, FRIBA, Surrey County Architect, George Watt Partnership
Name of Librarian	Mrs J Tilling, BA, ALA
Special features:	
a) site	In multi-storey college building on 5th floor
b) architecture	Reinforced concrete frame
c) function	College library and audio-visual library
Mechanical Services:	
a) heating	Low pressure hot water radiators
b) ventilation	Windows both sides
c) lighting	Fluorescent
d) acoustics	Carpet; acoustic tile ceilings
e) other	—
Areas: in square metres	
a) lending	—
b) reference	362
c) reading	—
d) special activities seminar	23 audio-visual 84
e) children	—
f) control	8
g) library staff admin.	31
h) exhibitions	—
i) lecture hall	80
j) circulation	—
k) services	—
l) lavatories	—
m) stack store	9
Total area:	597
Book volumes:	
a) adult lending	23,000
b) adult reference	4,000
c) children	—
d) stack	—
e) other	2,360 items audio-visual
Total:	—
Costs in £ p:	
a) site	—
b) building	Part of large block — proportion not known
c) furniture & fittings	6,500
Total Cost (ex fees):	—
Cost per square metre:	—

Didsbury College of Education is in a pleasant residential neighbourhood 5 miles out of the centre of Manchester close to the southern boundary of the city. Founded in 1946 it has grown to its present size of 1,500 students. The College offers courses in a wide range of subjects leading to a BEd degree.

The College has grown up around a series of courtyards with buildings running in an almost unbroken chain. This produces a pleasantly varied environment enhanced by much good mature planting. The library, on three floors is partly open at ground-floor level. It is built in a soft red-brown brick with narrow concrete bands at floor level with alternating pairs of horizontal and vertical strip windows with splayed brick jambs at upper-floor levels. The ground floor is largely composed of glazed window walls.

Entrance to the block is under cover on one of the College's main pedestrian routes. Generous cloakrooms have been provided where students are encouraged to leave briefcases and bags for security reasons. The counter has controlled entrance and exit turnstiles and a magnetic security device has been installed to make sure that only books that have been properly issued can be taken out otherwise the exit gate locks automatically. There is ample room behind the counter for the two staff normally on duty and this is needed for not only books but audio visual materials are returned at this point. Books are placed on trolleys and AV materials in a variety of plastic baskets designed to suit their shape and size. All returned stock is then taken by staff either by the passenger lift or despatched by book lift to the appropriate floors. Display cases for restricted loan stock (selected by academic staff) and those in constant demand are placed where all students pass the counter and these items can be borrowed for 48 hours only. The counter area is lively and busy. It is unfortunate that it is rather cold but improvement is being made to the heating. The problem arises from the large area of glazing which, whilst useful for drawing attention to the library, is excessive.

The main staircase, with its metal spine carrying open timber treads finished with cushioned rubber sheet, rises from the hall but leaves an untidy and unusable space beneath it just where most space is required.

The school services library is laid out to demonstrate how an ideal school library could be arranged. Housing 20,000 children's books (including textbooks) this area is popular for students studying curriculum development and children's literature. The central area can be curtained off for teaching practice, groups or seminars. Librarians' offices lead off this library where they are close to the counter. A staff workroom area, in which all work on books from acquisitioning to repairs is carried out, adjoins the Librarian's office. This is accessible from a staff car park at the rear and is planned to give considerable flexibility for changing needs.

The first floor houses the main catalogue, enquiry desk and quick-reference books, Lending and Audio Visual Library, as well as a large number of semi carrel desks, and a 90-seat private study room which is accessible from a separate entrance when the library is shut. Two librarians' offices are situated close to the trolley hoist. Lavatories are provided alongside the staircase lift block together with a cleaner's room.

Whilst the planning is sensible and quite spacious, the lighting, both natural and artificial, leaves much to be desired. The adoption of alternate pairs of floor-to-ceiling slit windows on either side of the perimeter columns with pairs of high-level horizontal slit windows are particularly inappropriate since it in no way relates to the layout of the rooms. It appears rather to have been the result of external aesthetic consideration. Where vertical windows occur the run of carrels is interrupted whilst the high-level windows serve neither to give good lighting nor outlook from the carrels. Artificial lighting is adequate in design but owing to restriction on running costs nearly half of the lights are kept switched off. As a result the carrels particularly are dimly lit and very claustrophobic.

The acoustic tiled ceiling and nylon carpet make for quiet conditions. Metal book shelving is by Reska with clear projecting notices at the ends of bookcases; tier guiding, however, is done by lettering on the top shelf and this is too small to be easily legible.

The Audio Visual Library copes well with the wide range of media. Pictures, posters, charts and maps are stored according to shape. A loan picture collection of art reproductions is also available. Projection materials, filmstrips, cassette loops, films and slides available for loan are well arranged and stored. Gramophone records and cassettes for loan or use on the premises in headphone booths are controlled by a full-time technician assisting the librarian. The technician will make temporary cassette recordings from records and cassettes on request, which helps to make for better use of limited stock. In addition many samples and kits for use in teaching are stored in specially designed cupboards. In this room the tall slit windows are again quite inappropriate for every inch of wall space is needed. Most of the windows are obscured anyway up to normal sill level by cabinets and desks.

The second floor layout follows the lines of the first floor with more carrels and the main lending stock as well as a stack area housing special collections and rare books. Eight hundred periodicals are available together with a local history collection, a Brontë Collection bequeathed by John Seymour and a microfilm collection.

Use by students has grown steadily and the library is evidently popular. Issues run at 125,000 books and 7,500 other items annually. A total staff of 18 run the library for a 55-hour week with some Saturday and vacation opening.

GKVT

Authority	Manchester Education Committee
Designation	Didsbury College of Education
Date of opening	September 1973
Population served	2,000
Name of Architect	E Besant Roberts, City Architect, G Walton, Job Architect
Name of Librarian	W H Shercliff, FLA
Special features:	
a) site	Central within campus between teaching and admin. blocks and accessible by underpass
b) architecture	Three floors but single storey over hall and counter area; RC frame at 24′ span in each direction
c) function	Supports college's work on teacher education
Mechanical Services:	
a) heating	Low pressure hot water system with panel radiators
b) ventilation	Mechanical extraction to workroom
c) lighting	Diffused fluorescent
d) acoustics	Nylon carpeting except hall, stairs and counter
e) other	—
Areas: in square metres	
a) lending	—
b) reference	—
c) reading	—
d) special activities	—
e) children	—
f) control	—
g) library staff admin.	—
h) exhibitions	—
i) lecture hall	—
j) circulation	—
k) services	—
l) lavatories	—
m) stack	—
Total area:	2,312
Book volumes:	
a) adult lending	58,168
b) adult reference	6,188
c) children	25,236
d) stack	3,354
e) other	30,800; 30,000 AV plus periodicals
Total:	123,746
Costs in £ p:	
a) site	—
b) building	150,000
c) furniture & fittings	24,000
Total Cost (ex fees):	£174,000
Cost per square metre:	£76

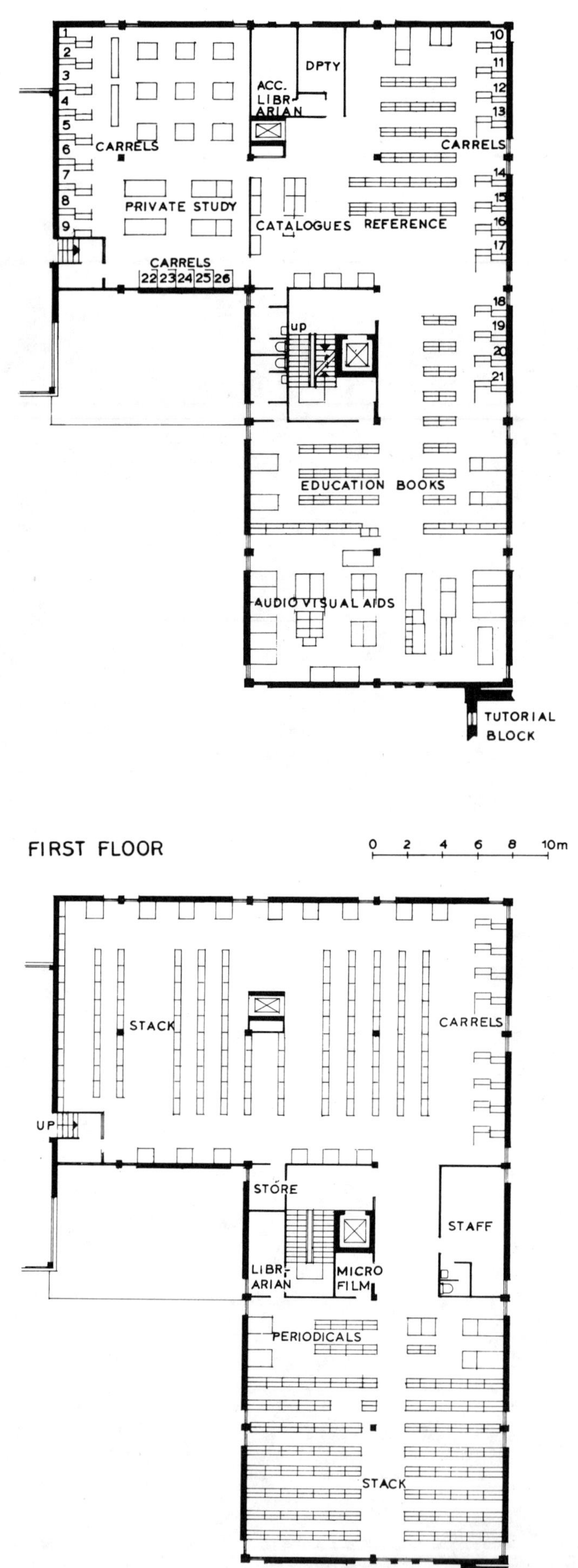

Surrey County Council:
Brooklands Technical College

Brooklands College is situated in a delightful parkland setting in Weybridge with an approach drive through banks of rhododendrons, which are such a feature of the area. The College, which might be described as a Sixth Form College, has about 4,000 students of whom about 1,000 are full-time. A wide range of courses is offered including technology, production and mechanical engineering, catering, as well as 'O' and 'A' GCE subjects. There are a small number of adult students on retraining or mid-career refresher courses with special emphasis on local industries.

The original library was in two rooms in one of the old buildings and it was fortunate that the Librarian who had run that library for years was able to formulate the brief for the new building on the basis of extensive experience of the needs of the students. From the evident success of the new library the brief must have been very much to the point so that, functionally, it is efficient whilst the architects have managed to produce a solution of almost classical simplicity and serenity. The single-storey building enjoys a spacious and beautiful setting with the dark background of well chosen shrubs, skilfully enhancing the very simple, elegant architecture.

For the exterior of the building a limited range of materials is used: white painted softwood windows in full-height panels, a brown painted horizontal boarded fascia and a broad band of brown, brindled paving bricks surrounding the building. The fascia overhangs the façade affording a degree of protection from the rain. The detailing of the timber sills gives cause for concern as the lack of any slope leads to water penetration and deterioration of the joints which will prove to be a tiresome maintenance problem.

In times when fuel costs have risen so steeply the decision to face the whole building with single glazed screens might appear wilful if not irresponsible, but it must be remembered that this building was planned before the Middle East oil crisis of 1973. The solution today might well be substantially different, though undoubtedly the appearance of openness with views into the library giving the publicity which is so necessary for a college library is vital. The views out from the building make it a very pleasant place in which to work.

The choice of a flat roof for such a large rectangular building was no doubt dictated as much by economic as by aesthetic considerations. Unfortunately there have proved to be serious problems with leaks which spoil the otherwise good record of client satisfaction. The library has been flooded on numerous occasions and much investigation and remedial work has been applied to try to cure this problem, but so far without complete success.

Turning to the planning, the building takes the form of a large rectangle with a recess in the south side, a garden court planted with low shrubs. The entrance is from the west side with a small lobby leading into a pleasantly furnished entrance hall where students may meet and talk. There are easy chairs for 23 people with low tables and plant containers. One wall has display panels where posters of college and outside activities can be shown.

To the left of this area are men's and women's lavatories, well planned and equipped and with high-level windows. Beyond the lavatories two doors lead into a large seminar room which can be partitioned by means of a plastic covered sliding, folding screen into two smaller rooms. This area can be used in the evenings, when the library is shut, for Open University sessions or meetings and at lunchtimes recorded music recitals are frequently given.

To the left of the entrance hall common room is a large square study room with 98 individual semi-carrel desks with screens between and on each side of each workspace. This room is fully glazed on all sides and is known affectionately as the 'fish tank'. Silence is maintained and supervision from the desk ensures good behaviour. This has proved to be a very successful feature of the library despite doubts expressed by the architects initially. The Librarian's experience had led her to believe that the reading and study room should be entirely separate from the main library so that it can be used at times when the library itself is shut. During the daytime the majority of readers using the reading room seem to arrive with most of their study material and to need to sit for long periods without needing library material immediately to hand. For those who have to work with the books adjacent there is provision at tables in the body of the library where a further 36 seats are available. An attractive cruciform arrangement is used for the reading room for 40 of the places, the desks arranged so that whilst well screened from one another, students do have a view out sideways which produces pleasanter work spaces without the slightly claustrophobic feeling of the long straight rows of desks with high screens on three sides.

Beyond the entrance hall the control desk projects into the opening to the library from one side and a low glazed screen from the other. The screen, which is open towards the entrance hall, directs students with bags and briefcases into the cloakroom where these containers must be deposited in the 36 pigeon-holes which can be seen from the desk.

Across the opening between entrance hall and library, a large sliding screen can be drawn at closing time, sealing off the library whilst leaving the reading room and seminar rooms open.

The counter, which is planned on the generous lines of the whole building, has plenty of space for two members of staff to work side by side. A slight snag is that 'In' and 'Out' circulation routes are not separated and at busy times some confusion arises. This counter allows a 'returned books' trolley to stand without being in the way, has adequate shelves and drawers, and the whole appears to work well.

The degree of control resulting from this arrangement is demonstrated by the fact that annual book losses average only about 60 volumes, which compares well with many academic libraries. Beyond the counter, in the narrowest part of the library, are the catalogues and display stands for the 150 periodicals taken, with small wall desks for quick reference materials.

On the north side a row of rooms provide accommodation for the Librarian, librarians' workroom, periodicals store, audio visual aids store and finally carrels. The bulk of the library, with open stack accommodation for 20,000 volumes, is in the south-east corner with two large areas of bookshelving separated by the nine tables each with four chairs. The spacious layout of the tables and chairs contrasts with the dense mass of bookshelving but because the lighting everywhere is excellent there is never any feeling of oppressiveness which might have resulted.

The offices, workroom and store are all sensibly laid out and generously equipped with shelving and cupboards and enjoy an attractively secluded outlook. The use of full-length windows is questionable, as it restricts the layout of furniture near the windows, a limitation which could have been avoided by the use of a translucent bottom pane of glass below sill level. There are places where the overall simplicity should have been modified to ensure the best functional performance.

The internal design is uniformly consistent with a very small range of materials. All ceilings are of acoustic tiles with a fissured pattern in metal angle suspension. The bays of ceiling are divided by immaculately detailed black strips of beams which are supported by slender, square, black steel columns on a regular grid. Two centre rows of rooflights run the length of the building. These have a small, square, egg-crate pattern plastic diffuser at ceiling level which serve to conceal fluorescent lighting strips, but get very dirty and trap dead flies and spiders, making for a rather sordid appearance.

Rows of precisely spaced white plastic, shaded tungsten lights and some spotlights help to provide a varied and warm scheme of artificial lighting. A brown nylon carpet unites all public areas whilst offices have grey plastic tiles. Walls are of a red-brown brick to door level height only, matching that used externally. Small black skirtings take any marking by the vacuum cleaners which can be such a problem.

Windows, which are mostly of the full height of the room, have a deep rail at sill height with a row of opening lights at high level which can be opened under the protection of the eaves, for ventilation. Windows facing east, south and west are fitted with full-height, white venetian blinds, allowing sunlight to be controlled.

Internal partitions have a row of borrowed lights at high level above doors and these correspond in height with the opening external windows. Doors have heavy white painted frames and are painted a dark brown with strips of aluminium with black lettering indicating the function of each room, placed above eye level. Library shelving is by Libraco with metal shelves; black uprights with hardwood ends are used with narrow matching fascias.

This is, in many ways, a model college library with many details worthy of study–though the building failures, leaky roof and poorly detailed windows mar the result.

It is interesting to contrast the completely different policy on student study areas and audio visual materials with that adopted by Kingston. Visual aids in Brooklands are completely excluded as it is hoped to build a completely separate visual aids centre elsewhere in the College at a later date.

GKVT

Authority	Surrey County Council
Designation	Brooklands Technical College Library, Weybridge
Date of opening	February 1973
Population served	—
Name of Architect	Raymond J Ash, DipArch, RIBA, County Architect, Howell Morgan, DipArch, RIBA, Job Architect
Name of Librarian	Miss B Weaver
Special features:	
a) site	Flat site in college grounds
b) architecture	Steel frame, brick and glass walls
c) function	Technical college library
Mechanical Services:	
a) heating	Hot water radiators and fan convectors
b) ventilation	Natural
c) lighting	Mixed fluorescent and tungsten (400 lux)
d) acoustics	Acoustic tile ceiling; carpet
e) other	—
Areas: in square metres	
a) lending	418
b) reference	in (a)
c) reading	232
d) special activities	28
e) children	—
f) control	10
g) library staff admin.	99
h) exhibitions	93
i) lecture hall	56
j) circulation	—
k) services	—
l) lavatories	52
m) stack	—
Total area:	988
Book volumes:	
a) adult lending	28,500
b) adult reference	1,500
c) children	—
d) stack	—
e) other	—
Total:	30,000
Costs in £ p:	
a) site	—
b) building	92,500
c) furniture & fittings	—
Total Cost (ex fees):	—
Cost per square metre:	£90

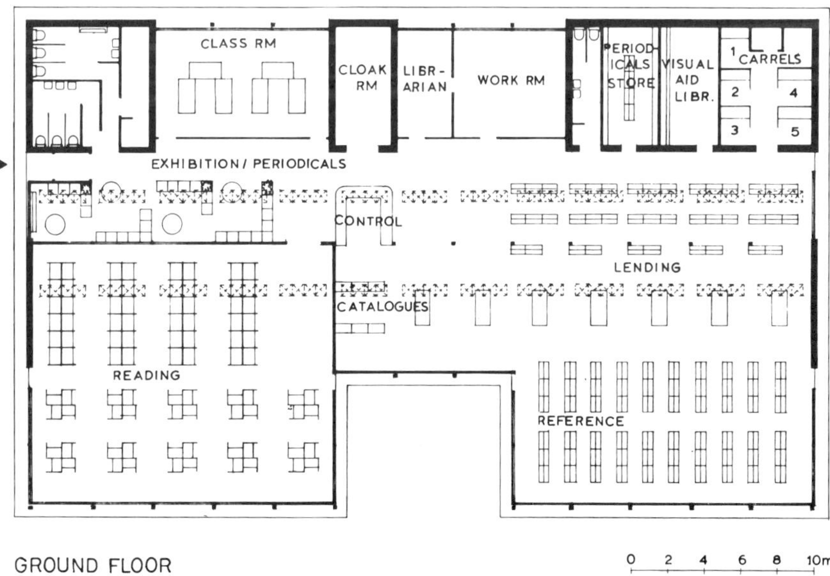

GROUND FLOOR

University of Bradford Management Centre: Yvette Jacobson Library

The University of Bradford is in the centre of the city (its new library is incomplete at the time of writing). The University's Management Centre, however, is in a fantastic Victorian ex-training college for Baptists in the suburbs. Tucked away at the back of this mansion, among other new buildings, is a most charming new Management Centre Library. At first sight it is like a very pleasant low-profile expensive house overlooking a garden, the only incongruity being a startling chimney out of all proportion to the size of the rest of the building. This was apparently a Local Authority requirement under the Clean Air Act: it is almost worthwhile for its shock value!

The library has two floors, the lower and larger having open access bookstacks, a reader area with 80 seats (including 26 Reska semi-carrels, and 10 private study carrels). The upper (ground floor) area which contains the counter and periodicals has a window which overlooks the lower area but does not really give the opportunity for supervision. The library is designed for minimal staffing but this can only mean a great deal of hopeful trust about what is going on at the lower floor level. Surprisingly, in contrast to this, are the quite definite turnstiles at entrance and exit to the building.

The counter is coated with a white plastic laminate and screened at the rear to make an enclosed short-loan collection. An unusual feature is a row of locked glass-fronted cupboards which hold the thesis collection. In all, the feeling on immediate entry is that the room is overcrowded with shelving–but necessity no doubt dictated this. The periodicals area is more spacious and has a beautiful window niche enclosing a charming ornament; it was not surprising to learn that this was a separate gift of the donor. Official funds seldom run to this kind of ornamentation.

The lower ground floor is more formal and spacious and appears to be very suitable for management trainees at all study levels. The readers' chairs are cloth-covered, very pleasant, but are they practical to keep clean? I really admired the guiding which is apparently carried out by a 'headliner' machine in the University's printing department. In the current periodical area, strips made by this machine are fastened magnetically to the backing.

The public areas are air-conditioned but in order to save money, radiators were introduced in the offices, staircase and study carrels. Indeed I had the impression that there was virtually no ventilation whatever in the carrels which have their own separate hot water heating. One carrel is used for the projection of an audio visual introduction to the library but this is a poor expedient as the room is much too small for the purpose.

This is a thoroughly practical library with an attractive exterior, good finishes and some thoughtful touches. It serves to show that the place of the private donor in public buildings can still be of considerable importance.

GT

Authority	University of Bradford
Designation	Yvette Jacobson, Management Centre Library
Date of opening	September 1974
Population served	65 academic staff, 300–400 students
Name of Architect	Building Design Partnership in collaboration with E Kemp, ARIBA, Resident Architect, University
Name of Librarian	N R Hunter, BA, ALA

Special features:

a) site	Sloping landscaped wooded grounds
b) architecture	Steeply sloping roof; tall chimney
c) function	Serves management centre which is far distant from university campus

Mechanical Services:

a) heating	Oil-fired low pressure hot water
b) ventilation	Air-conditioning plus some natural ventilation
c) lighting	To IES standards
d) acoustics	Incorporated in ceiling
e) other	—

Areas: in square metres

a) lending	} 432
b) reference	
c) reading	—
d) special activities	—
e) children	—
f) control	10
g) library staff admin.	23
h) exhibitions	—
i) lecture hall	—
j) circulation	18
k) services	40
l) lavatories	22
m) stack	—
Total area:	545

Book volumes:

a) adult lending	—
b) adult reference	—
c) children	—
d) stack	—
e) other	—
Total:	20,000

Costs in £ p:

a) site	—
b) building	57,000
c) furniture & fittings	14,000
Total Cost (ex fees):	£71,000
Cost per square metre:	£128

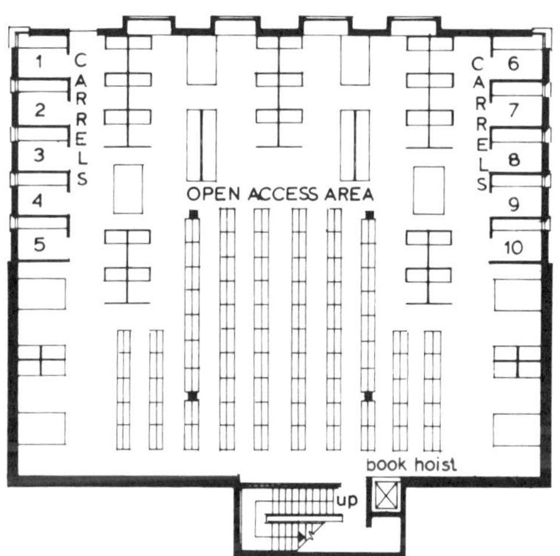

GROUND FLOOR

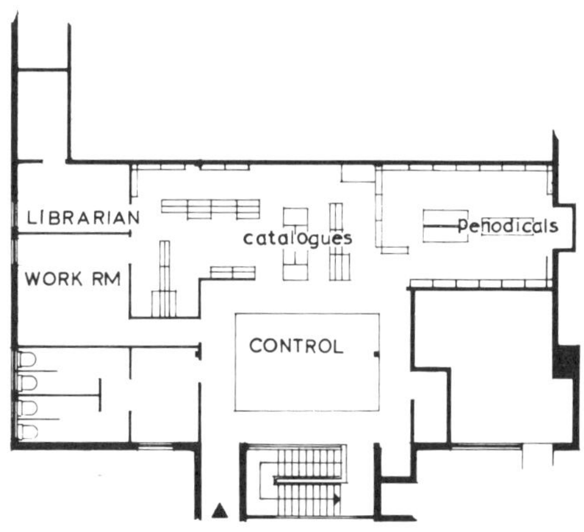

FIRST FLOOR
(entrance level)

University of London:
School of Oriental and African studies

The overwhelming problem posed by this library is not its sheer size, although space for a million volumes and 5,000 borrowers is not negligible, but the fact that the stock of books is in more than 2,000 languages and dialects. To a librarian the problems of selection, cataloguing, readers' advisory work and so on are frightening: it cannot have made the planning of this building easy. The building is an extension to the existing School which was constructed in 1940. The extension is part of the redevelopment by the University of an area of Bloomsbury which is proceeding in stages, with this the first to be completed.

The extension is, in fact, considerably larger than the existing school building. It is really two buildings in one: the core is occupied by the library, while wrapped around it are teaching and academic staff accommodation. The extension provides 220 rooms for teaching staff plus lecture rooms, laboratories and so on; the library seats 550 readers and provides working accommodation for 60 library staff.

Entrance is from the school, the library being in effect a dead end. Passing a display and bag-deposit area one reaches a huge open counter surrounded by metal ribbed matting which further cleans shoes already cleaned by their progress through the school. The top of the counter is of high quality hard wood: not everyone's choice but apparently wearing well. There are positive turnstiles on both 'In' and 'Out' sides.

The library is roll-carpeted throughout. Despite the 80/20 wool/made-made fibre mixture there are still static problems, but it looks good, gives quietness and seems to be wearing very well. Nevertheless replacement will one day be a headache.

There are five floors including the lower ground floor. The general principle is location of stock by regions, the regional specialist and a particular reading room being associated with each regional section of the stock. The ground floor houses the control counter, an open seating area beyond, the offices of the Librarian and administration as well as some of the stack. The first floor has a catalogue hall and a general reading room which also houses the short-loan collection. This is the point from which to view the library. An open square room lit from on high through grids, with each of the three floors above progressively stepped back, giving a feeling of space. This is enhanced by the narrow (1 ft) strip of open glass above the shelving which gives a feeling of greater depth as the eye travels into stack areas.

The first-floor cataloguing hall, approached by the only staircase and forming an ante-room to the general reading room, is a good example of the real thought which has gone into the design. The square wooden catalogues are echoed by a series of squared concrete openings from area to area. Inset coloured lino on the cataloguing consultation tables is repeated in the shelves below them. This hall leads on to the current periodicals room with a goldfish-bowl workroom, inevitably too small.

The two cores, at diagonally opposed corners, provide forced air ventilation and lifts to all floors and toilets for most. Ventilation is theoretically added by motor driven opening windows in the top lighting above the open well, but this is seldom used. There is only one staircase, enclosed, carpeted and lit by a very neat emergency light operated by a time switch.

There are a dozen generous double carrels with large glass windows, in odd places; in some cases near the stacks and, in others, off corridors. Naturally there are far too few for the demand. In addition to the bag-deposit station there are 220 lockers within the library. As always, carrel and locker administration eats staff time.

The second floor holds the biggest single stack area and is fairly conventional, with seating around the perimeter; it is unusual in that individual regional specialist offices substitute for the normal readers' advisory desks. As each floor higher gets smaller, the third floor is merely stacks of periodicals with a small number of seats around the rim of the void while the fourth is entirely closed (or sliding door closable) stacking for special books. Here also is a strong room which is locally air-conditioned but this has not been free from trouble. The lower ground floor is somewhat of a ragbag; sociology, law and maps, together with an improvised and locally air-conditioned storage room for microforms. This is the least interesting part of the building.

The appearance throughout is very pleasant. Precast concrete, as ever, but in this case, on the whole, very well-finished and far less brutal than most. The grey carpet goes well with the red of the seating, of the deep lounge seats in salient points and even of the waste paper baskets. Sankey Sheldon bracketed stacks stand (usually on the screed) at 4 ft 6 in centres. As only a half of the planned one million stock is yet held there is the luxury of plenty of empty shelves. The stacks on the perimeter areas are illuminated by ceiling fluorescent strips but those in the open well have a built-in canopy for holding lighting strips. In order to make use of natural light also, the canopy is skeletal: this is clever but looks rather bitty and, more seriously, prevents the use of the top shelf.

The furniture is well thought out. Tables have 18 in high dividers and tops of grained plastic: these will need cleaning—but is there any better solution?

This is a very irregular building and one difficult to grasp. Guiding is tasteful and there are good plans at intervals, but a stranger could be easily lost in it. There is so much to admire and one has to look hard to find things to criticise. The counter top of the bag-deposit area is not tough enough for its job and is fast wearing out; the concrete is becoming dirty around the lift entrances (although the lift interiors are sensibly covered with ribbed aluminium); smoke detectors are provided only in the strong room—elsewhere there are fire hoses. All these are small and unimportant quibbles: the only serious one is that there are large and entirely unusable balconies on two sides of the building. One appreciates that they help to give a more balanced view of the building from Woburn Square but surely this must be considered something of a luxury today.

GT

Authority	University of London School of Oriental and African studies
Designation	School library and national lending collection on the subjects
Date of opening	July 1973
Population served	250 staff, 1,000 internal students, 2,000+ outsiders
Name of Architect	Denys Lasdun and Partners
Name of Librarian	B C Bloomfield, MA, FLA
Special features:	
a) site	Restricted site; extension of existing building in Woburn Square development
b) architecture	17'6″ square grid. Concrete (mainly exposed) central space roofed by concrete diagrid with top lighting
c) function	—
Mechanical Services:	
a) heating	Perimeter hot water radiators; interior mechanical warm air
b) ventilation	Perimeter natural, interior mechanical
c) lighting	Natural top or side to all reading rooms, diffused fluorescent 300+ lux
d) acoustics	Carpeted throughout public areas; sound absorbent ceilings
Areas: in square metres	
a) lending	—
b) reference	—
c) reading	—
d) special activities	—
e) children	—
f) control	—
g) library staff admin.	—
h) exhibitions	—
i) lecture hall	—
j) circulation	—
k) services	—
l) lavatories	—
m) stack	—
Total area:	7,250
Book volumes:	
a) adult lending	} 450,000 capacity 1 million
b) adult reference	
c) children	—
d) stack	—
e) other	10,000 maps, 5,000 microfilms, 30,000 microfiches, 800 prints, 1,000 discs, 25,000 slides, 20,000 photographs
Total:	450,000 (ex av)
Costs in £ p:	
a) site	Part of complex; figures not available
b) building	—
c) furniture & fittings	—
Total Cost (ex fees):	—
Cost per square metre:	Not available

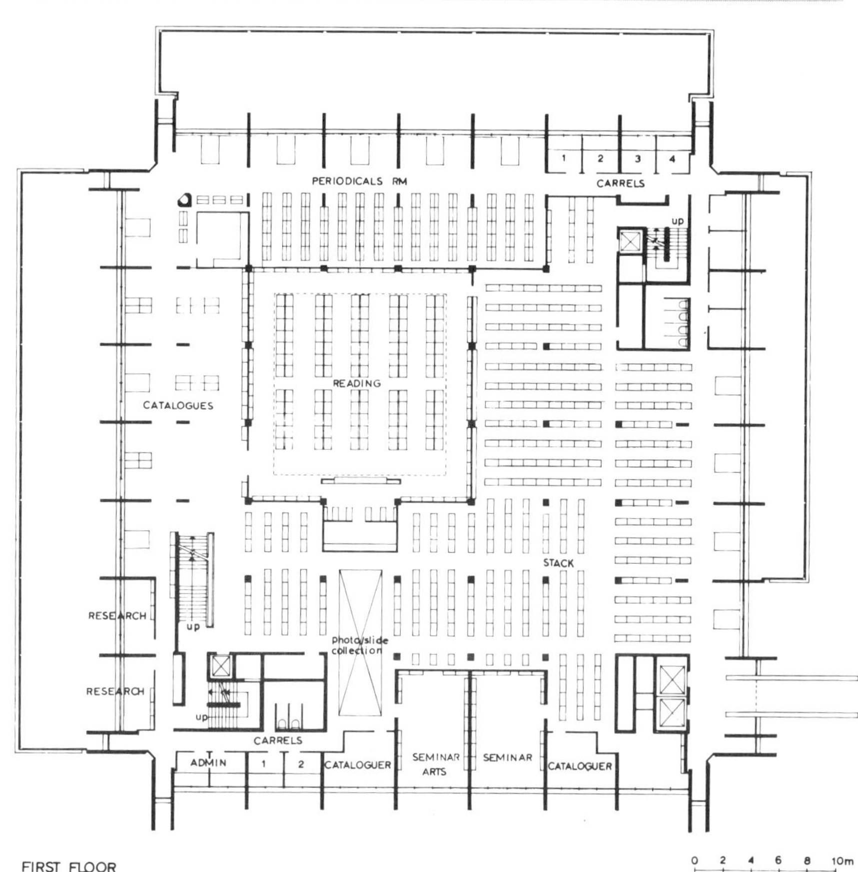

FIRST FLOOR

Glasgow District Council:
Jordanhill College of Education

Jordanhill College is the largest teacher training college in Great Britain and stands in its own attractive grounds of about fifty acres. The many new buildings reflect its rapid expansion in the last ten years. The most recent of the new buildings is the college library which opens off the entrance hall of the main building extension. This is the most heavily populated building in the college and the library is therefore ideally situated for maximum use.

The library, a square on plan, is two-storeys high, the upper floor being in the form of a wide gallery around three sides. The ground floor is allocated to lending and periodicals around the perimeter under the galleries, with a large reading area in the central double height space flooded with daylight from the roof. The first floor houses reference and study areas. The disposition of the various spaces generates a need for four circulation stairs in addition to the fire exits and three book hoists to ease vertical movement. No windows are possible on the lower floor because of the slope on the ground and the few windows on the upper floor are permanently covered by closed curtains. There are many other areas of curtains on the external wall covering slabs of brickwork. The total effect is inward looking but there is also a feeling of spaciousness resulting from the fact that from any point almost all of the rest of the library can be seen. One space encloses everything.

Structurally there appears to be a limitation of flexibility as evidenced by notices throughout the upper floor restricting numerous sections to either 732 kg/m^2 or 1,270 kg/m^2 superimposed floor loading.

Heating is by means of low pressure hot water with electric underfloor heating in the central area. Ventilation is mechanical and is provided at the rate of three air changes per hour and although this seems low the building has a large volume and the installation is perfectly adequate. No cooling is provided but the building is well insulated. Lighting levels in the central area are excellent due to the daylight from the large area of roof-lights but when this source is cut off at night the artificial lighting is not quite adequate. There is a high level of illumination in the bookstack where continuous fluorescent fittings run at right angles to the shelves. As previously stated there are three book hoists; one goods lift capable of accommodating a book trolley would have been more effective and would have allowed wheelchair users to reach the upper floor. The noise level is higher than normally expected in such a library and it is fortunate that there is a gentle hum from the ventilation system which has a masking effect.

Floors are carpeted throughout and furniture generally is comfortable and efficient. The use of white laminated plastic on the table dividers, however, does produce an uncomfortable glare. The signposting is consistent and very well done.

The librarians at Jordanhill provide an individual service to each student, tailored to suit his specific requirements which invariably range over a wide spectrum of subjects. The new library provides an excellent environment in which to perform this function.

AM

Authority	City of Glasgow
Designation	Jordanhill College of Education
Date of opening	October 1973
Population served	4,000
Name of Architect	Keppie Henderson and Partners, Glasgow
Name of Librarian	Peter S Clarke, MA, FLA
Special features:	
a) site	Within 50 acres of grounds; opens off main building in the extension
b) architecture	Square on plan, two storeys; the upper with wide gallery on three sides
c) function	To serve students and staff
Mechanical Services:	
a) heating	Low pressure hot water plus underfloor electric off-peak
b) ventilation	—
c) lighting	Mainly fluorescent
d) acoustics	Carpeted throughout
e) other	—
Areas: in square metres	
a) lending	930
b) reference	56
c) reading	28
d) special activities	—
e) children	—
f) control	—
g) library staff admin.	278
h) exhibitions	46
i) lecture hall	60
j) circulation	93
k) services	—
l) lavatories	23
m) stack	556
Total area:	2,070
Book volumes:	
a) adult lending	} 10,000
b) adult reference	
c) children	—
d) stack	—
e) other	115,000
Total:	125,000
Costs in £ p:	
a) site	—
b) building	137,258
c) furniture & fittings	25,631
Total Cost (ex fees):	£162,889
Cost per square metre:	£65

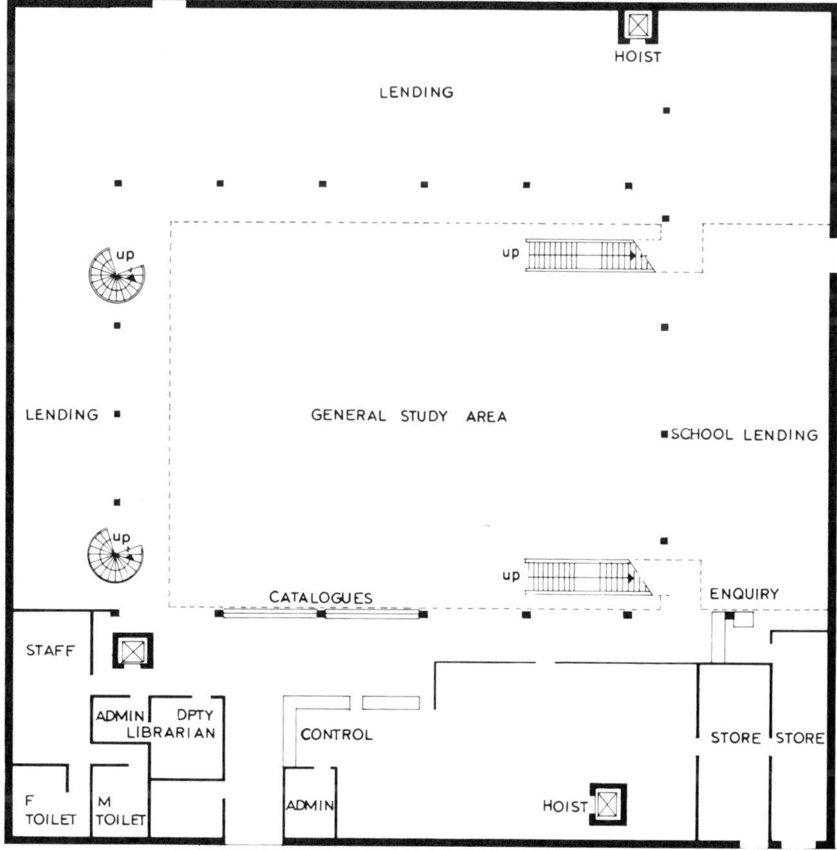

GROUND FLOOR

0 2 4 6 8 10m

Gwynedd, Clwyd and Powys Joint Education Committee: Coleg Normal

Coleg Normal, Bangor, has a long history, having been founded under the auspices of the British and Foreign Bible Society in 1858 for the training of men teachers. In 1908 control was transferred to the Education Authorities of Anglesey and Carnarvonshire and women students were first admitted in 1910. By 1934 it had become the official teachers' training college for North Wales and is now governed by a joint Education Committee representing Gwynedd, Clwyd and Powys.

The College occupies two sites, a mile apart, both beautifully situated overlooking the Menai Straits. Since the Second World War the later of these two sites, in Upper Bangor, has been extensively developed and the Library forms part of a complex of new buildings erected here. The purpose of the College is identical with that of any other teachers' training college except that, in the curriculum, special emphasis is laid on an ability to teach in both Welsh and English. Of the 800 students at present in the College more than half are Welsh speaking. This bilingual situation had considerable influence on the grant available for building and equipping the library as it was on a more generous scale than would otherwise have been the case.

The College site slopes towards the Menai Straits and the library is situated at a somewhat lower level than the road serving the various departments of the College. It is pleasantly approached by shallow steps through a lawn bordered by rose-beds. Rather severely functional, on two floors, the building serves to unify other college buildings adjacent to it. It is steel-framed, flat-roofed, and faced with grey brick, the latter being relieved only by the high-level windows lighting each floor.

The entrance, which also serves the adjacent building, leads into the quick-reference section of the library where the control desk, card catalogue and current periodicals are also to be found. This area has seating for 48 and is not intended for quiet study. Placed as it is in the centre of the ground floor it has no natural lighting and is artificially lit by tungsten light fixtures which give only a direct light downwards over a limited area. This produces a most unfortunate impression of gloom on entering the library. Lack of natural lighting also gives rise to problems of ventilation. One valuable feature of this section of the library is that all the Terrapin Reska furniture, including the catalogue cabinets, is mobile, thus enabling displays to be mounted or meetings to be held with a minimum of difficulty.

To the left of the quick-reference area is a reading room devoted to bound periodicals and a corresponding room on the right forms a reference library of 5,000 children's books in Welsh and English. This is a most attractive room and, again, all the furniture is mobile, enabling rapid rearrangement for various activities. This section is increasingly used by parties of children from schools in the locality and is provided with a separate entrance, thus avoiding any disturbance to the remainder of the library. Adjacent to the children's library is a similarly sized and well-equipped room concerned with all non-book materials.

Also on the ground floor are offices for the Assistant Librarian and Cataloguer, staff work and restrooms, all on a generous scale, for a comparatively small total staff.

The first floor is occupied almost entirely by the main library, reading room and bookstack but also includes the Librarian's office. The present book stock is 60,000, of which about 10% is in Welsh and is classified by Bliss. Shelving is available for a planned book stock of 100,000 and is arranged in alcoves with parallel centre bookcases. Fluorescent lighting between the latter and in the alcoves leaves much to be desired and the whole area would greatly benefit from top lighting, which could surely have been installed, at very little additional cost, in the flat roof. Remploy were responsible for all furniture on the first floor and must be given credit for their skilful masking of such awkward architectural features as the steel framing and pillars.

Seating is available for about 100 readers and is disposed in excellent fashion in a combination of a large formal reading area, with quieter areas in alcoves and between bookcases. This arrangement would seem to secure the best of both worlds. One has the general impression of a business-like large reading room, but at the same time reading desks are available for those who find study difficult when surrounded by other students. Adjacent to the main library is a room with accommodation for six microfilm readers with facilities for photocopying.

As the great majority of the books are on display the bookstack is comparatively small. It is equipped with manually operated sliding bookcases. There is some staff disappointment that the area occupied by the bookstack, which could have afforded a magnificent view over the Menai Straits, was not put to better use.

Whilst architecturally the library may be somewhat undistinguished and open to the various criticisms detailed above, it must be said that its shortcomings are to a large extent redeemed by an overall feeling of spaciousness. Floors are carpeted throughout and, although all sections were being well-used at the time of inspection, the generous space available produced an almost total silence everywhere. In other words one was left with an overriding impression that here was a library which functioned smoothly and efficiently.

DGT

(No photographs, plans or statistics available)

London Borough of Barnet: Hendon Central Library

The Library is adjacent to the Hendon Town Hall. The original, neo-classic building, completed in the late twenties consisted of a large, glass-domed double-height Lending Section flanked on either side and to the front with two-storied ancillary accommodation containing Stacks, Reading Room and Reference Library.

The architect's brief was to increase the available area in order to improve and extend the facilities and services the library offers to the public.

This has been achieved by re-utilising the internal volume previously occupied by the lavishly proportioned Lending Library with two upper floors of new accommodation in addition to a remodelled ground floor. A small extension across the full width of the building at the rear was added, (capable incidentally of taking two additional upper floors by way of future extension), and thus an increase of some 50% floor area was achieved.

The existing two-storey wings on either side were successfully linked to the new floors inserted in the central portion. The various floor levels were ingeniously adjusted and reconciled by interposing flights of continuous stairs on either side and linking levels at the half landings.

Of the two-storey parts one of the side wings was adapted for use as stack (with compactum-type metal sliding shelving) and workshop block, by adding an extra floor. The wing on the opposite side is adapted without structural alteration for staff and cloakroom accommodation at ground floor level and the first floor houses the Local History Section. Both these wings are linked by ingenious use of the half landings to the three levels of the central area as described above. The front portion which contains the original staircase is retained without structural alteration and the first floor level is adapted to provide the Music Library on one side of the staircase and a dual purpose lecture-cum-exhibition hall on the other.

The ground floor is planned on greater freedom combining the front wing and old central library now extended into an open plan Adult Lending section with loosely related Children's Library; this is linked with a more enclosed children's activity room in one of the wings equipped with television but capable of doubling up as a quiet room.

The existing central entrance and staircase have been retained but enclosed.

Adjacent is the central control desk which is accessible on all four sides and incorporates the Plessey 'Library Pen' data capture system linked to the Council's computer.

Altogether an ingenious and successful adaptation of an out-of-date building to modern use and extended provision of services. Some may argue against the conservation of the old library building but the success of this conversion contradicts this.

NTD   HW

drens Library

Authority	London Borough of Barnet
Designation	Hendon Central Library Extension
Date of opening	December 1973
Population served	152,000
Name of Architect	B Bancroft, RIBA, DipTP, MRTPI, Borough Architect; K Lim, RIBA, Job Architect
Name of Librarian	S T Butcher, FLA, FRSA
Special features:	
a) site	Adjacent to Town Hall on main road; separate from library administration offices
b) architecture	Remodelled 1929 building
c) function	Extension of lending and reference services
Mechanical Services:	
a) heating	Oil-fired boilers; panel and skirting heating strips
b) ventilation	Natural
c) lighting	Fluorescent strip with tungsten highlighting
d) acoustics	Acoustic suspended ceilings
e) other	—
Areas: in square metres	
a) lending	478 (and Music)
b) reference	368
c) reading	see (i and j)
d) special activities	in (e)
e) children	138
f) control	in (a)
g) library staff admin.	94
h) exhibitions	184
i) lecture hall	
j) circulation	328
k) services	28
l) lavatories	114
m) stack	102
Total area:	1,834
Book volumes:	
a) adult lending	75,000
b) adult reference	increased to 38,000
c) children	15,000
d) stack	in (a)
e) other	12,000 gr
Total:	140,000
Costs in £ p:	
a) site	—
b) building	131,990
c) furniture & fittings	35,000
Total Cost (ex fees):	of extension only £166,990
Cost per square metre:	£91

GROUND FLOOR

Humberside County Council (formerly Borough of Bridlington): Central Library

This is no new building but it is interesting, as October 1973 saw the second extension to the 'original' library, which took over bank premises more than thirty years ago. These premises are in King Street and still provide the main entrance, while the rear of the building, now completed, is in Queen Street which runs parallel. Bridlington is a popular and attractive seaside town with a resident population of 26,000; the main occupations are agricultural in the surrounding villages and the catering for holidaymakers within the town.

The bank premises adapted for a library service were soon inadequate but it was 1965 before a first extension was to provide separate Reference and Children's Libraries. This last extension has involved a break through from the Reference Library at second-floor level to provide a Music and Gramophone Record Library and a well-planned bibliographical room, a staff room and kitchen and store. On the first floor one now goes beyond the Children's Library, into a multi-purpose hall which is capable of being divided in a two to one proportion by a concertina floor-to-ceiling screen made of sapele and rubber. This, however, is not very effective sound proofing (the screen is, at no point, fixed to the floor, which is carpeted), with the result that there is some interference here. The combined room, at full stretch, is capable of seating 95 persons for large meetings of 'cultural and educational societies', lectures, etc, and for any exhibition of reasonable size; ceiling tracking and movable spotlights are provided. The walls are covered in hessian and the ceiling is tiled to be advantageous acoustically, while extractor fans keep the atmosphere comfortable.

At ground floor the lending area has been doubled; even so the much increased use is still taxing the staff. The counter area, sited between fixed columns, is becoming insufficient for the present Browne charging and the possibilities of moving the counter arms from 90° to 60° (approx.), and extending them, was suggested. The public lending area in the new extension has a ceiling height of nearly 20 ft and a thought again occurred that a mezzanine balcony might just be a possibility.

The final result, after the two extensions, is a great improvement, tastefully and thoughtfully achieved; but the constraints of the original bank building are perhaps more noticeable at the 'neck' of the building before it opens out into the more spacious areas. The greater public use which will now result may increase the flow problems at that point, even if the library's plans for computerised book issuing do materialise.

HW

Authority	Humberside County Council (formerly Borough of Bridlington)
Designation	Bridlington Central Library Extension
Date of opening	October 1973
Population served	26,000+
Name of Architect	A W Chaplin, MIMunE, Borough Engineer; V Poole, RIBA (Gelder & Kitchen, Hull), Architect
Name of Librarian	S T Thompson, ALA
Special features:	
a) site	Town centre; frontage fronts on to pavement
b) architecture	Brick piers with RSJs to each floor; timber roof to match existing building
c) function	To provide extra space and services
Mechanical Services:	
a) heating	Gas heated hot water
b) ventilation	Natural with extractor fans
c) lighting	Twin fluorescent strip
d) acoustics	Acoustic tiled ceilings; hessian wall covering in hall
e) other	—
Areas: in square metres	
a) lending	82
b) reference	—
c) reading	—
d) special activities	33
e) children	—
f) control	—
g) library staff admin.	67
h) exhibitions	—
i) lecture hall	95
j) circulation	70
k) services	—
l) lavatories	17
m) stack	—
Total area:	364
Book volumes:	
a) adult lending	
b) adult reference	
c) children	Not applicable
d) stack	
e) other	
Total:	—
Costs in £ p:	
a) site	9,415
b) building c) furniture & fittings	55,850
Total Cost (ex fees):	£65,265
Cost per square metre:	£179

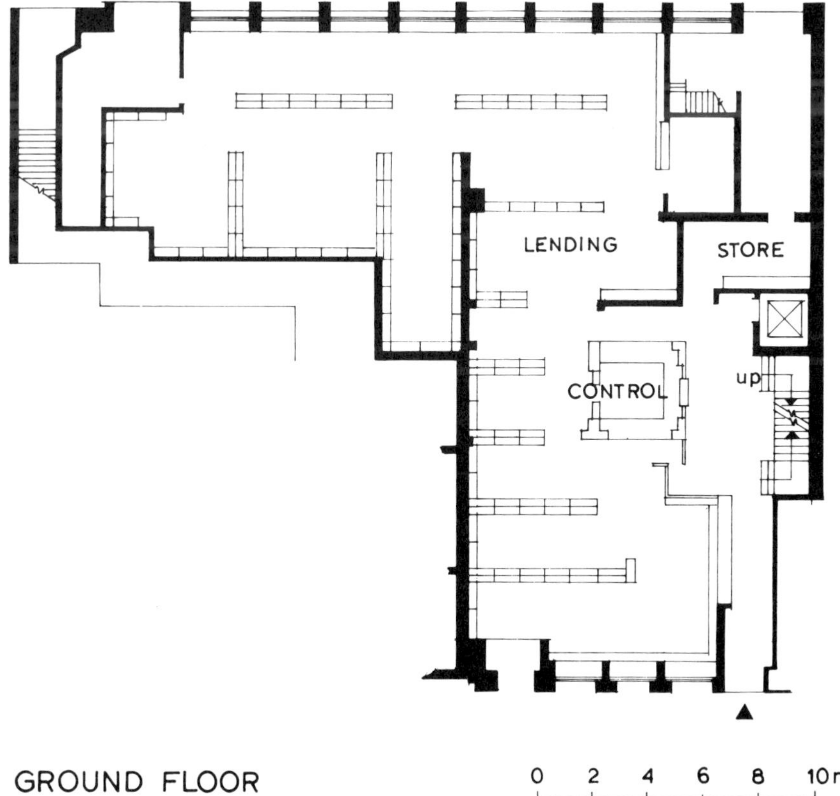

GROUND FLOOR